MW00795225

Seapower as Strategy

Seapower as Strategy

Navies and National Interests

NORMAN FRIEDMAN

Naval Institute Press
Annapolis, Maryland

Naval Institute Press
291 Wood Road
Annapolis, MD 21402

Library of Congress Cataloging-in-Publication Data
Friedman, Norman, 1946-
    Seapower as strategy : navies and national interests / Norman
Friedman.
    p. cm.
    Includes index.
    ISBN 1-55750-291-9 (alk. paper)
    1. Sea-power—United States. 2. Sea-power. 3. Naval strategy.
4. United States. Navy. 5. United States—Military policy. 6. World
politics—1989- I. Title.
    VA50 .F75 2001
    359'.03'0973—dc21

                                                    2001032649

Printed in the United States of America on acid-free paper ∞
08 07 06 05 04 03 02 01 9 8 7 6 5 4 3 2
First printing

Contents

Acknowledgments

Many friends helped with this book, providing invaluable advice and criticism of early drafts and other assistance: Dan David, Chuck Haberlein, Thomas Hone, Jock Gardner, James Goldrick, David Isby, Fu S. Mei, Christopher Page, David Stevens, David Steigman, and Christopher C. Wright. Errors remaining are my own responsibility. Portions of this book evolved from seminars on various aspects of naval warfare, which I have given over the past seventeen years. The feedback from participants in those seminars helped me formulate the ideas presented here. As in past projects, this one was made possible by the loving support my wife Rhea provided. She also contributed some essential editorial advice.

As this book went to press, J. David Brown, the longtime head of the British Naval Historical Branch and a good friend, died. This book is dedicated to his memory. For many years David Brown very successfully personified the application of historical lessons to modern naval strategic issues. In the interest of better modern decision making, he sponsored new research in the history of the primary global navy of the early twentieth century—the Royal Navy. He will be sorely missed.

Seapower as Strategy

Introduction

AT THE DAWN of the twenty-first century the U.S. Navy is the foremost instrument of U.S. military diplomacy. We seem, moreover, to be entering an era in which seapower is more, rather than less, important, not only to us but to many other countries. This is partly because our own national strategy more closely matches classical forms of maritime-oriented strategy. However, it is also because post–Cold War changes seem to make seapower more important for all countries able to maintain it. In effect these changes are devaluing airpower and ground power while increasing the impact of seapower, and of a maritime approach to national strategy. This book explains why this is happening, and it describes the kind of strategy and the kind of navy that is evolving.

The world has changed drastically since the end of the Cold War. Not only is there currently no great-power enemy comparable to the old Soviet Union, the United States apparently no longer contemplates using nuclear weapons in war, except in response to nuclear or equivalent attack. From a military point of view, the loss of nuclear weapons as a war-fighting option is surely the greatest single consequence of the end of the Cold War. Without them, the United States no longer has the sort of military power that in the past could simply have wiped out a medium-size enemy. Without the stimulus of a great-power enemy, we are unlikely to maintain the sort of ground forces that can occupy a small or medium country. We can no longer seek the sort of absolute victory that ended the two world wars of the twentieth century. In some important ways, then, the new world of the early twenty-first century recalls the world before the two world wars (and the Cold War, in a way the third world war), a world in which wars were generally limited, and in which seapower was dominant. This book is about the role seapower is likely to play in our changed world.

Seapower has certainly been vital in the wars the United States has recently fought. Aircraft carriers in the Gulf and in the Red Sea contributed heavily to the air defense of Saudi Arabia, which became the base for much of the coalition effort within a few days of the Iraqi attack on Kuwait. Without that contribution it would have taken several months to erect an adequate integrated air defense. Ground-based airplanes arrived quickly, but not their radars and command and control, nor the spares, munitions, and maintenance equipment that were needed to make them truly effective. The carriers offered instant capability because they provided not only the airplanes but also everything the airplanes needed; heavy objects can move easily when they are supported by the sea. In 1991 the carriers' strike aircraft contributed heavily to the coalition effort. Their fighters protected the coalition's seaward flanks, one of them under potential threat from Iran.

About 90 percent of all the materiel brought to the Gulf for the 1991 war came by sea. Again, heavy weights go easily by sea—but not by air. For that matter, marines using equipment prepositioned at sea provided much of the initial ground defense of Saudi Arabia. It is easy to forget that, without Western dominance at sea, much of that materiel might have been blocked as it traveled past the coasts of pro-Iraqi powers. It was not, after all, so very long since a Libyan merchant ship had mined the Red Sea (1984) in an attempt to destabilize the Saudi regime. Because the coalition did enjoy effective sea control, it was able to enforce an embargo against Iraqi sea traffic, which materially damaged the higher-technology end of the Iraqi defenses during the run-up to the war and thus also contributed significantly to the coalition victory. During the war, the credible threat of a U.S. Marines assault from the sea dominated by the coalition substantially dislocated the Iraqi defense of Kuwait.

Efforts to contain Saddam Hussein continued after the war, but not all the coalition partners were altogether willing participants. In at least one case the Saudis and other Gulf states refused to allow U.S. and British bombers to attack Iraq from their bases. Strikes were possible only because the U.S. and Royal navies could operate independently of those ground bases. Reluctant partners thus had no effective veto. It appears that the British government decided to build new aircraft carriers largely because of this incident. Navies are the only truly sovereign military instruments.

Because the former Yugoslavia is so mountainous, at times the main access to Bosnia and then to Kosovo was from the sea. As happened in the Gulf, a sea-based embargo proved valuable. Its effects, as much as any physical damage to Serbia, encouraged the Serbian electorate to oust Slobodan Milosevich. During the North Atlantic Treaty Organization (NATO) bombing campaigns against Serbia, carrier aircraft were often best placed to mount tactical strikes. In such operations promptness was vital, and the carriers could evade weather conditions that grounded land-based air forces. One reason NATO did not use ground forces during the Kosovo campaign was because poor roads drastically limited land access from Albania. Port problems seriously delayed any buildup of ground forces, including attack helicopters. Neither problem would have precluded an assault from the sea, by forces based aboard ship.

These considerations apply to any operation against an overseas target. Transport aircraft can quickly move troops into position. Even vehicles may come by air. To sustain operations, however, an army needs enormous masses of ammunition, fuel, and spare parts, not to mention maintenance facilities. This mass has to come by sea. For example, the Royal Australian Navy made possible the Australian army operation in East Timor in 1999. Without shipping little could have been done. If the Australians had encountered opposition at the outset, only the navy would have been in any position to fire back. Effective air support could not have been provided from bases in Australia because the transit time to the battle area would have precluded any sort of quick reaction. Bases on the scene could not have been seized without naval support. Such considerations presumably made the absence of heavy gun capability and the absence of any sort of floating air base (i.e., carrier) a matter of considerable concern for the Australian army going ashore.

These considerations apply to military operations other than war (MOOTW), quite as much as to war itself. Mobility allows us to engage when we choose, and to disengage when necessary. Ships can enforce embargoes that can make a difference because countries import so much of what they want by sea. Similarly, the navy/coast guard role in the drug war, which is a type of embargo, is worthwhile because the sea is often the easiest route for smugglers. It is also significant that this embargo can be mounted from what amounts to sovereign U.S. territory. Our ability to do so makes it much easier for friendly governments to join us. Otherwise they would have potential vetoes, and they might feel intense pressure to exercise those vetoes.

Although this book is necessarily directed at the U.S. national and naval situation, the reasoning it embodies should apply to all countries. It explains and advocates a particular kind of maritime-oriented national strategy that has proven remarkably successful in past centuries. Using complementary military arms, it capitalizes on the mobility and flexibility offered by sea transport and sea-based forces. It has a distinctive flavor, it carries distinctive requirements, and it offers distinct advantages to any country capable of using it.

The character of maritime strategy shows a remarkable consistency over time. Chapters 6 through 10 describe how seapower was wielded under a variety of circumstances, in fights between sea powers, between sea powers and states whose interests were predominantly on land, and as an adjunct to wars fought mainly ashore. These case studies make clearer the choices that governments have (and have made) in using or failing to use the seapower at their disposal.

Seapower, in the broad sense of power centered on and projected from the sea, matters because so much of the world is so close to the sea; most of the world's commerce travels by sea and natural resources are increasingly extracted from the sea and from its bottom. For years the U.S. Navy has used a dramatic night-time photograph of the earth to make this point. The centers of population and industry are well lit, and the lighting nearly matches the coastlines of the continents. Only in a few countries, mainly the United States, Russia, and China, are major cities far from the sea. If the point of military power is to influence other countries' governments, then what can have greater influence than something that can touch their most valuable resources? Those resources are both what is visible along the world's shores and the seaborne traffic uniting the countries of the world.

The key, and the theme of this book, is a very old idea. About four centuries ago, Francis Bacon wrote that "he that commandeth the sea is at great liberty and may take as much or as little of the war as he will." Seapower offers choices that land power cannot make. "As much" of a war means being able to exert maximum power far from home, because it is so easy to move vast weights by sea. "As little" may mean simply precluding invasion, but it also means limiting liability when intervening abroad. The sea can be either a barrier to attack or a highway leading both to our enemies and to us. Naval power creates the barrier and naval power exploits the highway, but naval weakness makes the sea an invitation to attack. A deployed fleet tends to keep problems at arm's length. It is much better to fight, if fight we must, in the Gulf or in Asiatic waters than anywhere near home. Bacon was thinking of England, whose position as an island power depended so obviously on naval dominance. In his day the only effective threat against Britain was invasion, so control of the seas was both defensive shield and offensive opportunity.

Britain generally chose to concentrate her forces to meet a potential enemy close to that enemy's port rather than spread her forces around her coasts. To do the latter would cause her to be weak everywhere and thus vulnerable to any concentrated enemy force. Similar choices apply to any other state faced by possible seaborne invasion. Because the geography of maritime operations is not fixed, flexibility flavors naval or maritime strategy. It is why coast defense is so difficult: the enemy can land almost anywhere, but the defending force is relatively immobile. The great hope is that technology limits the seaborne attacker to a few beaches, and the attacker hopes that technology can widen choices. Should the effort involve guarding a few key beaches, or should the defense emphasize an inland mobile reserve? How much reliance should be placed on naval operations offshore? The answers should critically affect policy for modern island countries like Australia, Japan, and Taiwan.

In our case, the advent of long-range nuclear missiles in potential target countries is another possible threat, potentially a means of deterring us from projecting our power. In most cases what will matter is the credible threat to project power, more than actual combat. Our credibility may ultimately rest in part on our ability to brush aside the threat of small-scale strategic missile attack. The U.S. nuclear deterrent may suffice, or it may be that some form of missile defense is a necessary complement to our ability to project force around the world. Incidentally, this question touches on *any* form of U.S. intervention abroad, not merely naval. One vital question is whether the cost of a credible missile defense will preclude the investment necessary to maintain the ability to project U.S. national power abroad.

Unlike Britain the United States has land borders over which, at least in theory, we can be invaded. Thus a necessary condition for U.S. maritime power is tranquil borders with both Canada and Mexico. Without them, the United States would have to maintain an enormous home defense army. We would no longer be an effective maritime power. In the past, countries with threats on their borders generally had no choice but to emphasize land power at the expense of seapower. Conversely, sea powers have found that one valuable way to cripple an enemy's attempt to use the sea is to promote a serious land threat on its borders. That was certainly the case in many of England's wars against France. Britain nearly faced disaster in the war surrounding the American Revolution because she failed to distract the French with a land threat. It is often tempting to see seapower as a sufficient solution to national security. The historical examples in this book show that adding a coalition partner makes seapower far more effective. Often being perceived as a sea power makes it possible to attract potential coalition partners.

As an extension of Bacon's idea, early in the twentieth century Adm. Sir John Fisher encapsulated much of the British experience of maritime strategy by saying that the British army was the projectile fired by the Royal Navy. Britain had been most effective when she had used maritime mobility to project her army at will and, as implied by Bacon, to withdraw it as necessary. The British had avoided open-ended ground commitments. Implicit in Fisher's formulation was that a relatively small, hence transportable, army was an excellent complement to an effective navy. Britain did not follow Fisher's dictum in World War I; Chapter 7 examines whether that was a good choice.

Rear Adm. Alfred Thayer Mahan, USN, pointed out that seapower, much more than other elements of military power, acts indirectly, often silently. In peacetime naval presence may keep a crisis from exploding. By encouraging friends, the same presence may allow us to assemble decisive land-based forces in a way otherwise impossible. An embargo, based largely on sea control, may deny a potential enemy, like Iraq, the wherewithal to run a nuclear missile program. In war, sea control offers national mobility, which may be decisive, as it was in both the European and Pacific theaters of World War II. Much of the time such results are achieved without combat: the history of seapower includes many fewer battles than the history of land warfare. The crisis that never escalated, the program that was aborted, and the landing that was not prevented reflect the subtle but decisive contributions seapower can make. As Chapter 6 shows, our understanding of the outcome of a major war, the Crimean War, depends on whether we take into account the effect of a credible but unrealized British seaborne threat on the Russians. How much did credible U.S. seapower affect the course of the Cold War, again without combat?

Seapower is probably most important, in this era of instability, because it limits the problems the United States must face. It helps shape the world, maintaining a world broadly friendly to us, and to the trade on which we live. That means encouraging our friends and discouraging potential enemies; it is more than simply holding down instability to a tolerable level. Simply because it is less intrusive, naval presence may well cause far less friction than deploying ground or ground-based air forces. Through the nineteenth century, after the defeat of Napoleon, the Royal Navy maintained a vital degree of stability in areas that came to be known as the Third World. That was vital for British economic health because Britain lived by her trade and investments around the world. The Royal Navy formed a backdrop to British prosperity; its mere existence tended to maintain a valuable degree of peace. Much the same can be said of the only current global navy, the U.S. Navy. In neither case is it easy to quantify the contribution the navy—and the peace that it maintains—makes to national prosperity, but in both cases that contribution is quite apparent.

This book begins with national strategy because ultimately military forces are valued only to the extent they serve it. That is not to say that a government chooses a strategy and designs forces to match. In reality, forces evolve organically and steadily, whereas statements of national strategy change frequently. Despite changes in stated strategy, however, national strategy itself tends to be fairly constant. Moreover, the forces that best suit long-term national goals tend to survive while less useful ones often fall victim to inevitable budgetary problems. Thus it is worthwhile to deduce a national strategy, or a strategic pattern, from actual national behavior, rather than from what one administration or another may express as its strategy.

The basic realities and the flavor of maritime strategy are explained. The chapters on national strategy and on the character of naval strategy are replete with historical examples taken from the great maritime wars of the past, from the age of sail through the Cold War. Clearly, technology has changed enormously during the past half-millennium. Some of the basic facts of geopolitics and seapower, however, have remained surprisingly constant. Historical cases are worth reviewing because, unlike theoretical scenarios of the future or the products of careful simulation, the past can be examined fully. Knowing how the involved actors, with incomplete information, reacted under stress is crucial in helping us understand any wars we may have to fight in the future. The flavor of maritime strategy turns out to be far more constant than one might imagine.

The ways in which naval forces are used, for example, to gain and exploit sea control, are discussed next. Seapower offers mobility, but to gain that mobility the mass that quickly can be deployed must be limited. Thus the rise of mass armies and mass air forces seemed, in the past, to limit the utility of the equivalent forces navies could wield. Chapter 5 suggests that the situation is now changing rapidly in favor of small sophisticated forces that are well adapted to sea-based mobility.

The way in which U.S. naval strategy has changed to meet the peculiar challenges of the post–Cold War period is explained in the last chapters. The appendices describe the current state of naval technology and detail current issues in the structure of the U.S. fleet.

One more point is worth stating. Much is often made of the dramatic changes in warfare that faster and faster computers and improved networking can bring. Some speak of a "Revolution in Military Affairs," others of network-centric warfare or the Joint Chiefs' Vision 2010 (and 2020). The basic concepts of naval warfare are entirely compatible with such changes; indeed, in some important ways network-centric warfare is a scaled-up version of the computer-linked tactics that evolved in Western navies during the Cold War. However, there is a deeper connection. In some important yet abstract ways network-centric warfare *resembles* naval warfare. The lessons of past naval warfare may be directly relevant, if they are properly translated, to the new world of network-centric warfare.

Quite aside from any such analogies, naval warfare in the classical sense is likely to continue to matter. Our ability to transmit information quickly over long distances has not changed the fact that immense tonnages of cargo have to be moved in order for people to live and to fight. If anything, countries are less self-sufficient than in the past, so they are more dependent on what they get by sea. Most of the time military forces are effective because they present threats, not because they carry them out. It still seems, moreover, that the threat of violence is much more effective than more subtle abstract threats against information infrastructure. The combination of presence and firepower, which navies offer, is still central to what we hope to achieve using military means.

1
National Strategy

STRATEGY IS ABOUT ends and means. During the Cold War the end—national survival—was quite clear, even though it was much less clear whether we could actually win the war in a finite time. The Cold War largely defined U.S. interests. Whenever a crisis arose, it was relatively simple to decide how the United States should act: which outcome was better for our side, or worse for the Soviets? Moreover, the Soviets were only the latest in a line of potentially mortal enemies, whose threats defined U.S. strategy: the British; then various European powers, which might have tried to seize access to the New World and against which the United States would have been a barrier; then the Germans and the Japanese in various combinations. The Soviets have had no successor. It will probably be decades before any threat comparable to that posed by the Soviet Union emerges.

There are enough tensions in the Third World to cause wars virtually everywhere. We are unable to predict them, or to decide which ones merit U.S. intervention. That is quite natural, and it is unlikely to change until (and unless) another great-power enemy appears. Strategists can set down criteria for intervention, but this is pointless unless they describe what the U.S. government actually has done and will do. It is relatively easy to explain intervention in Kosovo (to preclude a wider European war), but much more difficult to explain why the United States intervened in Somalia but not in Rwanda, or to explain just why the United States acted when and as it did in Sierra Leone. It is, of course, entirely possible that intervention in Somalia was driven by press reports of the horrors there, whereas few reporters ventured inland to Rwanda until after the disaster had occurred. In the case of Sierra Leone, the key may have been ignorance of the personal connection between a friendly head of another state, Liberia, and a local warlord. Both explanations suggest that U.S. foreign policy will often turn on decidedly case-by-case considerations. There is no particular reason to imagine that future administrations will be more consistent, or indeed that they should be; other countries have not done much better. All we really know is that, as a superpower, the United States will often find itself involved abroad.[1]

Over the next few decades, we will inevitably face numerous armed challenges, none of which in itself probably suffices to threaten our well-being in any major way. We cannot fight every challenger, but if all the challenges go unmet, the world will gradually become a much more dangerous—and much less friendly—place. Ultimately, then, the mass of minor security challenges can add up to major one. To the extent that we periodically crush challengers, like Saddam, others may be discouraged, and we may find it easier to keep a fragile peace. That suggests that it is very much in U.S. interests to maintain the ability to fight—or to threaten to fight—at our choice, far from home.

For Americans this is an unusual and confusing situation. American history is a poor guide, because we enjoyed a world order before World War II that was maintained in unruly peace by another superpower, the United Kingdom, mainly through the agency of the Royal Navy. This connection was largely ignored in the United States. As a consequence, Americans imagined that they could limit their peacetime involvement abroad, and that their military forces could be shaped almost completely by the prospective needs of major war. The situation was comfortable because, to a remarkable extent, our needs in the world paralleled those of the British and we were quite furious when they did not. That cushion no longer exists, but the Cold War clearly justified a worldwide engagement and delayed recognition of American security needs separate from major war. Without a Cold War, we have to face the fact that we still need engagement. Isolationism is no longer a realistic possibility.

Strategy and Ideology

U.S. foreign policy has always had a strong ideological component. One of the ironies of the Cold War was that our adversary, the Soviet Union, was explicitly an ideological power, yet the United States was every bit as determined to spread its own ideology, which might be described as free-market democracy.

This aspect of American power is reflected in recent claims, both by politicians and by academics, that democracies do not fight each other: a democratic world would be a peaceful, stable one.[2] Many Americans, if pressed, would say that this country has a mission of spreading democracy throughout the world. Probably many Americans would go so far as to say that undemocratic governments are per se illegitimate. These ideas go back to the founding of the United States. They are only rarely expressed as a national ideology, probably because they are so widely accepted and understood within the United States. Without a major enemy, our ideology often takes center stage. We have, for example, used our power to force several African governments to abandon one-party rule in favor of open multiparty elections.

Given the U.S. ideological sense of mission, despotic governments often see the United States as a natural enemy, to be feared and resisted—and fought. As a variation on this theme, the United States is widely seen as the prime mover of modernization, the capital, if you like, of the twentieth (or twenty-first) century. Many people and governments throughout the world find modernization frightening. By our existence, we are their enemy; in their view, we are attacking them. Thus there is little or nothing the U.S. government can do to avoid all challenges. Moreover, those who dislike us sufficiently are likely to try to attack us at home, using terrorist techniques. We cannot, then, avoid engagement in the Third World.

There is also a pragmatic goal: to safeguard our economic interests, which now often involve foreign countries. For example, we wish to maintain our access to reasonably priced oil, which often involves the United States in Middle East countries. Our country has a real interest in maintaining some degree of world order, not least because without it the U.S. economy, which is based on world trade, would suffer.

The two drivers of American policy necessarily collide at times. The Gulf War is a good case in point. The Gulf matters because it is the main source of the world's oil—and oil is still the world's lifeblood. If Saddam been allowed to keep Kuwait, he would have dominated Saudi Arabia, and with it much of the world's oil supply. Saddam presumably would not have cut off oil entirely, but he would have reduced the supply. The resulting sharp rise in the price of oil would have sapped the Western economies, as the oil shock did in the 1970s. He would surely have tried to use the resulting leverage to gain further goals, such as U.S. acquiescence in the destruction, for instance, of Israel. It was to avert such disasters that the United States backed the Saudis and Kuwaitis. We were embarrassed, however, that the regimes we were protecting in the Gulf were, to put it mildly, undemocratic. We appeared to be abandoning our fundamental principles in the service of the big oil companies or, at the least, American consumers. Many Americans were convinced that the enterprise was acceptable only because it was moral: it would destroy the most evil ruler in the Middle East, Saddam Hussein. Whereas the coalition achieved enormous success in ejecting Saddam's army from Kuwait, and thus stabilizing the region, Saddam retained his power. To many Americans, that undoubtedly felt like defeat, and this defeat may help explain the catastrophic loss of popularity President George Bush experienced in 1992, which cost him that year's election. The tension between ideology and economics—which is, after all, an important national interest—will surely bedevil us more, rather than less, as the Cold War recedes from view.[3]

To the extent that the Iraqi regime was contained, the war could be seen as far more successful. That success has made for an open-ended commitment, however, and no such situation can be very popular. A future administration may want to limit the forces it uses in a second Gulf War, to avoid the sort of issues raised before the first Gulf War. In this sense the scale of the buildup that seemed necessary to fight the Gulf War was ultimately quite counterproductive. Overall, the more mobile and deployable the forces, and the more quickly they can act, the easier it may be to use them without invoking outsized and unrealistic expectations.

The current defense decision-making process, which dates from the 1960s, uses a series of set scenarios to test alternative kinds of forces. Such a process automatically prefers forces optimized for the chosen cases, whereas the very uncertain future would seem to make maximum flexibility, which is difficult to measure, more valuable. Thus the process is inherently self-deceptive.[4] For example, one of the two main planning scenarios, a possible war in Korea, is a Cold War holdover. If, as seems possible, the two Koreas unify peacefully, this particular scenario will no longer be valid. Yet the United States will retain major interests in the Far East because Korea is one of our largest trading partners. Many of the tensions in the area, for example, between Korea and Japan, were not consequences of the Cold War, and they will not dissipate quickly or, probably, easily. It is difficult to say what our position should be if such tensions worsen.

An Historical Analogy

Tense international situations are not new. Our present situation is not too different from what the British faced after the end of the Napoleonic wars in 1815. Like them, we are now the only world power with a truly global reach.

Like the British in 1815, we have to find a new way to identify our national interests. Although we would hardly recognize that country as a U.S.-style democracy, it is clear from histories of the period that British foreign policy had U.S.-style components. There was a real desire to spread liberal democracy (or at least to support those fighting for what they considered democracy).

Because Britain was the greatest trading nation in the world, she also had strong commercial interests, which sometimes demanded military support. Commercial demands sometimes clashed with the needs of British military, particularly naval, forces. For example, as the leading sea power, Britain was clearly the leading exponent of blockade as a wartime weapon. Yet to many British liberals, who lived by trade, blockade was anathema. In 1856, as part of the Crimean War settlement, Britain voluntarily surrendered important blockade powers by international treaty.[5] Americans interested in parallels may note that the U.S. military is currently the world's leading user of the electromagnetic spectrum. American businessmen feel that this scarce resource absolutely must be made available on a commercial basis; therefore portions the military wants and probably needs are being auctioned off. To some extent the British paid in 1914 for the loss of blockade power they had accepted half a century earlier. However, to the extent that free trade, and the prospect of free trade, so enriched Britain that she could more easily weather the 1914–18 hurricane, perhaps the trade-off was worthwhile. Will the loss of spectrum result in some future disaster? Or will it result in the creation of capabilities that we will find extremely useful in some future war?

Similarly, in the mid-nineteenth century many in Britain saw little possibility that commercial arrangements could ever be disrupted by war. That was one reason the British were initially quite content to leave the Suez Canal, surely one of the most vital links in their seaborne empire, under largely French control (later they bought a controlling share from the Egyptians).

The British government also sought little say in arms sales to foreign powers. Undoubtedly the British reasoned, as we have, that the close relationship forged by, for instance, a mission modernizing a country's navy would translate into a more generally friendly relationship. Also, arms sales helped pay for a larger British arms industry than the Royal Navy could afford in peacetime. During this period of free arms trade, British shipyards produced the bulk of the world's export warships. When war came in 1914, several important ships already under construction for foreign buyers were taken over. Equally important, the industrial capacity built up to supply both the buyers and the Royal Navy was available for mobilization.[6] In some important cases, foreign sales could finance new developments.[7] A central question, which is still relevant, is whether a foreign country can make particularly good use of the advanced hardware it buys. Sometimes it could even be asked whether arms sales were not preferable to encouraging the growth of a local arms industry, which would ultimately cause even more trouble. Americans who see trade with China as a double-edged sword will surely see parallels.

With the defeat of Napoleon, France—Britain's longtime enemy—was prostrate, although not as prostrate as the Soviet Union is now. The end of the Napoleonic wars shattered what had been, for more than a century, the basis for British national strategy. Generations of Royal Navy officers had been brought up to understand the details of blockading the French coast, because for so long France had been the main enemy. After 1815 that knowledge was effectively obsolete. It took the British almost a century to come completely to terms with their changed strategic environment, in which France became a wartime ally rather than an enemy. Not until the end of the nineteenth century, about ninety years after Napoleon had been banished from Europe, did the British once again find themselves facing a potential mortal enemy, Germany. In the interim, they had numerous security challenges, and their forces experienced considerable combat, but always of a limited type.

The Balance of Power Concept

The fundamental fact of British strategy was that any mortal threat would have to come by sea. The British theory was that no single continental power had the wherewithal to maintain a sufficient army to stand off its neighbors and to build a fleet powerful enough to take on the Royal Navy. It would take domination of the entire continent, or at least its most productive countries, to mount a mortal threat. Hence the classic British policy evolved: to keep any single country from uniting Europe against Britain. Britain generally backed the weaker continental power against the stronger, unless facing a country that might, in itself, destroy the seapower that precluded invasion. Thus the fight against the Netherlands, a sea power, occurred during the seventeenth century.[8] When Spain was the principal European power, she was the main enemy, and the British backed her rivals. When Spain was eclipsed by France, France became the main threat. When Germany eclipsed France, Britain backed France against Germany. These choices were never ideological; they were matters of national survival. For example, in 1914 France was clearly more democratic than Hohenzollern Germany, but not nearly enough to justify the choice of allies on ideological grounds. Only after war broke out did the Germans demonstrate just how brutal they could be. The British choice, to ally with France, was not preordained; it grew out of German ambitions, and also out of a direct German threat to British seapower.

On the other hand, on a year-to-year basis, at least after the defeat of Napoleon, Britain felt reasonably safe; the Royal Navy insulated the British from problems within Europe. Thus British statesmen spoke of "splendid isolation," which in effect meant that they could limit any commitment—they could limit the price that Britain had to pay, particularly in blood, in any struggle on the Continent. That was not isolationism; the British were well aware that what happened across the channel and the North Sea affected them. Rather, it was a determination to keep their power to choose when and whether to become directly involved. For example, in 1854 the British did become involved in the ongoing war between Turkey and Russia, because it was important to maintain a balance of power in Europe. They nearly went to war for much the same reason in 1878. On the other hand, despite considerable domestic sympathy with the French, the British carefully avoided involvement in the Franco-Prussian War of 1870–71. Conversely, British involvement with France before World War I seems to have grown out of a sense that Britain could not afford isolation, which British statesmen feared would be the outcome if the French did not feel British support in the face of German antagonism.

A modern American can see suggestive parallels. The basis of U.S. foreign policy, at least since World War I, has been the recognition that the only mortal danger is likely to come from a hostile power that is able to unite other main productive centers of the world. Only then can an enemy gain sufficient strength to turn the natural barrier of the oceans into an invasion route, and to use that route to place a decisive force in North America. In 1914 the kaiser certainly had that potential, if ever he defeated France and Britain. Much the same could be said of Hitler after the 1940 blitzkrieg. The great Soviet threat was always that, by overrunning or cowing the nations of Western Europe, so much hostile strength would be built up that the United States would be directly threatened. In each case, merely to stave off the threat would require the United States to militarize to such an extent that our society would be ruined.

In neither case did the potential winner already possess sufficient maritime power to expand into the New World. Many have taken that lack to suggest that the supposed threat was not real. However, the issue was not whether

Hitler or Stalin could immediately invade the United States. It was whether either could gain enough raw economic power to convert into future maritime power. It seemed far better to face such threats before they could mature. There is evidence that the Germans hoped to build the ability to expand into the New World.[9]

For the British, the Napoleonic wars marked the end of an era in which Europe was the center of world power. By 1815 the British could see the United States as a possible future power, albeit an embryonic one. The War of 1812 had shown the British that they could not dominate the United States militarily.[10] It may also have been clear that eventually the United States might seek to eject the British from the Western Hemisphere, including both Canada and the more informal empire then emerging in South America. These were clearly distant prospects. The British, however, did have to decide just how to deal with the Americans. They might opt for an ability to contain the United States in wartime, using naval forces based offshore, for example, in Bermuda. They might opt for a degree of cooperation, perhaps based on a more or less common culture. A growing United States also attracted British investments, but it must have been clear that no U.S. government would brook British political interference: the country could never become part of an informal British empire. Through the nineteenth century there was an uneasy combination of cooperation (for example, in supporting the Monroe Doctrine or in demilitarizing the border with Canada), and friction (for example, during the American Civil War). The tension never quite dissipated; during World War II, when the two countries were closely allied, the United States tried to break up the British empire in Asia.[11]

For an American, this history recalls (but clearly does not mirror) the current relationship with China. When an administration calls for a "strategic partnership" it hopes that the Chinese will ultimately be friendly. When the Chinese seek hegemony in the East, is that posturing (like the United States when it announced the Monroe Doctrine in 1823), or is it another assault on us? Currently Chinese power is far more limited than Chinese appetites. What happens when (if?) the power grows to match? Clearly this is not 1815 or 1823. The Far East is much less a power vacuum than the New World was at that time. China is a far more massive power than the United States of the early nineteenth century. Even so, the parallels are worth noting. Should we be inspired by the way the United States allied herself with the British in two world wars and during the Cold War, or dismayed at the price exacted for those alliances?

Although in a sense Britain—the only state with truly global reach—was the only superpower of the late nineteenth century, in many other ways she was hardly preponderant. For example, without a massive army (the development of which was precluded by investment in the Royal Navy), the British could not overrun any other European country. When needing to act in or around Europe, Britain needed friends, at least temporary ones. Statesmen developed the skill of building and maintaining peacetime coalitions. To prospective partners Britain offered peacetime versions of the inducements that had proven useful in the Napoleonic and numerous earlier wars: the access guaranteed by the Royal Navy and financial backing guaranteed by an economy enjoying unparalleled access to the world. To some extent the fact that Britain was *not* a major land power was also an attraction, because she was unlikely to swallow up any partner.

Modern U.S. power is also limited. We lack an army on the scale of many in the Third World. We are most unlikely to exercise the ability, developed during the Cold War, to destroy a medium-size country completely using nuclear weapons. Like the British, however, we alone have truly global reach on an effective scale.

Thanks to seapower Britain could intervene overseas at will, without help from coalition partners. Paradoxically, such a solo ability tends to attract partners, as the U.S. government has found several times since the end of the Cold War. A potential partner who has an inherent veto on U.S. action is open to considerable pressure to exercise that veto. If it lacks an explicit veto, however, it can follow its natural self-interest and combine with the United States in a given operation. The Gulf War was a case in point. After Saddam Hussein overran Kuwait, he told the Saudi government not to welcome U.S. troops, on the ground that admitting infidels to the most sacred soil in Islam would destroy its legitimacy. The Saudis found the threat quite compelling, even though they knew that without U.S. help they might well fall victim to the Iraqis. U.S. carrier-based aircraft, however, could provide a degree of defense without Saudi agreement, because they were based in international waters offshore. Once the carriers were in place, the Saudis were in the happy position of having to accept protection whether or not they formally requested it; they were free to welcome U.S. troops. It is an interesting but unanswerable question whether the known U.S. ability to mount a major amphibious assault (using marines in the Gulf), in the event that base area had been denied, helped the Saudis agree to provide the base area from which the attack on Iraq was ultimately launched.

Naval-based theater missile defense may be an extension of such practices. Many potential victims of missile attack cannot possibly afford massive national missile defenses. Nor, in many cases, are they likely to welcome substantial U.S. ground-based forces bearing such defenses. However, the situation is far simpler if they can be defended from the sea. The option of offering a defense then falls entirely on the United States. That may be useful if the threat is mounted by another U.S. ally. Our access from the sea uniquely favors the United States to act as peacemaker.

Coalitions cohere partly because each partner gains some control over the overall operation, a control it would lack altogether if it did not participate. For example, during the Cold War the British deliberately integrated their strategic nuclear force with the U.S. force on the ground because this would give them "a say in the end of the world." It now seems that the future may well be filled with naval operations, for example, for what is now called peace enforcement (as in Bosnia and Kosovo). Countries with navies that can participate will have a say in what happens. This consideration probably explains the Belgian, Norwegian, and Danish decisions to build relatively large surface warships well suited to overseas deployment. The new units cannot by themselves be used to project power, but they are clearly well suited to roles within larger naval operations.

Obviously, the more crucial the contribution, the greater the say. In the Gulf, for example, the Saudis offered not only their own forces, but also the staging and base areas without which the ultimately decisive land war could not have been conducted. They presumably gained a veto over at least some aspects of the conduct of the war. For example, supporting a Western-led coalition that deposed an Arab government (i.e., unseated Saddam himself) might have endangered the Saudi government. Presumably it vetoed, at least implicitly, any such possibility.

These considerations certainly applied to the Cold War coalition the United States led. Only the United States could offer sufficient strength to destroy the Soviet Union if war broke out. On the other hand, U.S. views of just how Europe should be defended, particularly U.S. fascination, beginning in 1961, with building the ability to fight a conventional (i.e., horribly destructive) war in Europe, were most unwelcome there. The Europeans' security demanded that they maintain the coalition, but at the same time they wanted to veto what they feared might be precipitate U.S. action. Hence the observation, common during the Cold War, that the Europeans would do just enough to keep the United States in Europe, but not enough to fight the sort of war the United States envisaged. It helped enormously that the United States lacked the power to fight the war without substantial European help. Thus, much of the story of NATO, beginning about 1958, consists of U.S. attempts to convince the Europeans to provide enough military power to win the largely non-nuclear war the United States preferred. Cynical Americans sometimes said that the Europeans' favorite war would be a spectator affair, in which missiles passed over Europe en route to the Soviet Union and to the United States.

Simply having coalition partners verifies our values to ourselves. Early in the Cold War some American policy makers remarked that the United States could not survive in a world in which we were the only democracy, whether or not the Soviets physically or economically destroyed us. We may even imagine that forming coalitions is a valuable way of exporting our democratic ideology. We may, then, value some military capabilities largely because they help attract coalition partners. For example, theater ballistic missiles are a growing threat to many of our friends overseas, yet in most cases the countries cannot field adequate defenses even if they decide to do so. A mobile U.S. ability to defend against such weapons is valuable on two quite different levels. First, a country, like Saudi Arabia, that joins a U.S.-led coalition is telling its population that it has chosen the winning side. It is in our interest to make sure that includes denying the coalition enemy the ability to do much damage. In that sense the deployment of Patriot batteries during the Gulf War was vital to continued coalition cohesion. Second, governments faced with the missile threat may be attracted to us simply because we can protect them. The Cold War coalition, NATO, cohered because the United States, which many of the Europeans distrusted or disliked, could protect them against a worse threat, the Soviet Union. This logic is still valid.

More generally, it is vital that we understand just what it is we wish to offer prospective coalition partners. They may be interested in a far deeper and less temporary relationship than we would like to offer, simply because they can then wield our weight against their local enemies. For example, one drawback to the current concept of a mobile offshore base is not, as one might imagine, that so many countries would consider a U.S. base a few hundred miles offshore an unacceptable threat. Rather, it is that they would regard such a base as evidence of deep U.S. involvement, hence a *threat to their own enemies,* which we may have no desire whatever to fight. The Spratly Islands, which many think are located over vast oil deposits, are claimed by six countries, including China. The others are all quite weak by comparison, and all but one (Vietnam) are friendly to the United States. In a fight with China, each would probably lose unless, of course, it had some way of making sure that the United States was its ally.

It would be misleading to imagine that coalition partners necessarily share our basic views. For example, we justified our participation in the Gulf War on grounds of international law: aggression could not be allowed to proceed unchecked. We acted as though the coalition was held together by like views. Yet our view of international law is shared by few other governments; it may be a figment of our basically Anglo-Saxon political culture. Many of the partners were simply worried that they would be included among Saddam's future victims, or at the least that victory for him would transform the Gulf into his sphere of dominance. These partners were unwilling to take the next step, to agree to destroy Saddam simply because he was an aggressor. Among other things, they, too, had hopes of someday claiming land from their neighbors, so some kind of absolute prohibition would do them no great good. Much the same could be said of the attempt to disarm Iraq on the ground that it is fatally immoral for a country outside the current nuclear club to develop nuclear weapons. Similar problems can be seen in the coalition that fought Slobodan Milosevich in Serbia and Kosovo.

The British ended the Napoleonic wars as part of a victorious coalition; their partners were the Austrians, Prussians, and Russians. In theory, all four partners had fought to restore prerevolutionary Europe. In fact their motives were quite different. The British fought in self-defense, to preserve the balance of power that they considered the first element of their defense, and to keep the French from overthrowing their government. Even so, many Britons initially welcomed the French Revolution, and sympathized with its attack on French autocracy; what bothered them was French expansionism. The other coalition partners were absolute monarchs. The French Revolution endangered them directly, and in its aftermath they wanted any whiff of revolution or liberalism suppressed. The British did not find this particularly attractive, or even acceptable. On this basis the winning coalition was doomed, and it had little impact after 1815. In particular the British had no interest in suppressing the popular uprisings of 1848, whereas the Russians enthusiastically supported Austrian suppression of the Hungarians that year (creating, incidentally, lasting bitterness). Just how different is this situation from the splintered NATO confronting the crisis in Kosovo? Even governments that nominally share our values may not do so in practice.

After Waterloo the British felt safer than they had for decades; so much of the previous century had been filled with wars, mainly against France.

They were painfully aware that peace could not be permanent, but in peace-time the main function of government was to promote prosperity. Defense spending had to be minimized. The British already had a large battle fleet, but it had no active enemies at the moment. The British also had a large merchant marine. The government's solution was to lay up most of the battle fleet against the threat of a future war; in an emergency it could be manned by the experienced sailors of the merchant fleet.[12] Unfortunately for the British, technology changed so rapidly that their expensive fleet became obsolete about mid-century. After that, even though they did not face any immediate war, the British felt trapped into constantly rebuilding their fleet against the possibility of eventual war. Technology continued to change so rapidly that ships generally became obsolete long before they wore out.

Overall, through much of the nineteenth century the Royal Navy was quite expensive—in cash terms. We would describe the navy as technology intensive. On the one hand, Britain was a wealthy country, probably the wealthiest in the world. On the other hand, British naval defense was very inexpensive in terms of men—potentially, in terms of blood. That made sense: Britain was a wealthy liberal state, in which the individual mattered far more than on the Continent. The land powers of Europe could mobilize vast armies at a relatively low cost per man, but the real cost of maintaining those armies was a drastic devaluation of the men who constituted them. For example, as late as 1916 the British government found the idea of conscription unacceptable, even after it had raised a mass army. No other European government of the time would have found that scruple comprehensible.

The combination of seapower and geography made relaxation possible. We tend to see the Europe of 1815 through 1914 as peaceful, but that was true only for Britain, insulated from the Continent by the sea and the Royal Navy. For Britain, war was expeditionary, in the Crimea, Africa, or India. For a country like France or Germany, war was a much more immediate proposition, and the consequence of military failure could be disastrous—as it was for France in 1870. One reason Britain was drawn into European alliance politics after 1904 was that one of the continental states, Germany, appeared to be on the point of overcoming British seapower by building a powerful fleet. Similarly, the German advance through Belgium in 1914 entailed seizing exactly that part of the continental coast the British most associated with possible invasion. In some sense, then, in 1914 the Germans threatened to subject Britain to much the same sort of threats that normally afflicted a continental power such as France.

Surely this sounds familiar. In the wake of the Cold War the United States downsized its forces because, in the absence of a mortal threat, our economy became a paramount interest. That is reasonable even from a military point of view: ultimately it is the economy that determines how well a country can support future military action. Overarming in one decade may cause a devastating slump when a new generation of weapons is needed a few decades later.[13] Because technology is moving so fast, we are even more aware that what we stockpile today may well be insufficient tomorrow. Thus a choice was made to discard numerous serviceable ships at the end of the Cold War in hopes that maintenance money saved could be invested in new technology and, perhaps, in ships better suited to using the new technology. We also surely have the sense, which the British had, that the end of a great war is a great and fleeting opportunity. We can afford temporary weakness, as long as we face no immediate mortal threat, and that military weakness can be turned into the beginning of later strength. Beyond such considerations is a great question, whether the technology bought to fight a central war (had the Cold War turned hot) is entirely suited to the more limited wars we now face.[14]

Like the nineteenth century British, despite downsizing the United States currently pays a high monetary price for defense, because our wealth and technology are used quite freely. We are far less willing to use our population. In this we sometimes contrast ourselves with, for example, China, with its mass army. The great question, both for the British in the past, and for us now, is whether our technology affords us enough leverage to overcome sheer mass. During World War I the answer seemed to be no, and as a consequence the British felt forced to field a mass army and to accept the resulting mass casualties.

As long as the Royal Navy was supreme, the British government enjoyed enormous latitude in its policies. It could follow its basically liberal ideology. For example, the British strongly supported the Greek fight for independence, on entirely ideological grounds. Similarly, they were willing to intervene in the Third World for humanitarian reasons. One of the principal Royal Navy missions was to help suppress slavery by running down slave traders in the South Atlantic. The U.S. Navy cooperated in this endeavor because the trade—but not slavery in the United States—was illegal. One early reason for British intervention in Africa was to stop the slave trade with the Arabs. Much of what the Royal Navy did during the nineteenth century equates to our current interest in military operations other than war (MOOTW). That applies to the other British arms as well; much of British colonial warfare was not too different from the constabulary operation currently existing in the former Yugoslavia.

There was also a commercial logic to British national strategy. Among other things, the Napoleonic wars broke up the Spanish colonial empire in South America. Through the prior centuries, the Spanish had shut British trade off from their rich colonial empire in South America, and periodically the British had tried to dislodge them. With Spain overrun by the French, colonial governments weakened and, after the end of the war, the countries of South America became independent. They were now free to trade with Britain, and indeed to accept British investment. In effect the Royal Navy precluded any attempt by Spain to reclaim the empire after the war as well as any attempt by any other European country to colonize any of the former Spanish colonies. The main exception, which Britain did not resist, was the French intrigue in Mexico during the American Civil War. As the leading commercial country, thanks to a combination of the Industrial Revolution and sea-based access to the world, Britain naturally gained economic ascendancy in much of South America. This position was often equated to an informal kind of empire. Power was limited, however; for example, the United States in 1892 blocked a British assault against Venezuela, which had defaulted on bonds. As it happened, the British South American policy fit well with the desires of the rising United States. In 1823 the U.S. government proclaimed the Monroe Doctrine: it barred European powers from recolonizing the Western Hemisphere. Given rather limited U.S. seapower, the proclamation was hollow —except that it was backed by the overwhelming power of the Royal Navy.

From a British perspective, the informal situation in South America was often preferable to formal empire. It promoted British prosperity, and it cost very little in military terms. No garrisons were needed. No administrators had to be supplied. However, it mattered enormously that British forces, mainly naval, were available to help the informal partners. The British naval mission went well beyond countering specific threats to British possessions. For example, when a Peruvian ironclad, *Huascar,* went on what was seen as a piratical spree, a pair of British cruisers stopped her.[15] The British understood just how important tranquil use of the sea could be; it did not really matter whether the ironclad had interfered with British-flag ships. It was important that any minor despot know that any attack on a British merchant would lead to retaliation from the Royal Navy. The usual expression was that "trade follows the Flag."

These considerations explain why, until the latter part of the nineteenth century, Britain had few large colonies apart from India. The West Indian islands had been taken over for their sugarcane crops, but by the mid-nineteenth century that was not worth nearly as much as it had been. Other colonies were valued mainly for their contributions to worldwide British naval power or, as in the case of Hong Kong, as commercial centers providing market access. Some possessions, such as Canada and Australia, were clearly en route to self-government, more as client states or coalition partners than as true colonies. Much of the imperial expansion of the latter part of the century could be attributed to a mix of commercial and humanitarian concerns. Many places were taken over to ensure access to resources, at a time when other European countries were taking over colonies and, among other things, monopolizing resources. Presumably the British would have preferred that they remain as trading partners. Thus much of the informal empire was never converted into de jure empire.

The demise of the Soviet Union—actually, of the Soviet empire—opened up important economic opportunities. Possibly the former Central Asiatic republics are a sort of twenty-first century South America, fertile soil for U.S. investments, just as places like Argentina and Chile were for the British. For them, too, the central issue is whether our economic interest will be accompanied by security assistance, by guarantees of their borders with, for instance, Russia itself. Obviously nothing in history repeats exactly, and there is no local equivalent of the United States of 1823. The combination of difficult terrain and poor roads connecting Central Asia to the more populous parts of Russia may play something of the role of the Atlantic Ocean, inhibiting Russian repossession. The United States has guaranteed several borders deep in the former Soviet Union specifically to encourage governments to give up their stocks of Soviet-era nuclear weapons, generally to Russia.

The humanitarian impulse, which in the past sometimes led to colonization, explains U.S. intervention in Somalia. For a time that country was sometimes called the first likely United Nations (UN) colony. Will Kosovo be the first NATO colony? Or, eventually, the first European Union (EU) colony? If in fact the occupation of Bosnia and Kosovo is an open-ended obligation, then these areas are in effect protectorates. Like the colonies of the past, they tie down a significant fraction of the shrinking army strength of the occupying power or powers. Occupation duty, moreover, is unsafe and increasingly unpopular. In the United States it is said to contribute heavily to retention problems. How many Kosovos can the United States or NATO occupy at the same time? Is the British experience of operating a large empire using a small but mobile army relevant to us? Britain's seapower offered her army considerable mobility; the British could easily concentrate at a threatened point, but there was still a limit to how many crises could be handled simultaneously. Is that so different from the current U.S. defense problem?

It is also possible to envisage a modern equivalent of the impulse that led the British into much of Africa. Although governments generally claim to agree that they must opt for free trade and globalization, that may be a passing phase. There is increasing resistance to both. For example, some in the European Union argue that globalization threatens its social system. There is, therefore, a real possibility that the world will split into competitive trading blocs, each seeking at least privileged access to particular raw materials. The word *colony* probably will not be revived, but some equivalent to colonial empires may re-emerge. Again, the issue may ultimately be whether we can maintain peace in many relatively unstable places without bankrupting ourselves. It used to be said that the British empire ran a net loss. If so, the need to maintain government and peacekeeping forces everywhere probably explains why.

The British never had enough ground forces to deal with all potential sources of unrest. Their control over a vast empire rested ultimately on their prestige, and on the expectation that they could and would put down any rebellion, defeat any attack.[16] That is not too different from the prescription that the United States can maintain a congenial world as long as those who dislike us fear that we can swat them down at will. Such action, which must be possible anywhere in the world, rests ultimately on maritime mobility, because the decisive force is unlikely to be in place when the crisis erupts. In the British case, it helped that most colonies were not contiguous. Their crises were geographically separate; a failure in one place did not instantly ignite trouble across the border.

The modern United States faces an unruly world somewhat analogous to the unruly British colonial world. We, too, want to keep order by maintaining sufficient prestige. Sometimes that requires us to swat an enemy. More often we, like the British, hope simply to deter those opposing us, using some sort of presence rather than by actual combat. The threat that causes others to change their behavior must be credible; we may prefer not to fight, but we must be able to do so if challenged. Because we are not in a colonial posture, we do not always have to fight. Our prestige, however, cannot afford many defeats. Therefore, we need some means of engaging when and where we want to, without accepting so much involvement that we cannot pull back if we decide that our interests are not so vitally engaged. Sea-based forces offer exactly that option.

Moreover, the meaning of engagement on land is different for the United States than for the British. The British were already more or less permanently engaged, because they were operating in their own colonies. The United States can choose whether or not to deploy forces in any particular country. It is well understood that any fixed garrison can become embarrassing, Okinawa being a case in point. What is probably less obvious is that, to many countries, a U.S. garrison of some sort is a valuable, hence welcome, asset. If that government expects to become involved in war, having U.S. service personnel on the ground at the outset may well ensure that there are early U.S. casualties. Thus our decision whether or not to intervene takes on strong emotional rather than altogether rational tones. For example, in 1963, the prime goal of the then South Vietnamese government was to get Americans into combat. Americans were already fighting covertly, but that did not count. The U.S. government resisted, to the extent that it did, because it wanted to preserve its options. As it turned out, the U.S. government locked itself into Vietnam in another way, by becoming involved in a coup and thus by determining what sort of government the country would have. It then became a matter of U.S. prestige whether the postcoup government could do any better against the ongoing Communist insurgency, and within a year that led to an open-ended involvement on the ground.

The more basic point, that it pays enormously to be able to pull out, remains. Naval forces can be withdrawn far more painlessly than land forces. *A primary but unfortunately unquantifiable test of military forces is the extent to which they allow a government to retain its freedom of action.* If a crisis winds down, or if the cost of engagement proves disproportionate to the benefits, naval forces can be withdrawn at a low cost in national prestige. Withdrawing a garrison or even land-based aircraft, which may have been costly (at least in political terms) to put in place, is a very different proposition.

The British did sometimes need mass forces. They usually opted for a mixed strategy. The British treated India like a coalition partner, with a large army stiffened by British forces, whose mobility was provided by the Royal Navy and its subordinate shipping. British units also provided most of the higher-technology end of the army in India. The large Indian army provided the bulk of British forces between the Gulf and Malaya. It protected India itself, largely against the threat of Russian attack from the north; helped protect the British rule of India; and projected British power. When tensions flared with Russia in 1885, Indian troops concentrated at Malta for a possible attack in the Black Sea. Indian forces attacked the German African colonies in 1914. India was so important to the British that it was sometimes said, before 1914, that the British empire had two capitals, London and Delhi.

The policy had two major drawbacks. First, India was hardly a true coalition partner; she was a colony. When Indian troops mutinied in 1857, the British brought a massive force to India. Occurring immediately after the massive foreign engagement in the Crimea, this would have been impossible without British seapower. Indian troops performed willingly enough during World War I, but that experience apparently awakened Indian nationalism. After World War I, the British found it more and more difficult to use Indian troops abroad, due partly to rising Indian nationalism. For example, it was considered dangerous to use them in Moslem countries.[17] Some of the disaster in Malaya in 1941 was later blamed on disaffected Indian units attracted by the Japanese appeal of "Asia for the Asians." One reason the British had to promise India independence during World War II was to convince Indians to fight; another was to mitigate local unrest, which among other things would have required large numbers of British troops to control. A second drawback was the sheer size of the Indian manpower contribution—in effect, the success of the coalition strategy. After World War II several British politicians argued that once India was gone the British would need a peacetime draft simply to make up the numbers needed to control the remaining parts of the empire.[18] It did not help that the British had to fight to defend what was left, in places as far apart as Palestine and Malaya, and then in Africa.

Clearly the Indian contribution was not massive enough to fight a major war. During both world wars, the British empire's volunteer forces, including large forces from the independent Dominions, made vital contributions. These forces can be classed as coalition partners or allies. As for the Indian coalition solution, it failed because the coalition partner was coerced rather than voluntary; ultimately India rejected coercion. After World War II, with India independent, the British tried to create an equivalent colonial army in Africa, called the King's African Rifles, but that was never very successful. Little more than a decade after India left the empire, the sheer cost of maintaining a large British draftee army was perceived as crippling. Without the draft, hence with the British army drastically cut, there were no longer sufficient troops to police the empire while maintaining a sufficient force in Europe, and the African colonies had to be abandoned.

The requirement for empire defense had another, subtler, effect. The

British shaped their army largely for colonial security missions, because (apart from India) they faced few real cross-border challenges. In the interwar period the need to maintain sheer numbers of units, based in so many places, retarded mechanization. The costs would have been borne by cutting the size of the army. Repair facilities were scarce in remote places; therefore, in the 1920s and 1930s it was much more practical to retain horses and even mules for mobility. Under such circumstances it was difficult for the British army to adopt the sort of mechanized all-arms tactics needed to fight a major war in Europe. Splitting the army into small units limited officers' experience with large-unit command and control, in ways particularly evident at the outset of World War I. In case this appears to be nothing more than arcane history, ask whether adapting the U.S. Army to peace enforcement in places like Bosnia and Kosovo (the U.S. equivalents, perhaps, of the old British empire) might affect that same army's ability to fight an armored battle similar to the Kuwait battle in 1991.

The British benefited enormously from the fact that their empire was seaborne. The sea made it easy to shift the small ground forces the British could assemble from place to place. Permanent garrisons could be limited. The sea also separated British colonies from each other, and thus buffered each from the effects of any reverse suffered in any other. That was particularly true before the era of modern mass media. The Boer War is a case in point. It erupted at about the same time that British-led forces were fighting, literally at the other end of Africa, in the Sudan, against the Mahdi. There a British force had been destroyed thirteen years earlier, in 1885.[19] Buffering, and the ease with which troops could be brought in by sea, had limited the effect of that earlier defeat, although for the sake of imperial prestige it had ultimately to be reversed. The war in the Sudan was one of choice, whereas the Boer War farther south was imposed on the British government, at least partly by local settlers interested in gaining territory. This situation seems comparable to a future sequence of near-simultaneous crises the United States could face.

Without seaborne mobility, the British would have had to rely on troops already stationed at the Cape of Good Hope to fight the Boer War. Without any a priori reason to imagine the explosion at the cape, the garrison there would have been small. Troops would have been fed into the war of choice, in the Sudan, and little or nothing could have been added at the cape. The result probably would have been victory at one end of Africa and disaster at the other. Other troops would have been fixed in other parts of the empire.

Given peace everywhere but the Sudan and the Cape, *and* maritime mobility, the British could handle the two simultaneous crises. They could quickly reinforce the cape from other parts of the empire. As important, other potential enemies did not try to seize this opportunity, because they knew that Britain could use its seapower to redeploy troops to deal with them. In a greater emergency, the British could have reduced the Boer War to a holding operation while solving a distant problem, then come back to finish off the Boers. No matter how badly the troops at the cape were battered, they could still be supplied by sea, and the sea would still have been a refuge. British financial and shipping control, moreover, limited any advantage the Boers might have taken of the breathing space thus created. Seapower was also key to victory in the Sudan: the British force was carried down the Nile by boat.

Many Germans regarded the Boers, whom the British fought, as an allied ethnic group. As tension built toward war in South Africa, a British raiding party under L. S. Jameson struck at the Boers in the Transvaal in hopes of igniting a pro-British rising that would allow the British to incorporate the Transvaal into the British Cape Colony. The Transvaal was already under British suzerainty, but it was not a colony. When the Jameson raid was defeated, Kaiser Wilhelm II of Germany sent the Boer president, Paul Kruger, a congratulatory telegram, which infuriated the British. In effect the kaiser was saying that he identified with the Boers against the British, and that he supported their independence from the British. The episode was far more significant for the Germans, however, because it highlighted their inability to intervene in a war far from Europe. Without serious seapower, they could not possibly block British access to South Africa. A telegram, however incendiary, was a poor substitute. The kaiser's response was to favor the naval buildup that ultimately convinced the British that Germany really was a threat, and thus ensured British participation in World War I.[20]

Ironically, the Boer War helped convince the British that their own economic and military power was inadequate. They could not defend themselves adequately while also defending the empire against all comers. They began to seek accommodations outside Europe, initially with Japan in 1902. The entente with France two years later began as an agreement to settle differences in Africa. Meanwhile influential British policy makers were concluding that Britain must escape diplomatic isolation in Europe. That was soon taken to mean that she had to side with France against Germany. Maintaining the coalition with France became a major British foreign policy goal. The compromises the British found themselves forced to endure illustrate the extent to which a coalition partner can become dominant. This process began with the British agreement that any expeditionary force sent to France in an emergency would come under French command.

Consider an imperial war *without* much seapower, the Russo-Japanese War of 1904–5. Manchuria, the site of the war, was effectively a Russian colonial possession. Because the area of the country between Manchuria and European Russia was so sparsely populated, it might as well have been empty sea —with one important difference; it did not offer nearly the same good communication. The Japanese effectively cut off actual sea access to the Russian Far East by defeating and then blockading a Russian fleet. That left the Russians with the Trans-Siberian Railroad, which was mostly single tracked. Given limited railroad capacity, it took them a long time to build up their Manchurian force, and during the war they could not do much to reinforce, supply, or withdraw it. Moreover, like most armies, it could not redeploy easily. The Japanese in effect besieged the Russian force, destroying both it and the bottled-up fleet. The Russians' only real hope was to reopen sea communications by destroying the blocking Japanese fleet and thus freeing the Far East fleet trapped at its base, Port Arthur. Hence the desperate expedient of sending the Baltic Fleet halfway around the world, to what turned out to be its doom at Tsushima, became particularly pointless when Port Arthur fell while the fleet was still en route.

Even so, the Japanese found it very difficult to maintain the winning combination of land power and seapower. In 1905 the Russians actually had more troops in Siberia, and the Japanese were exhausted. In theory, the Russians could have struck back, or at least could have prolonged the war and extracted a better settlement. In fact the Russians lacked the will to continue. The Japanese victories had convinced many Russians that their government was so incompetent that it did not deserve to remain in power. Further Russian resistance became impossible when revolution, fed by that sense of incompetence, broke out. By that time the Russian government was almost bankrupt; it would have been hard-pressed to maintain a big army in Siberia for much longer. The high cost of supply, due to the lack of a sea route to the Far East, worsened the bankruptcy. The Russians lacked the seapower to maintain a route through waters the Japanese would try to control. To many Russians, the fleet steaming halfway around the world must have seemed a kind of last chance at victory, and the disaster at Tsushima ended that hope.

The situation was not too different from that at Dien Bien Phu in Vietnam in 1954. The French had been doing badly for years, but the Viet Minh had hardly succeeded in destroying them. The numerical balance of forces in the country, however, was not nearly as important as the widespread sense in France that the war could not be won. Adding more French troops merely provided more potential casualties. When the French added Vietnam to the agenda of an international conference in Geneva, thus signaling that they were nearing their exhaustion point, the Viet Minh understood that one last push, however expensive, would win. They therefore staked everything on victory at Dien Bien Phu. The logic of the French position there had been that without risking disaster elsewhere in the country the Viet Minh could not overrun it. In much the same way, Japanese victory at Tsushima was decisive because it capped a series of other Russian disasters.

For the Japanese, the war taught two strategic lessons. First, without seapower they could hope neither to land on the Asian mainland nor to win there. Second, seapower was not sufficient. The Russian army in Manchuria was supplied mainly by rail. No blockade could starve it, and it always had the option of drawing back from the coast. To destroy that army the Japanese needed a mass army of their own. What the Japanese did not learn was that it is exhausting to maintain a first-class navy *and* a first-class mass ground force. Through the period after the war, they were never able to choose between seapower and land power, not because they were so wealthy but because their political system was inherently so weak. As a consequence, the wars the Japanese army and navy fought in World War II were largely separate and uncoordinated, with terrible consequences for Japan. Because their ambitions in Asia ran so high, the Japanese never seriously considered forming a supporting coalition to solve their economic problem; any potential partners would have seen themselves as likely victims. Yet a strategist would have to say that the Russian army would have been in much greater danger if the Japanese had managed to gain support from the Chinese on the Manchurian border, and the Japanese might have won far more easily. Conversely, when the Japanese invaded China in the 1930s, they always had to guard against a Soviet attack from the north. That effort absorbed troops. The Japanese did manage a nonaggression treaty with the Soviets, after losing a campaign against them in 1939. As World War II turned against Japan, troops had to be siphoned off, leaving the Manchurian border almost unguarded. The Japanese hoped that the treaty would protect them. The Soviets, however, overran Manchuria at the end of World War II.

In modern terms, the Boer War was a major regional contingency (MRC); the war in the Sudan was a smaller-scale contingency (SSC). During the first few post–Cold War years, U.S. defense policy was generally predicated on the ability to fight two nearly simultaneous MRCs, such as a new Gulf War or a rerun of Korea. The unstated assumption is that forces built for such wars can be split up to handle all sscs. However, victory in an MRC generally requires massed power, and the only way to bring mass to bear is to move in heavy ground-based air and land forces. Naval forces are very mobile, but that mobility limits what a naval force can carry with it. Given a space ashore, ships and aircraft can bring in as much as is needed, to be regrouped and deployed after it has been landed. An SSC, on the other hand, is a small finite problem. The unstated assumption is that many SSCs may arise more or less simultaneously. It does not take as much power to head off or win an SSC, but that power had better be able to reach the scene of the action quickly. A world of MRCs favors mass forces and concentration. A world of SSCs favors dispersed forces, probably naval or naval-like ones.

It is generally assumed that no SSC can be as important intrinsically as an MRC. In the case described, however, the SSC was much more important than the MRC. In the Sudan the British fought a Moslem fundamentalist leader, the Mahdi, whose victory over them might have ignited revolt in the many Moslem territories of the empire, including large parts of India. Britain's enemies well understood this sensitivity. For example, British feared that Turkey, the hereditary leader of the Moslem world, would manage to turn World War I into a holy war (a jihad). The Germans tried hard to disable the British empire, which they could not really reach by sea, in just this way.[21] Similarly, in World War II they cultivated various Moslem clerics, such as the Grand Mufti of Jerusalem, in hopes of ejecting Britain from her largely informal empire in the Middle East.

It may well be that the optimum force for the United States is one that can split up to provide deterrence, by the mere fact of its presence, when faced with numerous sscs, partly in hopes that they do not metastasize into MRCs. For example, if the United States had deployed strong naval forces to the Gulf in, for instance, June 1990, would that have deterred Saddam Hussein? A military establishment optimized for one or the other end of the spectrum of conflict is probably inefficient at the other. One solution to this problem would be to optimize active forces for the split-ssc role, which is more likely to matter on a day-to-day basis. A large fraction of the MRC force would be maintained in the form of reserves. To some extent that is current policy in the army and the air force, which are MRC forces, but it is hidden by the services' natural desire to be involved in all SSC actions: reservists are now called up more or less continuously.

So what does the British imperial example suggest? We cannot escape stationing some forces abroad, but in doing so we have to limit their size ruthlessly, relying heavily on mobility, probably sea-based, to bring our limited stock of heavier forces to bear. Like the British, the United States cannot afford enough heavy forces to forward-base them in sufficient strength. Our great difference from the British is that we do not own forward bases. We rely on coalition partners to provide them, and permission to use the bases can be denied. We have already experienced problems when trying to use NATO facilities to support our policies, which many NATO countries rejected, in the Middle East.[22]

War Winning

An important question is unanswered. We fight wars to compel others, be they governments or subnational groups, to change their behavior. Only rarely, if at all, does the United States fight to gain or even to retain territory; others often have different objectives. Just what does success require? In a world of shrinking military resources it is by no means clear just what it takes to win. In the recent past the answer seemed obvious. In World War II Germany was overrun and the United States threatened Japan with total destruction. During the Cold War we threatened the Soviets with nearly total destruction. We now lack the mass necessary to overrun, let alone to occupy, even a moderate-size country. We cannot threaten sheer destruction, using nuclear weapons, unless our enemy threatens nuclear or biological attack against us.

At least for Americans, another factor—the shadow of Vietnam—was also at work in Iraq. During the Reagan administration, Secretary of Defense Caspar Weinberger announced a "doctrine" to guarantee that the United States would never again fall into that sort of quagmire. U.S. forces had engaged in Vietnam with neither a clear-cut war aim nor a clear-cut exit criterion. The stated goal of protecting South Vietnam was far too vague to be a war aim, and there was no way of saying when it had been accomplished. The problem of the open-ended commitment was magnified by the human cost of the war. If there been few or no casualties on a daily or weekly basis, the open-endedness probably would not have been nearly so onerous. That was certainly the case with the continuing U.S. presence in Korea, and it is also the case with the reduced, but quite active, presence containing Iraq a decade after the end of the war.

The Gulf War exemplified the sort of maritime strategy discussed throughout this book. Access by sea made it possible for the coalition, particularly the United States, to concentrate an overwhelming force against Iraq. Given other U.S. security concerns, that sort of concentration was allowable only because the sea could also be used to withdraw the force as soon as it won, for use elsewhere (the troops flew in and out, but the materiel did not). This sort of attack fit well with Weinberger's doctrine: the coalition fought a war of limited duration to achieve a finite war aim, to eject Iraqi forces from Kuwait. However, there was also an open-ended goal, which was to ensure the survival of friendly regimes willing to supply oil. Kuwait was a symptom of the much greater problem of Iraqi aggressiveness fueled by oil money. The unstated hope was that by reversing the Iraqi invasion of Kuwait, which seemed to threaten other friendly regimes in the area (particularly the Saudis), the longer-term goal could be promoted. In a longer-term sense the Iraqi attempt to acquire missiles and weapons of mass destruction also threatened local stability. There was an unstated hope that victory in Kuwait could some-how be translated into the elimination of this longer-term threat. Moreover, there was an unstated assumption that Saddam Hussein himself was the cause of the problem, that is, simply removing him would solve the long-term prob-lem.[23] Saddam is certainly extremely obnoxious, and he has been far too ready to start wars, but his most objectionable foreign policies can also be seen as a continuation of broader trends in Iraqi history. Any successor granted the same unified Iraqi state would pick up on these trends. That successor would probably also want to dominate the Gulf area, and would probably try to keep developing the Saddam's weapons.[24]

The assumption was that the short-term victory would automatically buy the long-term solution: the ascendancy demonstrated by smashing the Iraqi army within a few days could later be exploited to compel Iraq to follow the dictates of the coalition. Surely Saddam would accept whatever was demanded of him, because he had so clearly lost (and would lose again if he resumed the fight). It did not matter whether Iraqi soil was occupied. Little care was exer-cised in drawing armistice terms because it seemed that any errors could eas-ily be corrected. Hence the disastrous decision was made to allow Saddam to use helicopters freely over Iraq.

Saddam, who is probably typical of likely future Third World adversaries, apparently saw matters quite differently. Not occupying Iraq was perceived as Western weakness. Most important, the main props of the regime, such as the secret police and the Republican Guard, remained intact. Moreover, it was obvious that the massive coalition force would soon be withdrawn; reassem-bly would be difficult if not impossible. Saddam announced that he had won, in that he had stood off vastly superior foreign power. He grudgingly allowed inspections and arms control, of a sort, but he was really playing for time, in the sure knowledge that his enemies' coalition was gradually eroding. Unfortunately, some fellow dictators may well agree with Saddam. During the Gulf War it was clear that Saddam had supporters among his fellow Third World governments. They tried to help by increasing tension elsewhere to tie down forces that might otherwise have gone to the Gulf. For example, the North Koreans increased tension on cue. By pressing Pakistan, India precluded the dispatch of a Pakistani armored division earmarked to help in the Gulf. What happens to the force tied down by Iraq if, for instance, a war erupts in Korea? A decade later Saddam is still in power, and the coalition is beginning to fall apart. As long as he is still in power when the embargo ends, Saddam can resume the earlier adventures, which led to the Gulf War in the first place.

In the aftermath of the war, the main instruments of coercion left to the remaining active coalition members were a combination of embargo and sporadic air attacks, the latter essentially to enforce a "no-fly zone" and thus to keep Saddam's air arm crippled by precluding any flight training. There were also periodic air and missile strikes, although it is difficult to say just how significant they have been. The embargo, which is enforced largely by sea, has proven horribly costly for individual Iraqis caught up in the country's economic collapse. However, Saddam is its ultimate target, and as long as he can feed his secret police, his army, and his Republican Guard, he can remain in power. No embargo is perfect, and smuggling surely suffices for this purpose. Gross poverty due to the embargo probably helps him retain power, because he controls distribution of the remaining scarce goods or cash.

The theory of the embargo was that a rational (i.e., Western-style) government would have compromised rather than destroy its population and its industry, as Saddam is doing. Certainly the damage the coalition has already done would have appalled any Western government. Actually the situation has become a double-edged sword, because many Westerners are beginning to ask whether it is moral to visit such horrors on a population entirely unable to influence what Saddam does. The counterargument is that if the embargo is lifted, the resources made available will go into rearming Iraq rather than into feeding Iraqis. Saddam is well aware of such arguments, and he has tried to use them against the United States. As for possible compromise, by demanding that Saddam remove himself, we have made that effectively impossible. Yet we have painted him as the cause of the problem, so removal has become an irreducible goal of successive American presidents.

The lesson is that U.S. power is limited. As we move away from the more terrible instruments of twentieth century total war, we find it difficult to impose anything resembling total victory. The many historical examples in this book suggest that this is in the nature of maritime forces, including land forces that descend temporarily on an area thanks to sea access, as in the Gulf. Sea powers have been most successful when they secured coalition partners with powerful land forces. Perhaps, then, effective long-term containment of Iraq requires some sort of agreement or accommodation with the other main regional power, Iran. Our main land coalition partner, Saudi Arabia, is far too weak to contribute much on the ground, although the access she contributed prior to the Gulf War was vital. Prior to the Gulf War, the United States used Iraq as a coalition partner to contain what was then considered a worse threat to regional stability, revolutionary Iran.

Limited power is not a new problem. For example, consider the dilemma the British faced when they fought the United States in 1812–14. The Americans, at least those on or near the frontier, had gone to war largely in hopes of seizing Canada.[25] The British objective was not only to secure Canada at the present time, but also to preclude any later invasion by a growing United States. Yet the British could not maintain any large permanent garrison in Canada. Resources were limited, and other places, such as India and Europe, would always be far more important to British policy makers. For the moment, the situation was complicated by the ongoing war in Europe that was consuming the bulk of British forces on land and on sea. Yet continued possession of Canada was vital for the European war, because it supplied much of the timber and other materiel the Royal Navy needed to remain operational.

At the outset, the Americans threatened the British in two ways: by invading Canada overland, and by attacking British shipping. With limited forces available, the British confined themselves to beating off the invasion of Canada and to protecting their seaborne trade.[26] The Chesapeake and the Delaware were blockaded, mainly to neutralize the U.S. Navy. Little attempt was made to interdict trade, partly because American produce was helping feed not only Canada itself but also the British army on the peninsula in Europe. The British had no hope of striking any decisive blow; they could only hope that the Americans would exhaust themselves and tire of the war.

As the Napoleonic War wound down, the British could move more ships into the Atlantic and could stiffen the blockade, imposing an economic price on the Americans. They now blockaded New York, Charleston, Savannah, and the Mississippi Delta. Because the United States had poor roads, much of its domestic trade moved by sea, and was therefore subject to this economic blockade. As a developing country, moreover, the United States depended heavily on foreign trade. By 1814 the blockade and the stress of war were severely damaging the American economy and making the war quite unpopular.[27]

By the fall of 1813 Napoleon was defeated. Because the British controlled the sea, and had the necessary shipping, they could swing large ground and naval forces into what had earlier been a peripheral war. Soon after Napoleon went into exile, a British force sailed from Europe to relieve pressure on Canada at Niagara. In September 1814 it tried and failed to overrun Platts-burgh, New York. To divert American forces from this theater of war, the Royal Navy raided the American coast. In the face of British naval mobility, the Americans had to raise disproportionate land forces, which could not be mobile, to deal with the seaborne raiders. Raiding operations included the burning of Washington.

This strategy was still unlikely to be decisive. The British might have hoped that the Americans would have surrendered to save their coastal cities, but they had not given up after the successful attack on Washington. What military effort could end the war on British terms? What vital center could be identified? The Americans were, moreover, heartened by their one victory against raiding forces, when Baltimore held against a naval attack (providing the background for the U.S. national anthem).[28]

In September 1813 the British decided on two measures for the coming year's campaign. One was to gain control of the mouth of the Mississippi, cut-ting communication between the interior settlements of the United States and the sea. This was a shrewd political move. The frontiersmen were the main supporters of the assault on Canada. Coastal states, particularly in New Eng-land, depended heavily on overseas trade, and were suffering from the inten-sified blockade in the war they already opposed.

The second objective was to seize some prize so valuable that the Amer-icans would have to make concessions to get it back. With British forces already in place off the mouth of the Mississippi, and with British troops available from the West Indies, New Orleans was the obvious target. The attack on New Orleans was initially conceived as part of the raiding strategy, but the city then became an important strategic prize, the culmination of a campaign waged on the U.S. Gulf Coast. The British thought they had the advantage because they believed most inhabitants of New Orleans would not identify with the United States. They had been Spanish subjects, briefly French citizens, and then had been sold to the Americans in 1803 as part of the Louisiana Pur-chase. To the British, who in 1814 were allies of Spain, the sale of the Louisiana territory, which was far more than the current state of Louisiana, by France to the United States had violated the terms of the transfer of the territory from Spain to France; therefore the purchase was illegal. The British encouraged the inhabitants to revolt, but their commander was ordered not to promise that freeing Louisiana, or restoring it to the Spanish crown, would be a condition for peace with the United States.[29]

By the time the attack on New Orleans was being planned, the British were negotiating with the Americans at Ghent. Their main objective was to secure Canada, and to do that they needed a permanent ally on the American border. They chose the Indians of the Old Northwest, and demanded a large Indian reservation there.[30] They also demanded some parts of the border states of Maine and Minnesota, and demilitarization of the Great Lakes. Without a fleet on the Great Lakes, the Americans would find it difficult to attack overland. The territorial demands were to secure the Canadian border. The Americans found these terms altogether unacceptable. The British then retreated to a proposal that each side retain the territory it had at the end of hostilities, subject to adjustment. The British hoped in this way to gain northern Maine, the attack route against Halifax and Quebec in Canada, as well as some forts in Minnesota. If the attack on New Orleans had succeeded, such a peace would also have left the British in possession of the mouth of the Mississippi, and perhaps ultimately much of the Mississippi River valley.

A treaty was signed—but not ratified—before the attack on New Orleans. The British had been forced to agree to return to the unsatisfactory prewar status quo; they had lost any hope of strengthening their position in Canada. The sheer cost of the Napoleonic War made it difficult for them to contemplate continued warfare in North America, and their failures at Plattsburgh and Baltimore limited their ability to pressure the American negotiators. They apparently did not realize the tenuous American position, a fairly common situation in wartime. The British feared that, as in two recent cases, the Americans would insist on changing the treaty between signature and ratification. They therefore specified that peace would come only after ratification, which could take several months. Thus the attack on New Orleans would presumably have gone ahead even if news of the peace treaty had been known; seizure of the city would have been an invaluable piece of insurance. Moreover, during the recent wars in Europe several treaties had been canceled after signature.

Possession of the main port of the western United States would have provided the British with enormous leverage. Also, the British seem to have considered that no treaty could cover Louisiana, because it was not legitimately

American. For their part, the Americans wanted the treaty to create a commission to determine the border between the northern part of the Louisiana Purchase territory and Canada; the British recognized that as a ploy to force them to recognize the legitimacy of the purchase.[31] The treaty stipulated that all territory taken by one party had to be returned. Given the British interpretation of the Louisiana Purchase, this could have meant returning Louisiana to Spain. The presence of a strong British army there would have reinforced this interpretation very powerfully.[32] If the British had managed to pry the Louisiana Purchase from American hands, they would have limited American growth to the west and thus crippled the sectional party that had caused the war in the first place. The United States would have been largely dependent on seaborne commerce, hence at the mercy of the Royal Navy. The problem of Canadian defense would have been solved. In this sense New Orleans became absolutely vital. When the British lost the battle to seize it, they could no longer imagine any solution to Canadian defense.

In late 1814 the British could at least imagine deploying their powerful forces against the Americans, and doubtless this threat helped convince the Americans to sign. For the British the question was the expected cost of an 1815 campaign. Napoleon, however, escaped from Elba just about when the treaty was ratified, and the British were fortunate that their forces were available to deal with him.

In 1812–14 the British possessed unequalled strategic mobility, thanks to their seapower. Their army was more competent than what the United States could raise, although it could not always deploy in sufficient numbers. Even a limited British effort exhausted the United States to the point that the U.S. government had to seek terms, although not to the point of giving the British what they badly wanted. In retrospect, it may seem that the compromise peace reached in 1814 really was satisfactory, because the United States never again attacked Canada, despite the absence of a strong British garrison there. The situation looked different at the time, however. For example, when the British became embroiled in the Crimean War four decades later, they feared that the United States might take the opportunity to seize Canada.[33] British seapower, which in 1812–14 had done considerable damage to the United States, was the only available counterweight. The British never found any military solution to the American problem, and Canada never grew sufficiently in population to solve it for them. The coalition solution, represented by the proposed Indian reservation, failed because the British did not have sufficient strength in 1814 to impose it on a very unwilling United States.

2

The Flavor of Seapower

The Sea as Highway and Barrier

THE BASIC FACT of seapower is that is much easier to move anything heavy by sea than in any other way. Mahan called the sea the great commons, the open space open to anyone with a coast. The sea as a whole is, in effect, an interior line of communication, in the terms armies use. In this sense New York and Glasgow are closer together than, for instance, Paris and Warsaw. It is still sometimes less expensive to ship goods across the Pacific than to move them a few hundred miles by rail. Certainly people now rarely move by sea; airplanes are far faster. However, for heavy weights the sea is still, and is likely to remain, the only efficient means of transportation between the continents. That includes heavy military forces. That is why self-contained naval forces can easily supply operational airpower on demand, operational and sustained reconnaissance, or heavy short-range missile salvoes. This consideration also applies to mobile antimissile batteries. Similarly, vital resources such as oil generally travel by sea. It follows that denial of sea transport—embargo or blockade—can be quite effective.

The great goal of naval forces is to ensure sea control: a guarantee that the sea can be used freely, and that the enemy is limited to fugitive use (the sea generally cannot be completely denied to an enemy). Sometimes sea control is transitory; often the area controlled is limited. Sea control is sometimes contrasted to a lesser goal, sea denial, in which neither side can use the sea fully. For example, during the Cold War the West saw wide-area sea control as a prerequisite for success in case the war turned hot. The Soviets seemed to be interested mainly in promoting sea denial. Similarly, the German U-boat forces of the two world wars sought sea denial, not sea control; they could not guarantee free passage for German surface ships, except by destroying enemy warships blocking that passage.

Clearly, much depends on what a dominant sea power does with its sea control. Seapower can keep problems at arm's length, even in more or less peaceful times. Conversely, anyone trying to leap a water barrier—as the Germans wanted to do across the channel in 1940, and as the Allies succeeded in doing in 1944—needs not only ships but also at least local sea control. For centuries British control of the English Channel precluded any effective invasion. In turn, Britain had a freedom of action in continental affairs, which no country on the Continent enjoyed.[1]

As for sea denial, it is extremely difficult for an enemy actually to block sea passage; there are usually too many paths around any blocking force. That makes phrases like sea lanes, and the defense thereof, largely meaningless.[2] Naval combat is usually about attacks on particular moving ships or groups of ships, and merely finding those targets is an important theme. If the path is narrow enough, however, it can be blocked. Just how narrow depends on available surveillance and strike assets. Properly used, they could make passage of convoys through the Mediterranean (for example, during 1940–42) or around the North Cape to Russia (1941–44) extremely hazardous. Similarly, there was a real concern that the Libyans might oppose passage of ships en route to the Gulf in 1990–91 via the narrowest part of the Mediterranean. It is important, therefore, to distinguish oceanic sea control from the contested sea control of coastal areas.

These ideas are as old as oceangoing ships, but they remain important, perhaps even more important for the twenty-first century. They are as valid in a world of limited wars, which is the world in which we find ourselves, as in the era of total war just passed.

All U.S. services have adopted the concept of expeditionary warfare, which implies global mobility comparable to that offered by the sea. Thus the U.S. Army is developing a lightweight brigade that can be airlifted anywhere in the world by appropriate transport aircraft in ninety-six hours and the U.S. Air Force has formed Air Expeditionary Forces. However, these concepts are limited in important ways. Tactical aircraft and tanks can move quite fast, but their reach is limited because they carry only limited fuel and other loads. On the ground, sustained overall mobility requires dumps of supplies, from which supply vehicles can shuttle to the fighting or moving force. Ground units tend to leap between logistics dumps, which must be assembled laboriously if they are to support a large force. Even long-range aircraft often need aerial refueling, in effect a shuttle from a fuel dump. Air delivery cannot provide the massive logistical backup required for extended combat because airplanes have limited payloads. For the Air Expeditionary Forces, the solution is to fly into an existing base, and to use its facilities and its supplies. That in turn places drastic political limits on the places the force can use.

Seaborne forces offer something different. Ships can carry thousands of tons of payload for long distances at respectable speeds, about thirty miles per hour. Thus they can deliver, or support, not only the fighting machines but also the wherewithal for sustained operations. The hallmark of a maritime force is that it does not need local assistance—and that is likely to become more important in the future.

For a ground force already in place, moreover, fast movement requires roads or railways, which often do not run where a ground force wants to go. For example, roads more often go to a coast rather than along it. Such limitations affect the rate at which a defense can be erected against a surprise assault from the sea, in ways not altogether different from those familiar to the strategists of the past.

Navies are, indeed always have been, highly capital and technology intensive, and are expensive to replace. Capital intensity carries with it a need for expertise, which may be even more difficult to replace than the ships themselves. In mid-1916 the British fought two very bloody battles, Jutland at sea and the Somme on land. It was often said that the British commander at Jutland, Adm. Sir John Jellicoe, was the only man who could lose the war in an afternoon, because his fleet, once destroyed, could not quickly have been replaced. As devastating as the Somme was, however, the British mass army quickly made up its losses and continued to fight equally horrific offensive battles. No British general could have lost the war in a day or a week. In World War II, the American naval victory at Midway in June 1942 was decisive because the Japanese could not easily build new aircraft carriers or, more important, train new pilots. Two years later, in the Philippine Sea, the Japanese had barely assembled a new carrier force, and their new generation of pilots was not as effective as those who had been killed at Midway. Most of these pilots were killed in the Mariana "Turkey Shoot" in June 1944 and they were never replaced. The lack of skilled naval pilots was a major reason the Japanese adopted kamikaze tactics.

Given the combination of capital intensity and mobility, sea-based forces offer (or at least have offered) far more leverage per man than armies. For a highly industrialized country able to choose between land power and sea-power, seapower is a natural expression of national power. Conversely, a country dependent on seapower does not develop the political institutions associated with the regimentation implicit in maintaining mass armies. Historian Peter Padfield has gone so far as to associate this choice with the rise of liberal political institutions in the great sea powers: first the Netherlands, then Great Britain and the United States.[3] Others have pointed out that there are many army dictators but few naval dictators, because navies are ill-equipped to mount coups against existing governments. Clearly many countries, with long land frontiers facing enemies, cannot freely choose to invest in naval rather than land power.

Mobility and Ambiguity

Perhaps the key historical puzzle of naval warfare is why small numbers of ships have had such enormous impact on the outcome of wars. The answer lies largely in the ambiguity achieved through seaborne mobility.

Ambiguity means that the point of attack is difficult to predict. Because it is so mobile, a naval force beyond the horizon can attack in many different places. Land forces are not nearly so mobile as ships, at least over long distances. An enemy finds itself deploying numerous units ashore to deal with a few attacking units at sea. Sometimes this effect is called "virtual attrition," because the land units that are inevitably misplaced cannot join the fighting. It follows that an important measure of the effectiveness of naval forces is the range of credible possibilities they impose on an enemy. The wider the range, the more effective the force, because the more dispersal it imposes on an enemy.

Ambiguity also derives from the fact that it is difficult to find ships in the vastness of the sea. That is why, at least in the past, naval battles were generally fought near land, because there was a reasonable chance of encounter. Even surface ships are difficult to detect, simply because they are mobile and the sea itself is so vast. Merely finding the enemy's ships in the open sea becomes a key theme in naval warfare. Intelligence and reconnaissance are far more important than on land, where geography often determines where troops can be, and where massive forces are relatively difficult to conceal. Because the intelligence or remote-sensing aspect of naval warfare is often shrouded in considerable secrecy, it tends not to receive due attention. That in turn distorts our understanding of how and why battles and wars are fought. A navy's effectiveness depends heavily on its ability to conduct sea surveillance. Conversely, a navy can be crippled if its surveillance resources are destroyed or neutralized. With the exception of extremely elaborate sea surveillance systems fielded by the United States and, in the past, by the Soviet Union, it is still quite difficult to find a ship at sea. As explained later, commercial satellite systems are most unlikely to solve the problem for any other navy.

Ambiguity and mobility give seapower much of its leverage. For example, during the Cold War the U.S. Navy threatened the Soviet Union with strategic attacks mounted from aircraft carriers and then from strategic submarines. The U.S. Air Force's Strategic Air Command (SAC) heavy bombers and U.S.-based missiles carried far more nuclear tonnage. However, the routes available to SAC were quite limited, particularly after U.S. forces were ejected from many of the bomber bases around the southern Soviet Union borders. For their part, the Soviets had limited resources. Had they faced only SAC, they could comfortably have concentrated defenses in the north. For example, ballistic missile defenses needed to cover only a limited part of the perimeter around Moscow. That was unacceptable, because even without bases the U.S. Navy could mount a credible threat from the Mediterranean and the Pacific. No credible defense could exclude even the small attacks a navy could mount; near the end of the Cold War period, the strength of any attacks would not have been small. At the very least, submarine-launched missiles could destroy any missile defense facing the wrong way, and thus open the way for SAC's greater tonnage.

Coalitions

Given its inherent leverage, a sea power can attract coalition partners to add the massive land power it lacks. Few, if any, countries have managed to build dominant seapower and land power at the same time. A coalition combining the two can often be extremely effective. For example, during the Cold War the United States and Britain provided the bulk of NATO naval forces. Other countries, such as Germany, provided the bulk of land forces. Neither contribution was exclusive, but relative weights of investment were clearly quite different. Each partner offers something the other lacks. Seapower offers mobility that amplifies the effect of an army. The mobility of that army forces the enemy to disperse its own land forces, thereby assisting the land partner wielding a less mobile but more massive army. Conversely, the land partner can create conditions that make seaborne attack, for example, by blockade, much more effective. That was certainly the case with the blockade of Germany during World War I.

The idea of coalitions between sea powers and land powers has an interesting modern echo. Seapower always operates on interior lines, so distance is much less important at sea than on land. Moreover, because the sea is so broad, in most cases it cannot be blocked. In the last few years, there has been much discussion of warfare in which distance is much less important than in the past, including discussions by network-centric warfare, the "Revolution in Military Affairs," and the Joint Chiefs' Vision 2020 advocates. Many warfare strategists today emphasize that, instead of fighting our way through enemy forces (attrition warfare) or through the depth of enemy territory, we will strike at the center of gravity of the enemy; once this target has been overrun, our war aims will be met. The current concept of network-centric warfare is to some extent analogous to sea-based warfare. The modern hope is that long-range precision weapons can skewer an enemy in its "center of gravity" and cause it to collapse. In effect the weapons circumvent geography. In the past, it might be argued that ships circumvented land geography, because sea travel was so much easier than land travel. In a few cases seapower by itself might be decisive, but much more often victory required a coalition of land and sea forces.

Just as conditions often do not make seapower decisive, in many cases it may be difficult to identify a center of gravity susceptible to network-centric attack. That does not negate the network-centric concept, but it does suggest that much of the time success will require a partner. The obvious complement of seapower is land power. In the case of a network-centric attacker, the complement is probably a mass force designed for the opposite of network-centric attack, which is attrition warfare. Again, by analogy network-centric attacks throw the enemy off balance enough to open it to attack by coalition partners, and the coalition partner's attack makes the enemy more vulnerable to network-centric attack by stressing it or even by creating specially rewarding targets.[4]

A Maritime Style of Strategy

A maritime or naval approach to a strategic situation carries a distinctive style or flavor. As a case in point, compare the U.S. Army and U.S. Navy approaches to the problem presented by Japan before World War II. It was generally assumed that war would break out when the Japanese decided to seize the U.S. possessions in the Pacific, particularly the Philippines.

What was the likely war aim? To the U.S. Army, the issue was the defense of U.S. territory, particularly the Philippines, from a Japanese attack. The solution was to fortify the islands, and to install enough armed power to keep the Japanese from seizing them. That was extremely difficult; the pre-1941 U.S. Army was quite weak. Treaty agreements drastically limited fortification. Moreover, the Japanese had a wide choice of potential landing places—a typical theme in naval operations—so it was difficult to imagine stopping them at the water's edge. By the mid-1930s U.S. planners admitted that the Philippines probably could not be held. In 1935 the U.S. Congress decided to give the islands their independence, specifically to keep them from being used as a pretext for war. Yet at the outset of war the local army commander, Gen. Douglas MacArthur, acted on the theory that the islands could and should be held at all costs.

The naval position was quite different. As early as 1915, the U.S. Navy's General Board had concluded that the Philippines could not be held. Nor was independence a solution: less than two decades after they had become American territory, the islands were clearly a U.S. responsibility, and they could demand U.S. protection even after they were freed. The navy's view, then and later, was that in the event of war in the Pacific Japan would have to be defeated. Once that had been accomplished, Japan would disgorge any U.S. territory she had seized. With Japan as the objective, the question of means could be raised. It was unlikely that the United States could ever build up an army large enough to occupy the country. On the other hand, Japan was almost uniquely dependent on imports. A blockade could cripple her. Japan depended on her fleet to protect her against just such an assault. It would have to be destroyed. Thus the problem of fighting Japan turned into the problem of projecting an American fleet into the Western Pacific to defeat the Japanese fleet in a decisive battle. In the 1920s an additional possibility, using bombers to burn down Japanese industry, was added to the war plan. Both blockade and bombers would require that bases be established near Japan.

The difference was profound. The army concentrated, as armies do, on the occupation of particular territory as the goal in war. At sea there is no territory. Areas of sea cannot be occupied. Naval warfare is about the destruction of enemy forces as a prerequisite to mobile operations—in this case, as a prerequisite to a blockade.

The difference between army and navy views can be seen in the sharp controversy, in mid-1944, over future Pacific strategy. General MacArthur pressed for the invasion of the Philippines, not least on the ground that not to do so would be to betray the citizens of this American territory. His critics suggest that he was mainly interested in personal prestige; in 1942 he had rather dramatically promised to return, and that would hardly have been impressive as part of a postsurrender mop-up of Japanese forces. The U.S. Navy argued that the Philippines were quite large, and that liberating them altogether would soak up massive U.S. forces. Better to opt for a further operating base, perhaps on the China coast or on Taiwan, from which the blockade of Japan could be tightened and from which bombers could destroy Japanese industry. In either case, all that was needed was an enclave; the Japanese could be left holding the hinterland. In the case of the Philippines, however, it would be politically impossible to settle for anything short of total reconquest. The issue was whether any particular territory was worth the blood that it would cost to regain it, when all Japanese-held territories would inevitably fall into U.S. hands once Japan fell. MacArthur won his point. Incidentally, large U.S. forces were still being tied down in the Philippines the day the Japanese surrendered. In 1945 the navy still resisted plans actually to invade the Japanese islands, again on the ground that such operations entailed far too much sacrifice. Blockade and bombardment should suffice—as indeed they did.[5]

Obviously not all wars can be fought this way, just as opponents of network-centric warfare have asked whether there is always a center of gravity to attack. Attacks against the periphery of a major continental power may well fail to be decisive. It seems unlikely, for example, that in World War II the Allies could have defeated Germany without overrunning that country. On the other hand, from a purely military point of view it was not obvious which allies had to do the overrunning. Francis Bacon's comment is still relevant today: just how much of a war should a sea power take?

U.S. Strategy as a Case in Point

Classical U.S. national strategy has always had a maritime focus because most potential enemies are separated from, or connected to, the United States by the sea. From the founding of the republic to World War I, the assumption was that major war, if it ever came, would involve a European power trying to take over the United States or, later, to overthrow the Monroe Doctrine by seizing colonies in the New World. Americans noticed that the Prussians had apparently precipitated the Franco-Prussian War of 1870–71 almost literally for profit. Under Chancellor Otto von Bismarck Prussia (and later the German empire) ensured social peace by providing generous social programs, but very low taxes were levied. Government was financed largely by heavy borrowing. Defeated, France was forced to pay a heavy indemnity, which in turn paid off Prussia's national debt.[6] A wealthy but almost completely undefended United States would be an attractive prize; perhaps a foreign power could hold the rich coastal cities to ransom. The British had, after all, burned Washington in 1814.

Militarily, the United States was quite weak compared to the European powers. What could be done? It was unlikely that a fleet powerful enough to stop a modern European navy could be built. Nor was there any reason to imagine that such a fleet would find itself in the path of the oncoming Europeans. Instead, through the 1890s, coast defense forts were built to defend the approaches to major cities. In wartime, as in the American Revolution and the War of 1812, the main naval effort would be commerce raiding, in hopes that the rising cost of war would sap popular enthusiasm in the aggressor country. Commerce raiding failed during the American Civil War, and there was little reason to imagine that it would be terribly successful against any determined enemy.

In 1889, however, Secretary of the Navy Benjamin Tracy assembled an advisory board to rethink U.S. national strategy. Capt. Alfred Thayer Mahan had only recently formulated the principles of naval strategy, and he was assigned as an advisor to the board.[7] The board proposed that, instead of waiting for foreign powers to assault the New World, the U.S. Navy (the only armed force that could act abroad) should be capable of extended battle fleet operations in foreign waters. A foreign navy would find itself so occupied in dealing with such operations that it would have little ability to attack the United States. To execute this policy, Tracy's board proposed a massive fleet, about the size of the Royal Navy, which was then the most powerful in the world. The board's report was published, presumably as an attempt to justify a big U.S. program, and contemporary newspapers roundly attacked it as extravagant. Yet it became the basis for a national strategy that has endured to the present, a strategy of forward presence and engagement. Within two decades the United States had a first-rate fleet with which to execute Tracy's strategy. The next step, which was taken tacitly during World War I, was to admit that, given such a fleet, the only really daunting threat would be the combination of a massive land power and sea power—a threat offered in 1914–18 by Germany's kaiser if he won.

Tracy's national strategy necessarily had a naval focus in 1889 because the United States lacked any foreign possessions on which to base troops. It is still a naval strategy, because only ships can remain at sea off other countries' coasts for a protracted period, without those governments' permission. Troops require basing agreements, not to mention sustained support. Aircraft can fly across an ocean, albeit often only with the assistance of tankers for which bases must be obtained. Aircraft cannot maintain a presence, however; they fly out, attack, and return, or they fly out to a forward base.

Tracy's strategy was to create a fleet that could, in wartime, destroy an enemy's fleet near that enemy's home waters and thus secure sea control for the United States, rather than wait for the enemy to cross the Atlantic to attack. Even after World War II, policy was reactive: the U.S. Navy planned to maintain powerful Atlantic and Pacific fleets, based on the U.S. coasts, with limited forward forces. Task forces would deploy as needed. Forward deployment as it is understand today began with the Sixth Fleet in the Mediterranean in 1946, to stiffen Greece and Turkey in the face of Soviet threats. The United States began forward basing strategic bombers in 1948, in response to immediate Soviet threats in Germany. The modern Seventh Fleet was created to fight the war in Korea. Yet these forward deployments clearly reflect the basic ideas of Tracy's board.

Intervention by Sea

Recalling Bacon's comment that a sea power "may take as much or as little of a war" as it likes, it is difficult to know which battles we want to fight in the rather ambiguous post–Cold War period. We also do not know just how much victory in any one place is worth. That is not a defect in American thinking; it is inherent. There will be times to pour in more treasure and more blood— and times to leave when we wish to, not when we are thrown out. It will matter more and more that naval forces can apply force as needed, with minimum fuss, and can withdraw as needed, also with minimal implications.

It matters that U.S. naval forces are currently forward deployed. Ships already at sea can easily be redeployed elsewhere, particularly if they are supported by an afloat logistics force. No publicity automatically attaches to a decision to move an amphibious ready group from somewhere south of Singapore to somewhere off East Africa. Ships not forward deployed are a different proposition. It is obvious when a carrier battle group at piers in Norfolk, Virginia, is suddenly sent to sea, although its destination may be a matter of speculation. This difference, between an agile naval posture well-adapted to sudden decisions and an inherently reactive posture, is likely to become very important in the turbulent period ahead.

Somalia is a case in point. Although the situation was widely known, there was no particular reason why the United States could be expected to intervene, compared, for instance, to other crises in Africa. The U.S. government found intervention convenient because its sea-based forces, which were already at sea, could easily get to Somalia. Because those forces were self-sufficient, it did not matter whether the Somalis wanted us or not. The marines aboard the ships could easily set up their temporary base ashore, and later they could just as easily withdraw it. Any other form of intervention, for example, with airlifted troops, would have required local permission (the troops would have used the main airport), or at the least the agreement of a neighboring state (plus land access to Somalia, which might have been difficult). In fact the marines from the ships set up facilities that were needed for other troops to operate. When intervention began, it appeared to be a simple humanitarian mission, a charitable application of overwhelming American wealth and power. The Somalis saw it differently, however. After American troops were killed, intervention was no longer so attractive an option, and the U.S. government decided to pull out. That was easily done, because ships could steam away. American prestige, by no means an unimportant commodity, took only limited damage; the world was not treated to the spectacle of an overrun American base, or of Americans holding back a mob while the last few clung to helicopters, which is what happened in Saigon in 1975.

Now imagine a slightly different case, in which a U.S. administration cannot decide whether to intervene in a future Somalia. Amphibious forces can be moved into position so they can intervene *if* that choice is made. Because it is still quite difficult for anyone to detect and locate ships at sea, the world may well never be aware of this concentration of force. Imagine, now, that the decision goes against intervention, perhaps because the crisis has eased. The ships simply steam away. Deploying the force did not involve any sort of negotiation, which it would have if a base for ground troops was required. Using amphibious forces as a way of preparing to intervene did not heat up the crisis. Withdrawal did not carry any major cost, thereby allowing the U.S. administration to make its choice quietly and coolly.

Comparing the above imaginary scenario to actual events demonstrates the advantages of intervention by sea. In 1977 the Argentine government pressured the British in hopes of gaining control of the Falklands Islands, which Argentina has long claimed. The British did not want to complicate negotiations by visibly deploying military forces, yet they wanted to be prepared in the event the Argentines went ahead and seized the islands. Unlike the United States, Britain did not have forward-deployed naval forces. Thus a surface fleet deployment to the South Atlantic would be far too public. There was one important alternative. Movements by nuclear submarines were so secret that their departure for the South Atlantic carried no publicity whatever. Nor could the Argentines know that these craft were en route. They were soon on station, ready to help defend the Falklands if the Argentines tried to land troops there. In this case, the crisis was defused. It helped that there was no public British challenge to the Argentines; emotion did not build up. The Argentines never knew the submarines had been put in place, and they were quietly withdrawn.

Five years later, the Argentines had much less interest in backing down. The crisis mounted quickly, and the submarines arrived on station after the islands had been seized. It does seem clear in retrospect that it was far easier for the British government to deploy submarines than to deploy the surface fleet that was ultimately sent, because the submarine decision was much more reversible. When it was made, the British cabinet was still hotly debating whether to take back the islands. Once the submarines were on station, they could act; one of them sank the Argentine cruiser *Belgrano*, which had the incidental effect of discouraging any future Argentine naval action.

Of course, the virtues of forward deployment carry disadvantages as well. In 1940 the U.S. government wanted to deter the Japanese from further expansion into areas of Southeast Asia considered vital to U.S. interests because of their resources.[8] President Franklin D. Roosevelt ordered the U.S. fleet moved from San Diego to Pearl Harbor, from which it could presumably much more easily descend on the flank of any Japanese assault to the south. That also moved the fleet within range of Japanese attack, to a degree the president probably did not imagine. Ironically, the U.S. Navy had often practiced surprise carrier air strikes against Pearl Harbor, and had stopped doing so when shore-based patrol aircraft (PBY Catalinas) appeared with such long range that they could generally expect to find enemy carriers well before they could launch aircraft. By December 1941 the Pacific Fleet had been run down to supply assets such as Catalinas to fight the increasingly hot, albeit undeclared, naval war in the Atlantic. Now the Japanese could do exactly what the U.S. carrier force had done in earlier exercises. *Any* forward deployment, by its nature, exposes U.S. forces to attack. Recent examples include the destruction of air force barracks in Saudi Arabia in June 1996 and the attack on USS *Cole* in October 2000.

Command at Sea

At least in the West, naval operations have a distinctive flavor based on the way command is exercised. Unit commanders share a common tactical picture, on the basis of which they make their decisions, but they operate independently; they do not receive very detailed orders. The assumption is that the more information a local commander has, the better the commander can function, because only he or she is fully aware of local conditions. This command style is derived from the practices of pre-radio days, when a ship on a distant station might be out of touch with a government for weeks or months at a time. A captain, it was said, could start a war or conclude a treaty, subject to his government's reaction when he got home. Until then, what he did was his responsibility. This attitude translated into the saying that the navy set goals, to be reached without breaking a set of fixed rules. Just how the goals were to be attained was the officer's problem. In the new language of network-centric warfare, this is called "self-synchronization."[9]

Armies are necessarily different. A senior army commander might be in the same position as the captain of a ship, isolated from home authority, but subordinates, commanding separate units, have always been under the commander's control. An army consists of large numbers of more or less equivalent units, operating in close proximity for mutual support. Individual initiative can be dangerous rather than praiseworthy, because it can bring one such unit so far out in front that it can be cut off and destroyed in detail. Moreover, to command a large force of numerous units, a senior officer has to know what subordinates will do. It is best if all of them conform to standardized practices. Similarly, logistic support for the army constantly has to be arranged, and it cannot easily be tailored to the needs of numerous independent units. The army, therefore, has in effect a "book" stating what to do. Hence the old joke, that there is a "right way, a wrong way, and an Army way" of doing anything. Information is also handled differently. The navy tries to distribute information horizontally, but an army provides the most senior officer with the fullest data, and carefully limits what subordinates see.

Thus a navy is dominated by "line" (operational) officers, whereas an army is dominated by "staff" officers who develop the "book" and who work out the implications of general commands so that subordinates know exactly what they have to do. Alternatively, the command culture of a navy fosters independence and individual initiative to a degree no army can brook. Naval culture, then, tends to be pluralistic. Armies are more likely to choose and enforce a particular point of view. This difference can have real consequences. In both world wars Germany had powerful army-oriented general staffs. They produced excellent war plans, but only for the contingencies they had chosen. They chose wrong in both wars, and their main errors involved the potential of their overseas enemy, the United States. In 1986 the U.S. Congress chose to increase the prerogatives of the chairman of the Joint Chiefs, partly on the theory that the staff could evolve into something similar to the widely admired German-style General Staff. The U.S. Navy argued vainly that the existing Joint Chiefs structure should foster a more pluralistic outlook so it would have a better chance of corresponding to reality. For all the talk of German military prowess, they won only one big war (against France in 1870) and then lost twice, the second time worse than the first. It could be argued that in each world war the rather narrow army focus of the German General Staff blinded it to naval realities, such as the impact of enemy sea control and sea-based mobility.

During the Cold War, the Western concept of decentralized command was obscured by frequent high-level intervention. Beginning with the Kennedy administration, the view in Washington was often that the world situation was so delicate that the slightest misstep by a military commander could easily bring about a nuclear war. We now know that the Soviet leadership was less than anxious to chance nuclear disaster, and the view from Washington seems at best to have been an expression of egotism. High-level intervention, however, became ingrained. At times the White House Situation Room actually sent out rudder orders, which were deeply resented—but were obeyed. This practice is likely to end, simply because its rationale is gone. With the end of the Cold War, the sense of a world teetering on the edge of catastrophe is gone. At the same time, it seems much more likely that the United States will have to deal with numerous simultaneous but unconnected crises abroad. It will be impossible for the White House Situation Room to handle all the details of each crisis. The current popularity of network-centric fighting concepts, which stresses the need for independent (self-synchronizing) decision making, reflects the need to move away from such high-level intervention; this change is clearly widely accepted.

The Soviets' Cold War naval philosophy was similar to the U.S. Army's structure: top-down detailed command. That was, after all, the way Soviet society as a whole was constructed. It seems likely that navies trained by the Soviets, such as the Chinese navy, adopted much the same command philosophy. In the Soviet case, army orientation was fostered not only by the dominance of the army, but also by the main naval role of coast defense during the navy's formative years when an army style of operation seemed appropriate. Only at the end of the twentieth century did the Chinese begin contemplating extension of their naval role beyond coast defense.

The difference in command styles is reflected in the different ways wide-area surveillance systems were exploited. In the U.S. and NATO navies, the emphasis was on creating and disseminating a picture of naval activity beyond the horizon of the deployed ships, making it possible for commanders to make better tactical decisions. Initially the U.S. Navy set up fleet command centers (FCCs), and there was much talk of whether it was acceptable to move fleet command ashore. In fact the FCCs were data fusion centers, and they were concerned mainly with assembling information needed by the fleet. There is every reason, however, to believe that the Soviets assembled their information ashore, and that their fleet commanders made key decisions based on it—ashore. Some information was transmitted to the fleet, but the emphasis was on sending out the appropriate orders.

3

The Geopolitics of Seapower

THE SEA IS TRACKLESS. Except near the shore, it is deep enough for ships to pass freely. To that extent, it is without geography. Ashore, geography is destiny; it determines where armies can go, where they can mass, and where they can attack. There is, for example, a world of difference between a flat open plain conducive to tank operations and the cramped narrow valleys and mountains of Korea or the former Yugoslavia. Such differences determine not only the course of land operations but also, it is often suggested, of cultural development. There is no naval equivalent, which is exactly why navies can operate so flexibly, why they have such freedom, and why simply finding the enemy's fleet is so central to naval warfare. Much more of naval warfare than of land warfare, then, is maneuver. Yet geography does deeply influence what navies can and cannot do.

When a country or a place is considered "strategic," it is generally meaningful only in relation to a particular type of potential war. The Turkish straits would have been of great strategic value in a war between the Soviet Union and the West. They have little significance in a war between China and the United States. Indeed, after the end of the Cold War the United States abruptly cut aid to several countries that it had previously supported for their strategic value.

There is one exception, at least for the present. So much of the world's oil is tied up in the countries around the Gulf that the area—and access to it—

55

remains very strategic. Even though there are large oil reserves outside the Gulf, the flow from the Gulf is so large that Middle East countries control the price of oil. If that flow were cut off, the price would rise so sharply that it would probably throw the industrialized world into an economic crash. The strategic significance of the Gulf extends to access routes such as the Red Sea, the Suez Canal, and the Straits of Malacca (the shortest route between the Indian Ocean and Japan). The significance of the Gulf in the world oil market might decline, however, if large fields were developed elsewhere, for example, in what used to be Soviet Central Asia or in the South China Sea.

Trade Routes

In one important sense the sea does have geographical features that affect navies. In the age of sail, sea traffic depended on the wind, and some places enjoyed fairly steady wind. For example, the wind normally circulates around the North Atlantic, east to west in the south and west to east in the north. That is why European explorers such as Christopher Columbus found the Caribbean islands before North America. Once the islands had been found, winds running along the shore allowed easy access to the main continental masses north and south. Known wind patterns in turn imposed a sort of road system on the North Atlantic, and thus made it easier for a privateer to guess where prey might be found. Similarly, the seasonal pattern of winds in the Indian Ocean determined when fleets could pass from east to west or from west to east.

Modern merchant ships generally follow the shortest paths between ports to save fuel and time, so in this sense there are defined sea lanes. The paths, moreover, converge in certain places, which are called focal points. Ordinarily, then, ships are hardly randomly distributed at sea. In World War I, U-boats could confine their searches for merchant shipping to likely paths and, even better, to focal points. Much the same could be said of merchant raiders during both world wars. Thus many antiraider measures entailed patrolling known trade routes and focal points, on the theory that a raider would go there. There is nothing, however, that forces powered ships to follow particular routes. During both world wars, knowledge of U-boat operating areas often allowed the Allies to route ships evasively, saving them from attack. There was, to be sure, a hitch. There was little hope of individually rerouting the hundreds or thousands of ships at sea on any given day. For much of World War I, evasive routing was effectively limited to major ocean liners, which were among the few merchant ships with the radios necessary for them to receive updated course instructions. This system was, incidentally, in use when the liner *Lusitania* was sunk; apparently she fell victim in part to poor staff work and to her master's refusal to lose time by zigzagging.

When convoy systems were instituted in World War I, evasive routing became much easier, because convoys always included naval escorts equipped with radios and relatively few entities had to be maneuvered at any one time. Suddenly the usual trade routes were swept clean, and U-boats found fewer targets. When they did find convoys, they could not sink ships fast enough to do much damage, and of course they had to deal with counterattacks by the escorts. Systematic rerouting lengthened ships' voyages, however, and represented a kind of virtual attrition of shipping. Ports could not easily handle the sudden appearance of a convoy, and that, too, reduced the efficiency of ships. Both disadvantages were sustainable, whereas numerous sinkings of merchant ships were not.

These considerations led the Germans to institute wolf packs—group tactics—in World War II. Evasive routing entailed radio contact between a controlling authority and a convoy. By 1939 the Germans were confident that they could read the British merchant code, hence they could track attempts to maneuver convoys at sea. Given approximate track data, patrol lines of U-boats could locate convoys, and the boats could be directed to converge and attack them, overcoming the multiplicity of targets that had defeated World War I attacks on convoys. In the early phase of the war, the Germans had so few U-boats that evasive routing was still largely successful; by 1942, however, there were so many U-boats that few if any convoys escaped attack. By early 1943, the Allies could read the U-boat command center's messages that directed U-boats to intercept convoys. Convoy battles were now preceded by duels in which the convoy was routed according to the most recent estimates of U-boat positions, then the U-boats were repositioned according to broken convoy-routing messages, and so on.[1] The wolf-pack technique required considerable radio traffic both from the U-boat command center and from the U-boats themselves. For example, when assembling an attack force, the command center had to know the status (e.g., fuel reserves, spare torpedoes) of each U-boat. All of these messages made the U-boat force vulnerable to Allied radio interceptors and code-breakers.

Once navies became involved in antisubmarine warfare, patterns of ocean currents and temperatures became very important. Both currents and underwater geography can act as walls, sealing out sounds that might otherwise travel thousands of miles. For example, in 1950 the U.S. Navy reviewed the state of antisubmarine warfare and concluded that it was fairly desperate. Sonar functioned much more effectively in some places than in others. One implication was that it would be best to run convoys as far south as possible. Later, when the U.S. Navy discovered that it could use fixed listening devices in the SOSUS system to detect submarines at enormous ranges, the Mid-Atlantic Ridge, an underwater mountain range, became a substantial barrier. SOSUS stations had to be set up on the European side of the ocean specifically because those on the U.S. side could not see (actually, hear) past the ridge. Even then, SOSUS coverage of the Atlantic was hardly uniform. An antisubmarine warfare (ASW) instructor was a member of the Walker spy ring, so the Soviets probably became aware of the extent and quality of coverage in the 1970s. The U.S. Navy began to commission surveillance ships (T-AGOS) that could effectively change the geography of the underwater surveillance system, for example, by filling gaps in the coverage offered by the fixed sensors. With the end of the Cold War, SOSUS itself became far less useful, because it was unlikely that the United States would have to deal with Soviet submarines. Conversely, like other elements of the fleet, T-AGOS ships could be deployed to other U.S. operational areas.

Access and Strategic Straits

Sea access is blocked by the continents; there are only so many paths from ocean to ocean. Generations of American officers were taught that the Panama Canal was central to American seapower. Without it, the United States could not unite fleets maintained in the Atlantic and the Pacific nearly as quickly. That was not a serious problem before 1914, because the most likely enemy was Germany; the U.S. fleet and the industrial plant backing it were on the Atlantic coast. American attention turned to Japan in 1919, however, and the fleet moved, via the canal, to San Diego. The industrial base was still overwhelmingly on the east coast, and it remained there through World War II. Even today the only U.S. carrier-building shipyard is in Newport News, Virginia. The problem of maintaining fleets in both the Atlantic and the Pacific became serious when the United States faced war in both oceans simultaneously. The two-ocean navy act passed by Congress in July 1940 specifically intended to provide enough major warships so that the United States could fight such a war; otherwise, at least in theory, it could fight offensively in only one ocean at a time.

Before World War II all U.S. warships were limited by the dimensions of the locks at Panama. Indeed, the Japanese estimated the design consequences of the canal-imposed limits when they designed and built their *Yamato*-class superbattleships; they believed no U.S. battleship limited by the canal could match them. By 1942 plans were well advanced to build new locks specifically because the canal limits were crippling; the *Midway*-class carriers were designed to use the new locks. The canal project was stopped during the war and it was never revived. Indeed, in the 1977 agreement surrendering control of the canal to Panama in 1999, the United States specifically promised Panama that it would not support construction of any new canal. At the time, it was not a sacrifice to accept the limits the United States had faced since 1914, when the canal opened. We had adjusted to the fact that since 1945 many American carriers were unable to use the canal. In the 1970s it was assumed that war, if it came, would be swift and sudden—far too sudden to allow for ships to steam from one ocean to another. Forward-deployed ships would have to handle any crises. Now that U.S. resources are stretched, this sort of limit is less attractive.

Other countries with multiple coasts have been less fortunate. France, for example, always based fleets in both the Atlantic, usually at Brest, and in the Mediterranean at Toulon. Given finite finances, neither fleet could be overwhelmingly powerful, and a central problem of French naval strategy in the age of sail was how to combine the Brest and Toulon fleets, sometimes with Spanish fleets as well, to deal with a British fleet. The British seized Gibraltar specifically to support a blockading squadron to preclude such a union; for a time in the eighteenth century they also used Port Mahon, in Minorca, for that purpose.

The Soviet Union was the worst example of such unfortunate geography. During the Cold War, it operated four fleets: Northern, Baltic, Black Sea, and Pacific. The Northern Fleet had the best access to the open sea, but the Baltic and Black Sea fleets were based on, and presumably helped protect, some of the most important parts of the Soviet industrial infrastructure, at Leningrad (St. Petersburg) and Nikolaev in the Ukraine. The Pacific Fleet had access to the open sea, and it had to deal with both a U.S. and a Chinese threat. Presumably it had a wartime offensive mission to distract the Chinese from trying to cross the border in force. None of these fleets could effectively reinforce the others. Submarines could sometimes transit the Arctic from the Pacific Fleet to the Northern Fleet, however, and bombers could presumably redeploy, but the bases might not have sufficient capacity. The Russians

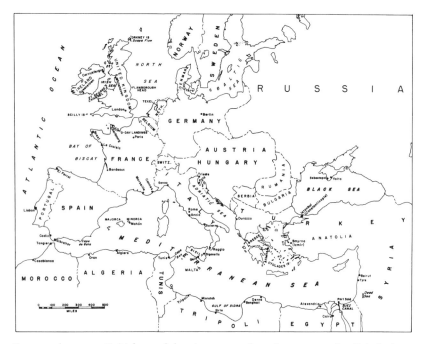

Europe, circa 1910. British naval dominance was based on geography: Britain is a stopper in the North Sea. The French fleet at Brest presented the British with special problems because that port lay to windward of the main British bases. Toulon, the main French Mediterranean base, is near Marseilles. Note how convenient Port Mahon, once a British base, is to it. In 1910 Austria-Hungary was a major naval power on the Adriatic, and Germany's seapower extended along much of the Baltic coast. Tripoli, modern Libya, was an Italian colony, and Turkey controlled most of the Middle East. In 1912 Turkey lost much of her European territory in the Balkan War; Serbia, Bulgaria, and Greece gained at her expense. This map also shows the site of the 1944 Normandy invasion, which illustrates the way in which maritime and ground geography interact. The Germans expected the allies to land in the Pas de Calais, the area closest to Britain. They did not appreciate that a slightly longer sea run would make little difference for the British, who had command of the sea. Because the area around the Pas was heavily fortified, the Allies chose to go as far from the Pas as they could. Ultimately they were limited by the range of Spitfire fighters based in England; they would provide much of the air support needed for the landing. It was impractical to move from the Pas north into Belgium or the Netherlands, because neither offered a clear path inland. Belgium led into the dense Ardennes forest. By opening dikes to the sea, the hinterland of the Dutch coast could be flooded easily. On the other hand, inland from the invasion beaches the French terrain was fairly flat, and the port of Cherbourg could be captured, it was thought, to supply the drive inland. To some extent the Allies could alter geography. They erected artificial ports, including breakwaters, off the invasion beaches, to serve the troops until Cherbourg was captured. *U.S. Naval Institute*

had also built a canal that permitted submarines built at Gorkiy, on the Volga, to join the Northern Fleet rather than the Black Sea Fleet; unfortunately its dimensions limited craft that could use it.

In 1914 Britain's First Sea Lord, Adm. Sir John Fisher, exulted that "we control the keys which lock up the world." By that he meant the vital straits and passages. Besides the exits from the North Sea, the British controlled the Straits of Gibraltar and the Suez Canal, which led to the two ends of the Mediterranean; the Cape of Good Hope, which led from the South Atlantic to the Indian Ocean; and the Malacca Straits, from the Indian Ocean to the China Sea. British islands in the Caribbean effectively controlled the eastern end of the Panama Canal, the only short safe route from the Atlantic to the Pacific. Although the British did not hold any colony at the southern tip of South America, a British base, the Falkland Islands, effectively controlled the trade route from the Pacific to the Atlantic via the Straits of Magellan or Cape Horn.[2] To these strategic straits and canals could be added the Dardanelles, from the Black Sea to the Mediterranean, which the British found, to their discomfort, that they did not control; the Sicilian Narrows, between the two Mediterranean basins; and the Straits of Otranto, which close the Adriatic. During World War I the Straits of Otranto blocked Austro-Hungarian access to the Mediterranean from Pola and Trieste.

In 1914 the Germans had a substantial cruiser squadron, commanded by Vice Adm. Maximilian Graf von Spee, in the Pacific. It headed east as its bases and coaling stations were systematically overrun by the Australians and the Japanese. Trying to get home, it could not transit the Panama Canal, so it had to take the much more difficult passage around Cape Horn and hopefully capture fuel—at the British colony of the Falkland Islands. Because von Spee had no alternative route, the British could concentrate their own force at the Falklands in time to deal with him. The entire episode was determined by naval geography.

Position and Dominance

Geography is closely linked to sea control. The Royal Navy achieved the dominant position it enjoyed through the nineteenth century because the British Isles lie athwart the sea routes from Europe to the rest of the world. The Royal Navy might not be able to find enemy fleets on the open ocean, but it could largely block the entrances to the Atlantic, both around Scotland (out of the North Sea and the Baltic) and through the English Channel. For example, any French attempt to invade Britain was likely to be mounted out of Brest, and to come up through the channel. In their lengthy series of wars against France, the British learned that by interposing a fleet off Ushant, at the southern (western) end of the channel, they could preclude any such attack.[3] The French had an additional outlet, via the Mediterranean and the Straits of Gibraltar, but once the British had Gibraltar that, too, could be blocked. Once the British had the Cape of Good Hope, moreover, they were able to block European access to the Indian Ocean until the Suez Canal opened.

Blockage could preclude both forays out into the wider oceans, and also access to the world's commerce from beyond Europe. During the long wars of the seventeenth, eighteenth, and early nineteenth centuries, the effect of British control of the sea exits from Europe made it possible for the British to seize the colonial empires of the other European powers, while protecting their own from most seaborne attacks. At the end of the Napoleonic wars in 1815, Britain controlled most of the colonies ever seized by any of the European powers. The most important exceptions were the Dutch East Indies (now Indonesia) and the Spanish Philippines and the South American states, now independent of Spain and Portugal. Most of Africa was as yet uncolonized.

The British position worked as long as a continental power could not credibly threaten to invade. British geography makes the Low Countries a particular threat, because they lie opposite flat areas of England, across which an army, once ashore, can easily spread out. In contrast, the part of southern England facing France is backed by hills that may present a barrier. The British therefore traditionally sought control or at least neutrality in the Low Countries; for example, Britain was one of the guarantors of Belgian neutrality in 1830. On this basis the British saw the 1914 German invasion of Belgium, which the German army saw simply as a way of outflanking French defenses, as a direct threat to them, particularly when taken in conjunction with their aggressive prewar naval building program. This perception helped the British decide to declare war.

Basing

Naval geography is often expressed in terms of bases. Although in theory ships are relatively autonomous, in fact they still require a degree of support. Battle-damaged and sometimes storm-damaged ships need havens toward which they can steam; the closer the haven, the worse the damage a ship can sustain before she must be abandoned. British Napoleonic War naval fiction describes ships putting into isolated coves, and the crews using onboard timber to make repairs. Even then the Royal Navy preferred established dockyards, with repair and refit facilities. Isolated coves could not supply essentials such as cannon balls, powder, rope, and what were then called naval stores, such as tar and turpentine. Rigging in particular required frequent repairs due to weather damage, and that required naval stores.[4] Sustained fleet operations demanded a base; in the absence of a base, they became impossible. For example, during the War of the French Revolution, the British seized Corsica specifically to support a blockade of the French naval base at Toulon. Later they had to evacuate it. Without a nearby base, coverage of the approaches to Toulon was much weaker, which is why the French fleet at Toulon managed to evade Lord Horatio Nelson in 1805. Similarly, the British seized and held Malta specifically to support a Mediterranean fleet capable of blocking French access to the Eastern Mediterranean and Egypt, which the British saw as a key to India. The French demand that Malta be evacuated helped precipitate renewed war against France in 1803. In much the same way, the British valued their alliance with Portugal largely because they could base a fleet in the Tagus, to watch the major Spanish base at Ferrol.

Machinery, unlike masts and sails, requires frequent repairs involving machine shops. Early in the steam age, machinery was unreliable and few harbors had the facilities to repair a steam warship. Destruction of even one of its specialized bases could cripple a fleet. Naval warfare might soon revolve around attacks, not on the ships themselves, but on the naval bases on which they depended. This perception helps explain intense British interest in coast defense (actually, coastal attack) ironclads in the 1870s.

Ships now have greater endurance, so the loss of a particular base is usually not nearly as devastating. Nevertheless, ships periodically need base services. For example, between the two world wars the U.S. Navy developed a transpacific strategy to deal with Japan. At the time, it was estimated that a fleet lost about 10 percent of its fighting power for every thousand miles it steamed beyond its base, for reasons as diverse as machinery trouble and marine growth. Part of the U.S. solution was to develop a mobile base, which could be moved among Pacific islands as they were secured. The U.S. fleet also benefited from more reliable machinery, which needed much less attention from base facilities. Once the fleet entered combat, it needed local havens at which damaged ships could be patched. For example, prior to the attack on Okinawa U.S. forces secured a small nearby island, Kerama Retto, specifically as a forward base. It proved invaluable for ships damaged by kamikaze attacks.

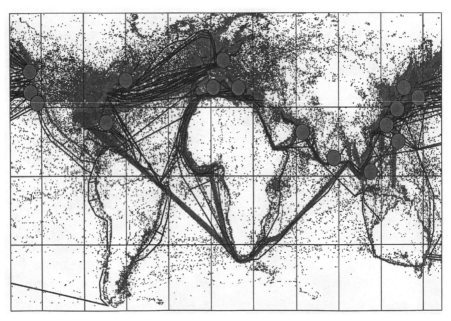

Current major shipping routes. This U.S. Navy map superimposes major shipping routes and the locations of superports (the large dots) on a digitized version of the "world at night" photograph, which broadly indicates world population distribution as well as seaborne traffic. World trade is widely seen as the main engine of world economic development. Countries reach the take-off stage toward modern development by selling products to more developed countries, because their internal markets cannot support their growth. As countries develop, trade between countries grows dramatically; it is currently growing 2.3 times faster than world output. In the year 2000, 99 percent of world trade by volume (84 percent by value) traveled by sea. The volume of world seaborne trade has risen one fifth since 1990, and that growth is accelerating. It is forecast to grow by two-thirds by 2010. Moreover, 95 percent of that trade by volume (70 percent by value) traveled through nine key choke points: the Bab-el-Mandeb (at the southern end of the Red Sea), the Cape of Good Hope, the Danish Straits, the Malacca Straits, the Panama Canal, the English Channel, the Straits of Gibraltar, the Straits of Hormuz, and the Suez Canal. For example, 43 percent of the world's internationally traded oil passes through the Straits of Hormuz at the mouth of the Persian Gulf. As of 1998, the major superports, in descending order of numbers of ship calls, were Singapore, Hong Kong, Rotterdam, Antwerp, Kaoshiung, Yokohama, Pusan, Hamburg, Nagoya, Europort, Kobe, Port Keelung, Jakarta, Osaka, Felixstowe, Piraeus, Houston, New Orleans, Barcelona, London, Shanghai, Le Havre, Tokyo, Genoa, and Los Angeles. Port data are from Lloyd's Maritime Information Services (London, February 1998). Other measures, such as total deadweight tonnage processed, give somewhat different results. *U.S. Navy*

Modern diesel-electric submarines, particularly, need specialized base facilities. The mouths of harbors containing those bases become choke points that other countries' submarines can patrol. If patrolling submarines arrive early enough, they can effectively neutralize the adversary's submarine force simply by waiting outside the base and trailing any submarine that chooses to come out. Because the endurance of diesel-electric submarines is limited, it may not matter if the other side's submarines are initially at sea; they still have to come back into port to replenish. When they do, they are trapped.

Overseas basing can change naval geography. Until the late nineteenth century, the Royal Navy in European waters could block the French fleet. Small commerce raiders could slip out, but they could be countered by numerous small British cruisers scattered around the empire. However, in 1884–85 France conquered Indo-China (now Vietnam), and thus gained a naval base in the Far East, near key British trade routes. A decade later Russia allied with France, opening the possibility of further Far East bases. Both the French and the Russians began to build large cruisers especially well adapted to commerce raiding. The new threat ruined British naval economics.

To deal with large cruisers, the British had to build a substantial fleet of their own ships of this type, fast enough to run them down. Each battleship-size armored cruiser cost more than a battleship. Yet an armored cruiser could not replace a battleship; she lacked both firepower and protection. Thus the Royal Navy had to maintain a predominant battle fleet as well as the new ships, which were valued mainly for their ability to protect trade. By 1904 the Royal Navy was in financial crisis. Admiral Fisher proposed that a single new type of warship, essentially an armored cruiser with battleship guns, replace both armored cruiser and battleship—if it could somehow survive combat with battleships. To Fisher, this new type, which became the battlecruiser, was the key to overcoming the Royal Navy's crisis.[5] His solution proved too radical, and he found himself ordering large fast battleships instead, to the point that his name has been identified with that type (the Dreadnoughts) rather than with the battlecruiser, which is what he really wanted.[6] Even then Fisher kept looking for some alternative to the high cost of a conventional battle fleet, whose main role would be to keep enemy battle fleets from getting into the Atlantic and the vital British trade routes there. A strong believer in technology, Fisher came to see submarines as a solution, which is why the Royal Navy had the largest submarine fleet in the world in 1914.[7]

A crisis occurred when it was no longer possible for the British to translate control of European waters, for which geography helped enormously, into control of the world shipping routes on which Britain depended. Similarly, at the outbreak of World War I the few German cruisers based in the German Pacific colonies had a disproportionate effect on the Royal Navy. They threatened to block the military contributions the empire, particularly Australia, New Zealand, and India, could make to the war in Europe and in the Middle East. Extraordinary efforts were mounted both to hunt them down and to eliminate their colonial bases.

Now imagine a rerun of the Gulf War against an Iraq with, for instance, a few submarines. As long as those submarines are based in Iraqi waters, they can be bottled up by a force in the Northern Gulf. Although the submarines have a long cruising range, the presence of the U.S. force, if it is effective, guarantees U.S. shipping worldwide. We can also imagine, however, a wiser successor to Saddam who makes an alliance with, for example, Libya. Before any hostilities, hence before any bottling-up, he moves his submarines there for safe-keeping, as Saddam sometimes did with his air arm. As in 1990, our position in the Gulf depends heavily on materiel flowing through the Mediterranean, past Libya. How serious a problem would we face? How much of our limited national power would we have to devote to dealing with a remote, yet still quite relevant, Iraqi threat outside the Gulf area? Incidentally, if Libya chose to remain neutral, and if the Iraqi submarines never came out, we would still have to assign massive forces simply to watch them. Indeed, we assigned forces to watch Libya in 1990–91.

A base structure generally reflects a guess as to the sort of war a navy expects to fight. For example, during the Cold War, the Royal Navy helped block Soviet submarine access to the North Atlantic via the Greenland–Iceland–United Kingdom (GIUK) gap. Submarines towing acoustic arrays were particularly well adapted for surveillance of the gap. They could be based in northern Scotland, quite close to their planned patrol areas. Because their role was surveillance rather than attack, they did not need nuclear power. On this basis the British built four *Upholder*-class diesel-electric submarines, which were far less expensive than nuclear submarines.

The Cold War ended almost at the same time the submarines were completed. Suddenly the GIUK surveillance mission was relatively unimportant. The Royal Navy certainly needed submarines, but for power projection over vast distances. Without an empire, the British could not depend on bases anywhere near where their submarines would operate. The *Upholder*s, whose characteristics had fit so well with the planned Cold War mission, were suddenly a drain on British resources, and they were laid up and ultimately sold.

Overall, greater reliance on bases can cut the cost of ships and other naval units. For example, a ship designed to operate from a base closer to a combat zone can be smaller because she needs less ability to repair herself at sea and she needs less steaming range. Nor does she need as high a standard of habitability, because she will spend shorter periods at sea. Conversely, she enjoys less of the overall mobility that makes navies valuable. The interwar Royal Navy, for example, designed ships with relatively short steaming ranges because it had a worldwide network of bases in British colonies. When some of those bases were lost during World War II, the Royal Navy sometimes found itself nearly immobilized. Without a comparable base structure, the U.S. Navy had built much greater steaming endurance into its ships and developed a sophisticated supporting fleet train. The main sensor supporting U.S. ship-based missiles, which are supporting troops ashore, is the radar aboard land-based Joint Stars (E-8) aircraft. There was a conscious decision *not* to place a somewhat equivalent radar on carrier-based aircraft. U.S. forces in Bosnia and Kosovo made extensive use of long-endurance unmanned aircraft (UAVs), which are land based. There is, however, active U.S. Navy interest in long-range ship-based UAVs. The current U.S. carrier attack fighter, the F/A-18, has limited range; in operations such as Iraq and Kosovo, it has often benefited from tanking—by land-based aircraft. In each case, basing offers foreign governments a partial veto over U.S. operations. Operations in Kosovo, many of which were mounted from land bases in Italy, were much affected by vetoes by both the Italians and by other coalition partners.

Many of the limits of current U.S. operating practice, due to the need for basing, are not yet widely appreciated, perhaps because we are still far more independent of bases than are our allies. Our operating practices will be better understood, however, as our forces engage more often, which will be inevitable in a post–Cold War world. Governments will come to appreciate how much we need their facilities. Conversely, measures to maintain our independence of action may become more and more vital. The two alternatives to land basing, to expand or redesign carrier assets and to move some systems into space, are both quite expensive.

Some developments have gone in the opposite direction. In the past, navies relied heavily on ground-based radio stations. Although high-frequency radio could, in theory, be heard throughout the world, a navy's reach was determined largely by its access to repeater stations ashore. In the 1950s, the U.S. Navy designed a special radio relay ship specifically to operate in radio "deserts," the places lacking shore facilities; ultimately two such ships were built, and they were heavily used in the 1960s to support carrier forces off the Vietnamese coast. This particular requirement has now been overcome by the use of satellites. Similarly, satellites have replaced shore-based radio navigational aids (Loran and then Omega) and some ground-based electronic and imaging reconnaissance forces.

Merchant shipping offers another version of the base issue. The trend has been away from break-bulk cargo, which is easy to unload with simple equipment, to containers, which require elaborate port facilities. As in the case of naval bases, such facilities are expensive; only a select few of the world's many harbors have them. At present as few as fifteen to twenty superports, such as Houston and Rotterdam, handle about 75 percent of world trade. Much the same can be said of bulk cargoes such as oil and iron ore. In each case development is driven by the economy of scale; it is far more efficient to build a single superport with efficient inland transportation, than to rely on numerous small local ports. The same argument justifies larger and larger merchant ships, because the new kinds of facilities can unload them far more quickly than break-bulk facilities could handle much smaller ships. The U.S. Navy does maintain shipboard facilities capable of unloading container ships at an unimproved port, but at only a fraction of the rate that a modern port can maintain.

Particular ports become tempting targets. The entire buildup for the Gulf War depended heavily on only three ports, al-Jubayl and ad-Dammamm in Saudi Arabia, and Bahrein, which had very modern facilities. Although the Iraqis lacked the naval force to attack the shipping pouring materiel through these ports, they did, at least potentially, have the ability to knock out the ports. For example, Scud missiles with chemical warheads would have sufficed if they had been accurate enough. No other target would have offered as much leverage. As it was, the U.S. Coast Guard mounted patrols to ensure that the Iraqis did not mount midget submarine attacks on the ports.

Economics will probably dictate further automation. There is currently interest in faster merchant ships, with speeds as high as thirty-six knots. That speed is valuable only if it can drastically reduce total voyage time, including unloading time. At present it takes about twenty-four to forty-eight hours to unload a big container ship, a substantial fraction of the total voyage time for a thirty-six-knot transatlantic ship (about one hundred hours plus turn-around time in port). The next stage would be to package containers, or anything else, on massive pallets that could be unloaded in, for instance, two to five hours. Any facility that could handle pallets weighing thousands or tens of thousands of tons would require massive capital investment. Presumably few such ports would be created, and thus they would become extremely attractive targets in war or in blockade.

With the coming of steam, ships needed fuel. Coal capacity was usually limited, and transfer at sea was virtually impossible.[8] Strings of coaling stations largely determined the mobility of fleets. The worldwide British empire offered coaling facilities almost everywhere, although there was some question as to how easily they could be defended. In peacetime, however, the British could in effect veto other countries' operations. For example, in 1898, before steaming to seize the Philippines, Adm. George Dewey's fleet coaled at Hong Kong, a British colony. The British might easily have aborted the operation simply by denying Dewey his fuel.

The Russians found out how important coal was when they sent their Baltic Fleet halfway around the world to its end off Tsushima. Given their alliance with the Japanese, the British denied them coaling facilities throughout their worldwide empire. The Russian alliance with the French did secure the Baltic Fleet facilities in Africa and at Cam Ranh Bay in what is now Vietnam. Even so, the fleet's battleships had to steam much of the way with excess coal piled on their decks. One consequence was that they could not conduct any sort of gunnery practice, with fatal results once they reached the battle area.

It proved very difficult to transfer coal at sea. Even in port, coaling was laborious. In addition, as it burned, coal formed an ash. Ships had to stop periodically to dump it at sea. Oil solved all these problems. It was also much more efficient; a given tonnage of oil could drive a ship much farther than a given tonnage of coal. Some countries, such as Britain, however, enjoyed good coal supplies but had no oil reserves. It became vital to safeguard not only overseas supplies, but also the ships carrying oil from the wells and refineries to the fleet at home.[9] For example, during World War I, German U-boats drastically curtailed oil shipments to Britain. When the United States entered the war in 1917, many American battleships burned oil fuel, largely because the United States produced much of the world's oil. When American battleships were assigned to reinforce the British Grand Fleet, only the older coal-burning dreadnoughts were sent, because, like most of the British ships, they could burn coal mined in Wales. For much the same reason, the Germans kept building coal-burning battleships through World War I, despite the technical disadvantages involved. During World War II, the Japanese lost most of their tankers to U.S. submarine attacks. In 1944 they moved their battleships to the only secure source of oil, the captured Netherlands East Indies (now Indonesia). Although the new location had no other strategic virtues, the ships would have been immobilized if they had been based anywhere else.

Geopolitics during the American Revolution

The American Revolution exemplifies the interlocking effects of coalitions and geography on seapower. After losing the great eighteenth century world war (the Seven Years' War of 1756–63), the French decided to seek revenge. They were well aware that seapower had been crucial. France could not match British seapower, however, as long as she had to maintain a large army to face British coalition partners in Europe.[10] The French mended fences on the Continent, while the British failed to maintain their wartime alliance with Prussia or to form a northern German coalition based on Hanover, which their king owned. The same Bourbon family ruled both France and Spain, the two greatest continental sea powers. The French promoted an alliance, the Bourbon Family Compact. Both countries made special efforts to build up their fleets. In a futile attempt at reconciliation, the British had returned to the French the West Indian islands they had seized, thereby providing the French with potential wartime bases. Neither continental power, however, considered naval warfare practical as long as the British could concentrate their fleet in European waters. They needed some coalition partner that could divide the British fleet. They found it in the American colonists, who rebelled against the British in 1775. Their advantage was geographical: the colonies lay outside the European area the Royal Navy normally controlled.

The Seven Years' War left the British heavily indebted. They laid up much of their fleet, but even in this state it retained considerable deterrent value.[11] In theory, ships could quickly be mobilized using the vast resources of the British shipbuilding industry and the large number of merchant seamen in British service. However, it was widely imagined in Britain that unless the debt incurred during the Seven Years' War was sharply reduced, the country could not afford to mobilize the fleet. Thus deterrence depended on British tax policy. To help solve this problem the British raised taxes on their American colonists; these taxes helped precipitate the revolution. The tax issue exemplified a recurring problem in imperial defense. To the colonists in North America, the main threat was a French invasion from Canada. Victory in the Seven Years' War ended it. On an imperial scale, however, the threat was French seapower, which might cut Atlantic trade links. The defense of North America rested heavily on the Royal Navy in European waters. Colonists found it diffi-cult to imagine that this invisible force was vital to their existence. The same could be said of Australians or South Africans who could not imagine that their defense depended on global British sea control, exercised largely in Euro-pean waters. To them, as to the colonists, threats were local, and they were met mainly by troops. Conversely, without a local threat, there was little point in paying for defense, particularly distant defense.

The colonial revolt strained British seapower in two complementary ways. One was direct: ships assigned to North America were not available to main-tain sea control in European waters. Geography did not help. The colonists were the first major maritime threat to Britain that could not be contained by blocking the exits from the North Sea, the English Channel, and the Mediter-ranean. Any blockade would therefore carry a high naval price. In this way the colonists were exactly the coalition partners the French needed. Second, there was an indirect drain: the colonies accounted for a large fraction of overall British empire naval resources. The colonies were the major source of masts and naval stores; during the Napoleonic wars supplies had to come from the Baltic, through waters contested by the French.[12] The demands of the Seven Years' War largely completed the ongoing exhaustion of British forests. When war broke out again the Royal Navy found itself desperately short of spars and timber with which to refit ships coming out of reserve or to repair ships after arduous sea duty. It did not help that many ships had been built of unseasoned timber, both during and after the Seven Years' War; they rotted while in reserve. The scale of resources lost by the American rebellion is noteworthy. As of 1775, colonial shipyards had built a third of all British-registered merchant ships. Moreover, the colonies were a source of seamen; about eighteen thousand became unavailable to the Royal Navy, equivalent to more than a fifth of full war strength.[13] When war began, the loss of American seamen made it difficult to expand the Royal Navy quickly enough to match the French and, later, the Spanish, at least in numbers.

There was no physical center of gravity that the British could attack and thereby end the American rebellion. Because the colonies lacked vital indus-tries or financial centers, the loss of the cities was unlikely to be fatal. On the other hand, enthusiasm for rebellion was limited, and it might be argued that the destruction of the rebel army, coupled with a generally conciliatory policy, would have ended the problem. Seapower could have contributed to that end in two ways. First, it could have provided British armies with far better mobility than the rebels enjoyed. Second, because the colonies had never industrialized, they lacked sources of arms and ammunition. Blocking imports, then, might have doomed the colonists' army. Initially the British hoped that the European powers would agree not to supply the rebels, which would be a nonmilitary equivalent to a blockade.[14] European monarchs had good reason to dislike the precedent the Americans were setting, but it turned out that they were clearly willing to risk the precedent if the rebellion weakened the British. To the extent that the American Revolution inspired the French, the French would have been wiser to take a longer view. As it was, in May 1776 the French decided to help the rebels with funds for arms. They saw such aid as a prelude to a renewed war, so they began to refit their fleet. For their part the British maintained a growing force in home waters both to deter the French from further involvement and to capture ships carrying munitions from France to the colonies.

The Royal Navy blockaded the long American coast. Operations were complicated by a basing problem; the only British dockyard in North America was in Halifax, Nova Scotia, and it was subject to land attack by the rebels. The loss of the dockyard would have crippled the British naval effort. The blockade crippled American trade with the West Indies, and badly damaged the American whaling industry. The British, however, were unable to cut off American access to Europe, which provided the small continental army with its weapons and ammunition. Indeed, British stocks of ammunition in the New World became prizes to be captured by American warships, the main example being the successful raid on Nassau in the Bahamas in March 1776. The Americans were also able to maintain their tobacco trade with France.

Given their heavily maritime economy, the colonies were able to mobilize numerous privateers and some commissioned warships to prey on British trade. The blockade did not contain them, and the British found it necessary to convoy trade, even on some routes that had not required such protection during the Seven Years' War, such as the linen trade across the Irish Sea. Also, the French welcomed American privateers into their ports even before they entered the war.

In addition to lighter units used to enforce the blockade, the British had to maintain larger warships in the American theater of war, both to convoy army units up and down the coast and as covering forces to resist foreign intervention. This requirement in turn made it difficult to maintain a sufficient deterring force in European waters; it also weakened the naval effort to cut off American trade at the European end of the routes.[15]

As long as the Americans lacked coalition partners with navies, British seaborne mobility was extremely effective. For example, an amphibious assault seized New York in 1776, and almost caught and destroyed George Washington's army. Other assaults carried Newport, Philadelphia, Charleston, and Savannah, but none of these victories proved decisive. Then the British decided to split the colonies, cutting New England off from the rest. To do that they had to seize control of the Hudson River, the mouth of which they controlled. The colonists managed to gain control of Lake Champlain, the body of water the British had to cross, long enough to hold back the British for the 1776 campaigning season. The following year the rebel army enjoyed one of its few military successes at Saratoga, which convinced the French that it would be worthwhile to enter the war.

The French signed a secret treaty of alliance on 6 February 1778, although they did not announce a state of war until July 1778. Presumably in hopes of releasing some ships from blockade and convoy duty, in March 1778 the British fleet in American waters was secretly ordered to attack the privateers at source, in American ports.

In the spring of 1778 the French fitted out a fleet at Brest to threaten Britain with invasion and thus, at the least, to tie down significant British naval forces. Another fitted out at Toulon to operate in the New World. The Royal Navy felt itself thinly enough spread that its force in European waters had to concentrate on the single greatest threat—invasion. That left the Toulon fleet free to reach the New World, arriving off Delaware Bay on 8 July 1778. The mere appearance of this fleet drastically reduced British mobility in North America. When the British decided to evacuate Philadelphia and bring their force back to New York, they sent heavy materiel by sea, but troops by the slower but safer land route. Failing to intercept the British supply ships, the French fleet appeared off New York, but chose not to attack the weaker British force in the harbor. This weaker force prevented a French assault on Newport. A pursuing British fleet missed the French at Boston. With the approach of winter, it sailed for the West Indies, taking a French island there. Presumably the British saw this action as a way of bringing the French fleet to battle in order to destroy it. From the French point of view, the sugar islands in the West Indies were the main prize. The French sailed in pursuit of the British fleet, failed to retake the lost island, but took two British colonies. They refused battle with the British fleet, and early in the new year returned to the American coast for a failed joint assault on Savannah.

The French presence off the American coast did block British reinforcement of Savannah, an omen of what would happen at Yorktown. Moreover, fear that the French fleet would support an American attempt to retake New

York led the British to abandon Newport in order to concentrate troops at New York. The French fleet returned home, however, because it had no base in the New World.

Just like the Royal Navy in American waters, the French fleet could not maintain any kind of sea control or even sea denial. In particular, the British could still use the sea freely to supply and to move their army. In 1781 a British army under Gen. Charles Cornwallis was sent to Yorktown, Virginia, probably hoping it would attract the American rebels into a decisive battle. Unfortunately for the British, by this time another French fleet had reached the New World. This fleet had sailed from Brest, which would normally have been covered by the British fleet in the English Channel. The Admiralty had ordered its channel fleet to the Irish coast, presumably to block a threatened invasion. The British were also unable to prevent Adm. Pierre André deSuffren from taking a powerful fleet into the Indian Ocean.

After delivering troops to Newport, the French fleet was ordered to reinforce the American and French troops besieging Yorktown. Defeating a British fleet on 5 September, it gained temporary but decisive local sea control, blocking the mouth of the Chesapeake Bay, the route to Cornwallis' position. In addition, the French fleet conveyed strong American forces to reinforce those facing Cornwallis. Cornwallis found himself in trouble. The French blocked both British reinforcement and his escape route. On 19 October he surrendered. The American Revolution was, in effect, over.

Similarly, during the Indo-China War, the French relied on another kind of mobility, support by air, to maintain a concentrated force deep in enemy territory at Dien Bien Phu in 1953–54. The loss of mobility, due to massed antiaircraft fire (using guns supplied by an ally, China), doomed not only the concentrated force but also the entire French position. Like the British in 1781, the French in 1954, when Dien Bien Phu fell, were demoralized by a long and apparently pointless war. Again, like the British, the French still had substantial forces available to them. The shock of a major military disaster, however, was enough to convince them to settle.

Had the French and their Spanish allies been more aggressive during the American Revolution, they might have achieved more. In the West Indies, they consistently preferred to seize particular islands rather than risk decisive battle with British fleets. In British home waters, the two allies managed to combine their fleets to achieve what should have been overwhelming superiority over a British home fleet badly weakened by the demands of the American war.[16] The French commander was loath to fight, arguing that he could not undertake an invasion, which might have been decisive, until the out-numbered British home fleet had been destroyed. There was little attempt, moreover, to bring this fleet to battle.

Because France and its Spanish ally never destroyed any of the deployed British fleets, they could not win the war. At war's end, the British regained the islands the French had captured. The only permanent effect of the war was to pry the American colonies from the British empire. Because the British lived more by trade, which their seapower protected, than by exploiting colonial resources, that was a survivable blow.

Losing Favorable Geography: The Pacific

British naval dominance was threatened when powers outside Europe—hence not subject to the geographical disadvantages imposed by the British Isles—began to build powerful navies. Russia posed particular problems, with its bases in the Pacific that the British could not block. From those bases Russian cruisers could prey on the vital shipping of the British empire in the East. By land, the Russians threatened the British empire in India. Quite possibly the sheer cost of defending India would make it impossible for the British to maintain a sufficiently strong fleet to defend other parts of the empire. The British sought a diplomatic solution, an alliance with a country that could tie the Russians down. Beginning in 1900, they approached France (Russia's ally), Germany (Russia's potential enemy in Europe), and Japan (Russia's potential enemy in the Far East). Only Japan proved amenable, and an alliance was signed in 1902.

It was already clear that rising Japanese nationalism brooked no foreign power rival anywhere in the Far East, hence Japan ultimately would not tolerate the British Empire there. The Russians were a greater impediment to Japanese expansion, however, with their near-control of Manchuria and Korea. Thus the alliance with Japan pushed the Japanese to deal with the Russians rather than the British. It guaranteed the Japanese that France, Russia's European ally, would not become involved in a Russo-Japanese War, because the French would want to avoid British involvement. By the time war broke out, the British and French were concluding an entente. The alliance solved the central British problem of naval geography: the Japanese home islands lay between the main Russian base, Vladivostok, and the Pacific. Japanese ambitions on the mainland of Asia threatened the other main Russian fleet base, at Port Arthur in China. The British could hope that, at least for the moment,

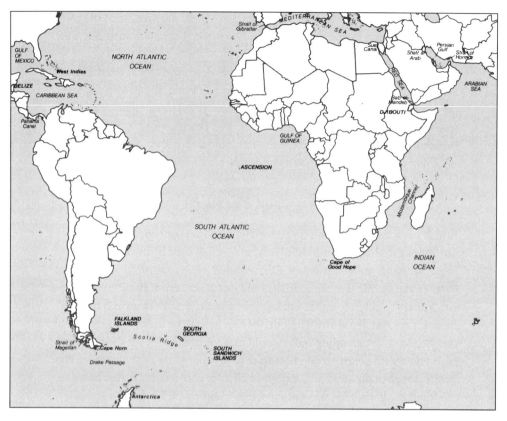

British seapower, 1914. In 1914 Britain controlled many of the "keys which lock up the world," some of which are shown here. British bases in the West Indies blocked the exits from the Panama Canal. Less obviously, the Falklands blocked the route around Cape Horn or through the Strait of Magellan from the Pacific to the South Atlantic. The Cape of Good Hope, in British-controlled South Africa, controlled the shipping route around Africa to the Indian Ocean. The alternative route, through the Mediterranean, passed through British-controlled Gibraltar and then through the British-controlled Suez Canal and down the Red Sea past Aden, which the British also controlled, toward India and the Far East. Not visible here are the Straits of Malacca, through which traffic passed from the Indian Ocean toward Japan. The British controlled Malaya, at the southern tip of which lay the future base at Singapore, at the entrance to the straits. During World War I the British seized German colonies in East Africa, north of the Mozambique Channel, largely to prevent the Germans from basing cruisers there to attack shipping passing around Africa. *U.S. Naval Institute*

the alliance would turn the Japanese against the Russians rather than themselves. They probably expected the two Far Eastern powers to neutralize each other. That did not happen; the Japanese defeated the Russians in 1905.

The British had to face the fact that their alliance was only a temporary expedient. They still had to protect the Far Eastern part of the empire without incurring the cost of maintaining a powerful Far Eastern fleet. Fisher believed that fast task forces could do much of the job. Individually they could run down and destroy commerce raiders. Combined, they could form an Empire Fleet. Even if it was not as powerful as the Japanese fleet, it could act as a deterrent (as a fleet-in-being). Each tactical unit of the fleet would consist of a battlecruiser supported by three fast light cruisers acting as out-running scouts, the smallest ships with roughly the same seakeeping qualities and long endurance as the battlecruiser.[17] The prototype unit was purchased by the new Royal Australian Navy. Plans originally called for four fleet units: a Canadian unit based at Vancouver, an Australian unit at Sydney, and two Royal Navy (at Singapore and at Hong Kong) units. New Zealand would help to pay for the Hong Kong unit. Plans for India to buy at least two fleet units were deferred due to financial problems. The Admiralty hoped that South Africa would eventually buy a fleet unit. All of the Pacific dominions were expected to help pay for a new fleet base at Singapore. The units would normally act independently, but they would unite in an emergency to hold until the main British fleet could join them.[18] The two battlecruisers bought under the scheme served in the Grand Fleet during World War I, and the fleet unit program was not revived afterwards.[19] To some extent the fleet unit idea was revived when HMS *Prince of Wales* and HMS *Repulse* were sent to Singapore in December 1941.[20]

During the period leading up to 1914, with both Japan and Russia as allies, the British could reasonably argue that a battle fleet in home waters, blocking the Germans, protected not only Britain but also the empire; a few lighter units abroad could deal with whatever commerce raiders might operate in distant waters. On this basis the Australians, for example, could send ships and men to fight in Europe as defenders not only of Britain but also of the empire of which they were part. It was entirely reasonable for Australian troops to fight to defend the Suez Canal, because it was an important link between Australia and the United Kingdom. Conversely, if Japan became a primary threat, any such cover was irrelevant. In World War II, Australia contributed heavily to British forces fighting in the Middle East, only to feel entirely uncovered when Japan entered the war.[21]

4

Using Naval Forces

Sea Surveillance

A CENTRAL FACT of naval warfare is that ships are difficult to find and identify in the vastness of the sea. It might seem that the advent of aircraft solved this problem. Obviously ships are visible from the air. The requirement, however, is not merely to detect some ship; it is to identify particular ships among the vast number at sea at any one time. That is difficult from any distance, and for an airplane to close in on each ship it detects in order to identify it drastically slows any search it attempts to carry out. The situation for a space satellite is even more difficult.[1]

Much depends on a navy's surveillance systems, many elements of which may be fixed ashore or in the command and control net that connects ships, aircraft, and surveillance. This is not a new idea. As soon as ships began to use radios for communication, messages were intercepted. Even the fact of communication revealed a ship's position. Code-breaking offered far more. In 1914 the British cut German cables throughout the world, so that all German naval communication outside Germany had to be by radio. At about the same time they obtained the German naval code books. Partly because the Germans were blithely unaware that their codes had been compromised, the British read their radio traffic through World War I, and thus were often able to follow their operational plans. The fruits of this effort went directly to the British

Grand Fleet. For a variety of reasons this rich source of information was underused, but the practice was the beginning of operational surveillance. Unfortunately for the British, their World War I code-breaking success was openly described after the war. The Germans took it to heart, both defensively (they adopted machine ciphers, in the form of the famous Enigma machine) and offensively (they worked hard to defeat British naval codes, the result making a vast difference in the Battle of the Atlantic).[2]

Based on the lessons of World War I, the Admiralty created an Operational Intelligence Centre for World War II. It is impossible to understand the performance of the World War II Royal Navy without taking into account this vital shore-based sensor center.[3] The U.S. Navy also created surveillance centers. These centers, for example, used code-breaking intelligence to deal with the German U-boats. The British were painfully aware of the potential of radio-based surveillance. As a consequence they enforced strict radio discipline, which sometimes had adverse consequences. For example, it appears that HMS *Hood* maintained *radar* silence during the approach to the *Bismarck,* with terrible consequences. Postwar, the British apparently preferred not to use radio data links, for much the same reason, until they learned in the Falklands War just how valuable they were.

Both main Cold War combatants were intensely interested in long-range surveillance, but initially in different contexts. Concerned mainly with defeating Soviet submarines, the U.S. Navy developed a combination of underwater acoustic surveillance (sosus system) and HF/DF (high-frequency [radio] direction-finder) stations, the latter to exploit periodic reports the submarines made. Given data, long-range patrol aircraft could be vectored out to locate and attack Soviet submarines. They were, in effect, interceptors.[4] Conversely, without long-range means of detection, the patrol aircraft really does have to patrol, and its main hope is that the submarine turns on a radar or radio. Aircraft cannot possibly carry enough sonobuoys to search continuously during a lengthy flight and the chance of picking up a submarine falls dramatically. Since the end of the Cold War patrol aircraft are used far more for surface surveillance.

The Soviets tracked what they saw—the U.S. surface fleet, including carriers—as the main threat. When the U.S. Navy became interested in tracking the Soviet surface fleet, its understanding of the techniques the Soviets were using improved enormously, and it developed sophisticated countermeasures, ultimately including elaborate deception schemes.[5] Conversely, as the Soviets became more interested in tracking U.S. submarines, particularly strategic ones, they came to understand how their own were being tracked. They invested more heavily in countermeasures. New submarine designs emphasized silencing, and the Soviets invested in improvements to existing craft.[6] They also probably learned to make better use of underwater geography to defeat fixed systems.

The U.S. Navy found that it could fuse available data to form a reasonably current picture of world ship movements. The U.S. forces could then evade contact with the Soviets, target long-range missiles, or plan air strikes. The shore centers at which the data were fused were as important as the sensors, many of them in space. The centers formed one end of a system; the other end was computer centers on ships. The two were linked by space-based communications to ensure that they were always available, and to provide sufficient capacity. This combination—sensors, data fusion, and a reliable link between shore and ship—gave the U.S. Navy a degree of sea surveillance unique among the world's navies. It radically changed the capabilities of surface ships armed with long-range antiship missiles, in a way that navies that buy equivalent missiles—but not equivalent backup—cannot match. In a way, then, the sensor/data fusion combination separates truly oceanic fleets from those that currently have pretensions to oceanic reach.

The U.S. sea surveillance system was demonstrated during the embargo leading up to the Gulf War. With only a few frigates available, enforcement depended heavily on knowing the exact location of ships suspected of carrying contraband. The shipboard terminal for the system, which was then called JOTS, was approved for service in June 1990, and in August it was supporting the embargo on coalition and U.S. ships.[7]

One conclusion that can be drawn from Cold War experience on both sides is that open-sea surveillance is expensive, including the satellites themselves and the intelligence support required. For example, ships are tracked passively not merely by detecting their radar emissions but by determining that a particular ship has been detected. That in turn requires radar fingerprinting; successful fingerprinting requires that each ship to be tracked be revisited periodically so that her radar emissions, which can change over time, can be recorded. It seems unlikely that there are civilian requirements for the sorts of sea surveillance satellites that the Cold War adversaries fielded. In direct contrast, imaging satellites are unlikely to offer much in the way of open-sea surveillance because the swaths they cover at any one time are inherently quite narrow. If they are made much wider, ships detected will probably be unrecognizable. This situation is in stark contrast to that of armies, which must build up large static dumps of materiel in order to move. The dumps are easily seen and usually identified by commercial imaging satellites. One might, then, conclude that navies are likely to retain their current degree of invisibility much longer than armies preparing for assault. Conversely, the existence of imaging satellites may well encourage the existing, although little-developed, trend of armies to split into smaller, more mobile units.

Some space resources are making sea surveillance much more difficult. In the past, ships depended on high-frequency radio to communicate at long range. The signals were relatively easy to intercept, and fleets could be tracked. Many countries operated nets of high-frequency radio direction-finders and intercept stations. The shift to satellite communications makes interception almost impossible. In some cases location data can be deduced from signals in the satellite down-link, if they can be picked up, but that opening is unlikely to last very long.

Perhaps the key Cold War naval surveillance lesson is that the value of weapons, particularly long-range ones, is limited by the ability to find and track moving or easily moved targets. The longer the weapon's range, the more heavily the shooter must rely on information from remote sources, such as space-based ship detectors. Conversely, merely buying long-range weapons does not buy long-range capability. For example, in the early 1960s the Royal Navy planned a new class of aircraft carriers, but it was understood that they might well be canceled as too expensive. To defend the project, the navy estimated the cost of a non-carrier fleet. Radar aircraft aboard carriers could detect surface ships a few hundred miles away and direct carrier-based aircraft to destroy them. The Royal Navy could develop ship-launched missiles offering similar range. Aircraft were still needed to detect targets, however. This was before the U.S. Navy fielded space-based sensors, formed a shipping picture on the basis of which targeting was possible, and apparently shared the picture with its closest ally, the Royal Navy. As another case in point, the Indian navy is taking delivery of Russian-built submarines and surface ships carrying antiship missiles with ranges up to three hundred miles, but India has no comparable surveillance system. Most countries are content with reasonably good surveillance out to the radar horizon, supplemented by intermittent coverage by a few maritime patrol aircraft operating farther out. It is striking, moreover, that attempts to sell longer-range radars and acoustic surveillance systems, both of which would extend the sensor horizon to a few hundred miles, have apparently largely been fruitless.

Sea Control and Power Projection

Often a navy capable of projecting its power over great distances (in the case of the United States, across the world) is contrasted with one limited to home or adjacent waters. The former is often described as a power projection or sea control navy. The latter is seen as a local sea denial navy, because it often concentrates on preventing anyone else from operating in the area it tries to dominate. Power projection refers to the ability to attack land targets, either with weapons, which may be carried by aircraft, or by landing troops. Sea control is the ability to maintain use of the sea, which in turn usually means keeping an enemy's attackers from sinking friendly ships.

During the Cold War, for example, U.S. aircraft carriers were often described as power projection assets, because their bombers could strike land targets. The frigates operated by NATO navies, on the other hand, were often described as sea control assets, as were maritime patrol aircraft such as P-3 Orions. In war against the Soviets the argument has been expounded that sea control forces would have been key, because they would have maintained the transatlantic supply line vital to NATO forces fighting on the aptly named Central Front. Thus, when the United States abandoned interest in the Third World following the Vietnam debacle, there was interest within the U.S. government in abandoning power projection forces, particularly expensive carrier battle groups. Unfortunately the frigates and the patrol aircraft would have dealt with only one facet of the Soviet antiship threat. The other threat, against which they were powerless, was an increasingly powerful force of missile-equipped land-based bombers. Carrier-based fighters were needed to shoot the bombers down. Even if the frigates could have shot down the missiles, Soviet bombers would have survived to return to base, rearm, and attack again, eventually exhausting the frigates' stocks of defensive weapons.

How, then, could a carrier's F-14 fighters be characterized? Did they simply protect the carrier herself, as the outer layer of her defenses, or were they an offensive arm seizing sea control by wiping out an important element of the Soviet fleet, the bomber force? Clearly they were both. Moreover, the carrier was hardly the only element of the force designed to deal with the bombers. For example, some bombers might well launch their missiles before the F-14s attacked. If the fighters had to concentrate on those missiles, many bombers would escape to fight another day. The U.S. solution was to surround the carrier with effective antiaircraft ships, either Aegis cruisers or upgraded versions of earlier missile ships. These escorts were backstops against any missiles the bombers managed to launch, freeing the F-14s to concentrate on the bombers—an important element of the Soviet fleet, albeit a land-based one.

The carrier presented the Soviets with the offensive threat of attack aircraft, which had to be neutralized. The Soviet forces might otherwise have been used against NATO shipping less able to deal with them: missile-bearing bombers and missile-bearing submarines in particular. The carrier's defenses, then, had a decidedly offensive flavor. Indeed, the point of running the carrier force toward potential Soviet targets, as the U.S. Navy planned to do, was to incite the Soviets to fight what the U.S. Navy hoped would be a decisive battle.

The offensive use of the carrier exemplified an important truth: sea control and power projection can be two aspects of the same thing. They need not be; frigates enforcing sea control against submarines certainly would not be useful for power projection. The U.S. emphasis on carrier battle groups was a conscious choice. One advantage was that the same fleet could be used to project power to deal with Third World crises. When the Soviet Union collapsed, leaving the requirement for power projection but not for sea control against hordes of Soviet submarines, the U.S. fleet built during the Cold War was still quite relevant to the new circumstances. Oddly, that proved somewhat embarrassing; the other U.S. services clearly had to redesign themselves for the new world situation, whereas the Cold War navy was already largely adapted to it, yet appeared to many to be resisting necessary change.

Maintaining Sea Control

The power projection method of gaining sea control combines two tactics: decisive battle and attack at source. Ideally the carrier battle group would have destroyed so much of the Soviet sea denial force in one or more decisive battles that it could never have threatened any other NATO use of the sea. If the Soviets refused to come out, the battle group could, hopefully, have projected power in such a way as to destroy Soviet bombers on the ground. Both were particular ways of gaining sea control in the face of potent sea denial forces and considered necessary partly because other NATO forces could not have dealt with these forces.

Attack at source is particularly attractive if the raiders cannot easily be countered when they are at sea or, in the case of the Soviet bombers, in the air. At the end of World War II new submarine technology supposedly outclassed wartime antisubmarine escorts. The U.S. Navy argued that it needed carrier-based nuclear bombers specifically to gain sea control by destroying advanced Soviet submarines at source.

In the past, a concentrated main fleet was often contrasted with dispersed trade-protection or trade-attack craft. It was assumed that only a main fleet could destroy another main fleet in battle. The main fleet was built around capital ships, the assumption being that only a capital ship could expect to destroy another capital ship. Capital ships were, therefore, big and expensive —and they could not be numerous. Trade warfare, on the other hand, covers the world's oceans, so units built for it, on either the offensive or defensive side, must be numerous; therefore, the unit basis cost must not be too expensive. To further complicate matters, the ships designed for trade warfare are often also secondary elements of main fleets. In Lord Horatio Nelson's time, for example, frigates were used both as fleet scouts and as convoy escorts. Today, destroyers and frigates are both fleet elements, usually as carrier escorts, and trade-protection craft when they act as convoy escorts.

Convoy is a better-known sea control strategy. In a sense, it is a form of the decisive battle strategy.[8] The theory is simple. Because the ocean is vast, commerce raiders such as submarines are difficult to detect at any distance. The raiders have to find their targets, which can be gathered into compact convoys and surrounded by antisubmarine ships. Raiders can attack a convoy when they can find it, but they reveal their presence and open themselves to counterattack by the escorts. Convoy offers a series of battles of annihilation on a small scale. Alternatively, one might see the carrier battle group as a gigantic convoy, combining the most attractive targets with the deadliest countermeasures. In both world wars most U-boats were sunk in the vicinities of convoys.

Convoy is effective only if there are enough escorts, and the number of escorts is set not by the strength of the opposing force but rather by the number of convoys that must be protected. Huge numbers may be needed. To be affordable, each escort can have no more than the minimum capability needed to handle a raider. It cannot deal with main fleet units. The main fleet makes convoy tactics possible by covering the escorts from possible depredations by the enemy's main fleet. For example, during World War II the British ran convoys to resupply the Soviet Union. They faced both classical antishipping forces (aircraft and U-boats) and a sort of main fleet, in the form of battleships like the *Tirpitz*. Typically a convoy had a close-in escort capable of dealing with the antishipping craft. The main British fleet, the Home Fleet, provided distant cover against any German capital ships (in effect, main fleet units) that might be sent into combat. It was well understood that if a capital ship found a convoy, it could and would destroy both the close-in escorts and the convoy. The convoy would have to scatter in hopes that some of the ships would survive. Scattering would, however, negate the value of the escorts, so the ships would easily fall victim to any aircraft or U-boats that happened to be present. In that case the convoy might be destroyed, but the British hoped that their Home Fleet would destroy the German capital ship, ending its threat to future convoys.

In mid-1942 convoy PQ-17 was en route to the Soviet Union. The British Admiralty received signals intelligence revealing that the battleship *Tirpitz* was about to come out. The Admiralty ordered PQ-17 to scatter, because there was no chance that the heavy covering force could have come into action soon enough to save it. As it happened, the sortie was abandoned, and the U-boats and aircraft wiped out most of the ships of the convoy. For the Germans, then, *Tirpitz* exemplified a fleet-in-being. By her mere existence she tied down important Allied naval forces, generally at least three battleships plus lesser craft, which might more usefully have supported major invasions. A feint on the German battleship's part, moreover, could have devastating consequences, as in the PQ-17 battle. For the British, then, the destruction of the German battleship became vital, not least as a means of freeing important resources. Attacks were physically difficult, because the ship lay up a fjord that was easily defended. The British tried midget submarines and carrier air attacks. Eventually heavy bombs, dropped by land-based Lancaster bombers, succeeded.

The Germans well understood the connection between main fleet and convoy escorts prior to World War II. As a major land power, they could not hope to build a main fleet comparable to the British. They could build individual ships of considerable power, partly by violating prewar naval arms limitation treaties. By 1939 their planned wartime strategy was to deploy four powerful surface task forces or battle groups while maintaining a battle force in home waters to tie down the British fleet.[9] They learned the lesson from World War I when the mere existence of the German fleet had tied down the British Grand Fleet. The British could not provide each convoy with a heavy covering force; at least some of the battle groups would be able to tear up convoys. If the British abandoned convoys in hopes of evading surface attack, they would open the ships to U-boat attack. As it was expressed prewar, the strategy did not quite explain how the task forces would evade British geography. Adm. Erich Raeder, the navy chief, talked of an Atlantic Ocean–North Sea "two-pole" strategy. Possibly the strategy was framed in the expectation that the German army would seize the necessary French bases. To some extent the 1941 sortie by the battlecruisers (fast battleships) *Scharnhorst* and *Gneisenau* and the abortive sortie by the battleship *Bismarck* exemplified the offensive element of the German strategy. By that time the German army had provided the necessary geography.

Convoying was used extensively during the sailing ship era, but it was dropped with the advent of steamships. The argument was that raiders would now be less efficient. Sailing ships were bound more or less by the wind, so a raider could simply run down wind-determined trade routes. Steamships, which could choose their courses more independently, would be more difficult to find. Raiders would surely have to concentrate at focal points, in which typical trade routes converged near key ports, and antiraiders could also concentrate there. Shipping routes proved all too predictable during World War I, with gruesome results for the Allies. After an intense debate, the British reintroduced convoying in 1917, with gratifying results.[10] One great irony was that many World War I naval officers raised on Mahan's concepts (i.e., on the primacy of decisive battle as a way of seizing sea control) rejected convoying as defensive; surely the offensive was the stronger form of warfare at sea. Yet much of the value of convoying is exactly that it forces the enemy to accept battle.

One might analogize convoy to the sort of protection offered by a bodyguard. Although the bodyguard is trained to place his body in the line of fire, in fact he is a deterrent. A determined enough assassin can expect to get through bodyguards, as long as he is willing to die in the process. Most submarine commanders will say that they can find a way in through escorts, but that once they have announced their presence by attacking, they will inevitably be counterattacked. One U.S. Cold War diesel submarine commander summed it up by saying that in wartime he would have to choose between living (i.e., avoiding attack) and sinking enemy ships—and that he was paid to sink enemy ships.[11] Thus convoy is part of a statistical or attrition strategy, in which enemy submarines get to sink some ships but die off in the process. For example, a 1960 U.S. study estimated that Soviet submarines could sink about one hundred merchant ships a month; however, after the first three months of a war, all them would have been sunk.[12] It was assumed that such losses of merchant ships would be tolerable. That might not always have been true; surely the loss of a fast ship carrying a large fraction of the tanks of an armored division would have been a serious blow, because the West had only a limited number of tanks. In a post–Cold War context, in which virtually all the escorted units are extremely valuable, it is not as clear that such exchanges are acceptable, and some other antisubmarine strategy may be mandated.[13]

Adm. Sergei Gorshkov remarked during the Cold War that the true significance of World War II's Battle of the Atlantic lay in the huge ratio of Allied resources required to neutralize an inexpensive German U-boat fleet. He was presumably trying to justify the cost of a Soviet submarine fleet to Soviet land-oriented commanders; in World War II the Allied resources might have been used instead against the German army. However, it is not clear that the Allies actually spent more than the Germans.[14] After World War II, as submarines became more sophisticated, the unit cost of escorts rose to the point where it might not be possible to provide nearly enough. Alternative shipping protection strategies, therefore, were developed.

If the enemy enjoys some form of wide-area surveillance, clearing the sea may even be counterproductive because it may concentrate targets where attackers may find it profitable to mass. The enemy may no longer need vast numbers of antishipping craft, so unit capability can be much higher. A weakly escorted convoy becomes, in effect, a meal laid out for the submarines. In the Pacific, U.S. submarines supported by surveillance—actually, by code-breaking—were able to find and destroy many Japanese convoys.[15] During the Cold War the U.S. Navy often argued that much the same could be said of Soviet nuclear submarines vectored by the Soviet sea surveillance system.

The two main alternatives to convoy are barriers and hunting. A barrier or blockade is interposed between the commerce raiders and their targets. During the Cold War NATO planned to place submarines in the strategic straits through which Soviet submarines would have to pass en route to their patrol areas. Groups of surface antisubmarine ships would perform similar duty. The expectation was not so much that no submarines would reach the open sea. However, a substantial percentage would be destroyed both going out and returning, thereby reducing the load on other measures. This was not too different in principle from British sailing-era attempts to blockade ports at which privateers were based. The obvious alternative to blockade, both in the sailing ship era and later, is attack at source, before the commerce raiders have any chance to spread out on the ocean.

Hunting gained an evil reputation during both world wars. U-boats could usually dive before being spotted, so few if any were caught by surface ships. As soon as the surface ship left, the submarine was free to surface again. Yet hunting by submarines was a very different proposition. During World War I, when antisubmarine measures were often ineffective, British and, later, U.S. submarines patrolled the Irish Sea, the North Sea, and other areas. To make good distance, U-boats had to run on the surface. Normally they could do so safely; they were so small that they could spot surface craft before being seen.

A surfaced U-boat, however, was unlikely to spot a submarine lying in wait for it. The mere threat of such submarines might well cause U-boat commanders to spend more of their time submerged, and thus rob them of their mobility. Much the same was said for air patrols. In the Pacific, U.S. submarines were faced by Japanese air patrols, but their ability to detect Japanese airborne radar before being detected largely negated the Japanese tactic.

During the Cold War NATO had long-range submarine detectors, such as the sound surveillance system (SOSUS) net. SOSUS could cue hunters, which could then redetect the submarines it found. It was, for example, the basis of long-range maritime patrol aircraft operations. Because SOSUS could detect a Soviet submarine in the open ocean, each Soviet submarine had a statistical chance of being sunk each day, no matter what it did.

The Main Fleet and the Fleet-in-Being

In theory a battle between main fleets could be decisive because it would be difficult to replace a devastated one in wartime. For example, at Trafalgar in October 1805 Lord Horatio Nelson destroyed a combined French and Spanish fleet. Although the French built numerous ships throughout the remaining decade of Napoleon's rule, these units all found themselves closely blockaded in harbor. They could not go to sea to train crews, and thus could never become effective. That was why Trafalgar was decisive. Although the post-Trafalgar Royal Navy had to continue to maintain its blockades of various European ports, Trafalgar freed the British to project power, for example, to use Wellington's forces to support Napoleon's enemies in Spain.

The obverse of the dominant main fleet, which can win a decisive battle, is the fleet-in-being, the inferior fleet that refuses battle but, by its existence, hobbles the stronger fleet. For example, in the Revolutionary War the weaker British fleet-in-being in home waters precluded a French invasion of England. In World War I the German fleet-in-being limited the extent to which the British could exploit their naval superiority. In each case, the counter to a fleet-in-being is either to force it to come out to fight to defend some vital interest, or to destroy it in place. Fixed defenses can make such attacks difficult or even futile, so in a sense they are part of the fleet-in-being. Both the French, in the age of sail, and the Germans, in the two world wars, were often criticized for caring too much about tying down their enemies (as fleets-in-being, in or out of port) to risk battle. Both navies were also criticized for avoiding battle in order to gain immediate objectives, for example, the West

Indian islands in the case of the French. In several World War II cases, German surface commanders broke off actions for fear of being so badly damaged that they could not carry on their primary mission of attacking British commerce. Apparently it did not dawn on them that destroying the Royal Navy would have opened up British shipping to attack.

Rear Adm. Alfred Thayer Mahan, USN, the father of modern naval strategy, became famous for his emphasis on main fleet engagement as a way of seizing sea control. He saw this as a decisive instrument in war. For Mahan, as with other naval strategists, seizing sea control was the initial step, to be followed by its exploitation. Mahan's ideas, however, were easy to oversimplify. In June 1944 the U.S. fleet seized Saipan in the Marianas; the Japanese attacked. In the initial phase of the battle, U.S. naval pilots destroyed the attacking Japanese aircraft. This destroyed Japanese naval airpower, because there was little hope of training replacement aircrew. U.S. fleet commander Adm. Raymond Spruance had a choice. He could uncover Saipan while the battle still raged ashore, in order to close with the Japanese carriers and sink them—in order to fight a decisive battle. Alternatively, he could be satisfied with a defensive victory and limit any pursuit, on the theory that his primary task was to secure Saipan. Saipan was wanted as a base within air range of Japan; a year later the nuclear bombers flew from it. To Spruance, the answer was clear: he covered the island. For that he was roundly criticized. In October, Adm. William Halsey led the same fleet, and he was responsible for the security of the beachhead at Leyte in the Philippines. He apparently did not realize the extent to which the Marianas victory, the famous "Turkey Shoot," had destroyed the Japanese naval air arm, because it may not have been clear that the Japanese had no pilots in reserve.[16] Lacking pilots, the Japanese used the carriers Spruance had not sunk as a decoy force to pull Halsey's fleet away from the invasion area, uncovering it to surface attack. They had, incidentally, had much the same idea in mind at the time of the Saipan operation, and their analysis had been captured by U.S. intelligence. This time Halsey took the bait, and disaster was narrowly avoided. Was he the truer heir to Mahan, or was he overly affected by criticism of Spruance?

Mahan's views were widely criticized after World War I because the main fleet model seemed irrelevant to the U-boat crisis. The British had the dominant battle fleet and the German battle fleet was shut in its base, but the U-boats almost starved Britain out of the war using a form of attack that apparently bypassed the British fleet altogether. Mahan's rejoinder might have been (he had died in 1914) that the convoy operations, which he certainly espoused, that ultimately defeated the U-boats had been possible only because convoy escorts were inexpensive. Otherwise they could never have been provided in sufficient numbers. That in turn was possible because the Germans could not mount an effective surface threat against the escorts—a threat that the British main fleet precluded. Imagine what would have happened had the Grand Fleet been defeated by the German High Seas Fleet. None of the convoy escorts could have stood up to German cruisers, let alone battleships. Moreover, big fast surface ships would have been far more efficient destroyers of commerce than U-boats.

The British feared that if the Germans secured control of the surface of the North Sea, they could have invaded Britain and so ended the war. The only German craft that could have crossed the North Sea unmolested were submarines; they could not have carried enough troops. Control of the surface of the North Sea, then, precluded any threat of invasion. Remarkably, the Germans never seriously contemplated it.

The U.S. carrier battle group clearly qualified as a main fleet during the Cold War. The Soviet combination of missile-firing land-based aircraft, surface combatants, and submarines also qualified, but less clearly. For example, it took long-range carrier-based fighters to destroy the bombers, because no other shipboard weapon had the necessary reach. The central problem of U.S. Cold War naval strategy was how to avoid the sort of dilemma the *Tirpitz* had imposed on the British. The Soviets were well aware of the potential value of a fleet-in-being. How could they be forced to give it up? As long as their fleet remained in place, NATO would get little value out of an expensive main fleet. U.S. strategists reasoned that the key was the U.S. main fleet's ability to project power—to destroy shore targets. The Soviets were likely to try to deal with the carrier, if only to protect targets ashore. The hope was that the carrier battle force would destroy the Soviet main fleet in a decisive battle. If it refused to come out, the fleet could project its power ashore to destroy the Soviet bombers and possibly the submarines and surface ships.

The problem of assaulting a Third World country may not be too different, in an abstract sense, from dealing with the Soviets. A country may well operate a substantial air arm, which threatens both troops who come ashore and shipping offshore. The troops and the ships may well be armed with antiaircraft missiles, but if the air attackers have stand-off weapons, as is increasingly the case, they will more likely be firing at the weapons than at the airplanes. Even if the weapons are destroyed, the attackers can keep coming back. In effect the enemy air force can be a country's main fleet. The only weapon likely to destroy that main fleet in the air, where destruction will really be effective, is our own air arm, and the most mobile form of that air arm is probably launched from a carrier. Because the carrier is also a highly effective offensive weapon, it is at least reasonable to imagine that its presence will draw out an enemy's best counterweapons, its aircraft—into a potentially decisive engagement. The same might be said of enemy submarines. The carrier is often the juiciest target, and its self-defense measures may be the best way to destroy the enemy's submarine force. Because that force is usually small, an engagement can indeed be decisive. Of course, the enemy may see matters similarly; we have few carriers, and sinking or disabling one is well worth the effort. It is our task to ensure that a decisive battle goes our way.

Moreover, just as in the Cold War, we have a considerable incentive to seek an early decisive battle. Now, as then, the main fleet can project power as well as fight for sea control. In a confrontation with a Third World country, power projection is probably much more important. Like the Germans and the Soviets, the opponent can choose between accepting battle and maintaining what amounts to a fleet-in-being. Rules of engagement may preclude attacks on the enemy's antiship force. That was certainly the case during the NATO war against Serbia, when the small Serbian submarine force enjoyed what amounted to sanctuary.[17] There is always a chance that after a time fatigue, wear and tear, and even accident will make our own force more vulnerable.[18] The U.S. Cold War strategy, to use the ability to project power to force the other side into action, is relevant.

The Cold War added an additional element, the strategic submarine. Both adversaries assumed that such submarines would be hunted and attacked in wartime. The Soviets assumed that the "combat stability" of their strategic submarines could be assured only by a measure of sea control, exerted in areas they called "bastions."[19] Indeed, in the 1980s the primary task of the Soviet main fleet was simply to defend the bastions. Thus a credible threat to strategic submarines in the bastions could tie down, or force into battle, a Soviet main fleet that otherwise might have been deployed against NATO and other vital shipping. At the least, Soviet concerns would probably significantly delay the onset of any main fleet antishipping campaign.

The U.S. view was that strategic submarines could survive in the open ocean without support. They were so quiet that the Soviet hunters were unlikely to find them. The Soviets would try to locate them, however, and they would expend considerable resources doing so. From a U.S. naval point of view, that was an advantage because every Soviet nuclear attack submarine wasted in the antistrategic role was not available to contest sea control. Every sortie ordered for this role exposed a Soviet submarine to attack as she passed back and forth through choke points controlled by NATO.

Blockade and Embargo

Sea control automatically confers the ability to stop most or all of an enemy's seaborne trade, in wartime by blockade and in peacetime by embargo. Embargo was formerly called "pacific blockade," as opposed to warlike blockade. In either case, the superior seapower sets up a barrier between the open sea and the enemy's ports. The main fleet shields the barrier against any enemy attempt to break it. Mahan believed blockade was the ultimate means by which a sea power could slowly strangle a land power.

The difference between blockade (or embargo) and commerce raiding is that blockade interposes a barrier, passage through which is the exception, whereas commerce raiding is hunting enemy ships on the open sea, which allows most ships to escape. From this point of view submarine blockades, which the German U-boats tried to execute in two world wars and the U.S. submarine force executed against Japan during World War II, are commerce raiding.

It is difficult to evaluate the effectiveness of a blockade.[20] Mahan wrote about the visible effect of cutting off trade, using the example that "grass grew in the streets of Amsterdam," the principal Dutch trading city, after the British destroyed Dutch sea control. However, blockades of supply, as imposed on the Confederacy during the U.S. Civil War and imposed on Germany during World War I, act slowly and subtly. Some supplies generally get through; the Confederates, for example, became very skilled blockade runners. Ingenuity often produces viable substitutes for imports. For example, the South industrialized under the pressure of blockade. Obvious shortages of goods within a country may be ascribed to inefficient distribution rather than to the blockade itself. When supplies are sharply reduced, however, those that do get through attract much higher prices, which is what motivates blockade runners and smugglers. The resulting inflation damages a wartime economy. It also damages social cohesion, because important goods, such as foodstuffs or acceptable clothing, may no longer be available to much of the population. That was evident in Germany by 1918. Ultimately, as in modern Iraq, virtually all the hard currency in a country may be exhausted, particularly if the blockade also drastically reduces exports. Under normal conditions there would be no point in expending energy and manpower to produce substitutes for inexpensive imports. Creating new industries, which may seem a graceful way to avoid the consequences of blockade, actually is a consequence, draining military potential (e.g., in the form of manpower). Blockade magnifies the effects of inefficiencies that would otherwise have caused no problems. Over several years, these factors may grow more important. Conversely, in a short war blockade or embargo is unlikely to have much impact at all, except for any special austerity measures the target government adopts.

Until the mid-nineteenth century the British maintained several pillars of maritime rights: the right of blockade, declaring as contraband any goods that might assist an enemy, and the right to seize enemy goods in transit on board whatever ships might be carrying them. The Royal Navy could declare an entire coast under blockade, even though it could not actually stop ships from going into or out of every port along that coast. Opponents demanded that blockade be considered legitimate only if it was effective, that is, if it were actually enforced everywhere along a coast. Otherwise it should be considered nothing more than commerce raiding. The British placed particular stress on the right to capture enemy goods; other powers naturally disagreed, because goods might be seized from their (neutral) ships in war-time. They preferred a doctrine of "free ships, free goods." At the Congress of Paris in 1856 the French offered to prohibit privateering (i.e., private-venture commerce raiding) in exchange for British agreement to the immunity of all goods under neutral flags and the immunity of all goods except contraband even under an enemy flag. Also, to be binding a blockade had to be effective. The British delegate, Lord George William Frederick Villiers Clarendon, later said that he agreed because Britain would never again be able to enforce her ancient rights without causing all the maritime powers to fight Britain. As it was, the United States refused to sign, and it was clear that a ban on privateering was meaningless, because any government could undertake to arm commerce raiders of its own. At the time the Declaration of Paris was widely seen as disarming British seapower. In 1871 Lord Robert Arthur Talbot Gascoyne-Cecil Salisbury wrote, whereas blockade had been a powerful weapon against Napoleon, "in your reckless Utopianism you have flung these two weapons [general blockade and searches of neutrals] away, and your fleet can only blockade the particular ports to which it is sent or bombard any fortress which may happen to be on the coast."[21]

It turned out, ironically, that the agreements at Paris actually strengthened the British position in 1914, because only a dominant sea power had any hope of enforcing an effective blockade. By placing cruisers, which were converted liners, across the mouth of the North Sea the British could intercept all seaborne commerce to northern Europe, even though they could not hope to block each port separately. The 1856 agreement considerably stiffened requirements that had to be met before a merchant ship could be seized or sunk. Each ship therefore had to be boarded and searched. That was no problem for a large cruiser, but it was virtually impossible for a U-boat, whose only option was to torpedo merchant ships. Thus not only could the Royal Navy enforce an increasingly effective blockade, but the attempt by the Germans to enforce a counterblockade by U-boats led them increasingly to infuriate the largest neutral of all, the United States.

During World War I the British blockaded Germany. This was the most intense blockade the Royal Navy had ever mounted. Its effects have been debated ever since. Prior to the war, it was generally imagined that industrialized economies were so interdependent that trade warfare, or indeed any sort of sustained war, would devastate them. In fact it turned out that the international financial system was quite closely interlocked, but that countries enjoyed considerable autonomy. The prewar idea was confirmed by a 1912 report prepared for the British Committee on Imperial Defense that claimed that blocking trade with Germany would damage Britain almost as badly as Germany. By 1913, however, the decision had been made to blockade Germany in the event of war. There was little analysis of just how this measure would effect the German war effort. The Royal Navy considered blockade valuable, but did not expect it to be decisive in itself. Certainly pre-1914 Germany did import a good deal of what she used, but many foodstuffs and raw materials were produced on her own.

To maintain good relations with the most powerful neutral, the United States, the British had to limit their attacks on some key items. Also, only contraband—material used directly to support war-making—could be stopped and seized. The list of contraband was widened as the war progressed and as the blockade apparently failed to bite (yet clearly did interdict shipping en route to Germany). Furthermore, some countries in Europe, such as Denmark, the Netherlands, Norway, and Sweden, were still neutral, so shipments to them could not easily be interdicted. They could transship goods to Germany either by land or, in the case of Sweden, via German-controlled waters. Ultimately the Allies tried to limit shipping to those countries to their own national requirements. Pressure was limited, however, by the need for products from neutral countries (e.g., French powder factories relied on imports from Norway). Blockade eventually required a combination of economic measures, such as buying 95 percent of U.S. copper supplies to keep them out of German hands, and actual stoppage of shipping. The issue was greatly simplified when the United States, the main exporter outside Europe, declared war on Germany in 1917.

The Germans developed numerous substitute materials. By 1918, however, German civilians were suffering, particularly for clothing and for food. That was partly because so much was reserved for troops, and partly because farmers withheld considerable stocks for their own use. Even so, in 1918 German army rations were severely limited, and presumably the situation would have worsened significantly if the war had continued into 1919. In early 1918 the Germans thought that the collapse of Russia had solved their problem. They arranged a wide variety of transport routes from Ukraine, which they pictured as a vast granary, only to discover that it was momentarily quite barren. Probably matters would have improved in 1919. By 1930 it was clear that any Germans contemplating a further war would see the Soviet Union, either friendly or conquered, as the key to sustained combat, because it could provide most of what the kaiser's Germany had normally imported from overseas.[22] After the armistice was signed in November 1918, the Allies lost their military means of maintaining pressure on Germany to accept peace terms the Germans considered repugnant. The "hunger blockade" remained, and apparently its threat forced the Germans to abandon any hope of resuming the war or of holding out for better terms. Senior Germans did claim that the blockade had beaten their country, but that may have been a way of shifting blame away from the German army.[23]

Evaluation of the blockade is difficult because of its relationship with the stress of combat. It can be argued that German economic collapse was due to the demands of the war. On the other hand, without any blockade much of that stress could have been alleviated by imports, as it was in the case of Britain. Interdiction is most effective when an enemy desperately needs supplies to keep fighting. Few countries depend so heavily on shipping that they can be starved by blockade. In the two world wars, Britain and Japan fell into this category. Under the impact of a German submarine offensive in 1917, the British literally felt that they faced starvation, although there is some question as to whether that was ever true.[24] By 1945, with her merchant shipping largely gone, Japan was certainly facing economic meltdown.[25] More recently, Iraq has suffered from the UN-imposed embargo (in effect a blockade), which includes attempts to cut off business dealings and thus to cut off supplies of hard currency.

Quite aside from direct starvation, blockade can have important economic effects. There was a long period, beginning in the fifteenth century, when Western national wealth depended quite heavily on access to what we now call the Third World. For example, the Spanish government depended on shipments of silver and gold from the New World and from the Philippines to finance its wars in Europe. Losing a convoy could cripple a planned campaign, even though the average Spaniard could live well enough without any shipments from abroad. In other wars, sea control allowed the British to seize islands in the Caribbean and in the West Indies, accounting for much of the income supporting French war efforts in Europe.

In recent times blockade has taken another turn. Besides countries dependent on seaborne supply, particularly of oil, some countries depend on sea routes to deliver those raw materials on which their economies depend. For example, during the Iran-Iraq War of 1980–88, Iraq was supported by countries heavily dependent on oil exports by tanker through the Gulf, and Iran also depended on tankerborne oil exports. The Iraqis closed the major Iranian oil port of Abadan in an attempt to cut the flow of cash the Iranians needed to support their war effort.[26] For their part, the Iranians attacked the tankers operated by theoretically neutral states that were financing the Iraqis. Both may well have hoped that Western countries, dependent on those tankers, would intercede to stop the war in order to keep oil flowing. Instead, the major Western sea powers, the United States and Britain, assigned naval forces to protect the tanker trade. The political desire to maintain neutrality precluded any attack on the land-based forces used against the tankers. Therefore, the naval forces had to try to shield tankers from attack, or at least to deter attacks.

Placing U.S. and British warships in a war zone offered Iraq and Iran an interesting possibility. An attack on a Western warship might well propel its government into the war. In 1987 the United States was backing Iraq against Iran, encouraging financial support and perhaps even providing intelligence. One night an Iraqi Mirage attacked, but did not sink, the U.S. frigate *Stark*. In the aftermath of the attack, the *Iranians* claimed credit.[27] It would appear that they had deceived the Iraqis into thinking that an Iranian ship was located where *Stark* was, and that it was carrying some senior Iranian whose death might cause the stalemated war to end on favorable terms. Certainly the Iraqi Mirage was carrying an unusually heavy missile load (two rather than the usual one Exocet), and the pilot was acclaimed when he landed—and made to disappear the next morning when it became clear just what the target was. The Iranians' motivation would have been obvious: had the Iraqis sunk a U.S. warship, it would have been extremely difficult for the Americans to continue their support, however covert, of the Iraqis. Fortunately the crew managed to fight the damage and save the ship—and leave the U.S. government to pursue the policy it thought necessary.

It is inevitable that wars will erupt in many places through which vital oil supplies flow. Besides the quiescent Gulf, there are the Malacca Straits between Indonesia and Malaysia, and the South China Sea, where the Spratly Islands are claimed by several countries. The assistance of the major Western powers is quite valuable, and our involvement in trade protection in such areas is virtually inevitable—without it, we will suffer horrific economic consequences.

In the run-up to the Gulf War, the coalition opposing Iraq found embargo an attractive way of doing something against Iraq while building up the wherewithal for the military offensive. Embargo was, at the same time, a clearly limited act and a way of maintaining pressure on Iraq. With an embargo in place, military action seemed a logical next step. Without it, Western governments would have been hard-pressed to explain just why they were suddenly attacking Iraq in January 1991, having done nothing about the invasion of Kuwait for the preceding months. In this case embargo was, to be sure, double-edged. Opponents of any decisive military action could demand time to allow embargo to become effective. In fact it was never likely that, in itself, the embargo would have caused the Iraqis to disgorge Kuwait. Rather, embargo was a valuable means of weakening Iraq before the war itself began. Similarly, the embargo erected against Serbia could not have toppled Slobodan Milosevich or forced him to abandon Kosovo. It did weaken support for him among Serbians, which helped him lose the critical postwar election.

Embargo is not a new way of pressing a country without fighting. For example, in 1935 the League of Nations imposed economic sanctions, in effect an embargo, to protest the Italian assault on Ethiopia. Fearing that Benito Mussolini would fight and that they would lose a potential coalition partner against Hitler, the British refused to block vital imports such as oil. The British claimed that sanctions had caused Mussolini serious domestic problems, and that his economy was suffering. There is no evidence that he felt any real pressure, however; a dictator can usually afford to accept some suffering on his population's part. Certainly that has been the case with Saddam Hussein in Iraq. Also, presumably the half-hearted British effort tended to convince Mussolini that the West would not fight, and thus helped him decide to ally with Hitler.

In 1941 the Americans, British, and Dutch embargoed oil and other strategic materials ordered by Japan. No naval action was involved because the three countries were the main suppliers and thus able to enforce embargo administratively. Japan went to war to avoid the expected crippling effect of the embargo. More recently, the Royal Navy enforced an embargo against the breakaway Rhodesian regime in the 1960s and 1970s (the Beira patrol). Its value was limited because the Rhodesians could obtain much of what they needed through South Africa.

Modern embargoes differ from classic blockades in a very important sense. In the past, the great issue in blockade was neutrals' rights. Countries being blockaded tried to import supplies on board neutral ships, and sea powers might or might not claim that a neutral flag was no protection for contraband on board. In the case of modern embargoes declared by the United Nations, in principle there are no neutrals at all; by joining the United Nations a country declares itself bound by Security Council resolutions. A particular government may well defy the announced embargo, but it cannot do so overtly. It cannot protest the seizure of its ships and cargo because seizure would be possible for a neutral facing an embargo or blockade announced by a few sea powers against another country.

Strategic Defense

The United States now faces mainly wars of choice, not compulsion. From any potential enemy's viewpoint, that means that we can choose *not* to fight. Many countries feel that they can relatively easily convince us to choose that way. For example, for some time People's Republic of China (PRC) officials have suggested that, in a crisis, we will not back Taiwan against China because we will not want to risk trading Los Angeles, for instance, for Taipei. Europeans, incidentally, asked much the same question during the Cold War. Charles de Gaulle argued that the United States could not be depended on because ultimately the choice would be whether to save Paris at the cost of New York. Many in the United States have argued that, on the contrary, no one aware of the U.S. nuclear stockpile would chance a nuclear attack on this country, for whatever reason. It was too likely that the United States would strike back extremely hard. No Cold War crisis ever deepened to the point where the other side had a real incentive to take that sort of chance, so this deterrent idea remains untested. Some possible adversaries may believe that the United States is too decadent to act. For others deterrence may be almost irrelevant, because they may feel that by our existence we are somehow attacking them; they are striking out in self-defense. In favor of active homeland defense, it can be argued that such investment offers leverage: many potential enemies may be unable to overcome even a limited U.S. defense unless they invest so heavily in strategic forces that they can no longer afford effective non-nuclear ones. It may not really matter that, for example, China can vaporize Los Angeles, if the occasion to do so never arises because the Chinese army is too weak to begin the crisis in the first place by overrunning Taiwan.[28]

This sort of possibility suggests that some form of homeland defense is a necessary complement to deployable seapower or other deployable forces. Most of the time, we would prefer not to fight, but rather to deflect a crisis by credible threats. Anything that destroys credibility is likely to deepen crises. Paradoxically, that makes it more likely that, in the end, we will have to fight. Obviously the most visible form of homeland defense would be some form of defense against ballistic missiles, including sea-based ones, but there are other defenses, too. Clearly the problem can be overstated, in which case expenditure for homeland defense can displace our ability to project force abroad.

Our possible solutions are threefold. One, we can rely on the deterrent power of our own strategic attack forces, which demands that more attention to these forces is required than is currently being given. A second possibility would be to plan preemptive attacks on enemy missiles, whose numbers would presumably be small, before actual intervention. A third would be a homeland defense program. Whether or not it would work in extremis, the mere existence of such a missile defense system would suggest that another country's weapons were not likely to deter us from acting. That is one reason the Chinese, who have a small offensive strategic force, have so vehemently attacked U.S. plans for national missile defense. If the U.S. system comes to fruition, it will nullify an extremely expensive Chinese investment. Buying enough missiles to overcome a U.S. system might well make it impossible for the Chinese to buy enough nonstrategic forces to cause the sorts of crises that might make the United States intervene.

Naval forces can contribute to any of the three possible choices. Strategic submarines offer an effective secure deterrent, particularly against countries with limited antisubmarine forces. Moreover, it is easier to test-fire submarine-launched, rather than land-based, ballistic missiles in such a way that would advertise the continued viability of the deterrent. The second possibility, the preemptive strike, would have to be non-nuclear, and might be mounted from the sea. Depending on just how vulnerable an enemy's missile force actually was, it might be conducted effectively by stealthy aircraft or missiles. As for the third possibility, a case can be made that mobile defensive missiles are more survivable than fixed ones, particularly against unconventional attack, and that the best form of mobility would be sea based, because the missiles would then be on sovereign U.S. territory. If the power projection fleet includes a missile defense capability, and if any ascending missile is within the fleet's range, then power projection and homeland defense would come together neatly. In a larger sense, a national missile defense based on any sort of fixed missile system might, at least in theory, be destroyed by non-nuclear attack, for example, by special forces or terrorists. Forward bases ashore would be subject to political attack. Unless an enemy possessed considerable seapower, however, a sea-based national missile defense might be much less vulnerable, simply because an enemy could never be sure of exactly where the missile ships are located at any specific point in time.

5

The Rise and Fall of Mass Forces

SHIPS OFFER EXTREME mobility, but they can carry only so much. For example, at the outset of the Gulf War buildup, the U.S. Marines' prepositioning ships quickly moved a brigade's worth of heavy equipment into Saudi Arabia. The marines themselves flew in. The brigade was faced by a massive Iraqi army, many divisions strong. Just how significant was the U.S. seaborne force? If forces quickly inserted by sea generally face overwhelming strength ashore, then no sea-based strategy is likely to succeed. After all, we have virtually abandoned our equalizer against mass, nuclear weapons. How do we deal with mass armies—if indeed they are what we will generally face—with neither mass nor weapons of mass destruction? In the Gulf, we were fortunate that Saddam halted at the Saudi border. That halt provided the time needed to bring massed coalition ground forces into place. It is still not entirely clear whether Saddam halted because his ill-maintained armor was worn out, or because he feared the small but well-armed Marine brigade and U.S. tactical aircraft in Saudi Arabia.[1]

Mass applies to air as well as to ground forces. Also in the Gulf, the initial air defense of Saudi Arabia was erected by a limited number of carrier-based aircraft. Ultimately most of the coalition air force in the Gulf was ground based. Similar to a mass coalition army, it took months to put in place. How adequate was the initial force? Could it have been effective if the coalition had not had access to Saudi air bases?

Without the ability to land effective ground forces, much of the value of seaborne mobility would be lost. The peripheral operations that enforce virtual attrition become pointless, because they cannot damage an enemy enough to make him prepare to repel them. During the Cold War, the U.S. Navy strenuously advocated threatening the Soviets with amphibious attacks in places such as the Black Sea. Critics asked how the brigade or even the division the Marines could quickly put ashore could possibly make much impact on a Soviet army that was expected to mobilize 175 or more divisions. It is often argued that it takes a mass army to deal with another mass army. Thus the United States maintained a heavy mass army in Europe, as part of a massive NATO response to possible Soviet assault. In a more turbulent post–Cold War world, however, it is difficult to say where U.S. mass armies should be positioned to match possible threats. Maintaining many of them around the world would bankrupt the United States. Alternatively, we can plan to fight holding actions while we feed in mass forces, on a time scale similar to that of the Gulf War. For example, in Korea in the summer of 1950, limited U.S. and Korean forces held the Pusan perimeter in the south while further units were fed in from overseas.

In the past, mass armies had another significance. They were virtually impossible to destroy at one blow; as long as a rump survived and the supporting population was large enough, they could regenerate. World War I demonstrated that a country could convert much of its overall wealth, human and material, into military power. That made the war both lengthy and costly, in human as well as financial terms. Before 1914, the mass aspect of armies was understood, but not regeneration, which is one reason all the combatants imagined that the war would be short, and that opening battles could be decisive.

The North Vietnamese side of the Vietnam War can be read as an exercise in regeneration. The United States fought a limited war, which meant that the commitment of resources was ultimately controlled. North Vietnam fought a World War I–style unlimited war of regeneration, with gruesome consequences for its own population. One result was that the United States fed in far more resources than the war was worth.[2] A lesson drawn at the time was that Western technology did not offer sufficient leverage to overcome a Third World government willing to commit on an unlimited scale. In fact the situation is somewhat ambiguous, as will be explained in the Cold War discussion in Chapter 9.

The lesson of regeneration and protraction has been driven home again and again, most recently during the seemingly endless massacres of the war between Iran and Iraq from 1980 to 1988. The ability to regenerate makes it is extremely difficult to win a war simply by defeating an enemy army; something more is needed than a victory in battle to convince the government and the population that it cannot continue. For example, in the 1940 blitzkrieg the decisive factor was probably French memories of what an earlier protracted land war had cost.

The essence of a maritime strategy is to limit the cost, which generally means the duration, of any particular land operation. It therefore matters a great deal whether a force delivered by sea can defeat an enemy army, and also whether the enemy can easily generate a new army to resume the war if the seaborne force is withdrawn.

Fortunately, mass armies are declining. One lesson of the Gulf War is that mass is not enough: an obsolete mass force can easily be destroyed. A U.S. force small enough to have been delivered rapidly by sea (or, as in the Gulf, by a combination of air for the troops and sea for the equipment) really might have sufficed.

Historically mass armies are a relatively new development. Until well into the nineteenth century they were impractical, simply because they could not easily be fed because agriculture was too close to the subsistence level. Armies were generally small and, prior to the French Revolution, professional. They were too valuable to risk lightly; engaging in attrition warfare would have been counterproductive.[3] Small also meant that forces enjoying full maritime mobility were unlikely to meet much larger forces when emerging on a beach. That made the combination of a navy and a mobile army extremely effective.

By the middle of the nineteenth century, however, the agricultural and transportation revolutions had solved the food problem, and the governments of continental Europe developed mass armies. These forces were inexpensive on a per-soldier basis; the soldiers themselves were drafted, and their main weapons, their rifles, were quite cheap. Training was relatively simple, and military skills did not become obsolete. The draft created a valuable reserve of trained soldiers, ready to be mobilized in any emergency. The potential strength of a country's army could be equated to the number of men of military age in its population. The rise of such armies coincided with the construction of railroads without which they could not quickly move long distances.

It appeared, moreover, that the combination of railroad mobility and mass armies trumped the old one of naval mobility and small armies. By

World War I, there had been no developments to increase the mass that a naval force could quickly project onto a beach. In the past, a small army could land effectively, partly because its land-bound enemy could not reinforce quickly. Railroads reversed the situation. If there was rail access to a beach, defending troops could be concentrated more quickly than ships could bring attackers ashore. This is one reason the British failed at Gallipoli in 1915–16. At that time, technology offered little leverage, certainly too little to allow a small but well-equipped army to take on a large but perhaps less lavishly equipped one, with the exception being colonial warfare. Even so, sea transport did bring the small British expeditionary force into position to play a decisive role in the initial battles of World War I.

These considerations explain how the World War I blockade of Germany affected the outcome of the war. By 1917 the Germans were desperate to achieve a decision because their own regeneration was exhausting them; the blockade made matters critically worse. They could clearly see that unless they found some way to win quickly, ultimately they would collapse. Thus the spring 1918 offensive became not just one of many attempts to maul the Allies, but very nearly the last possible attempt. The offensive failed because breakthrough was impossible; mass armies just could not destroy each other. The failure did not suddenly open Germany to invasion. The Allies had no greater chance of breaking through than the Germans. The failure, however, did signal clearly that the pressure of the blockade could not be broken, and that realization seems to have been fatal.

The Decline of Mass Armies

With World War II the economics of mass armies began to crumble. As armies mechanized, the cost per division (or, per properly equipped soldier) rose dramatically. For that matter, the numbers needed to maintain mechanized equipment also rose, so that the number of divisions that could be fielded for a given number of troops declined drastically. Countries that had easily fielded tens of divisions in the 1930s found it quite impossible to field four or six in the 1950s. Failed NATO attempts to match the number of Soviet divisions dramatize the problem. By the late 1950s, it was agreed that big draftee armies were quite expensive. The British abandoned the draft because they could not afford to train, house, or—more important—equip a mass army. It took much longer for the French to do so, because they had a national tradition of the "nation in arms," which produced far more draftees than they could afford to arm. Hence, in part, the French concentrated on nuclear weapons as an equalizer.[4] After the end of the Cold War, however, the French were forced to end the draft to maintain a modern and necessarily smaller army. The United States abandoned the draft for political reasons, but it is increasingly difficult to field even the current force.[5]

During the Cold War, the Soviets solved the problem by militarizing their entire economy. They managed to produce enough hardware to equip a truly massive army. Despite their claims, however, the Soviets had not invented a new kind of economy. As in the West, a mass army was horribly expensive to equip, and through the 1970s and 1980s the cost of continued production of floods of tanks, armored personnel carriers, and the other accoutrements of modern ground power began to tell. The Soviet economy produced less and less for its public. When Mikhail Gorbachev tried to revitalize the economy, mainly to match Western military computerization, he needed incentives for his workers. With no material ones available, he had to turn to political ones, and within a few years he found himself opening up his political system—with suicidal results.

Now that the Russian economy is more like those of the West, the cost of a mass army is far more apparent. President Vladimir Putin finds himself demanding deep cuts in manpower. To maintain any force at all, the Russians must produce new equipment. Existing weapons and vehicles are rapidly wearing out, due in part to the economic crash that often precludes maintenance and to dismal morale caused by low pay and poor conditions, which discourages troops from making much effort to keep equipment functional. Putin emphasizes, as his British and French predecessors did, the high cost per soldier of any modern force. Yet he still needs mass forces to deal with numerous border problems in Central Asia and with internal problems such as the war in Chechnya.

The Chinese are in a situation similar to Putin's position. Like the Russians, for years the Chinese managed to produce floods of the necessary equipment. As the Chinese economy matured, the floods became more expensive, and suddenly it became clear that the government had to live within economic constraints. For some years it has been stated Chinese policy to cut existing mass forces in order to modernize. The promised manpower cuts have not materialized, however. The Chinese government probably is uncomfortably aware of the extent to which it depends on its army for political control. Thus army officers, who would suffer badly from any cuts, can deter the government.[6] It is also possible that, as in Russia, an argument can be made that without a massive army minority regions such as Sinkiang and Tibet cannot be held, hence the choice is between internal control and external firepower. That may explain why the threats against Taiwan generally involve missile attack rather than invasion.

Dealing with Mass Land Forces

Many Third World armies are still massive, because they are living off stocks of equipment gained during the Cold War, essentially without payment. As the equipment dies, they will face the choices that currently bedevil the Russians and the Chinese. It may be that a small dose of modernization, for instance, in communications, makes such a transitional military effective. That seems unlikely, however. Such a failure will leave these governments with a choice between maintaining mass forces of a pre-1945 sort, armed mostly with rifles and machine guns, or making do with relatively small numbers of better-equipped troops. If the real reason for mass is the need to maintain internal security, which may include simply keeping officers employed rather than plotting, then the first choice will be forced on many governments. In that case the future of ground combat will belong to the sort of small professional—and inherently sea-transportable—army being built up in the West. The future will look similar to the pre-1914 colonial world, in which small Western armies generally routed large indigenous ones. Vietnam, of course, remains as a cautionary case.

A very unsettled world, in which navies provide much of the strategic mobility and armies are small and professional, resembles the pre–Napoleonic War era. It is a world in which armies are too valuable to be risked lightly, because they are so difficult to replace. They are, moreover, too small to occupy much territory. Instead, they seek decisive results, if at all, by destroying an enemy's professional army, which is equally difficult to regenerate. That may be quite enough. For example, in the Gulf War, Saddam depended on his Republican Guards to guarantee his own power. If they had been destroyed they could not easily have been regenerated, and Saddam's opponents might well have destroyed him. By way of contrast, it was never a viable objective for the coalition force to occupy Iraq.

In a world of small professional armies, it becomes particularly expensive to maintain substantial garrisons anywhere; the force cannot provide many of them against future emergencies. Bosnia and Kosovo, for example, sop up a large fraction of the small British army. On the other hand, simply because they are so difficult to withdraw, garrison troops carry particular political weight. For example, there must be an enormous difference, in Korean eyes, between about thirty-seven thousand U.S. troops on the ground and, for instance, a battle group operating in the Sea of Japan within striking range. The Koreans undoubtedly know that no U.S. government could explain non-intervention if an initial North Korean attack killed thousands of Americans, whereas a skittish U.S. government could easily withdraw the carrier group. Having been deployed, the troops cannot easily be withdrawn, not least because withdrawal would send an unwanted signal to both North and South Koreans, which President Jimmy Carter discovered when he proposed rede-ployment. How do we decide when the stakes are high enough for us to tie down significant forces?

Mass Airpower

Aircraft can operate from land or sea bases, but sea basing limits their size. It takes ground basing to concentrate large numbers of aircraft, or even small numbers of large ones. Before and during World War II it was obvious that aircraft carriers could not mount attacks on the same scale as land-based bombers.[7] This argument paralleled that between advocates of mass armies and those who favored smaller sea-mobile ones: mass (in this case, of attack against fixed targets) was promoted as decisive. With the advent of nuclear weapons, it was still argued that masses of long-range (i.e., massive) bombers were needed to achieve valuable results. For about the first decade of the Cold War the U.S. Navy accepted this argument; it thought its main contri-bution would be the virtual attrition of Soviet air defenses. As the result of the U.S. Air Force request for a larger nuclear stockpile in 1957, however, President Eisenhower asked the navy and the army to evaluate the air force's strategic war plan. The result was startling: the air force was indulging in gross over-kill, to the point that fallout from its planned attacks would kill millions of people in allied countries such as Japan. Mass alone no longer seemed impor-tant. This study convinced Chief of Naval Operations Arleigh Burke that a submarine-launched deterrent, Polaris, fielding about four hundred mis-siles, could suffice as a viable alternative to the mass nuclear-armed air force. Eisenhower did not go so far as to eliminate SAC, but the point was made: nuclear weapons offered sea-based airpower and missile power the sort of potential that in the past had belonged solely to large land-based air arms.

It still appeared that mass was essential in non-nuclear warfare. In the past, numbers were vital, first, to overcome attrition at the hands of enemy air defenses and, second, to drop enough bombs to ensure that at least some hit their targets. Large numbers of aircraft require large ground facilities to support them. In the Gulf War, for example, over 70 percent of all coalition aircraft were ground based. So many aircraft were present that merely keeping them coordinated was a major effort—and a major technical triumph.

The situation has been changing for some time. Just as in the case of armies, mass is becoming much more expensive: numbers of aircraft in land-based air arms are falling dramatically. In part, the rise in unit aircraft costs can be attributed to nuclear weapons, which justified the post-1945 shrinkage in aircraft numbers. This shrinkage in turn made dramatic improvements in aircraft performance affordable. It also encouraged the development of much better air defenses, on the theory that a single leaker might be fatal. This cycle of rising unit costs cannot easily be reversed. Any airplane inexpensive enough to be built in large numbers would quickly fall victim to defenses designed to deal with higher-performing types.

Dramatic cuts in the number of aircraft, and in worldwide production rates, make it possible to imagine decisive air campaigns, just as small and nonregenerating armies can be subject to decisive defeats. Similar considerations affect air defenses sophisticated enough to deal with expensive modern aircraft. This is not a new idea. For example, the U.S. Cold War maritime strategy, described in Chapter 9, sought to seize maritime air superiority by wiping out the irreplaceable force of Soviet Backfire antiship bombers. The campaigns in both Iraq and in Kosovo began with an air superiority phase, not too different in concept from the planned initial phase of the Cold War maritime strategy, in an attempt to secure free use of the air by wiping out, or at least seriously degrading, the enemy's ability to shoot back. In Kosovo, this phase was protracted because so much of the enemy's counterair capability comprised mobile and concealed antiaircraft missiles. The effort was derided at the time because it seemed to show just how frightened NATO was of casualties. That missed the point. Airplanes are valuable largely because they can return again and again to deliver their expendable weapons. Anything that puts them out of action seriously limits offensive capability, because they are difficult to replace.

Overall, to maintain appropriate and adequate air arms requires that airplanes last about as long as ships. Not only must they survive combat, they must survive obsolescence through the addition of new electronics and weapons. Anything that makes airframes inherently obsolete is inordinately costly. Stealth is a case in point, as, possibly, is the new capability (e.g., in the

F-22 Raptor) to cruise at supersonic speed. There must be a question as to whether it would not be better to place the required performance in add-on electronics and better stand-off weapons, rather than accept the obsolescence of a large part of the existing tactical air fleet and the need to spend so much for quick replacement.

Despite the development of stand-off weapons, it may still be vital that airplanes be able to penetrate enemy defenses. In the past, pilots generally visually acquired the ground targets they hit. Now more and more weapons are preset to fly to particular coordinates, which may or may not be a lasting trend. For example, it may be difficult to measure the coordinates of pop-up targets detected by remote sensors, such as those aboard unmanned vehicles. In the Kosovo campaign, pilots were provided with images of the target area and of the target, but they had to go in and acquire and attack visually. If pop-up targets are the most important ones, because they are the most tactically significant ones, then the pilot's ability to penetrate and survive remains paramount. If it becomes easier to designate targets remotely, for example, by inserting the target image in a missile, then airplanes will generally deliver stand-off weapons, and load-carrying ability and durability will become the dominant virtues.

These considerations make unmanned air combat vehicles attractive, but only up to a point. Many air operations occur in peacetime, and often the pilot's role is to observe some other airplane and apply judgment. This is often a form of presence. It cannot be accomplished by a remote pilot using a data link. Links do not always work as they should. There is also an interesting legal issue. As part of the agreement eliminating intermediate-range nuclear weapons in Europe, the United States and the Soviet Union agreed to ban land-based cruise missiles with ranges over six hundred kilometers. The United States may well be loath to abandon this limitation because it is the key to attempts to control missile technology abroad. Unmanned but armed air vehicles would arguably be classed as cruise missiles. The one loophole is that such missiles are perfectly acceptable if they are sea based.[8] Thus, if the United States fields unmanned combat air vehicles, they will most likely be based at sea.

If the future of airpower belongs to limited numbers of strike aircraft, mass may still be important—but it will have a very different definition. It will not be the mass of airplanes but the mass of munitions they can deliver. In that case sea-based aircraft may be more attractive than land-based equivalents, simply because they are easier to deploy. It is certainly true that with air-to-air refueling a land-based fighter can reach an airfield anywhere in the world within a day, but that airplane arrives without any backup. It is good, if at all, for one sortie. A carrier offers the complete support package for the airplane, for several days, and the package is easy to replenish using existing ships and techniques. For carrier-based aircraft to be effective in this role they will need the support of a large replenishment fleet.

The other great question is whether air forces, either land based or sea based, enjoy the sort of decisive impact with which they were credited in the past. If not, then air arms are probably valuable mainly for their tactical contributions. It is certainly difficult to envisage using nuclear weapons, except to retaliate against another power using them, or even using any other weapons of mass destruction. Advocates of continued reliance on strategic airpower argue that modern precision weapons can hit targets exactly, thereby eliminating the mass raids of the past that were necessary largely because so many bombs missed. In fact, however, surgical results are possible only when extremely detailed knowledge of what is being attacked is available. It is by no means clear that we understand foreign societies well enough to identify key targets. Our Cold War experience suggests that intelligence, even when it is concentrated on a single target country, is rarely good enough. The mass raids of the past were often effective because some bombs hit unintended, but vital, targets. Although in theory nuclear weapons were precisely targeted, in practice their overwhelming destructive power overcame many errors. The non-nuclear mass raids of World War II were sometimes devastating enough to affect civilian morale, although more often the survivors of the raids felt themselves more tightly bound to their governments. Because precision raids, such as those on Belgrade, avoid unnecessary civilian casualties, they sometimes foster a sense among civilians of relative immunity, which makes it even easier for them to be more supportive of their governments. Beyond all of these considerations, it is not clear that crucial point targets always exist. They may simply be inaccessible, given reasonable rules of engagement. What, for example, is the center of gravity target of the United States? Surely it is not Washington, just as it was not Washington when the British burned the city in 1814.

Unfortunately, many rulers may not find the prospect of industrial damage particularly frightening or, if it occurs, devastating, because the loss of a country's wealth may not threaten their own grip on power.[9] The old argument, that an attack on enemy industry would ultimately sap the enemy's ability to fight, seems almost irrelevant for the enemies we might face today, because their weapons are largely imported.

For Saddam Hussein's Iraq, it may be argued that the dictator himself is the center of gravity.[10] Presumably he must respond to threats against major props of his regime such as elite troops (e.g., the Iraqi Revolutionary Guards) and his secret police. However, it is not clear that any of these potential targets can effectively be hit. Dictators, for example, are under constant threat from their own domestic enemies, and there is little reason to imagine that we can find them more effectively than internal enemies can. That became obvious when U.S. targeters tried to mount air attacks on Saddam during the Gulf War. It is unlikely that we will do much better at any future time. There is considerable deterrent value, however, in having weapons suited specifically to destroying bunkers in which a dictator may choose to hide. It appears that Saddam and his generals found a spectacular U.S. Air Force attack on a deep Baghdad bunker, just before the end of the Gulf War, quite chilling.

Neither the dictator nor his secret police are easy to target from the air. Only the army may really be accessible from the air. At the very least, the loss of his armed force limits the damage the dictator can do outside his country, and the most we are likely to hope for is to moderate his behavior across his border. In such an attempt, airpower is still extremely important, indeed more effective than ever, given the new precision weapons. Applied tactically, it can go a long way toward making up for limited numbers of ground troops.

In a tactical role, moreover, it may be very important that the aircraft operate from a base close to the battle area. That would further favor a mobile sea base over any series of land bases, from which aircraft are difficult at best to relocate. Not only are many of the targets moving, but even the static ones derive their significance from a rapidly changing, essentially unpredictable, situation. Strategic air attacks are mounted against fixed preselected targets. The unpredictable tactical situation demands that aircraft be available almost constantly. It might be argued that a single large airplane, armed with numerous independently targeted bombs, could provide much the same degree of tactical support as many smaller ones. If the bombers must be based far from the battle zone, however, maintaining one orbiting over that zone will require large numbers constantly in transit.[11] Any loss will uncover the battle zone, perhaps at an unacceptable time. It may also be difficult to provide the single large bomber with sufficient communications to target all its bombs in a timely way; if the bombs are expended too early in the mission, no other bomber will be available soon enough.

For example, during World War II, long-range land-based bombers were often employed as air support for convoys in the Atlantic. Their situation was not too different from that of a modern heavy bomber orbiting over a battle area; their role was to attack surfaced submarines, to keep them from approaching the convoy while covered by darkness. Given the limited number of airplanes, it was impossible to provide more than one at a time, and that airplane had to remain on station for a full eight hours before another could arrive. Indeed, even if another bomber was launched as soon as the first came on station, it might be as much as eight hours from the convoy. Thus there was never much hope of reinforcing the airplane on station in the event of some misfortune. In at least one case, in March 1943, quite early in its coverage of a convoy, the sole bomber escort used up all of its depth bombs on surfaced U-boats—all the bombs missed. It then began making dummy attacks, in hopes of forcing down the U-boats. That worked, but only for a short time. Once the U-boat commanders realized the bomber was unarmed, they stayed on the surface, and the bomber crew watched the attack on the convoy. The situation would have been very different for smaller antisubmarine aircraft, on board an escort carrier, actually accompanying the convoy, simply because they could have flown back on board and rearmed if the bombs had missed. The same can be said of the difference between air support from a nearby field, and tactical air support mounted from five hundred miles away.

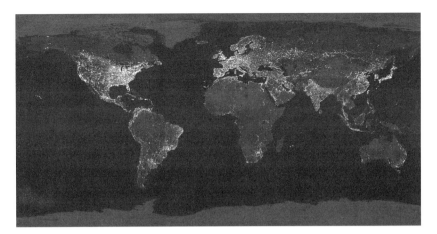

This image of the world at night, adapted from weather satellite photographs, demonstrates how little of the inhabited world is more than a few hundred miles from the sea. The brighter the area, the more populated it is. *Image by Craig Mayhew and Robert Simmon, NASA Goddard Flight Center*

Carriers exemplify seapower: they are mobile and self-contained. Here USS *John F. Kennedy* receives stores under way from the fast replenishment ship *Seattle*. *Seattle* typifies the "station ships" that can accompany battle groups to provide them with fuel and ammunition for sustained combat. *U.S. Navy photo by Christian Eskellund*

The combination of cruise missiles and satellite communications provided surface combatants like the destroyer *Curtis Wilbur,* shown here in the Persian Gulf, something of the reach of a carrier. The rectangle abaft the destroyer's 5-inch gun contains vertical launchers which can fire Tomahawk land-attack missiles. Radomes around the destroyer's bridge are for satellite communications. *U.S. Navy photo by Mahlon K. Miller*

Because they are nearly invisible, submarines offer navies a wide range of capabilities. USS *Maine,* shown in November 1998, carries ballistic missiles to deter nuclear attack on the United States. *U.S. Navy photo by* PH1 *Michael J. Rinaldi*

Navies are more than ships. Here an F/A-18F Super Hornet strike fighter rides a carrier's elevator. The F/A-18 was the first U.S. fighter to exploit computer technology allowing it to be effective both as a fighter and as a light bomber. *Boeing photo by Ron Bookout*

Many naval aircraft are land-based. That limits their strategic mobility. This U.S. Navy P-3C Orion of VP-45 is practicing dropping missile decoy flares in preparation for a mission over Bosnia-Herzegovina. Designed to hunt submarines, the P-3C is now valued for its overland reconnaissance ability.

U.S. Navy photo by PH2 Robert Fleugel

Most navies are limited to small surface combatants ineffective far from their coasts. The Chinese Jiangwei-class missile frigate *Huainan* is shown at the August 1998 Indonesian Navy review. The six-tube launcher visible forward contains anti-aircraft missiles; not visible is the ship's main offensive armament, six tubes for C-802 missiles amidships. *Allied Navy*

A Russian-built "Kilo"-class, diesel-electric submarine is delivered to the Chinese Navy on board the flo-flo merchant ship *Sea Teal*, 1998. The method of delivery illustrates the limited mobility of such submarines; the flo-flo is much faster. *U.S. Navy*

To the U.S. Navy, naval warfare is increasingly aimed directly at land targets. Here the missile cruiser *Shiloh* fires a Tomahawk at Iraq on 3 September 1996 in retaliation for an Iraqi ground assault on the declared Kurdish sanctuary area within Iraq. The vertical launcher from which the missile was fired made the ship extremely versatile: originally bought to fire antiaircraft missiles in rapid succession, it can also fire land-attack weapons and antisubmarine missiles. *U.S. Navy*

Naval assault includes amphibious warfare. Here U.S. Marines practice at Camp Pendleton, California, in April 1999. In the foreground is a Marine amphibious assault vehicle; in the background is a fast air-cushion landing craft (LCAC). *U.S. Navy Photo by PH2 Michelle R. Hammond*

The U.S. Coast Guard is another aspect of U.S. seapower. In peacetime its cutters enforce maritime laws, such as those against poaching in U.S. waters. Here the high-endurance cutter *Mellon* patrols off Kodiak, Alaska. *U.S. Coast Guard photo by PA1 Keith Alholm*

Warships and airplanes are the visible end of naval warfare, but they are tied together by communications. Without the largely invisible communications systems and the sensors feeding them, naval forces would be far less effective. Here a technician examines a UHF Follow-On satellite under construction for the U.S. Navy. *Hughes Space and Communications Company*

6

Seapower versus Land Power

How can a country's seapower affect the outcome of a war against a land power? Clearly a powerful navy can destroy an enemy's fleet, and it can blockade its coast. But what good does that do when the enemy has little need for either a fleet or for freedom of movement overseas? This issue frequently arose in strategic debates during the Cold War. The solution favored by the U.S. Navy, the maritime strategy, turned out to mirror Anglo-French strategy during the Crimean War of 1854–56, and even British strategy against Napoleon. The key elements were flanking operations, exploiting the mobility offered by seapower, and coalition warfare.

Britain against Napoleon

Except for an 18-month peace in 1801–3, Britain was at war against France almost continuously from 1793 until 1815. For much of that time Napoleon dominated French policy; he became dictator in 1799 and emperor in 1804. He seems to have seen Britain as the one great barrier to sustained domination of Europe. Thus for clarity the war may be considered Napoleonic, although the 1793–1801 phase is usually called the War of the French Revolution. At the outset, the British assumed that this could be a short war. France was nearly bankrupt and the revolution had killed off most of the experienced army officers. British strategists concentrated on cutting France off from her colonies in the West Indies and India in order to cut her colonial income.[1] France proved far more self-supporting, however, than Spain and Holland, both of which had suffered badly when cut off from colonial income.[2] As Napoleon began to win on land, moreover, he seized resources from conquered countries. It was also soon evident that the French revolutionaries, and later Napoleon, had created a very effective mass army. On the other hand, the destruction of the French naval officer corps apparently did cripple the French fleet; it was much more difficult to turn civilians into effective naval officers than into army officers.

Napoleon's land army could defeat any other army in Europe. However, it could not occupy the whole of Europe. Countries he had defeated in the field could periodically defect to join coalitions organized by, and financed by, the British. Thus the British decided when and whether the war would end. If they been unable to build and maintain coalitions on land, presumably their continued hostility would have been irrelevant. A key to coalition warfare was British finance, maintained by an economy that benefited hugely from control of the sea. Moreover, the British could limit their degree of national mobilization because they controlled the sea, the invasion route Napoleon would use against them. Thus the British economy could continue to grow, generating the cash needed to prosecute the war. British financial strength was coupled with access by sea to those who were being subsidized as well as being supported, in some key cases, by British troops. Finance alone did not suffice, because coalition partners would not risk their armies unless the British were willing to risk their own lives on the Continent.

Because the British commitment to any coalition was limited, the defeat of any partner on land could not end the war. The British did not callously use and discard partners; their partners joined and rejoined the coalitions to further their own interests. The coalition partners supplied the bulk of the troops who actually defeated Napoleon's army. The troops would never have been engaged, however, if Napoleon had managed to pacify all of Europe, as he tried to do. What blocked Napoleon from complete dominance was British seapower.

The French tried four ways to defeat the British, or at the least to bring them to terms. One was to attack England directly, by sea across the English Channel. A second was to lever existing Irish unrest, by using French troops to support an Irish uprising. Putting down the rebellion would, at the least, denude England of troops and so open her to invasion. A third, more indirect, was to attack the sources of British wealth overseas, particularly in

India. A fourth was a subtler attempt to destroy the British war economy by cutting off another source of wealth, the trade with continental Europe.

In 1796–97 the French tried to support a rising in Ireland. They nearly succeeded, because the British fleet mutinied in port while the French were preparing and the blockade of French ports was drastically weakened. The British commanders at sea managed to bluff the French, who did not discover the scale of the great mutiny until it had been quelled and it was too late to ship an army to Ireland.[3]

Several times the French tried to assemble an invasion force to attack England directly. To make an assault, they had to break British control of the channel, which in turn required them to assemble a strong fleet and get it to sea. A French alliance with Spain promised sufficient numbers to overcome the Royal Navy in the channel. To do that, the French had to unite their two main fleets, based at Brest and at Toulon, and join them to the two Spanish squadrons, at Ferrol and at Cadiz. Napoleon ordered the Brest squadron to break out and then to break the British blockade of Ferrol. The combined fleet would sail to the West Indies. There it would join the French Mediterranean fleet that, having broken out of Toulon, would have joined the Spanish Cadiz squadron. Given the threat to a vital British interest in the West Indies, Napoleon expected the British fleet blocking the channel would sail in pursuit of the Brest fleet. With the channel uncovered, the French could rush back and support an invasion.[4]

The plan made little naval sense. It demanded excellent coordination. Communication was poor, so each of the two widely separated forces had to follow a rigid timetable.[5] No account of the vagaries of the wind was taken. It was by no means certain that the French fleet returning from the West Indies would outsail the British. Indeed, during the campaign leading up to the French disaster at Aboukir, Nelson's fleet outsailed the French, arriving in Egypt ahead of them. In this case the attempt to raise the blockade of Brest failed, leaving only the Toulon fleet to run out to the West Indies and back. That it made the attempt despite the failure at Brest attests to poor communications.

In March 1805 the French Mediterranean fleet at Toulon managed to escape Nelson's covering British fleet, passing through the Straits of Gibraltar to unite with a Spanish fleet at Cadiz. After a long and fruitless run to the West Indies, hotly pursued by Nelson, the combined fleet returned to Europe. Although this was the strongest fleet Napoleon managed to assemble, it was not strong enough to break through the British fleet blocking the southern end of the English Channel. When Napoleon heard in August that the fleet had gone to Ferrol, in Spain, rather than into the channel, he abandoned his planned invasion of England. His army turned east to attack the Austrians.[6] That did not end the threat posed by the combined fleet. Napoleon planned to use it to support an attack on Sicily, which supported the British fleet, by the French army in Italy. Once the French controlled the Mediterranean, they could revive their old threat against India via Egypt (see below). The combined fleet sailed from Cadiz to enter the Mediterranean, but Nelson brought it to action and defeated it off Trafalgar on 21 October 1805.

Trafalgar did not end Napoleon's interest in seapower, however. He tried to assemble an alliance of northern European maritime states, including Denmark, Sweden, and Russia, which would provide enough ships to overwhelm the Royal Navy. He also pressed an aggressive program of warship construction.[7] For example, in 1809 when the British felt compelled to land a large force on Walcheren, at the mouth of the Scheldt, in the Netherlands, one motive was to destroy ships under construction at Antwerp, up the river. Similarly, one early motive for intervention in Spain was to gain control of the Spanish fleet, which might otherwise accrue to Napoleon.

The large number of ships under French control after Trafalgar did remarkably little. They made no attempt to intercept the lightly protected convoys that supported Wellington's army in Spain. The French seem to have suffered from low morale (too many of the experienced officers had died at Trafalgar) and lack of training on board ships confined to harbor by the British blockade. The effective size of the French fleet was far smaller than its apparent size.

Walcheren exemplifies the use of seaborne mobility to affect events ashore. In 1809 the Austrians had just defeated the French, and the Prussians offered to join the war if the British would create a diversion to draw French troops away from them. Seaborne mobility offered the British real options. Naturally the Prussians wanted direct support, but the British regarded the Prussian king as shifty. He might easily refuse to join the anti-Napoleon coalition (as in fact he did). They therefore chose a place where success would help them whether or not the Prussians entered the war. Destroying a major part of the French-controlled fleet would free ships to support the campaign beginning in Spain. The British also knew that Napoleon considered Antwerp very important; therefore that he would move large numbers of troops to defend it. Thus Antwerp offered the British more leverage than a landing in Germany. The expedition failed due to poor leadership and sloth; the attack at Gallipoli failed little more than a century later for much of the same reasons. Nevertheless, the expedition caused Napoleon great uneasiness, and the French pronounced it a brilliant stroke.

Overall, through the Napoleonic War period, the British feared attack from the Low Countries. Thus it was natural that the British force under Gen. Arthur Wellesley Wellington was landed there, meeting Napoleon on the road to Brussels after he had escaped from Elba.

Another attempt to break the British began with Napoleon's invasion of Egypt in 1798.[8] Like Alexander the Great, Napoleon believed he could lead an army from there against India.[9] Whether or not the British could defeat such an army, the effort would have left England uncovered. Moreover, to the extent that India was a major source of British wealth, cutting it off might have damaged British attempts to finance anti-Napoleon coalitions. Without sea control, the French had no other way of cutting off the flow of overseas wealth to England.[10] Unfortunately for Napoleon, Nelson destroyed the French fleet at Aboukir in 1798, ending this project.[11] Napoleon did not lose interest in India. In June 1802, for example, he sent an emissary to negotiate with anti-British potentates in India, and that September he sent another to Egypt; troops were assembled in Corsica for a new attack. By 1803, when the British declared war on France, Napoleon had openly stated his intention to retake Egypt.[12] The combined fleet destroyed at Trafalgar was to have seized control of the Mediterranean as a step toward a new invasion of Egypt en route to India. For that matter, after Trafalgar Napoleon maintained his interest in the Eastern Mediterranean. A British 1806–7 attempt to negotiate peace failed because he demanded Sicily, which would have become part of the Kingdom of Naples ruled by his brother. The British refused because they saw Sicily (and Malta) as keys to the security of Egypt, hence of India.

Finally there was more direct economic attack. Napoleon tried to sap the British war economy by proclaiming a counterblockade, the "continental system," against the luxury trade with French-occupied Europe, which accounted for much of the British wealth that supported the war. This form of attack became practical after France had defeated Prussia in 1806 and thus had gained control, in theory at least, of the entire European coast (at this time Spain was an ally). The embargo was accompanied by an energetic warship building program, on the theory that the British would be further strained to match the new construction. As is usual in blockades and embargoes, smuggling flourished—and so, as often happens, did the British economy. Moreover, Napoleon's concept of Britain's economic structure was outdated. Too much of it was domestic. The threat to overseas trade would have been far more effective a century earlier. By the time the continental system was set up in 1806–7, the British government had previously weathered a serious fiscal crisis in 1796–97. In this case, the Royal Navy helped support British trade, for example, in the Baltic and by protecting Malta as a trading outlet to southern Europe.

Many European customers refused to accept Napoleon's strictures.[13] Napoleon found himself seeking direct control over more and more of Europe simply to maintain his continental system, including Spain, especially after the Portuguese revolted in 1808. In 1810 the czar defected from his alliance with Napoleon, partly because French trade restrictions made it impossible to export Russian produce. By 1812 Napoleon was garrisoning the German Hansa ports specifically to prevent trade with Britain. These troops were the margin by which his Grand Army was defeated in Russia in 1812—in a campaign intended to shut down Russian trade with Britain. The overextension of French resources was the result of the inability to break British maritime power; British naval power really was a decisive factor in the war.

British seapower precluded Napoleon's victory, and it left open the possibility that eventually a coalition would prevail. Thus British seapower made it possible for Napoleon to stumble into the suicidal campaign in Russia in 1812, and it encouraged the Prussians to regenerate their army to the point that it was deadly a few years later. It is possible that both countries would have fought eventually, but the British were the organizing force. Apart from Britain, none of the countries fighting Napoleon stayed in the war continuously for its full course. Seapower made it possible to tie together coalition partners separated on land by French-controlled territory.

British seapower was not entirely immune from Napoleon's victories on land. Sailing ships required frequent repairs, and the material for much of that work came from the Baltic. When Napoleon defeated Prussia, he gained control of her Baltic coast and of the ports at Memel and Danzig, which normally were used to transship naval stores from the region.[14] For this reason the British maintained their second-largest fleet in the Baltic as of May 1810.

Nelson's victory at Trafalgar in 1805 freed the British to use their seapower *and their army* much more offensively. Trafalgar in effect ended the defensive phase of the Napoleonic war that had begun in 1803. Through 1803–5, the British policy makers' main concern was to build enough of a force to beat off an invasion. They sought coalition partners, but with little success. Prospective partners all wanted ground commitment, which the British could not afford. Once Nelson won, the threat of invasion was much reduced. Once the Royal Navy could operate freely off the European coast, it provided the small British army with such mobility that it could tie down and exhaust the much larger French ground forces on Napoleon's strategic flank. This was very effective leverage. It also carried only limited risks, because failure could not undermine British security. Only a seaborne invasion of Britain could have done that.

Some of these attacks were mounted against Spanish colonial ports, because Spain was a French ally and provided much of Napoleon's potential seapower. For his part, in 1808 Napoleon violently encroached on Spanish sovereignty. That excited a rebellion that the British, with their access from the sea, could exploit. The Royal Navy inserted and supported an army, led by Wellington. It kept the Spanish insurrection alive and gradually bled Napoleon.[15] By tying down large numbers of French troops, it precluded any French threat overseas, for example, against India or Canada. The rebellion also ended British fears that Napoleon might complete his control of Spain and thereby gain control of the Spanish colonies, particularly in South America.[16] The British presence in Spain also opened a large hole in Napoleon's continental system counterblockade. Luckily, Spanish terrain limited elements of the French army, its cavalry and its artillery, in which the British were weak, because they were difficult to transport by sea. Spain was always a secondary theater; there could be no hope that the whole of the French army would die there. When Napoleon's main army had been bled in Russia, the force tied down in Spain was no longer a surplus. Suddenly it became much more difficult for Napoleon to face other threats, and regimes that had lost in the past took heart. French disasters in 1812–13 made it difficult for Napoleon to keep Austria from joining a new alliance against him. Moreover, after Wellington ejected the substantial French army, Spain was dependent on the exhausted French economy; that additional burden helped sap Napoleon.

Spain was peripheral, however, and even access by sea was less than satisfactory. As Napoleon's control began to collapse in late 1813, the British government would have preferred to have its army in the Low Countries, which were of far greater significance, fighting alongside the coalition partners. Unfortunately there was no hope of quickly moving a large army around the European coast in mid-winter, even without any sort of opposition. Without an army in northern Europe, there was a real possibility that Britain would be frozen out of any settlement.

One key to victory in the Napoleonic War was that the British could focus on the target, Napoleon himself, rather than on particular bits of territory that Napoleon was bent on seizing. If they, for example, had decided that the issue of the war was territory in Germany, they might easily have sent in an army and lost it there. That loss in turn might have convinced them that the war was lost. Certainly the loss of armies caused continental powers to sue for peace. As it happened, focus was relatively easy in this case because of the widespread sense that Napoleon and the French Revolution were ideological forces bent on the destruction of the settled order of Europe, hence that they were the true enemy. The larger lesson is that wars often are not about territory, but rather about forcing a government to abandon some course of action—in this case, about turning France away from an attempt to export first revolution and then Napoleonic domination throughout Europe.

The Crimean War

In the Crimean War four decades later, the British and the French fought the Russians to maintain the European balance of power, in particular to maintain Turkish control of the Dardanelles. The immediate goal agreed by the two powers was to prevent the Russians from seizing the Turkish capital of Constantinople, located at the entrance to the Turkish Straits leading into the Mediterranean. The easiest route there from Russian territory was across the Black Sea from the Russian base at Sevastopol. If the Black Sea was blocked, Russian troops would have to take the far more difficult route by land around the shores, which also might be blocked. British war aims, however, were actually more expansive. In the 1850s Russia was the only world power other than Britain, hence Britain and Russia were natural rivals.[17] Russia was expanding into Central Asia toward India. Russian domination of the Turkish empire would have given her much better access to the approaches to India via what is now Iraq. In 1853, when the crisis erupted, the British regarded the Mediterranean as a route to India, and their Mediterranean fleet as its guardian, as in Nelson's day.[18] Any threat to the status quo there would have been seen as an implicit threat to India. The cold war between Britain and Russia for control of Central Asia and, therefore, India was later called "the Great Game." At the outset the British war aim was somewhat confused. Cabinet members' opinions differed, with goals ranging between simply forcing Russia to withdraw from attacking Turkey to pressing for a substantial reduction in overall Russian power, such as the restoration of Polish independence and transfer of the Crimea from Russia to Turkey.[19] It was, however, generally understood that it would probably take more than direct pressure in the Black Sea to force the Russians to give up their plans to attack Turkey. This perception explains why at the time the conflict was called the Russian War rather than the Crimean War.

British statesmen disagreed as to the best course of action. It seemed unlikely that the allies could defeat the vast Russian army, just as it seemed unlikely during the Cold War that NATO could ever match the endless Russian armies. One alternative advanced at the time was blockade and economic pressure, which the British thought would take two years or more. Russian trade could certainly be ruined, but (similar to more recent times) the country was largely self-sufficient. Moreover, the British wanted support from other governments, which in the past had been outraged by British blockade policy.[20] This alternative was therefore abandoned. Instead, a combined attack on land and sea was chosen.[21] A limited blockade, which did badly damage the Russian economy, was imposed.

Wartime British cooperation with the French was complicated by the fact that in 1853–54 the British fleet was designed primarily to fight France, and considerable sums were being spent on fortifications against possible French attack. Much of this effort was the result of an 1846 pamphlet by the Prince de Joinville, a prominent French admiral, to the effect that with the advent of steam power the French could easily invade Britain. One irony of the situation was that by 1853 the Royal Navy was beginning to develop the means, but not the tactics, to destroy French coastal bases from the sea; this would be needed later against Sevastopol—in support of the French. On the other hand, the Royal Navy was built mainly to fight a blue-water war against France, so it lacked any sort of inshore flotilla for coastal attack. Its special adaptations were all guns, or modifications of guns, to be mounted on board conventional warships. During the war, specialized coastal craft were built, mainly for service in the Baltic. These craft included floating armored batteries—the first armored ships—proposed by the French emperor, Louis Napoleon. After the war, with the French again the likeliest enemy, the Royal Navy quickly discarded the coastal force developed specifically to destroy the Russian fortresses, even though it would have to conduct very similar operations against French coastal fortresses if war with France broke out.

Within the British government, strategy was largely set by First Lord of the Admiralty Sir James Graham, who began developing a maritime strategy against Russia in March 1853. He planned two operations to destroy Russian seapower: an attack on the Baltic fleet at Reval (Tallinn) and a "grand raid" on Sevastopol, the Black Sea fleet base, in the Crimea. In each case, neutralizing the Russian fleet would lay Russian territory open to further attack.

Destroying the Baltic fleet would also eliminate any Russian threat to European allies (at the outset, the French feared for the security of their Atlantic ports). Because Sevastopol would have been the base from which a Russian seaborne descent on the straits would have been mounted, dealing with it would have ended the Russian threat to Turkey. The French therefore strongly supported an attack on it. Just why the British went along is not entirely clear; from the outset they seem to have considered the overall Russian threat to the empire, rather than the immediate threat to the balance of power in southern Europe, the issue. Graham initially hoped that a purely seaborne assault would suffice, but soon learned that Sevastopol was too strong for that. The grand raid degenerated into the siege that dominates accounts of the war. The raid was inspired by earlier attacks on Copenhagen in 1807 and Walcheren in 1809; the object in each of these cases was to destroy enemy seapower, not to seize and hold a particular place. Such raids generally required only small armies, thus the Sevastopol operation was attractive to the British, who had only a very small army in 1854.

The British cabinet came to believe that taking Sevastopol, a place of little significance to the Russians, would necessarily end the war; this belief made them take major risks. Perhaps as more and more troops were fed into the apparently bottomless pit of the Crimea the British ministers had to convince themselves that this rather peripheral operation could be and would be decisive. Much the same might be said, over a century later, about the significance Vietnam came to have in the larger picture of the Cold War the United States and her allies fought against the Soviets. The British government was clearly surprised that the Russians did not give up when Sevastopol finally fell. Probably concentration on Sevastopol (i.e., the Crimea) became self-justifying, crowding out any understanding of the wider meaning of the war.

As for the Baltic, the British were apparently entirely unaware that the Russians saw their Baltic fleet as reinforcement for the fortresses protecting Helsinki (Helsingfors) and St. Petersburg, rather than fleets-in-being that might help deny enemies the free run of the Baltic.[22] Graham's initial Baltic plan was frustrated by the withdrawal of the Russian battle fleet to the protection of Kronstadt. By 1855 the French were war weary, so the British were free to pursue larger naval-oriented Baltic operations. The Russians were tired, and their economy had been damaged quite badly, but they were not ready to quit. Yet the Russians would yield if continuing the war would cost them too much, if they faced the loss of something more valuable than the Crimea.[23] In 1854, when the British entered the war, the Baltic, particularly St. Petersburg, was the core of the Russian empire.

More significant, in 1854 the Royal Navy operated in the Baltic, gauging the strength of various Russian fortresses and gaining a forward base. The ultimate objective, chosen in 1855, was Kronstadt, at the time the strongest sea-fort in the world, guarding St. Petersburg. Through the winter of 1855 the Royal Navy built up an elaborate amphibious assault force specifically for the Baltic, including numerous specialized gunboats.[24] The Russians were aware of this effort, and they knew, from their experience in the Crimea, that their defenses could not resist a determined British naval attack. After the victory review, the London *Times* remarked that "a new system of naval warfare had been created": the Royal Navy could assault any naval base in the world. The Russians' likely gains in the Black Sea, moreover, were relatively marginal. They were certainly not worth the loss of St. Petersburg. The czar made peace, on Anglo-French terms, including an agreement to forgo rebuilding the Black Sea fleet, and thereby not pose a threat to Turkey again. The terms held for about twenty years.

The Russian army performed poorly in the Crimea, and its failure soon had dramatic effects on the czarist state. If the war been fought out on land, however, Russians might have been able to trade enough land for time (and allied blood) and thus eventually have ended the war more on their own terms. The triumph was due to the transformation of the war to terms far more favorable to the British, maritime terms in which a relatively small army could be projected into a decisive position, out of the Baltic Sea, far from the nominal theater of war. Was the war really Crimean at all, then?

When the British contemplated war against Russia in 1878 and again in 1884–85, they planned attacks in the Baltic—even though the issue of the crisis was Russian pressure against Turkey in the Black Sea, as in the Crimean War.[25] As in many other applications of seapower, this one was silent: Kronstadt was not seized, but successes elsewhere convinced the Russians that it could easily have been taken. As a consequence, few then or later realized just how decisive seapower in the Baltic had been. When Adm. Sir John Fisher proposed Baltic operations in 1905, the British War Office objected that that operation had no effect on the Crimean War, entirely misunderstanding both the character of the war and its ending.[26]

The American Civil War

The American Civil War is a classic case of the application of a country's seapower against a land power. Seapower was applied mainly by blockade and in providing the North with valuable waterborne mobility. Because the unindustrialized Confederacy could not create a fleet, it could not contest sea control beyond its coast. The South sought to develop some sort of equalizer, hence its early interest in ironclads, beginning with CSS *Virginia* and continuing through the war; intense interest in mines; and strenuous efforts to develop submarines, including the successful *H. L. Hunley.* The South generally used what armored ships it could produce to block Union access to coastal and inland waterways, that is, to limit the mobility of the Union army using those waterways.

The Northern industrial base more than matched Southern initiatives, particularly in the most successful area, armored (ironclad) warships. Because Northern industry was far more capable, it produced a superior (mechanically more complex) armored type, the turreted monitor, in greater numbers than its Southern counterparts. The more exotic Southern weapons, which had no effective Northern counterparts, were produced in small numbers and were not altogether successful, presumably in part because Southern industry was so limited in its capabilities.

Union strategy included the Anaconda Plan, a thrust down the Mississippi to split the Confederacy in half, coupled with a blockade.[27] When the Mississippi had been cleared, the eastern part of the Confederacy would be invaded and occupied, the Union army exploiting the major rivers branching from the Mississippi to gain mobility. In effect the Union followed this strategy in its western campaigns, but it also pursued a complementary strategy of more or less direct assault on the Southern Army of Northern Virginia covering the Confederate capital, Richmond. The Confederates tried to block the Union advance in the west, defending their territory, while threatening the Union capital and sometimes the eastern states with their army covering Richmond. The Union war aim was to destroy the Confederacy altogether. The Confederates hoped to inflict sufficient damage on the Union forces, and draw out the conflict long enough, to convince the Union to abandon the struggle out of war weariness.

Blockade was worthwhile because the South was not industrialized. It could feed itself, but before the war virtually all its manufactured goods came from the Northern states. After the war began, the South had to turn to European manufacturers, and the goods had to pass through the blockade. Conversely, the South's source of money was its cotton export trade, and the blockade largely stopped that as well.[28] President Abraham Lincoln never expected blockade in itself to destroy the Confederacy. Like all interdiction strategies, it made battlefield losses, particularly of weapons, more costly and more difficult to recoup. It is difficult, in retrospect, to say just how effective blockade was. It consumed considerable resources, and for a long time after the Civil War its success was accepted almost as an article of faith.

More recently the effectiveness of the blockade has been called into question.[29] Owners of suitable fast ships learned how to run the blockade; by the end of the war they succeeded at least 80 percent of the time. Blockade-running success amounted to an average of two ships a day clearing ports from which at least dozens had cleared before the war. Goods did get through, but in small quantities. The economics of blockade running favored low-volume luxury goods that could be sold at a high profit, rather than the bulk commodities an economy needs. The southerners did find substitutes for imports; for example, they industrialized to the extent of supplying many of their own weapons. Southern industrialization could not support the sort of shipbuilding needed to defend Southern ports and inlets against Union naval attack. The Southern army was poorly equipped, to the point that a major motive for the advance toward Gettysburg was to seize military supplies. The Southern economy declined tremendously, but it is not clear to what extent poor internal transportation was to blame.

There is evidence that the thin stream going through the blockade kept the South fighting substantially longer than would otherwise have been the case.[30] There has also been speculation that the South might have won the war if it could have broken the blockade, that is, if it could have gained sufficient endurance and sufficient supplies to keep its army going. In this sense the blockade gradually strangled the South. The stream going through the blockade suggests that the strangulation was slow, not that the blockade was ineffective. That the Southern navy never seriously considered building a force to break the blockade speaks more of the fragmented character of Southern resources than of any decision that the blockade was irrelevant to the country's fate.

Conversely, the prewar South was important to the British in particular as the source of 80 percent of the cotton on which their industries depended. The Confederate government hoped the British would support it, much as the French had supported the colonies during the American Revolution, simply in order to keep their industries alive. To this end initially the South blocked exports of cotton to Britain, in hopes of causing an industrial panic that would force the British into the war. This self-imposed embargo did cause damage to the British economy, but those most affected were absolutely unwilling to go to war to support slavery. It proved possible to find substitutes.[31]

Blockade was a legal as well as a strategic term. To make it effective, a navy had to maintain ships continuously offshore. Otherwise blockade degenerated into commerce raiding, an act of war against not only the intended object of the blockade, but also any neutral country's ships caught in it. In the face of such acts of war against third parties, foreign powers could assign warships to protect their merchant ships. The resulting combat might, at least in theory, cause intervention. The blockade therefore offered the Confederacy a hope of bringing powerful allies into the war, particularly in 1861–63, when the overall issue was in doubt. Unfortunately for the Confederates, Union diplomacy was astute, and British liberalism probably never would have accepted an alliance with the slave-holding South.

The potential use of a blockade, however, by the intended victim to gain a coalition partner has interesting modern implications. The modern U.S. Navy is in much the same position the Royal Navy occupied in the 1860s, because the United States depends heavily on foreign suppliers of raw materials, particularly oil. During the Iran-Iraq War we found ourselves convoying oil tankers. Can the weaker party in some future local war use a similar third-party mission to get us more actively into a war?

One way to make the blockade effective was for the Union to seize the ten major Southern ports by amphibious assault: Norfolk, Virginia; New Bern and Wilmington, North Carolina; Charleston, South Carolina; Savannah, Georgia; Jacksonville, Fernandina, and Pensacola, Florida; Mobile, Alabama; and New Orleans, Louisiana. New Orleans was particularly important because it lay at the southern end of the Mississippi River. Six ports, including New Orleans, had fallen by early 1862. The remainder—Charleston, Mobile, Savannah, and Wilmington—had shallow harbors limiting the size of any ships they served.[32] They remained in Confederate hands until nearly the end of the war. A naval assault on Charleston failed in 1863. Mobile was sealed by a naval assault in 1864, but an attempted naval assault on Wilmington failed that year.

Blockade was the strategy of the stronger sea power, the same strategy the British had used in the Revolutionary War and in 1812. The Confederates used the strategy the United States had used in both wars: commerce raiding, in hopes of diverting the Union navy from the blockade. Raiders were built and armed in Europe and, with the blockade in place, they operated out of European ports. Thus USS *Kearsage* was able to destroy CSS *Alabama* off Cherbourg in 1864. Overall, the Confederate strategy failed, because the Union navy never devoted much effort to hunting down the commerce raiders. A complementary program of buying ironclads in Europe specifically to break the blockade produced only one ship, the formidable CSS *Stonewall,* which appeared too late to affect the outcome. By the end of the war, the U.S. Navy was completing fast cruisers intended specifically to run down commerce raiders—or to function as commerce raiders themselves. Their technical success helped convince the British government to settle U.S. claims for damages done by the British-built *Alabama,* on the theory that they could outrun existing British cruisers. One side effect of the blockade was that the United States adopted a traditional British strategy. Creating legal precedents of its own, this strategy negated long-standing U.S. opposition to the sort of nominal "paper" blockades the British had erected in the past. These precedents proved quite useful to the British during World War I.[33]

The Confederate commerce raiding strategy conflicted with the hope of bringing Europeans, particularly the British, into the war on their side. Even though the United States had never agreed to the restrictions imposed at Paris in 1856, the Confederates decided not to attack European-flag ships, whether or not they might be carrying Union cargoes. Union shipowners could evade attack simply by transferring their ships to British registry, which they did in large numbers. The main effect of Confederate commerce raiding, then, was to draw down the U.S.-registered merchant fleet, with no real impact on the Northern economy.[34]

The greatest potential breach in the blockade was the land border with Mexico. The French, who were sympathetic to the Confederates, exploited the Civil War to place their own emperor in power in Mexico. Land communication, both across the Texas border and within the Confederacy, was extremely poor as a consequence of the lack of industrial development, so this possibility was never realized. Moreover, once the Mississippi was in Union hands by mid-1863, there was little hope of moving much tonnage from Texas to the main theater of war in the east.

The other side of the naval coin is seaborne mobility. The Anaconda Plan recognized the value of the great Western rivers. In particular, the Mississippi in effect split the Confederacy in half. It reached the Gulf of Mexico at New Orleans. Perhaps the Mississippi could be described as a pair of interior coastlines, since naval mobility against those coastlines proved extremely important. The Mississippi was so wide that it could not be blocked; troops could generally outflank fixed defenses, most famously at Vicksburg in 1863. The river also offered great mobility for assault artillery. Throughout the war, Union forces used riverine mobility effectively in the west, and combined army-navy operations were common. Rivers reached so far into the south that the mere presence of Union forces on them helped convince Confederates that the war was lost.[35]

Riverine mobility was not nearly as important in the east, although the area around Washington and the Confederate capital, Richmond, opened into Chesapeake Bay and was served by several major rivers. The one major attempt to use naval transport was the unsuccessful Peninsular Campaign, mounted from Hampton Roads. Richmond lies at the head of a peninsula formed by the James and York rivers. In March 1862 the Confederate ironclad *Virginia* nearly destroyed the Union force at Hampton Roads, and thus precluded any seaward approach to Richmond. However, the Union ironclad *Monitor* appeared and drove off the *Virginia,* in the world's first ironclad-on-ironclad battle. It in turn opened the way for superior Union sea mobility to be used. Given control of Chesapeake Bay, thanks to this battle, Gen. George T. McClellan moved his Union army down to the peninsula. Even then CSS *Virginia* blocked the James River, so he had to move up the less satisfactory York. Under pressure, the Confederates had to abandon Norfolk to concentrate forces around Richmond. *Virginia* could not move all the way up the James, and had to be destroyed. Union naval forces moved in, and supported the Union army as it fought up the peninsula. In the end, McClellan failed as a result of poor generalship. Even then seapower helped, because his failure was not fatal: his army withdrew by river and sea. Given the advantage of riverborne mobility, McClellan had come close to destroying the Confederate army covering Richmond.

McClellan's stroke was not repeated, partly because an army approaching Richmond along the preferable path, the James River, left Washington uncovered to any Confederate force marching north. Also, by 1863 there was some question as to whether the immense effort required to take Richmond would end the war. It was no longer certain that the Confederacy had a geographical "center of gravity," in modern network-centric terms. Without such a center, no single blow, however facilitated by seapower, could be decisive. Richmond itself held out to nearly the end of the war, enduring a long siege in 1864–65. That siege in turn was supported by waterborne supplies.

The key point was that Union war aims were unlimited. Even with Gen. Robert E. Lee's army defeated and Richmond seized, the Confederates still had the wherewithal to keep fighting, if they saw the alternative as total defeat. Under such circumstances it appears that the destruction of the Southern will to resist, partly by the effects of blockade but also largely by Gen. William Tecumseh Sherman's march to the sea, was probably crucial. Only at the very end did the Confederacy's president, Jefferson Davis, reject a proposal to keep fighting using guerillas. If so, then the South exemplifies the situation in which no single operation could possibly have been decisive, with important implications for modern ideas of center-of-gravity warfare. What if victory against a popular government requires that the enemy population simply be worn down, as the Southern population was by 1865? These questions matter because we are now so interested in using military effects precisely to gain victory at minimum cost. Assault from the sea certainly comes under the head of limited but precisely targetable military effects.

7

War with Limited Sea Control: Britain and World War I

IN RETROSPECT THE British conduct of World War I is shocking because it reversed a long-standing pattern.[1] Britain behaved not as a sea power, but as a land power with substantial naval assets. Bizarrely, the shift coincided with the widespread success of writers such as Mahan who lauded the earlier British maritime strategy. The British had always committed troops to the Continent, but this time the commitment was unlimited, and so, it seemed, was the cost, both human and financial. Britain had actually improved her position during the previous world war against Napoleon, but this time war was ruinous.

In part the Royal Navy was a victim of its historic successes. The old type of war in which it had succeeded so well, when colonies were vital prizes and victory was achieved largely by slowly exhausting an enemy economically, seemed passé. Its use and abandonment of coalition partners seemed dishonorable, even reptilian. It seemed that no country could afford to fight for very long; it was *necessary* that a decision be reached quickly. The only service that could offer a quick decision was a mass army, which could destroy the enemy's mass army and break through to occupy territory. With the staff system it had created after the Boer War, the British army appeared to be a completely modern service. The Royal Navy had created no such staff system, because none was needed; its unwillingness to match the army's reforms, however, made it vulnerable to charges that it and its thinking were archaic. Moreover, the army's arguments were far better attuned to the way British politicians thought. The indirect attack offered by a navy seemed far less useful than a straightforward campaign on land. Given what we know of the straightforward, quick, decisive land warfare of World War I, the British army's pre-1914 arguments were cynical and ridiculous, but that was not how it appeared in 1914.

There also was an increasing acceptance at the top of the British government that, with the advent of steam power, the Royal Navy could no longer preclude invasion. Several popular novels, such as *The Battle of Dorking* (1871), argued that without a large standing army Britain could easily be conquered.[2] The resulting furor led directly to massive army reform; henceforth a substantial part of the army would be retained on home service, to ensure security. It also led to the construction of more massive coast defenses. It was sometimes said that a "brick and mortar" school had displaced the "blue water" school of British defense.

It thus became more and more important for Britain to deny any enemy the nearby French coast, from which an invasion could most easily be mounted. Beginning with victory in the Franco-Prussian War of 1870–71, the Germans posed just such an implicit threat. If they ever overran France completely, they would unite the bulk of European productive power with a position on the English Channel from which Britain could be invaded. Traditionally, Britain had always sided with the weaker of the major European powers to prevent such dangerous hegemony. Before 1870, that had often meant wartime alliance with Prussia or Austria against France. Now Prussia was clearly the greatest military power in Europe.

The Royal Navy managed to win the fight over coast defense. That eliminated the army's coast defense and internal defense missions. The army was now free to contemplate expeditionary warfare, which at first it interpreted mainly as warfare on the frontiers of the British Empire.[3] As early as 1903, however, the British army was considering its possible role in an Anglo-German war. The defeat of Russia in the Russo-Japanese War seemed to remove the main possibility for a frontier war, the Russian threat to India. At the same time the entente with France presented a real possibility of continental warfare, which would justify a powerful British army. It was not too great a step to imagining a shift in British national strategy in which the balance between land and sea components might shift drastically toward the land, with a substantial British army fighting on the Continent.

In 1898 the Germans began to build their own major fleet. Adm. Alfred von Tirpitz justified it as a deterrent against British involvement in a future war. If Britain went to war against a Germany armed with a powerful fleet, she would risk substantial losses in the inevitable battle. Britain would be reduced to the status of a second-rank power, at the mercy of other powers such as France and Russia. Tirpitz posited a "risk theory": the British would do a great deal, such as avoid any alliance with France, to avoid risking such a fate. In fact, by 1914 the German policy had driven the British into partnership with all the major European naval powers except Germany. Tirpitz may well have posited the risk theory because his real goal, naval supremacy, would have been rejected by the German government and the powerful army. In April 1914 he wrote in a letter (omitted from his memoirs) that the risk concept had been a smokescreen, to be deployed while he advanced to his true goal of building the most powerful fleet in the world and making Germany the pre-eminent sea power as well as land power. Even so, the imperial navy considered the risk theory dogma: it was designed specifically to operate in the southern part of the North Sea, between the Heligoland Bight and the Thames, where Tirpitz expected his decisive battle. Misinterpreting Mahan, Tirpitz assumed that victory in this battle would automatically confer global sea control upon Germany.

Tirpitz was apparently blissfully unaware of German economic limitations. Like France before her, Germany could not afford both an enormously powerful army and a powerful navy. No German navy could solve the critical security problem presented by enemies, France and Russia, on both sides. Ironically, the same Kaiser Wilhelm II who enthusiastically backed Tirpitz also discarded the earlier German policy of befriending Russia so that at the least Germany would never have to face war on two fronts. Indeed, the kaiser's hysterical response to excessive reports of Russian economic growth helped him decide for what he saw as preemptive war in 1914. Because the naval program enjoyed the kaiser's direct support, for a time growth in German naval appropriations exceeded that for the army, encouraging Tirpitz's fantasies of out-building the Royal Navy. The situation reversed in 1912, however.[4] As in the past, then, the British benefited enormously from having coalition partners capable of pressing their enemy on land.

Tirpitz claimed that the British offensive spirit would propel them into an attack on the German fleet at the outbreak of war. Thus the British would inevitably fight where the Germans had built up both fixed minefields and flotillas of small coastal torpedo craft, in the eastern North Sea. Tirpitz, who had been trained as a torpedo expert, argued that such an attack would be suicidal yet inevitable. At the outbreak of war the German fleet cleared for action while in its base at Heligoland. In fact it never came; the British Grand Fleet almost never ventured into the southern part of the North Sea.[5]

After World War I a German strategist, Comdr. (later Vice Adm.) Wolfgang Wegener, argued that the British had no need to fight such a battle because they already dominated the trade routes from the Atlantic to Germany.[6] Moreover, an inferior German navy could not afford to fight. It might well cause serious damage to the British, but in the process it would probably be destroyed. The Germans had few second-line ships, but the British had an enormous fleet of them; victory in the great battle would leave the situation slanted more, rather than less, heavily against the Germans.

Wegener somewhat undercut his own argument by thinking through the likely effect of the destruction of the German battle fleet. During World War I he pointed out that the High Seas Fleet controlled the Baltic in much the same way that the British Grand Fleet controlled the North Sea. It backed the lighter forces that actually operated in the controlled area. Without that backing, the British would be able to cut the vital iron ore traffic from Sweden upon which Germany depended to sustain her war effort. If the Germans lost control of the Baltic, the British could easily resupply the Russians, and the Russian fleet itself could support flanking operations against the German army on the Eastern Front. In Wegener's view, any of these threats could have been fatal to the Germans. It was in the interest of the British to destroy the German fleet as soon as possible, and thus Tirpitz was not entirely unrealistic in imagining that they would try.

Moreover, parts of the Baltic were politically sensitive. East Prussia was the political core of the German empire. When Marshal Helmut von Moltke became chief of the German general staff in 1906, he was initially preoccupied with a possible British invasion in the Baltic.[7] He wanted to double-track railroads to the Baltic coast, update fortifications, and earmark reservists to defend the coast. The island of Borkum was fortified and extra guns were moved to the Baltic. The Germans had been through a war scare in 1904–5, and during the Algeciras crisis of 1906 the British explicitly backed the French, to the extent of threatening to stand beside them in the event of a European war.[8]

When the Russians invaded East Prussia in 1914, the Germans rushed troops from France to defend it, weakening what might have been a decisive blow against France. Germany was unwilling to tolerate major territorial losses for even a brief time. For its part, given its experience in the Crimea, the pre-1914 Royal Navy showed considerable, although ultimately abortive, interest in Baltic operations. The key objections were that Germany could close the

Northern Europe, 1914–18. The geography of naval war in northern Europe during World War I is shown on this map. The Germans sought sea dominance by controlling the North Sea from their base at Wilhelmshaven, off the Jade. They assumed that the British would not tolerate such control; to break it the British would run the risks of seeking a decisive battle. When that battle was lost, Germany would enjoy global sea control, because her only important rival would be gone. Vice Adm. Wolfgang Wegener pointed out that by blocking its entrances, the Straits of Dover and the gap between Scotland and Norway, the British could strangle Germany by blockade without engaging the German battle fleet. To Wegener, in order to contest control of the world ocean, the Germans had to advance toward the Atlantic, at least into the Skaggerak, the strait between Denmark and Norway, and preferably to the Norwegian coast. In 1916 the British and the German fleets met off Denmark (Jutland); the Germans called the engagement the Skaggerak battle, because it was fought off the mouth of the Skaggerak. Earlier the Germans had raided British east coast seaside towns such as Scarborough and Yarmouth, largely to raise German morale, but also hoping to bringing inferior parts of the British fleet to battle. Jutland resulted from a similar plan, although it was ruined by superior British radio intelligence that alerted the British so they could intercept the Germans on the way toward Britain. On this map, number 1 indicates Scapa Flow, the fleet base the British created to control the Scotland-Norway gap. Number 2 shows the mine barrage, created mainly with U.S. mines, to cut off U-boat access through the gap into the North Atlantic. Some British officers argued that it would be far better to mine the entrances to German naval bases such as Wilhelmshaven. The string of islands off Wilhelmshaven, however, protected a channel to the sea through Dutch waters, thus the channel could not effectively be closed by mining due to Dutch neutrality. The two Flanders U-boat bases, at Zeebrugge and Ostend, threatened the vital sea traffic supporting the British army in France. Their proximity to the stabilized Western Front encouraged British projects to overrun them, including a major abortive amphibious operation planned in 1916–17. Note the North Sea entrance to the Kiel Canal. This canal made it possible for the Germans to shift their fleet quickly between the North Sea and the Baltic, and thus to concentrate their fleet for a naval attack on the Russians in 1917 without risking a British assault on Wilhelmshaven while the fleet was in the Baltic. The project to widen and deepen the canal to take modern battleships was completed in June 1914. To many British naval experts, the project was a prerequisite for German involvement in a major war, although this timing seems not to have figured in German calculations, which were oriented toward a land war. Canal dimensions limited the size of German battleships, just as the dimensions of the locks of the Panama Canal, which had a somewhat analogous place in U.S. strategy, limited the size of U.S. battleships and aircraft carriers. *U.S. Naval Institute*

Danish Straits by invading (or pressuring) Denmark, and that the rail net along the Baltic shore made it too easy to reinforce troops opposing a landing. It is not clear to what extent the British war office, which saw a Baltic operation as no more than a continuation of its old role as an auxiliary to the navy, deliberately overrated these problems.[9] As deadlock developed on the Western Front in 1914, First Sea Lord Sir John Fisher raised the possibility of a Baltic operation to pry German forces from the French front. He pointed out that the navy might land troops within striking range of Berlin, an idea reminiscent of the proposed 1856 strike at St. Petersburg. The Germans would later joke that the British troops would have been arrested by the police if they had landed, but the evidence suggests that much more would have been required. The British war cabinet rejected Fisher's idea, although it did approve construction of several major ships earmarked for the Baltic.[10]

Wegener believed the German naval position in the Heligoland Bight was virtually pointless, because the distant blockade the British mounted across the mouth of the North Sea made that sea "dead," that is, without sea lanes passing through. Germany had to "advance to the Atlantic" to contest the control of vital sea lanes. Ports directly on the Atlantic should be seized. For example, German victory in the Battle of the Marne would have yielded French Atlantic ports, such as Brest; this was not, however, one of the German army's goals. When the navy did raise the issue, in October 1914, considerable but fruitless efforts were made. Given failure at the Marne, the next best thing would have been to seize Denmark and base the fleet in the Skaggerak (the Danish Straits) or, even better, to seize bases in Norway. On this basis Wegener was credited with inspiring the German attack on Norway in 1940. Remarkably, Wegener showed no interest in the extent to which a German fleet in the North Sea could threaten Britain with invasion, and therefore, at least in theory, tie down British troops as well as the British fleet.

Certainly German naval expansion attracted British attention and hostility. Winston Churchill, for example, called the kaiser's navy a "luxury" fleet, an unnecessary creation. The Royal Navy, which it threatened, was essential to British survival, however. First Lord of the Admiralty Churchill announced that the Royal Navy would seek to maintain a 60 percent margin of strength over the Germans; previously the doctrine had been to equal the next two navies. Even if the Germans had not begun an oceanic fleet, classic British balance-of-power doctrine might well have sufficed to bring the British into conflict with them.[11]

To senior British politicians, France became not merely a likely wartime coalition partner but a potential ally; the fall of France would be intolerable. In a world dominated by mass armies, a British army on the Continent was far more important than any dominant naval force offshore. Many British policy makers may have been very fearful of isolation; seapower no longer seemed to be enough to guarantee national survival. It was argued, probably under French pressure, that France, depressed by the defeat of Russia, might become a German satellite if Britain did not back her. Given the French passion for revenge against Germany after the 1870 defeat, this fear seems ludicrous. Certainly the British Foreign Office took the bait. Thus during the 1905–6 crisis British Foreign Secretary Sir Edward Grey warned Germany on 3 January 1906 that British opinion might make it impossible to stay out of a Franco-German war. The French, moreover, let it be known that backing had to mean substantial numbers of troops; a past policy of subsidies would hardly satisfy them.[12]

It did not help that the army officers who dominated foreign military establishments had little or no concept of the value of naval forces.[13] In 1904 the British formally agreed to back France against Germany, and the British government slid into a promise, beginning in 1906, to support the French with troops under French command in the event of war. This rather dramatic shift was largely secret. Prewar British governments viewed the understanding with the French as encouragement and, perhaps, deterrence rather than as a prelude to a likely war. It was heavily encouraged by the British army's General Staff, which had its own ambition of gaining true independence, thereby escaping the role of Admiral Fisher's projectile fired from the gun of the Royal Navy, and growing to the size of continental mass armies. The explicit commitment, which amounted to only six divisions, seemed finite, and British statesmen probably thought that they could take "as little of a war" as they liked. They apparently neglected to consider that land wars entail open-ended commitments unless it is accepted at the outset that the territory involved may have to be abandoned. After leaving a crucial 23 August 1911 meeting of the Committee of Imperial Defense, Brig. Henry Wilson, the director of military operations, admitted to a friend that he had in mind more than fifty, not six, divisions, but his political masters, who were responsible for the commitment, were clearly unaware of that.[14]

Entente with France carried an additional benefit: Russia was allied with France. In 1907 the British entered into an entente with Russia, which drastically reduced the land threat to India. This agreement did not upset the existing alliance with Japan, because the Japanese had already won their own war against the Russians. Thus the 1907 entente with Russia freed the British to concentrate on the German threat.

Rimland versus Heartland

The key argument that the age of any country being a dominant sea power was past probably originated from Sir Halford Mackinder, a British geographer. In the past, he argued, goods had generally moved by sea, and "rimland" (seapower) countries like Britain had the best access to the world's wealth. By denying that access to continental powers like France, they could slowly strangle them. However, by 1900 more and more of the world's goods were moving by rail. Mackinder believed that railroads offered access to the massive resources of the "heartland" of what he later called the world island (Eurasia). In the future a heartland state might realize its full potential and thus rule the rimland by building up both a conquering army and a dominant navy. The heartland power would not be vulnerable to blockade because it would be largely self-sufficient. In 1904, when Mackinder first published his rimland/heartland idea, his heartland state was Russia, but the message that a land power might rule the world was probably more significant.[15] He implied that Germany could become an impregnable enemy, if she could overrun Russia. Mackinder's distinction might currently be applied to China and the United States, with China cast as the heartland power and the United States, increasingly dependent on trade, as the rimland. Mackinder's reasoning explains why China is so often advertised as the future dominant power.

Mackinder concentrated on position, land mass, resources, and population. His argument was flawed, however. Effective government, far more than railroads or any other physical improvement, is needed to translate sheer size (of land and population) into real national power. In reality inefficient government doomed both czarist Russia and the Soviet Union. Neither ever realized its potential. It may even be that a country beyond some critical size cannot run itself efficiently; any attempt to run it from above is inherently so inefficient that it cannot win a heartland-rimland battle.

At first blush it might seem that railroads (and, in the modern world, roads) solved the problem of army immobility which in the past had given seapower some of its leverage. Both railroads and conventional roads, however, are expensive to build, and they cannot be moved. Peacetime economics dictated a hub-and-radius arrangement in most European countries. Few railroads were built along coasts. If amphibious operations were viable, they might be conducted away from a railhead, hence away from any point at which ground forces could quickly be concentrated. Naval feints along a coast could even cause an enemy to concentrate ground troops far from the actual landing site. Against this, in a pre-motorized age a force landed from the sea was not very mobile. It had to depend largely on horses, which were difficult to bring ashore. That affected Wellington in Spain and it affected amphibious thinking a century later. Thus amphibious warfare did not really revive until World War II, when armies were motorized.

Blockade and Decisive Battle

The Royal Navy failed to explain its own strategic position and importance. As in the past, its two most urgent defensive tasks would be to protect Britain from invasion and to protect British commerce from attack. It would also impose an offensive blockade on the enemy, although, as noted, few expected a war to last long enough for that to matter.[16] The great complicating factor was the submarine. It is widely, but entirely incorrectly, imagined that the Admiralty somehow failed to appreciate the submarine's potential. In fact the opposite was the case. Secret tests showed that antisubmarine measures were unlikely to succeed.[17] By 1904 the Royal Navy had accepted that it could not closely blockade the German coast in the face of submarines and underwater weapons such as mines. What was not said was that British submarines could block the North Sea against German invasion, shipping, and surface commerce raiders. To that end the Royal Navy aggressively developed first coast-protection and then long-range submarines. It built them in such numbers that in 1914 it had the largest and most capable submarine fleet in the world. At that time, too, the Admiralty was planning to scale back battleship construction drastically in order to build more submarines. In wartime a line of cruisers (later, mainly converted liners) north of Scotland, covered by the submarines in the North Sea, would block trade routes into German ports.

Experience showed that the British were overoptimistic. The submarine blockade of the North Sea was easy to penetrate. Those on board submarines could not see nearly as far as those on board surface ships, nor could adjacent submarines coordinate effectively. Thus the British submarine force was not enough to cover the distant blockade against a possible German surface attack. It took the British main fleet, the Grand Fleet, to do that. Fortunately for the British, the rather futuristic submarine-heavy strategy did not quite supplant earlier ideas.

As it appeared before 1914, however, the main naval problem left unsolved was that German submarines might operate in and beyond the North Sea. Just as the Germans were unlikely to be able to counter British submarines even in their home waters, the British would have little chance of destroying German submarines at sea. The only solution would be to close the German bases at the outset of the war. At the August 1911 conference on British wartime strategy, First Sea Lord Adm. Sir A. K. Wilson said that despite its high expected cost he planned a close blockade of the German bases. Most listeners were appalled; at least some of them apparently felt confirmed in their army-oriented view that the navy was still living in the presteam age. Wilson claimed that the close blockade was needed to prevent German torpedo craft, both destroyers and submarines, from getting into the North Sea. Apparently Wilson imagined, incorrectly, that surface craft really could stop submarines in shallow water. Wilson's concept was certainly not embodied in Admiralty war plans of the time. For example, he proposed seizing a forward base and conducting the blockade using light craft, yet some years earlier amphibious attacks on the German North Sea islands had been rejected as far too risky. Winston Churchill was appointed First Lord of the Admiralty, equivalent to the Secretary of the Navy position in the United States, in 1911 specifically to bring the navy into the modern age.

Yet Wilson had a point. If the submarine could not be countered at sea, it must be destroyed at its base: attacked at source. The German surface fleet in effect covered German submarine bases. Unquestionably any sort of close-in attack would have been costly to the British battle fleet. The cost would have been bearable, however, if the British had first managed to destroy the German fleet. An early decisive battle would have bought not only neutralization of German submarines, but also freedom of action on the seaward flank of Germany, both in the North Sea and in the Baltic. Risky coastal operations could have been undertaken because there would be no great fear that substantial losses would fatally compromise the essential command of the sea. For example, British control of the Baltic would have blocked vital iron-ore traffic, and thus have starved the German arms industry.

The Germans used their surface force as a fleet-in-being. The British could not afford many kinds of operations as long as it remained intact. Thus the Germans were unwilling to risk their fleet, although they were interested in smaller-scale actions that they hoped would ultimately even the odds between the two navies. That is why they never chanced a rematch after Jutland. Overall, the superior British surface fleet could certainly contain the German fleet; an American journalist wrote after Jutland that even though the Germans had sunk more British ships, "the jailer has thrown the prisoner back in jail." However, that containment was not really enough. Through World War I, the British pondered the problem of destroying a fleet that refused to come out to fight. For example, at the outbreak of war the Admiralty authorized conversion of three English Channel liners into primitive carriers specifically to attack the German fleet in harbor, but the technology was far too immature.[18] In February 1915 Fisher proposed amphibious operations in the Baltic, probably specifically to tempt the inferior German fleet to battle.

The British blockade strategy included no offensive element to satisfy either British political leaders or their new French allies. Without any naval offensive plan, the only way in which Britain could be seen to be participating actively in a war between France and Germany would be via a continental commitment of troops. The question was just how far such a commitment would be pushed. Initially the British carefully limited their commitment. During the first disastrous days of the war, they seriously considered withdrawal, either to the Belgian coast (to safeguard Britain from invasion), or from the Continent altogether, as in 1940. Withdrawal was impractical because the small British expeditionary force found itself caught up in the larger French retreat.[19] One lesson the British learned was that when committing troops to the Continent, they had to be prepared for disaster; their army always had to be deployed in a position with access to the English Channel. As long as the British controlled the sea, they could withdraw their army, thus limiting their commitment. The French saw that it was very much in their interest to preclude British withdrawal, so any disaster that befell them would also engulf the British expeditionary force. This conflict typifies the consequences of coalitions between sea powers and land powers.

The British were well aware of the maritime importance of the Belgian coastal towns the Germans were seizing. Soon after the outbreak of war they seriously considered a descent on the Belgian coast on the German flank. It was abandoned because the bulk of the British army was already engaged in France. Despite serious interest in landing it in Belgium to back the brigade of British marines already there, the sole available army division was soon fed into the battle farther south. Without that reinforcement, the marines also had to be withdrawn. They had caused the advancing Germans some anxiety, but not enough to abort their operation. Nor were the British able, a few months later, to support the Belgian effort to defend the fortress of Antwerp, which was another place of considerable maritime significance. The British offered a division, but were reluctant to deploy it unless the French provided a matching force; ongoing French operations precluded a French commitment. The British also became interested in moving their expeditionary force north by land, to the German flank, an operation that would be viable because it could be supported from the sea. After Antwerp fell, First Lord of the Admiralty Winston Churchill pressed for a combined operation to retake the Belgian coast. This "Zeebrugge plan" would exploit British seapower. It became official British strategy but it died because the French feared that if the British were allowed to operate on the sea flank they might disengage altogether and withdraw to England.[20] Churchill's proposal for an attack on the operational flank of the German army, which might have forced it to withdraw, was matched by a proposal for a purely naval attack on Turkey, the strategic flank of the Germans.

Because the British and the French were coalition partners, the French could never veto planned British peripheral operations, no matter how much they feared that such operations would reduce British support on the Western Front in France and Belgium. Fortunately for France, the British commander, Gen. Sir John French, agreed to participate in a joint offensive before the advance along the coast to Zeebrugge became official policy. Once his force was absorbed in the offensive, it could not be redeployed against Zeebrugge. French had to agree to complete the planned offensive before redeployment. The French seem to have been well aware of the British plan, and the joint offensive may have been intended specifically to abort it. When the operation had been delayed long enough, it was recast not as a local attack but as one of several alternative major strategic options for 1915. The idea of striking north toward the strategic Belgian ports, however, continued to interest the British. The failure of the joint December 1914 offensive led the British government to consider shifting from the deadlocked Western Front to other theaters, such as the Balkans and the Dardanelles. That possibility was available only because the British enjoyed sea control. In January 1915 the British abandoned the Zeebrugge plan, deciding to leave strategy for the war on the Western Front, in which their forces were involved, to the French, while they used their seapower to engage the Germans and their allies elsewhere.

Field Marshal Lord Herbert Kitchener, the war secretary, had already predicted that the war on land would stalemate. On this basis he convinced the British government to authorize a large volunteer "New Army" to be ready for action in 1917. By that time the Germans and the French would have worn each other down, and the big new British army would decide the outcome. In fact by mid-1915 both the French and the Russians in the east were in deep trouble; unless the New Army went into action, one or both would collapse. Given the government's tacit belief that the fall of France would spell disaster, the continental commitment became open ended.[21]

It was understood that there were two alternative strategies. One was to attack on the Western Front, on the theory that the main German army in the west had to be broken. It was also argued that unless pressure was maintained in the west the Germans could shift enough forces east to defeat the Russians. That in turn would release the forces initially tied down in the east, thus providing the Germans with sufficient superiority in the west to win there. This possibility was a direct expression of Mackinder's idea that a land area filled with railroads offered the same sort of easy transportation normally afforded by the sea.

The alternative was to emphasize potential Russian power. If the Germans could be held until Russian power was fully developed, it might suffice to defeat them. In this strategy operations on the Western Front would be limited to a holding action, and the resources thus released could be used on the periphery. This more maritime strategy led to the attack on the Dardanelles and to the attempt to reinforce Serbia via Salonika. The French naturally strongly favored a Western Front offensive that would liberate the areas seized by the Germans.[22] Conversely, it seemed that if the Germans won heavily in the East, they might be able to mount a successful offensive in the west, raising the possibility of an invasion of Britain, although this was never a possibility as long as the British exercised sea control. This possibility so exercised the British that it justified sending the first divisions of the new army Kitchener created not to France but to the Dardanelles, in an effort to open a route to assist the Russians.

The Germans' potential exemplified Mackinder's idea that seaborne mobility did not match mobility on land. The Germans had long been aware that they faced enemies on two fronts. They doubted that they could build enough forces to fight full-scale wars on both. They therefore built a railroad system specifically to shunt large armies between east and west. Their war plan called for a quick victory over the French in the west while a limited force in the east fought a holding action against the Russians. That made sense because the Russians were expected to take much longer than the French to mobilize their army. If the French could be defeated quickly enough, the Germans could, in theory, ship most of their army east in time to deal with the mobilizing Russians. In fact nothing of the sort was possible. The Germans found themselves deadlocked in the west. In 1914 their limited holding force did defeat a powerful Russian army, but the Russians managed to regenerate.

Even with their railroads, the Germans probably could not beat off powerful simultaneous offensives from east and west. Thus the Allied war plan for 1916 was to mount just such attacks, in hopes that they would simply overwhelm the Germans. Peripheral operations made possible by seapower did not fit this kind of plan.[23] Moreover, the quick offensive demanded the largest possible British military contribution.

By mid-1915 some in the British government rightly, as it turned out, feared that this sort of commitment would be disastrous. Instead of fielding a mass army, Britain would be better off providing limited numbers of troops backed by munitions and economic aid, as had been done in past wars.[24] By the fall of 1916 the British were buying two-fifths of their war materiel in the United States, and they had long exhausted their reserves of hard currency. In November the U.S. Federal Reserve Board advised bankers to stop lending to the British and the French. Although the British still produced much of what they needed at home, this financial threat was potentially devastating. The Germans do not appear to have appreciated the depth of the impending British and French financial crisis in the United States. In effect, beginning with the massive assault on the Somme on 1 July 1916, the British gambled that they would win before going bankrupt.[25]

The gamble failed; at the end of 1916 the Germans still occupied Belgium and northern France. Romania, which had joined the entente because her government was impressed by the coordinated 1916 strategy, was being defeated. The Germans had further mobilized their economy, promising to triple gun production by the spring of 1917. Even so, in November 1916 the Allies decided to continue their strategy of simultaneous attacks east and west into 1917. For the British, continuation of the earlier policy required increased support from the overseas dominions: Australia, Canada, New Zealand, South Africa, and India. The price exacted was influence over British strategy and war aims. For example, to improve their own security, the Australians demanded that they retain some of the South Pacific islands seized from the Germans. Such demands for colonial expansion ran counter to the wishes of the United States, which was the other overseas state the British badly wanted in the war. For that matter, American opposition to colonialism, as well as a number of entente war aims and practices, made it urgent for the Allies to end the war before the United States contributed so much of the manpower on the Western Front that it could dictate terms.

By late 1916 the Admiralty was pressing for the capture of the key Belgian ports of Ostend and Zeebrugge, on the premise that German destroyers and submarines based there could cut the sea line of communication between

Britain and the army on the Continent. The British war cabinet endorsed the operation, naming the occupation of, or at least the denial to the enemy of, Zeebrugge and Ostend its highest priorities for the coming year.[26] Plans called for an amphibious attack to the north to be mounted once an Anglo-French offensive further south had tied down German reserves.[27] Unless those reserves were immobilized, railroads could have shifted them north more quickly than troops could move along the coast or even by sea. That was another case in which Mackinder's perceptions proved important. Even so, after the southern offensive failed, the British did strike north into Flanders. The attack was mounted by land, the landing being abandoned, but even so the motivation was maritime. In the end, little was accomplished. As elsewhere on the Western Front, breakthroughs on land were virtually impossible.

The Germans had held their position during 1916, but they were also tottering. Like the Allies, the Germans had hoped to mount a knockout blow during the year, but success was elusive. Their attack at Verdun had been designed to bleed the French army white. It failed at enormous human cost to both sides. This failure demonstrated to the German general staff that there was no option for a quick military solution to the war in the west. The Germans saw Britain, with her overseas sources of supply (guaranteed by sea control), as the main obstacle to victory, as Napoleon had a century earlier. Calculations suggested that Britain could be starved out of the war if U-boats were permitted to attack unrestricted (by the rules of blockade) for even a few months. The foreign ministry warned that any such campaign might bring the United States into the war. An earlier campaign had been suspended in 1915 for just this reason. The general staff argued that this time the campaign would win before American strength could be mobilized.

To avoid the problem, the Germans decided to concentrate American interest in the only potentially unfriendly U.S. land frontier: Mexico. They offered the Mexicans the area they had lost in the Mexican War, in return for entering the war on the German side. The Mexicans already had reason to be hostile, partly because the United States had just intervened in the ongoing Mexican Revolution. In fact the combination of U-boat atrocities and the German offer to Mexico, embodied in the "Zimmermann telegram" that the British intercepted and decoded, brought the United States into the war. American manpower, brought to Europe thanks to British control of the seas (enforced, among other things, by convoying), helped tip the balance against the German army. Victory at sea was certainly a prerequisite for victory on land.

Through 1917 German hopes for victory by starvation faded. The British managed to fight their costly battle in Flanders, albeit without gaining control of the Belgian ports. They were even strong enough to hold the line in France when the French army mutinied that year. The Germans were thrown back on a ground forces solution. This time they hoped that if they could knock the Russians out of the war they could concentrate almost their entire army for a knockout blow in the west before the Americans, whom they had brought into the war, could contribute much of an army. The Russians were already battle weary. Offensives mounted in 1917 hurt them further, and it did not help that their pleas for assistance in the Baltic went unanswered. The czar was forced to abdicate, and the Germans found and financed Lenin, who was the most enterprising of the Russian revolutionaries. Lenin was sent into Russia on a sealed train in hopes that he would mount a coup and install a pro-German, or at least a neutralist, government. The Germans hoped not only to free the large army they maintained in Russia, but also to overcome the considerable shortages they were suffering due to the British blockade.

When the army had been freed, the Germans made one last attack in the west, in March 1918. They drove the British and the French back, but they failed to break through. Once the offensive had failed, German energies had largely been spent. Moreover, even if the offensive had succeeded, at worst the British would have withdrawn into an enclave supplied by sea. The war would not have ended, and increasing U.S. support would have made Allied recovery inevitable.

German success in Russia did have one other important effect on the British. It revived the old threat to India, which had always drawn British resources in the past. The British had joined the French and the Russians in hopes of solving the Indian problem with limited resources. Now many British troops had to be deployed to peripheral areas of southern Russia, to support buffer states between the Germans newly installed in Russia and Persia (Iran) and India itself.

At the end of the war Britain was economically prostrate. The great question was whether she could have fought the war more effectively, given her huge naval force. What had that investment bought? Could it have bought a better strategy? At a bare minimum, British naval power precluded any invasion of England that would have ended the war in the Germans' favor. When war began, the British used their seaborne mobility in classic fashion, to place the five divisions of the British expeditionary force in a key position to block the German advance. British naval superiority made it possible for the Allies to keep fighting, because it guaranteed them access to the world's resources. British command of the sea offered safe passage first to the empire armies and then to the mass U.S. Army that provided much of the decisive margin at the end. If the Germans had been able to exercise effective sea denial, these armies would not have come into play, and the German army would undoubtedly have won its battles on the Continent.

Command of the sea had other consequences for the British and their allies. In 1914 it mattered a great deal that the French were able to transport a large army from North Africa to fight in the initial battles on land. The French naval concentration supporting this operation, however, helped leave two German warships, the battlecruiser *Goeben* and the light cruiser *Breslau,* free to reach Turkey. Those two ships helped lever Turkey into the war—with enormous consequences, if the need to maintain access to Russia is accepted. On the other hand, Anglo-French dominance of the Mediterranean presumably helped convince the Italians to abandon their prewar alliance with Germany and Austria-Hungary and to enter the war on the Allied side.[28] If that alliance had not been abandoned, the combined Italian and Austrian fleets would have been more powerful than the French fleet, and the Allies would presumably have lost control of the Mediterranean altogether. At the least, the pressure created on Austria reduced Russian problems. Effective command of the Mediterranean did make it possible for Britain and its allies to mount a variety of peripheral operations, such as the lengthy occupation of Salonika. It is difficult to say whether such operations were a benefit of seapower status, or whether seaborne mobility made it too easy to dissipate limited Allied resources.

In retrospect it is clear that the British constantly were aware of maritime considerations. The war cabinet focused on the Belgian coast throughout the war, and often approved attempts to land on it or to seize it by a northward land offensive. On the other hand, the British built a mass army at ruinous cost, largely to ensure against possible French collapse. The ultimate fear was that French collapse would make a German invasion possible, yet the Royal Navy could almost certainly have prevented that. It is by no means clear that the British high command ever, at least after 1914, thought through the consequences of a possible French collapse.

The U-Boat War

British command of the sea was incomplete. German U-boats conducted their own blockade of the British Isles. Through much of 1916 the British had no effective surface ship antisubmarine weapon. Their own submarines could sometimes sink U-boats running on the surface in what they considered safe areas, but the idea of attack at source remained attractive. Thus, there was intense interest in 1917 in attacks on the Belgian coast. Plans for amphibious operations were abandoned for fear of losing enough capital ships to lose command of the North Sea. In 1918 the British actually did attack the bases at Zeebrugge and Ostend, but they achieved only partial success. When it entered the war, the U.S. Navy also supported the concept of attack at source. It deployed land-based naval air wings to France specifically to attack U-boat bases, although little came of this initiative.

Fortunately for the British, U-boat operations were politically restricted during most of the war. The German Foreign Ministry always feared that they would bring the United States into the war by accidentally sinking U.S. ships or even by killing Americans on board Allied ships. It was impractical for U-boats to follow the international law of blockade, as it had been set at Paris in 1856. In practice the rules required a blockading warship to stop and board any merchant ship, examine her cargo, and only then decide whether to seize or, if necessary, sink her. In the latter event, provision had to be made for the safety of passengers and crew. That was simple enough for an armed merchant cruiser. It was much more difficult for a U-boat to follow the prize rules. Submerged, she was relatively safe, but she could hardly board and search a ship. Surfaced, she was vulnerable because the British soon put concealed weapons on some ships, hoping to trap and sink U-boats closing to search them. U-boat captains found it far easier to sink merchant ships on sight. In so doing they would inevitably create civilian victims, as indeed the Germans did when they torpedoed the liner *Lusitania* in 1915. Whether that mattered depended on whether such acts impelled the most powerful neutral of all, the United States, into the war. Through 1915–16 the Germans vacillated between unrestricted submarine warfare—sinking merchant ships on sight—and adherence to prewar international law.

Only in February 1917 did the Germans finally begin unrestricted submarine warfare. It proved less successful than they had imagined, initially because the British made more efficient use of the resources on hand. A few months later convoy tactics greatly reduced the effectiveness of the U-boats. Even so, other antisubmarine measures were employed. British, and later U.S., submarines patrolled U-boat operating areas such as the Irish Sea, in hopes of catching and torpedoing surfaced U-boats. Consideration of a variety of schemes to close German U-boat bases with minefields led to mining of a broad belt of the North Sea between Norway and Scotland. U.S. entry into the war made this particular tactic possible, because only U.S. industry could produce mines in the vast quantities needed. Proposals to mine major German naval ports were rejected because submarines could have escaped via adjacent neutral waters.

An Alternative Strategy?

British, and later Allied, naval superiority was a necessary but not a sufficient condition for victory. The nature of the victory was clearly less than satisfactory. Was there any way in which British naval superiority might have made World War I more like the Napoleonic wars? Many in postwar Britain traced the disaster to the open-ended, and secretly agreed, continental commitment. Prewar trust in France now was thought to have been misplaced. The sheer cost, largely of mass war on land, in World War I severely damaged the British economy, not to mention its horrific human cost. For example, to help finance the war the British sold off many of the investments that had given them substantial political, as well as economic, power in places like South America and China—places sometimes described as their informal empire. The British also ran up a huge war debt in the United States, with consequences for potential U.S. assistance two decades later. These costs precluded effective rearmament in the face of new challenges in the 1930s. The human cost affected subsequent decisions. At first, it dissuaded the British from taking actions that might have headed off World War II. It also shaped British strategy during Word War II. In the 1930s it was too easy for British policy makers to wonder whether Britain should not have sought some arrangement with Germany, for instance, in 1904, rather than the entente adopted.[29] British memories of the disastrous commitment help explain why Britain was unwilling to commit an army to France until well into 1939.

The British were not the worst affected by the war; it crippled France. Perhaps because the war was not fought on its soil, Germany was less affected, and was better able to reopen the conflict. In that sense the expensive victory in World War I was a partial failure. Was that really because the British, who had real options because of their island position, failed to concentrate on the destruction of Germany as the objective?

The essence of earlier British national strategy was to concentrate on the oceans of the world while wooing coalition partners, without making an open-ended commitment to any one of them. They sought to limit risks, and coolly accepted the possible loss of coalition partners. During the Napoleonic wars the British were well aware that they had to further their economy, which depended heavily on world trade, because it was such an important weapon of coalition warfare. When World War I began, it appeared crass to concentrate on such things. By 1917 the British cabinet was certainly aware that it wanted to seize some key parts of the crumbling Turkish empire to form a new informal British empire in the Middle East, much as helping ensure Latin American independence proved so important to the British after the Napoleonic wars. Perhaps Baghdad should have been the focus in 1914, too.

For that matter, in contrast to British practice in past wars, at the outbreak of war there was no British plan to seize the German colonies, which provided bases to support surface commerce raiders and threatened nearby British colonies. Expeditions were extemporized, and quickly succeeded everywhere except in East Africa. The Germans later attributed the failure of the cruisers based overseas to the loss of these colonial bases. The British retained several of the German colonies after World War I specifically to preclude the establishment of bases that might have threatened their shipping.[30]

In 1914 Britain entered the war with two partners: France and Russia. Turkey blocked the easiest sea route to Russia. The northern route via Archangel was far too difficult, and Germany itself blocked the Baltic route. It was probably fairly clear, in 1914, that France would absorb the bulk of German army strength. The Germans clearly expected that a holding action in the east would suffice. Any reinforcement to the Russians might have had a disproportionate effect. The Russian Brusilov offensive of 1916 forced the Germans to pull significant forces out of the Western Front; perhaps this was enough to account for the failure at Verdun.

Surely, then, it was in Britain's interest to maintain the line of sea communication to Russia through the Black Sea. That might have been done by making a greater effort to maintain Turkish friendship, or even neutrality, at the outset. There was, to be sure, a problem; the Russians wanted Constantinople, which the Turks would not willingly surrender. By late 1914, the Allies were wooing the Greeks, in hopes of placing forces in Salonika to back up the hard-pressed Serbs. Like the Russians, the Greeks wanted Constantinople. The Russians wanted to preclude the Greeks from taking the city, so they extracted a pledge that they would receive it in the postwar settlement. Meanwhile the British tried to negotiate the Turks out of the war. Their ploy nearly succeeded, but the overt promise to the Russians doomed it. Without a Turkish agreement, the British had to fight to reopen the sea route to Russia through the Turkish Straits (the Bosphorus and the Dardanelles).

The strategic potential offered by aid to Russia was enormous. It surely justified the Allied attack on the Dardanelles. Indeed, it would appear that Gallipoli deserved far more in the way of resources than it received. Those fighting on the Western Front could not, in the end, imagine that events so far away could possibly affect their battle. It was the job of British maritime strategists to force home the point that distant events really did matter, that the battle in France was a means to an end—the defeat of Germany—rather than an end in itself.

If success at Gallipoli had opened a major supply route to Russia, that country's army might have received enough arms, or even stiffening by British units, to keep fighting. If that worked, the Germans might have moved much larger forces east, drastically reducing their forces in the west, and thus relieving pressure on the French. A German, or even Austrian, disaster on the Russian front, threatening, for instance, Prussia itself, would have been a very different proposition. Unanswered, the attack might have made it all the way to Berlin. To the extent that the kaiser's Germany was really a federation built around Prussia, Prussia became the key part of German territory. Admiral Wegener's speculation about the effect of loss of German control of the Baltic, discussed earlier, is also noteworthy.

Success at Gallipoli would have opened the Black Sea, including the mouth of the Danube, to the Allies. The British planned to move a force up the river into the heart of Austria-Hungary, relieving pressure on the Serbs and quite possibly knocking Austria out of the war.[31] Allied pressure on the Danube would also have blocked Rumanian wheat imports to Germany. Rumania did eventually enter the war on the Allied side, and was defeated by the Germans.

The promise to Russia violated a long-term British policy to safeguard the route to India by keeping the Russians out of the Mediterranean. The defense of India against Russia was considered the single most intractable imperial problem. When in March 1915 the Russians demanded a formal commitment to give them Constantinople, the British government concluded that Russian possession would threaten Egypt. The conclusion was that Britain should try to obtain Mesopotamia (Iraq), which was Turkish territory, as well as enough territory to provide access to Mesopotamia from the Mediterranean via the port of Alexandretta in Syria. One reason given at the time was that if the British did not take this territory upon defeating Turkey, the Russians would. That would bring them to the Gulf, and they would be able to press Persia (Iran) from both north and west. Beyond Persia lay India. A land route through Persia would be far easier than the mountainous route through

Afghanistan along which Russian pressure had been exerted in the past. Mesopotamia was also valued for its oil. At the end of the war, the British obtained a League of Nations mandate over Mesopotamia, but the French got the mandate over Syria, including Alexandretta. The episode is interesting for the light it sheds on coalition warfare; coalition partners are not, and cannot be, expected to remain friendly after the war.[32]

As for the Western Front itself, it is not clear that a more mobile British army could have affected the issue more directly. As the account shows, at times the British certainly did think that landing a substantial force in Belgium would have turned the Germans' seaward flank and thus would have forced back their entire line. Much the same reasoning was revived by the U.S. Navy in its Cold War maritime strategy. Each time the possibility was raised the operation was aborted for two reasons: a landing alone was considered too risky in terms of ship losses that might have cost dominance of the North Sea, and the Western Front itself demanded the forces that might have been used. The one case of a maritime-oriented offensive was the British attack into Flanders in 1917. It achieved little because it was a frontal assault during an era when defense was favored over offense.

The British also considered attacking the Baltic coast. British submarines operated out of Kronstadt with considerable effect. In 1915 Admiral Fisher proposed a Baltic landing, but his idea was rejected by the war cabinet. In the fall of 1917 the Russians asked urgently for a British naval demonstration in the Danish Straits to reduce pressure on them. The British found themselves unable to do much. A proposal to send a substantial force into the Baltic itself, when the German fleet attacked the Russians in Finland, came to nothing because analysis showed that it was too risky. Throughout the war, as long as the German fleet survived, the British could not afford major losses because loss of overall superiority would have given the Germans command of the North Sea and the approaches to the Atlantic.[33]

Quite possibly no peripheral attack would have been particularly decisive. None would have been as costly, however, as the Western Front meat grinder. As in the Napoleonic wars, all the alternatives would have left the British economy more or less intact to keep generating money to keep the war alive. If the human cost of the war could have been limited, Britain could have kept fighting, while constructing new coalitions. Meanwhile the blockade of Germany would be maintained.[34] Postwar analysis showed that the conquest of France would not have solved Germany's economic problems. Only Russia offered the necessary reserves of food. When the Germans finally did induce a Russian collapse in 1917–18, they gained almost nothing, because the revolution that had thrown the country out of the war had also destroyed her productive capacity.[35] Even with much of Russia surrendered to the Germans, the blockade continued to strangle Germany. As in World War I, in this alternative scenario the Germans would presumably eventually have mounted their own U-boat blockade of Britain, accepting the same risk of U.S. intervention and vulnerable to the same successful convoy counter-measure.

World War I was one more in a centuries-long series of wars the British fought to prevent any single European power from becoming preeminent. Preserving power did not mean preserving any other government; governments could be regenerated, as the Napoleonic wars clearly showed. It did mean preserving the country's economic power and the formal and informal empires that generated a great deal of that power. There was no reason to imagine that the kaiser would be the last such challenger. Thus it should have been an important element of British strategic calculation to fight in such a way to avoid exhausting the country's resources. As in Napoleon's case, more-over, it is not clear that German control of Europe could have been expanded indefinitely. As long as the British held the sea, they could have supported revolts and defections from the German ranks. From a British point of view, would such a strategy have been worse than what was actually done? Seapower made that possible, in a way that was not available to continental powers such as France and Russia.

In the end, the sole justification for throwing resources into France was that without them the country would collapse. Yet the British could have allowed France to fall; during the Napoleonic wars they allowed several coalition partners to collapse. France was considered different because she might have been the base for an invasion. Yet the experience of World War II showed that a cross-channel invasion would have been difficult to mount. Britain would probably have survived the defeat of France, as a much weaker Britain did in 1940.

During the Cold War, the United States often planned the sort of strategy the British adopted in 1911, accepting implicitly that a disaster on the Continent would be decisive. U.S. troops were concentrated on the Central Front, and that phrase carried the unfortunate connotation that the outcome there was central strategically as well as geographically. The kind of war imagined in the 1970s was not too different from the kind imagined just before 1914. If NATO won, would it have been impoverished, from both a human and a financial point of view, as the British had been by 1918? Would some quasi-ally, perhaps Japan, emerge as the true winner?

U.S. Strategy

To an extent, the United States followed a maritime strategy throughout World War I. As long as the Royal Navy contained the German fleet, there could be no question of the Germans crossing the Atlantic to embroil the United States. If the Allies lost, however, Germany would presumably combine her powerful army with crushing naval superiority, perhaps, for example, with captured fleets. In that case the Atlantic would suddenly become a venue for attack. There was real fear that a victorious Germany would finance its war partly by exacting payments from a relatively undefended United States.[36] That was logical. The German Imperial government financed itself by deficits, and it had famously used an indemnity from France after the 1870 victory to pay off its debts. Thus the United States had a real interest in precluding a German victory. U.S. neutrality had a strong pro-Allied bent, and U.S. banks helped finance the Allies' war. As a rising power, however, the United States also had an interest in preventing a total Allied victory. For example, the European colonial powers, including Britain, tended to enforce a monopoly of trade with their colonies. The British largely monopolized trade within their informal empire. If such connections were weakened considerably, the United States could benefit enormously. Many strategists of the time made exactly such deductions, which fit with the sort of social Darwinist philosophy then popular. Thus President Wilson attempted to mediate a peace "without victors" that would, incidentally, leave the United States preeminent. The key to such a policy was that Wilson could decide exactly what he wanted to do about the war if the U.S. Navy could turn the oceans into barriers. He could take "as much" or "as little" of the war as he wanted.

The German View

The Germans had a different view of the maritime side of World War I, and it, too, had Cold War implications. For them, the powerful but enormously expensive battle fleet had been entirely wasted; perhaps it had even proved malignant. It was often argued that what propelled the British into the arms of the French early in the twentieth century was the German naval program, with its implicit challenge not only to the balance of power in Europe but also to Britain's critical naval dominance. The German fleet was sometimes derided as a "luxury," the kaiser's personal extravagance. Many historians saw the Anglo-German naval arms race as the true road to war. It can easily be argued (as discussed above) that the naval arms race was not as relevant as the basic British interest in maintaining the balance of power and the fact that the French would bring with them the Russians, thus relieving pressure on India. Yet the German drive for naval supremacy certainly made it much easier for the British government to agree to the entente with Germany's enemy, France. As for the course of the war, it is not too difficult to argue that, particularly before large numbers of U.S. troops arrived in mid-1918, British Empire troops made up the difference between victory and defeat on the Western Front. For example, they critically maintained that front when the French army mutinied in 1917. On this basis the Germans could reasonably imagine that they would have won in 1914 or 1915 if the British had stayed out of the war.

After the war the German army argued that the cost of the German naval buildup had been failure at the outset of war; by not building capital ships Germany could have afforded the troops that would have provided the margin of victory.[37] In the spring of 1919 pamphlets, for example, "Tirpitz, Gravedigger of Germany," were widely circulated in Berlin. German naval officers were afraid to wear their uniforms on the street.[38] The claim that navalism had, thus, been suicidal may be seen as a far more palatable explanation than the truth: a decisive victory in 1914 was impossible, and the General Staff had fatally misled the kaiser. It did not help the old imperial navy that the collapse of 1918 began with a mutiny in the High Seas Fleet, which had just been ordered to make one more suicidal sortie.

An analogy can also be drawn between Soviet and German naval expansion and their consequences. There is no question that high technology was expensive for the Soviets. Under Leonid Brezhnev, military production seemingly expanded without control. The Soviet navy benefited heavily from this laissez-faire regime. Was its program the straw that broke the camel's back?

The Outcome

From a British geopolitical point of view, the most important outcome of World War I was that it apparently effectively ended any naval threat in European waters. In theory both the United States and Japan were potential naval enemies. In 1919 the British formally chose to accept U.S. naval parity.[39] This was partly an economic decision; World War I left Britain nearly prostrate, whereas the United States gained a dominant financial position. Moreover, rising U.S. naval industrial power would clearly eventually exceed that of

Britain. It was also geographic: U.S. access to the sea could not be blocked. That is one reason the U.S. Navy was never included in the Royal Navy's traditional "two power standard" requirement that it be powerful enough to deal with the next two largest navies. The geographic factor had set British policy even before the war, when Britain was still the dominant financial power, with a much better naval industrial base.

Japan was the main potential post–World War I British problem. As in the U.S. case, the British could not block Japanese access to the sea. In 1919, while the Anglo-Japanese alliance was still in force, Adm. Sir John Jellicoe, who had commanded the Grand Fleet at Jutland, toured the empire. His specific task was to find a way of protecting the Far Eastern part of the empire, including Australia and New Zealand, from Japanese attack. Neither the Australian nor the Canadian government felt particularly protected by the Anglo-Japanese Treaty.[40] Meanwhile, the Americans, who assumed that they would eventually have to fight Japan, saw the treaty as a threat of British intervention in such a war. Indeed, American war planners took the possibility of British intervention into account. At the 1921 Washington conference on naval arms limitation the United States, supported by Australia and Canada within empire councils, demanded the end of the treaty. The British felt powerless to resist. Yet the United States refused any substitute alliance. Instead, the British found themselves forced to accept a more or less meaningless multilateral security arrangement for the Pacific, which the Japanese felt free to discard in 1936. While it is unlikely that any treaty with the Japanese would have saved the British colonies in the Far East, it is interesting to what extent naval geography determined the outcome.

Without any naval threat in Europe, the British felt that they could concentrate on the Far East. They had to block a Japanese seaborne thrust south, and also to protect vital empire seaborne communications. Without any choke points, this was a difficult problem. Perhaps given World War I experience, the British saw a decisive battle against the Japanese fleet as a prerequisite for further operations. The question was how to entice an inferior Japanese fleet to battle. In this case the British reasonably imagined that the Japanese would have to advance by sea, so they would have to ensure the security of their own sea lines of communication. That would be impossible as long as a substantial British fleet operated freely in the area between Japan and her targets. Thus it seemed likely that the Japanese would feel compelled to come out to fight. The British believed that they could win the resulting battle, particularly if they could make sure that it was fought far from Japanese home waters. When they had won, the British would blockade Japan. Japan was peculiarly vulnerable to such maritime attack because she imported virtually all necessities. Particular British territories might not be defensible, but, once defeated, Japan would have to disgorge whatever she had conquered.

What is interesting about this strategy is that it was conceived after the British naval experience of World War I, which included the experience of widespread U-boat warfare and apparently little capital ship action. Japan had a substantial submarine force, and the British would have had to convoy shipping in the Far East. That the Royal Navy considered a battle fleet action a prerequisite for further action shows that it well understood that its own World War I trade protection and attack (convoys and blockade) had been possible only because of the covering action of the Grand Fleet.

To operate effectively, the fleet needed a base. The British selected Singapore, which seemed far enough from Japan to be reasonably secure.[41] It was, however, too far from Britain for a major fleet to be based there in peacetime. The British maintained a small China fleet, mainly to sustain their prestige and thus to support their informal empire in China. In an echo of their pre-1914 thinking, they maintained a strong submarine force in the Far East, in hopes that it could seriously retard any Japanese thrust south.[42] In an emergency, the main fleet would steam to Singapore, which, it was hoped, could hold out long enough for the fleet to arrive. None of this was possible because, by the time Japan contemplated war, the Royal Navy was already stretched to its limits by the war raging in Europe.

8

World War II as a Maritime Campaign

The Napoleonic Analogy

THE KEY TO THE COURSE of World War II in Europe was Winston Churchill's perception that the Germans, despite reaching the English Channel in June 1940, had not won the war. Churchill realized that a maritime strategy offered a reasonable chance of success, but his cabinet was divided on this point. Also, due largely to the impact of World War I, Britain had a far weaker economy than in 1914. That Churchill had real options was not obvious to the land-minded Hitler, who imagined that the war was over; he assumed the British would now accept some kind of settlement. Their army had largely been destroyed, and surely armies were the only way to win wars. In his writings, Hitler had ridiculed the pre-1914 German navalist writings. His surprise at British recalcitrance led first to the order to attack England by air, and then to prepare an invasion that was far more difficult than his army imagined. The power of the British fleet (and the Germans' failure to achieve air superiority over the channel, which might have neutralized the fleet) precluded any quick invasion by the Germans, although that was not quite obvious at the time.

Churchill deeply understood previous British strategy. He realized that, with maritime power, he could keep forming coalitions until the enemy was defeated. Churchill's behavior in 1940–41 reveals his reflection of the experience of past maritime-oriented wars. Moreover, as a major architect of the failed flanking attack at Gallipoli in 1915, he well understood the mobility that seapower could provide. It was no coincidence that in June 1940, at the height of the blitz, Churchill ordered the design of the first large British tank landing craft, specifically for the return to the Continent, and that later in the year he ordered fully seagoing tank landing ships, to support the kind of peripheral attack typical of maritime strategy. The success of this strategy clearly depended on maintaining sea contact with the empire and with the United States, which was now the greatest industrial power in the world. As in the past, the Asiatic part of the empire was an important source of power, including manpower, and the direct route from it to Britain lay through the Mediterranean. Strenuous British attempts were made to maintain control of that sea.

Thus Britain, and later its American ally, fought World War II much more like the Napoleonic wars than like World War I. As in World War I, the British began the war with a commitment to send a small expeditionary force to France. Fortunately for them, the French lost quickly instead of reaching stalemate against the Germans. The British, therefore, were relieved of any unlimited continental commitment.

Churchill's refusal to surrender puzzled Hitler; the British must have some particular reason for continuing the fight. By late July 1940 he was musing that the British must be counting on an alliance with the Soviets. Invading the Soviet Union, which Hitler already planned to do, became a means of cowing the British into surrender.[1] In this sense Churchill's seapower-based appreciation of the war led indirectly to the formation of the coalition he ultimately sought.

The Naval Geography of World War II

As at the outbreak of war in 1939, the British and the French controlled the outlets to the North Sea that German forces had to use. Submarines could slip past Allied surface forces, but only if they submerged by day. A submerged U-boat could not travel very fast or very far, so she needed much of her limited overall endurance simply to get to her patrol area. Slow transit speed also limited how far out into the Atlantic a U-boat could operate. The area was likely within the patrol areas of British aircraft based in Scotland and in Northern Ireland, thus further hindering the U-boats. In effect geography shrank both the U-boat force and the area in which it could operate. That was one reason why, at the outset, the British planned to provide convoys with anti-submarine escorts only for about the last five hundred miles of their runs. Corvettes, the planned escorts, could be made relatively small and inexpensively. Farther out, the main danger to a convoy was a surface raider, so the only escort needed was an armed merchant cruiser—a liner with cruiser-caliber guns.

Conversely, the German land victories of June 1940—the conquest not only of France but also of Norway—placed U-boats directly on the Atlantic. Without adding a single U-boat, the Germans added considerable patrol time, hence effectiveness. The rate of merchant ship losses rose. Convoys now had to be escorted all the way across the Atlantic. Corvettes perfectly acceptable for limited periods at sea became quite uncomfortable. Larger escorts (frigates) had to be built, at a cost in other warship construction. The British shipbuilding industry was strained both to build necessary warships and to replace lost merchant tonnage. Construction of heavier ships, such as carriers, had to be delayed.

For both the Allies and the Germans, Norway was important mainly for its geographical position. At the outset, the Allies hoped that a World War I–style blockade—practical due to British geography—would gradually crush the German war economy. Given their World War I experience, the Germans were well aware of this danger, and they had invested heavily in developing substitute (ersatz) materials. For some things, however, there were no substitutes. One was high-quality Swedish iron ore, which was shipped via the Norwegian port of Narvik in the winter when access via the Baltic routes, which the Germans did control, was lost. Narvik was ice-free, and it had protected access to the Baltic via an inshore channel, the Inner Leads. This same channel was used by German ships evading the British blockade. In April 1940 the Allies planned to invade Norway specifically to deny the Germans both iron ore and blockade runners, and thus make their economic pressure more effective. For their part, the Germans had to ensure access to ore and gain naval and air bases. As it happened, the Germans struck first, and they won.

Somewhat bizarrely, once he occupied Norway, Hitler imagined that the Allies were going to seize it. He therefore retained considerable forces, which could have been useful against the actual invasion in France, in that country. An Allied deception operation played to this fantasy. The deception was viable only because the Allies had the seapower that might realistically have mounted an invasion of Norway. That is, seapower offered the Allies enormous flexibility in their choice of invasion target, whereas the garrison forces the Germans maintained could not easily shift between widely separated places. The same could be said of deception operations mounted in the Mediterranean, for example, to protect the landing in Sicily.[2] Even in the case of the Normandy invasion, deception as to the precise place to be attacked was extremely important, because the geography of the sea allowed the Allies to choose their place.

Conversely, by the end of the Pacific war it was obvious to the Japanese that the Allies would land in the home islands, and most likely in the southernmost, Kyushu. An elaborate deception plan was activated to lead the Japanese to mass their troops away from projected landing sites. After the war it turned out that the Japanese had guessed correctly; their forces would have been massed at the right beaches. In this case, it was simple deduction. The inshore geography was such that none of the other potential beaches made much sense.[3] Seaborne forces are flexible, but they have definite limits.

The geography of British seapower at the outbreak of war in 1939 included the Pacific. By the mid-1930s, with Italy hostile and Germany rearming, the British could no longer assume that they faced naval war only against Japan. By the late 1930s, the British faced the prospect of war in Europe and in the Pacific simultaneously. The British service chiefs pressed for an understanding (appeasement) with the potential enemy either in Europe or in the Far East, because they doubted that the country could handle both. Yet the chance of any such understanding was slim. There seemed to be no concession that would avert a Japanese attack on the British possessions in the Far East. Any concession would probably encourage the Japanese. Moreover, if Britain became embroiled with Japan, Germany would probably act in Europe.[4] By the late 1930s the British faced not one, but three potentially hostile powers: Germany and Italy in Europe, and Japan in the Far East. Under the arms control treaties the British had accepted in 1922 and in 1930, they enjoyed a margin of superiority in battleships over the Japanese. If the Italians were added to the Japanese, the margin became extremely thin; if the Germans were added, it vanished altogether. Moreover, the British had accepted limitations because their economy could not support anything similar to the pre-1914 naval construction costs. Even when the treaties lapsed in 1936, they could not afford a two-hemisphere fleet, which would be required to deal with European and Far Eastern threats simultaneously.[5] However, their fleet was mobile. Given control of the Suez Canal, a fleet based in the Mediterranean could quickly steam east to Singapore. Given control of the Straits of Gibraltar, the same fleet could "swing" to reinforce the home fleet in northern European waters.

Until about 1935 the British faced no challenge in the Mediterranean,

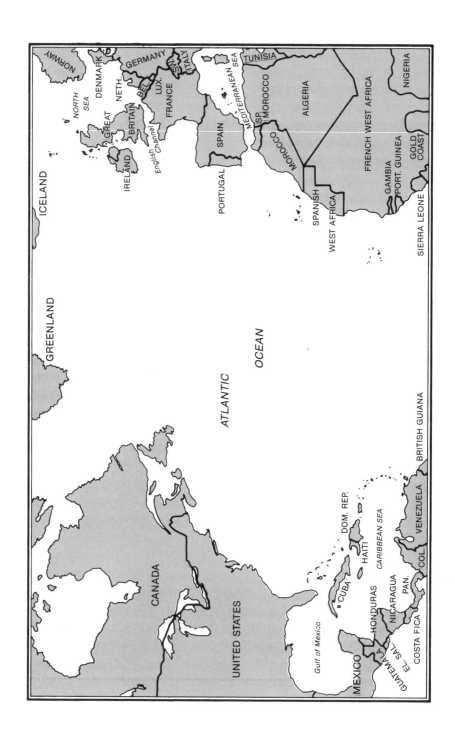

The Atlantic theater during World War II. In 1939 the Atlantic could be seen either as a highway uniting Britain and France with sources of supply in the New World, or as a barrier behind which American isolationists could shelter, safe from involvement in a European war. American involvement in World War II was based on the perception that the Atlantic was a highway, that there was an Atlantic community uniting the United States and Western Europe. The same perception justified the postwar creation of NATO. German seizure of Norway and France brought German seapower directly to the Atlantic, drastically changing the pre-1940 situation. At the same time the defeat of France eliminated the Allied margin of strength over the Axis powers, and thus greatly complicated any British attempt to reinforce the Far East prior to the outbreak of war there. Conversely, the Atlantic highway made it possible for U.S. strength to flow to Europe to overcome the Germans and the Italians. This map also illustrates the risk inherent in the North African invasion of October 1942, a large component of which was mounted directly from the United States. If the invasion had been repulsed and the amphibious ships disabled, the troops would have had no recourse. By way of contrast, the Normandy invasion of June 1944 was mounted from a nearby base, the United Kingdom. The position of Cuba, as a barrier, potentially could block egress from the Gulf of Mexico to the Atlantic. During the Cold War, much of the American materiel destined to reinforce armies in Europe would have come down the Mississippi and then past Cuba. Submarines based in Cuba could have inflicted heavy losses. Countering them would have been difficult, because the Gulf of Mexico is quite shallow. Cuba presented American Cold War strategists with a dilemma. If Cuba joined a Soviet attack on NATO, then a force could have been assigned to overrun the island, then "swung" to other tasks. The Cuban government, however, could choose to remain neutral. In that case, the substantial force required to overrun Cuba would still have been required, but not used until Cuba entered the war. As a consequence, it could not have been swung to other tasks. Yet the total U.S. naval force was not large; subtracting the large force required for a one-time attack against Cuba could have been crippling. Nicaragua's strategic position near the Panama Canal, through which materiel from the U.S. Pacific coast would have flowed to Europe, explains the urgent U.S. interest during the 1980s in the fate of Nicaragua. *U.S. Naval Institute* and the main issue in their strategy was which way to swing the fleet there. The Mediterranean was also attractive as a training area because it had less bad weather than home waters. When Italy attacked Abyssinia in 1935, the British backed the Abyssinians. They faced a real possibility of naval war in the Mediterranean. The British expected that they could easily defeat the Italian fleet. Given rigid treaty limits on the total number of British capital ships, and the limited capacity of British industry, any losses in such a war might well have had crippling effects in the event of war against Japan, which was a much more dangerous enemy. The British also saw the Italians as potential allies in the event of war against Germany, and they therefore limited their opposition to the Italians.[6] When Italy became a potential enemy, the British had to rethink the value of the Mediterranean. As a route to the Far East, it could, in an emergency, be replaced by the much longer route around Africa. That routing could be equated to a substantial loss of shipping tonnage, in effect a virtual attrition equivalent to major sinkings.[7] By the mid-1930s it was clear that the Middle East might be more important to Britain than the Far East. To abandon the Mediterranean in wartime would be to lose the prestige gained and maintained while the British had control of that area.[8] Unfortunately, if Italy went to war, then the Mediterranean Fleet would be fully occupied keeping that sea open to British communications.

The British envisaged two possible alternative solutions. One was political. It might be possible to appease either the European or the Far Eastern threat, at least long enough to allow the Royal Navy to build up to match it. Uncomfortably aware of just how powerful the Japanese were, and of just how determined they were to take over the whole Far East, in the 1930s the Royal Navy leadership supported appeasement of Germany.

Alternatively, the fleet might cripple one threat for long enough to allow redeployment against the other. Fighting only one enemy at a time, it was strong enough to have an excellent chance of victory. Thus, for the British, decisive battle was the only way to win a naval war with a one-ocean fleet. If that was impossible, as happened during World War I when the enemy chose to maintain a "fleet-in-being," then the British would be stymied.

This strategy required that the British be able to fight and defeat one enemy, then swing to the other. It assumed that both Atlantic and Pacific enemies would go to war at about the same time. Before 1939 the British promised the Australians and New Zealanders that no matter how great the pressure in Europe they would send the bulk of their battle fleet east on the outbreak of war to deal with the Japanese. It was reasonable to imagine that it could induce and fight a decisive battle, then swing back to the Atlantic to deal with the Germans and the Italians, whose fleets probably would not unite. As long as they remained separate, a limited British home fleet could deal with either threat, swinging between the Mediterranean and the Atlantic. Unfortunately for the British, the European crisis came first. Combat in European waters wore down the British fleet before any transfer east could be justified.

Given the dual threat, French support became extremely important. Conversely, transfer of the French capital ships to the Germans after the French surrender in June 1940 would have had devastating consequences. This potential explains Winston Churchill's determination to neutralize the French fleet in July 1940. He ordered his fleet to destroy the French warships at Mers-el-Kebir, in Algeria, and at Alexandria, the base of the British Mediterranean Fleet. The attack at Mers-el-Kebir poisoned Anglo-French relations.[9] Ships surviving Mers-el-Kebir retreated to the French naval base at Toulon, which was in the part of France not occupied by the Germans. As the British had feared, they were always vulnerable to seizure, if the Germans decided to replace the puppet regime at Vichy with direct occupation. When the Germans did so, in November 1942 (at the time of the Allied invasion of French North Africa), the French managed to scuttle their fleet, keeping the great bulk of it out of German hands. The French admiral at Alexandria saved his ships by agreeing that they be disarmed. The ships remained there, under British protection, until they were rearmed to join the Allied cause in 1943. They became the core of the postwar French fleet.

In November 1940 British carrier aircraft crippled the Italian battle fleet in its base at Taranto. Unfortunately that was not sufficiently decisive. Moreover, it proved impossible to destroy the German capital ships at their bases. The threat of German battleship action in the Atlantic, dramatized by the cruise of the *Scharnhorst* and *Gneisenau* and then by the *Bismarck* sortie, drew British naval strength from the Mediterranean. That in turn made it much easier for the Germans to insert Gen. Erwin Rommel's armored force into Libya than it might otherwise have been.

By May 1941 the Germans had moved large numbers of antishipping aircraft to the Mediterranean, and much damage was inflicted on the British fleet off Crete. Without carriers, the British could not destroy many German aircraft in the air. The perception was, moreover, that any aerial victories would have only a transient effect, because the Germans possessed so many airplanes and had so many trained pilots. This exemplified a wider perception that air forces were mass organizations comparable to mass armies. Airplanes were, after all, generally built in enormous numbers. In 1941, then, it seemed that no battle at sea could be decisive: the aerial threat to shipping in the Mediterranean would cease only with the capture of the bases from which the Germans flew. That was clearly impossible, given the limited strength of the British army.

The number of aircraft actually in combat service at any one time, however, was quite limited, partly because pilots were scarce and partly because airplanes themselves had very short lifetimes, due as much to accidents as to enemy action.[10] Antishipping operations required specialist pilots, who could not easily be trained. Indeed, throughout World War II the impact of killing off elite corps of pilots seems to have been underestimated.[11] The Japanese in particular seem to have found it very difficult to train replacement pilots quickly.

Thus the British, if they had been able to deploy a powerful carrier battle group to the Mediterranean in 1941, might have been able to win a sufficiently decisive series of air battles, thus ensuring more or less free use of the sea throughout the year. The same dive-bombers that so badly damaged the Royal Navy off Crete were badly needed for the opening of the Russian campaign, so the Germans could not have afforded major losses. During the later phases of the Cold War the U.S. Navy would look back at World War II and conclude that it was indeed possible to fight a decisive sea-air battle to achieve what it called maritime air superiority.[12]

The reality in 1941 was that the British lacked sufficient carrier forces to concentrate them for a decisive battle in the Mediterranean, even if they had imagined that such a battle would have been worth fighting.[13] By mid-1941 it seemed clear that nothing the British could do would allow them to release a substantial fleet to the Far East. The hope of deterring the Japanese evaporated.

U.S. Intervention

As in World War I, the United States would clearly have felt threatened if the Germans had overrun Britain. A German victory might well have put potentially hostile forces on the American side of the Atlantic, in British colonies and perhaps even in Canada, just as the fall of France gave Germany access to French North Africa. The British fleet, at least as powerful as the U.S. fleet, could provide the Germans with the sort of sea control that would make Western Hemisphere colonies effective bases for assaults on North America. In mid-1940 President Franklin D. Roosevelt tried to force Churchill to agree that, in the event of a collapse, he would send his fleet to the New World, to keep it out of German hands. Well aware that in this case Roosevelt would feel less impelled to back him, Churchill demurred; whatever he might say, a successor government trying to make terms with the Germans would find the fleet a valuable bargaining chip. None of this suggests that the result, an Anglo-American alliance capable of winning the war, was foreordained in the fall of 1940, just as victory against Napoleon was not foreordained, for instance, in 1795.

It was always clear that Germany was a direct threat to American survival, whereas Japan was, at worst, a threat to the U.S. position in the Pacific, a secondary issue. During 1941 American national strategy was "Germany first," on the ground that Germany could certainly survive the defeat of Japan, whereas the defeat of Germany would free forces powerful enough to crush Japan. Because Japan, not Germany, attacked the United States in December 1941, there was a real possibility that the United States would fight only Japan.[14] Fortunately for both U.S. national strategy and for Britain, Adolf Hitler took it upon himself to declare war against the United States.

British Maritime Strategy

If the example of the Napoleonic wars is a fair one, a key to maritime strategy in a major war is patience. If the maritime force can preclude enemy victory, then coalitions can be built and nurtured. Partners that collapse can be replaced; in some cases collapsed partners can be resuscitated. In the Napoleonic wars, moreover, the passage of time actually strengthened the maritime power, Britain, while the sheer cost of maintaining a mass army gradually weakened Napoleon. Unfortunately for Churchill, previous damage to the British economy and, more important, the denial of American credit, limited the available time.[15] On the other hand, Hitler was in a hurry, and he did not wait for the British economy to collapse. A year after the fall of France he presented the British with a possible new coalition partner when he invaded the Soviet Union.[16] As a historian, Churchill would have recalled that in 1814 Russian cavalrymen rode through Paris; the sheer weight of the Russian army was a major contributor to Napoleon's defeat. Churchill also knew from bitter experience, however, that Joseph Stalin would have welcomed this sort of development, and that, unlike the czar's men, his probably would not have gone home. In that case Soviet hegemony would have replaced Hitler's, and Britain would have been faced with much the same problem as the Germans presented. Thus he could not allow his coalition partner free rein.

Like Napoleon, the Germans had to defeat the British. As early as the end of June 1940 they had settled on the Mediterranean, seen as a flank of the British Empire, as an alternative theater in the event that direct invasion proved impossible.[17] This was not too different from Napoleon's idea of attacking the empire in India through Egypt. There was particular interest in attacking both Gibraltar and Suez, thus sealing off the Mediterranean altogether and protecting German conquests from British attack. As it turned out, Francisco Franco, the Spanish dictator, was less than enthusiastic; the British could, after all, attack his Atlantic coast. Italy was a different proposition. Her African colonies adjoined Egypt, thereby offering access to the Suez Canal and the Middle East. Hitler made the Mediterranean an Italian sphere of action, and all Italian projects received automatic German approval. That proved unfortunate.

Hitler chose to back the Italians in Libya, on the Egyptian border, with German forces, in this case with Rommel's Afrika Korps. On the other hand, it was easier for the British to reinforce their army in Egypt, by sea around Africa, than it was for the Germans to move convoys across the hotly contested Mediterranean, particularly when British naval strike forces operated from Malta.[18] In this sense Rommel was a drain on German strength, particularly when so much was needed in Russia. Rommel survived as long as he did mainly due to poor British army performance; the sea route certainly provided the British with far more materiel and fuel than he ever had. For the Germans, Rommel's operation was peripheral; it turned into a nearly open-ended commitment. For the British, the defense of Egypt was vital because beyond Egypt lay the oil of the Middle East. There is little evidence that Hitler ever planned to give Rommel enough resources to get that far. Nor is there evidence that he saw Rommel's thrust along the southern shore of the Mediterranean as complementary with the German thrust down through the Balkans toward the northern shore.

Churchill's ideal strategy in 1940–41 was to hold out while using his sea control to build national strength, by maintaining communications with the empire and with other sources of strength, such as the United States, and to attack his enemies along their periphery, not least to encourage real and potential coalition partners. Strategic bombing by the Royal Air Force (RAF) fit into the same category. Churchill could also hope that the Germans would find it necessary to defend their lengthening periphery and the resulting airspace, thus diluting forces available for further expansion. British seapower made the Mediterranean a particularly attractive operational area, because allies on its coasts could be supported. Thus British troops were funneled into Greece, which in mid-1941 was the last British ally remaining on the Continent. The Germans saw Greece as a potential menace to the crucially needed oil of Rumania, and apparently Hitler saw the opportunity for a potentially decisive victory over the British.[19] The Greek adventure helped inspire a pro-Allied coup in Yugoslavia, temporarily adding another ally. The Germans drove the British out of both countries, but that was not disastrous, although it was costly.[20] As long as the British retained sea control, nothing that happened on the Continent could actually destroy Britain. It turned out that the time the Germans lost in overrunning Greece and Yugoslavia delayed the assault on the Soviet Union to late June 1941, and that probably ensured that the Germans would reach full stretch just as winter struck that country. That may well have been decisive in precluding a victory over the Soviets.

At the very least, the British could hope that their potential ability to land anywhere along the coast of occupied Europe would dilute German defenses. Through 1942 they mounted numerous limited operations to demonstrate exactly this potential and, incidentally, to learn how to mount the major ones needed to regain major territory. One consequence of such attacks was to convince the Germans that the Allies could and perhaps would mount amphibious assaults anywhere around the long coast of occupied Europe, and in this way made numerous deception operations, mounted to protect real landings, possible.

After the United States entered the war in December 1941, Churchill found it difficult to maintain his slow-motion maritime strategy. The U.S. approach was much blunter and U.S. patience much shorter. The U.S. Army, in particular, believed that American forces had to get onto the Continent, destroy the German army, and overrun Germany. This was very much the World War I strategy revived, and it clearly horrified Churchill.[21] Surely it was better to use Allied maritime superiority to attack around the edges of the occupied area, limiting liability in any one assault, and forcing the Germans to stretch their resources? By December 1941, moreover, it was clear that the Soviets would continue fighting. Any stalemate in the east would grind up much of the German army. Given time, it might even be possible to undermine German control in Western Europe.

These considerations help explain the strategy that Churchill espoused in 1941–44. For him the Mediterranean was particularly important, because it was the shortest route to the vital supporting economies of the empire, particularly India. The combination of Axis occupation of much of North Africa and Italian participation in the Axis effectively blocked that sea. From an empire perspective, reopening the Mediterranean was an essential prerequisite for continuing the war. For that matter, regaining control of some of the Far Eastern territories the Japanese had seized, particularly Burma and Malaya, had a high priority because their resources could feed the war in Europe. There was also a coalition aspect. The empire gave Britain part of her economic muscle and thus offered the possibility of equality with her alliance partner, the United States. Conversely, with much of the empire cut off or in enemy hands American bargaining power within the wartime alliance was greater. The British were also uncomfortably aware that many Americans regarded their whole empire as illegitimate, and hoped to use wartime leverage to destroy it. Coalition partners do not necessarily share the same outlook; they come together, often reluctantly, for particular ends.

The U.S. perspective was very different. To American strategists, the obvious initial target was the German army of occupation in France, which blocked the direct route to Germany. The Mediterranean was a secondary theater of war. Operations there were initially approved only because by mid-1942 it was obvious that no near-term invasion of France was possible; it would be better to undertake an offensive somewhere than to appear idle while the invasion force was built up to assault France. Once Allied forces had landed in North Africa, the Mediterranean theater developed a momentum and a logic of its own, and no invasion of France became possible until 1944.

Ultimately the British and the Americans could not afford the kind of division of effort that had made Britain so successful in the Napoleonic wars, because they could not afford to leave the land war in Europe to the Soviets. If the Allies had not landed in France in 1944, evidence suggests that the Soviets expected to occupy the whole of Europe. Indeed, there is evidence that prior to the outbreak of war Stalin expected Germany and France to reach a stalemate, which would provide Communists, backed by his own army, a valuable opening. During and after the war the U.S. Army leadership was often criticized for political naivete, particularly for allowing the Russians to reach Berlin first. The decision to land in France in the first place, and to push as deep into Germany as possible, had enormously beneficial political consequences. It shaped Europe for the next five decades, and it precluded early disaster in the Cold War. To what extent was that obvious at the time? Through at least 1943, as the Germans severely punished the Soviets, Stalin demanded that a "second front" be opened in the west. By early 1944, when the Soviets were in the ascendant, Stalin probably began to regret this earlier demand.

As it turned out, this time the continental commitment was much less costly than in World War I. Seapower helped. For example, Allied seapower made possible not only the Normandy landing but also the quick follow-up landing in the south of France, on the Germans' strategic flank. German units had to be pulled out of southern France to deal with the post-Normandy breakthrough, which in turn allowed Allied forces a quick advance through southern and central France. Conversely, limitations on naval resources, particularly landing ships, made it impossible to conduct the two operations as close together as had been hoped. There is also evidence that landing the Mediterranean forces farther east might have brought greater benefits, because it might have dislocated the German defense of Central Europe.

As in the Napoleonic wars, much depended on having a coalition partner on the Continent. In this case that partner, the Soviet Union, was, paradoxically, both vital and potentially very hostile, so that its success was essential—but only up to a point.

Blockade

As in World War I, the British began a blockade of Germany at the outset of war. Having experienced the "hunger blockade" two decades earlier, the Germans predicated much of their strategy on the problems its successor could or would cause. Hitler sought a short war because he feared that the social strains caused by a blockade might destroy his regime. To limit sacrifices the German public would have to make, he adopted blitzkrieg tactics and limited military production in Germany until 1943–44. The blockade experience had already led Germans to see conquest of the Soviet Union as the only possible solution to their expected shortages.

It would be some time before the productive capacity of a conquered Soviet Union could be exploited, so the Germans had to plan for a short campaign there; they could not afford to expend much materiel. That requirement in turn led to a paradox. Hitler demanded that effort be concentrated on seizing resources in the Ukraine. His General Staff, however, sought a short war, and the only way to do that was to win a decisive battle, thus destroying the Soviet army. It was assumed that the Soviets would fight for Moscow and Leningrad, hence an advance to the north could be decisive. As a result, German efforts were divided, and neither drive fully accomplished its objectives.

Moreover, in their quest for a decisive battle the Germans ignored the lesson of World War I: mass armies could be regenerated as long as the will to fight remained and the national territory had not yet been occupied. Once the Soviets were fighting the Germans, Allied seapower contributed heavily to regeneration—to their ability to keep fighting—by providing them with equipment and also with machine tools required to produce weapons.[22]

At the least, the effect of a seaborne blockade provided the British with the coalition partner, the Soviet Union, needed to destroy the German army. British and U.S. seaborne support in turn proved vital to sustaining Soviet resistance.

Because the Germans were never able to conquer the Soviet Union and fully exploit its resources, their high command spent the war in what the wartime British ministry of economic warfare called "a state of mild hysteria" due to inability to supply material, munitions, transport, weapons, shipping, food, and warm clothing. In 1944–45, Allied advances, which were cutting the Germans off from their supplies of materials such as tungsten and nickel, threatened to stop German military production altogether, even if Germany itself was not occupied.[23]

The Germans did manage to continue to arm themselves, however, and fought until their territory was occupied. If there been no blockade limiting access to Western Hemisphere resources, they would presumably have been far more successful. As it was, probably the most important impact of the blockade was that its threat impelled them into the suicidal war against the Soviet Union. One irony of that war was that Stalin was supplying what the Germans wanted until they attacked the Soviet Union; at the same time the Soviet Union was functioning as a loophole in the blockade, through which cargoes from the Pacific could pass.

The Asian Connection

The sea created connections that may initially appear paradoxical. Through 1940–41 the United States armed against the possibility of war in Europe. That required raw materials, some of which were not available at home. Some of the most crucial came from Southeast Asia.[24] Britain also depended on these same raw materials. Thus the European and Pacific areas were inextricably connected, for both the United States and Britain. Japan sought control of the crucial area; if Japan controlled the area, she would cut off access. Through the first half of 1941, the United States tried a combination of deterrence and appeasement. The main U.S. instrument was the main fleet, which was moved from San Diego to Pearl Harbor, far closer to the area of Southeast Asia the Japanese might decide to invade. Although still distant, it had something of the role of the fleet the British would have liked to send to Singapore. U.S. domestic opinion precluded any Anglo-American alliance, so the U.S. government could not take the next step of moving the U.S. fleet to Singapore in the event matters worsened. Appeasement meant continuing to sell strategic material, such as oil, to Japan. There was still hope, at least within the U.S. government, that a Japan tied down in China would not yet move south.

To the Japanese, however, the European war offered a unique opportunity for Japanese conquest. Two of the main colonial powers, France and the Netherlands, had been defeated by Germany and thus were unlikely to resist attack effectively. The greatest Far Eastern colonial power, Britain, was occupied mainly with the war against Germany and Italy. Japanese suspicions that the British could not reinforce their forces in the East were heightened when a German surface raider captured secret mail, including War Cabinet minutes, on board a British steamer, SS *Automedon,* in the fall of 1940. Her documents, handed over to the Japanese when the raider reached Tokyo, were surely among the more valuable fruits of the German-Japanese alliance. As for the U.S. deterrent, by early 1941 Adm. Isoroku Yamamoto was planning to destroy the American fleet by attacking Pearl Harbor at the outbreak of war.

In mid-1941, the Japanese occupied French Indochina (later Vietnam), obtaining the bases needed to seize the British colony of Malaya. Clearly the U.S. and British attempts at appeasement had failed. The only hope of retarding the feared advance was to cut off the oil supply Japanese forces would need. No blockade was needed, because the United States and the Dutch government in exile controlled most supplies. They demanded that the Japanese withdraw from Indochina, that is, abandon their threat to the key sources of raw materials. A parallel demand that the Japanese withdraw from China somewhat clouded the issue, because a Japanese withdrawal from China, even if possible politically, would have freed forces for the southward attack. It is not clear to what extent the U.S. government hoped that the Japanese would accede to its demands. Recent evidence suggests that they were made only after the situation had turned hopeless; there was some hope that negotiations might hold off a Japanese attack for a few months, while more supplies were brought from Southeast Asia.[25] The embargo was probably the final straw for the Japanese. At an imperial conference, the delegates heard that U.S.

industrial potential was crushing, and that Japan had only eighteen months of oil left. The choice, as they saw it, was to live like slaves or to die like men; they chose to die.[26]

The U.S. War against Japan

By this time the U.S. Navy had had more than three decades to think through the problem of a Pacific war. As with the British, its strategy was to win by blockading Japan; blockade in turn required that the Japanese fleet be defeated, most likely in decisive battle. The alternative, to occupy Japan physically, was dismissed as entirely impractical. The Japanese saw matters roughly as the Americans did; they also thought that the issue of a Pacific war would turn on a decisive main fleet battle. Probably because their resources were more limited, they went much further than the Americans in optimizing their fleet for just that contingency, including a massive night torpedo attack preliminary to it. Much of this effort was wasted when the war turned out differently than the Japanese had imagined. Flexibility matters. The U.S. Navy was probably saved by the sheer variety of Pacific war scenarios it had considered.[27]

The U.S. fleet could not simply steam from Hawaii to the Far East. If it did, the Japanese could win simply by refusing to give battle until it had run out of fuel and other supplies. The fleet would need a base for postbattle repairs, without which even a decisive victory would gain little. Through the interwar period, then, U.S. naval strategists increasingly understood that a Pacific war would turn on acquiring and defending bases. Initially it seemed that a base in the Philippines would suffice, but there was no possibility that the United States could station a large enough force, either naval or army, in the islands to preclude their seizure.[28] In 1935 the official U.S. war plan was rewritten on the assumption that the Philippines would fall before relieving forces could arrive. The U.S. Navy would, then, advance stepwise, from advanced base to advanced base, across the Pacific.

Unfortunately, after World War I, the Japanese had received League of Nations mandates to govern many of the formerly German-owned islands of the Central Pacific, which lay along the likeliest route the U.S. fleet would take.[29] These islands gained enormous naval significance from the character of the interwar naval arms limitation treaties. Between 1922 and 1936 they set the number of capital ships, including aircraft carriers. Nothing, however, could limit the number of seaplanes that could operate from even unimproved Pacific atolls. Those aircraft could attack the U.S. fleet as it crossed the

Pacific. Similarly, submarines and light surface craft, largely unlimited by treaty, could be based on the atolls, with little or no prewar preparation. U.S. war planners therefore envisaged seizing islands not only for their own use, but also to deny them to the Japanese. Islands were valued entirely for their effect on the application of U.S. seapower.[30]

A fleet route through the South Pacific was rejected because the islands along it were mainly British possessions. In the interwar period U.S. naval planners thought that the British might well revive their earlier links with the Japanese. For example, in the early 1920s the U.S. Navy rejected a strategy of unrestricted submarine warfare against Japan, which was certainly quite vulnerable to it, on the ground that British merchant ships, by far the most numerous in the world, would inevitably be sunk. If unrestricted submarine warfare had levered the United States into World War I, would it lever the British into a future U.S.-Japanese war?[31] The U.S. planners were apparently unaware that the British were desperately trying to devise a way to bring the United States into an alliance *against* Japan as a way to deter the Japanese from seizing the British colonies in East Asia.

The U.S. Navy would have to seize and defend island bases along the route the fleet would take. Although this was a ground combat mission, it was radically different from operations normally carried out by the U.S. Army. Armies fight for territory of intrinsic value, or at the least adjacent to territory worth seizing. Neither description applied to isolated atolls in the Pacific. The U.S. Marines Corps, a land force allied to the U.S. Navy, became vitally important. Its ambiguous charter clearly included the seizure and defense of bases the navy needed to maintain and extend sea control, hence the Marines' intense interest in amphibious operations and their characteristic style of warfare, a quick assault to seize a limited base area. U.S. Army amphibious assaults were designed to seize a beachhead that opens a large continental area to ground assault.[32]

Particular bases were of transitory value. To maintain a garrison for each would waste valuable resources. Instead, the U.S. Navy counted on the mobility of ships. It designed a fleet train: repair ships, tenders, ammunition ships, oilers, floating (towable) dry docks. Anchored in an otherwise deserted lagoon, these ships created a temporary fleet base. Although no one could mistake the ships of the train for combatants, they were as essential to the fleet's progress across the Pacific as battleships, carriers, cruisers, or destroyers. The U.S. approach could be contrasted with that of the Royal Navy, which in peacetime relied on a worldwide string of bases. World War II showed that such bases are difficult to defend. Ironically, victory in World War II plus Cold War alliances gave the United States a worldwide network of bases not too different from those the British maintained before the war. Although the U.S. Navy continued to maintain a strong fleet train, it must have seemed more luxury than necessity, because it was cut deeply at the end of the Cold War. Now that base access is less certain, however, the fleet train is more important.

By 1944, the U.S. Navy had perfected techniques for underway replenishment that allowed it to operate much farther from a base, and for much longer. The British likened late-war U.S. operations to fighting a war off the U.S. Atlantic coast from a base at Gibraltar. Even so, bases such as Ulithi were absolutely essential; Hawaii was not nearly close enough.

U.S. conduct of the Pacific war demonstrated just how valuable naval mobility could be. The Japanese created what they thought was a defensive perimeter of islands. In fact it is virtually impossible to erect any such barrier against seaborne attack. During the weeks after Pearl Harbor, U.S. carrier task groups struck repeatedly at islands on the Japanese defensive perimeter. As in the Japanese attack on Pearl Harbor, it became painfully evident that carriers could literally vanish into the blue, to appear unexpectedly, strike, and then vanish again. At the very least, such operations convinced the Japanese to keep expanding in hopes of precluding further attacks. Given finite Japanese resources, such expansion could not be sustained. The ultimate raid was the famous April 1942 attack on Tokyo, mounted by U.S. Army bombers, normally land based, launched from the carrier *Hornet*. It probably was mounted primarily to maintain U.S. morale at a particularly dark time of the war, when the Japanese were completing their conquest of the Philippines. Yet it had enormous strategic effect, because the Japanese services considered any assault on Tokyo particularly unacceptable.

The raids convinced the Japanese that they had to destroy the U.S. carrier fleet once and for all; they had to seek a decisive battle. They sought it at Midway, the westernmost Hawaiian island, on the theory that the U.S. Navy would have to fight to defend it. As in the case of the bases, the point of the assault was not the intrinsic importance of the nominal target, but rather its naval significance, in this case as a target that would draw out the elusive U.S. fleet.

It is not clear to what extent the U.S. Navy of early 1942 welcomed such an encounter. Its leaders knew that within a year many more carriers, already under construction, would be entering service. On the other hand, the Japanese appeared unstoppable, and unless their carriers, the main engine of their advance, were destroyed, within a year they might have linked up with the

Germans in the Middle East, or attacked the U.S. west coast in strength. The U.S. Navy's doctrine was offensive; decades of War College classes had taught officers that naval wars could only be won by early offensive action. The histories of the Royal Navy in the Napoleonic wars showed that at times fighting spirit could make up for disparity in numbers. It was widely believed that carriers were virtually impossible to defend, therefore whoever found the enemy's carriers first would win.[33] Given the intelligence via code-breaking that the U.S. Navy enjoyed by mid-1942, there was a real possibility that its carriers could ambush a Japanese force. The U.S. view seems to have been that Midway might well be the best opportunity to win a decisive battle and, with it, the initiative in the Pacific. With the destruction of the Japanese carrier task force off Midway, the run of Japanese offensive sea-based operations, begun at Pearl Harbor and then extended in the Philippines and Malaya, effectively ended.

Also disastrous for the Japanese was the protracted battle in the Solomons, which, like Midway, began with the intent to expand the Japanese perimeter. Most of the Japanese carrier air arm not lost at Midway was expended in the Solomons. The Japanese disaster demonstrated once again that commitments on the ground take on a strength and intensity not related to the intrinsic or strategic value of that ground. The ultimate U.S. victory in the Solomons did not open the Japanese empire to any threat great enough to have justified the vast and irreplaceable sacrifices the Japanese made in 1942–43.

Despite these disasters, the idea that a chain of islands is somehow a barrier has persisted. The Chinese have clearly taken up the idea. Their official justification for building a fleet is that they must dominate first the inner and then the outer chains of islands off the Asian coast. Since the outer chain is thousands of miles offshore, roughly duplicating the World War II Japanese defensive chain, such requirements presumably imply a desire to dominate the Western Pacific. Stating them in terms of specific chains of islands, however, suggests a land-oriented mentality that bodes ill for Chinese naval development.

A Japanese View

Through the interwar period Japan painstakingly built a powerful navy capable of challenging the U.S. Navy even though Japan's economy was only a fraction as large. She could do so because the United States spent so little on defense between the two world wars. Just as important, naval technology was sufficiently static that steady Japanese investment could build power by accumulating ships. Naval aircraft technology certainly was not static, but aircraft were inexpensive, so they did not invalidate the idea. In the context of static technology, moreover, the Japanese could reasonably believe that specific technical surprises, such as excellent night optics and a super torpedo (the "Long Lance"), could be very effective.

If the U.S. government decided to do so, it could negate Japanese prewar investment simply by mobilizing its much larger economy. That began to happen in the late 1930s, and the Japanese navy began discussing the closing window of opportunity for successful war. During any lengthy war the United States, but not Japan, could easily make up losses. Also, probably because the United States did not militarize its economy, it was better able to develop new technologies that could bypass Japanese innovations. In effect the capital that would have produced new technology in Japan was consumed in producing the fruits of an older technology. One might, for example, equate the industrialization of Japan with iron and steel making technology and with iron and steel products such as ships and guns. By the 1930s the United States had added chemical and electronic industries, whereas Japanese investment in such areas was quite limited. The U.S. electronics industry was mobilized in wartime to produce radars, tactical radios, and sonars that the Japanese could not match, either in quality or in quantity. These new devices in turn made practical tactics that the Japanese could neither copy nor counter. The Cold War offered important parallels.[34]

Against such realities the Japanese could only oppose qualitative superiority. Their technical innovations were vulnerable to technological revolution, which the much larger and more advanced U.S. economy would almost inevitably produce. The Japanese also told themselves that their martial spirit made each Japanese the equal of several Westerners. On a less exalted plane, this meant that the Imperial navy trained hard and elaborately. Despite its professed indifference to human losses, it could not even make up its losses among such skilled groups as aircrew. Kamikaze tactics were mounted partly because the supply of trained pilots had largely run out.[35]

Two other key lessons of World War II for Japan were that land commitments tend to be open ended, and that it can be extremely difficult to achieve decisive results on land. The open-ended commitment was to the conquest of China. Once enmeshed there, in Manchuria, the Japanese found that they could not pull out. The Imperial army was unwilling to lose "face," and by 1936 it was quite capable of assassinating any politician who advocated withdrawal. Unable to achieve any sort of decision, the Japanese found themselves expanding the war, first from Manchuria to North China in 1937, and then to the seizure of the Western colonies in order to gain sole access to raw materials needed—to continue the war in China. Even the seizure of the Chinese capital, Peking (now Beijing), did not help; the Chinese government simply withdrew inland. Its territorial mass gave it immunity from military disaster similar to the protection the English Channel and the North Sea afforded Britain. The Chinese, like the British fighting Napoleon, had no hope of fielding a force powerful enough to secure victory. They could, however, reasonably expect that in trying to defeat them their enemy would keep expanding its war, eventually assaulting enemies that could win. Perhaps because the country was not heavily industrialized, there was no territorial loss that the Chinese considered crippling. In a way, this was the inverse of the Crimean War: the Japanese never could find a target so important that the Chinese would surrender rather than lose it. Surrender would have meant the loss of Chinese sovereignty, whereas in the Crimean War the czar surrendered relatively little. Japanese action in occupied China, moreover, convinced many Chinese that this was a fight to the death.

As in China, the Japanese were never quite sure how to end a war against the United States. They fell back on the hope that they could make counterattack so clearly expensive that the Americans, who they imagined were cowardly, would shrink from attempting it. Japanese who understood U.S. culture knew better. Admiral Yamamoto, who planned the Pearl Harbor attack, famously said that he could run wild for the first six months, that is, on the strength so painstakingly gathered, but that after that peace would be dictated in the White House.[36] Unlike Japan, the United States could be expected to regenerate its losses.

9

The Cold War as a Maritime War

THE WESTERN ALLIANCE that fought the Cold War was held together by sea routes, so the war necessarily had a significant maritime dimension. As in past conflicts, seapower offered the West a certain flexibility in applying pressure to the Soviets. On the other hand, Western dependence on the sea made Soviet acquisition of particular allies or client states particularly threatening. One great, and as yet unanswered, question of the Cold War was to what extent Soviet penetration of Africa and Southwest Asia was intended specifically to threaten crucial Western sea routes. For example, the lengthy Soviet courtship of Egypt could have been construed as a thrust to control the Suez Canal, and with it the tanker route between the oil states of the Middle East and Europe. On the other hand, President Gamal Abdul Nasser of Egypt had pretensions to leadership of the entire Arab world; by courting him the Soviets might well have imagined that they were approaching control of the oil itself.

The Cold War differed strikingly from earlier conflicts because actual fighting was quite limited. By the mid-1950s, both sides were acutely aware that nuclear and then thermonuclear weapons would make any war too devastating to contemplate. From a military point of view, mutual deterrence stalemated any direct conflict in Europe. It did not apply to the periphery, however. Virtually from the time of the Russian Revolution, the Soviets saw in the European colonial empires (later the independent states of the Third World) a major opportunity. Populations were often dissatisfied with the West.

They might be won over to Communism. Because the colonies and their successor independent states provided many of the crucial raw materials on which the West depended, it could be argued that an apparently peripheral approach through these countries would ultimately undermine the West without the risk of central war. Thus peripheral wars and the political subversion that often substituted for actual warfare were a major Cold War theme. Western access to the Third World was overwhelmingly seaborne. Most actual fighting during the Cold War was generally by Western expeditionary forces supported from the sea. In some cases, such as wars in Africa, Soviet or proxy access was also by sea. The effect of mutual deterrence was that neither side could afford to block the other's seaborne access. Peripheral conflicts included the Korean and Vietnam wars, the Malayan insurgency, and the confrontation between Britain and Australia on one side and Indonesia, acting as something of a Chinese proxy, on the other.[1]

Mutual deterrence did change the character of the main conflict. Both sides partly shaped their decisions according to their perceptions of what would likely happen if war broke out—and also of whether the other side was willing to chance such a war. Both sides built their military forces to fight the hot war that would have broken out if deterrence had failed, and debates over appropriate military forces focused on how well they might function in the event of war.

The difference between cold and hot wars might be likened to the difference between the two games, chess and poker, often used as models for warfare. Chess can be compared to a more formalized war, in which combat actually occurs, and the game ends in victory that is achieved by annihilating the enemy, or at the least threatening the enemy's king with certain annihilation. Poker is a game of perceptions; rarely are all the cards shown. Players act on their perceptions of what cards their opponents hold, and of their opponents' willingness to keep betting. Chess is a game of position; poker is largely a game of intentions, in which a player with a weak hand can often win by making his position appear much stronger. Nuclear weapons made a chesslike fight to the finish far too suicidal to contemplate. There was always, however, the possibility that one side or the other might be able to fight and win, using some new kind of technology or tactics. The content of nuclear poker, then, was each side's guesses about the other's capabilities, which might or might not be demonstrated realistically in exercises and in peripheral combat.

The sea was particularly important in this context. Naval forces often do not persuade by destroying other forces but rather by indicating their ability to destroy. That is why the British fleet in the Baltic in 1856 proved so persuasive to the Russians—without actually putting to the test its ability to take St. Petersburg. It was far safer to demonstrate resolve at sea than on a heavily fortified border in Europe, not least because the demonstration could be private, so neither side would lose much face in the process. That could even apply in the context of an ongoing war.

Europe

One of the great strategic questions of the Cold War was how NATO could stop a Soviet invasion of Europe, assuming that the Soviets had decided to gamble that invasion would not invite a disastrous nuclear escalation. If NATO answered a non-nuclear Soviet attack with a massive nuclear riposte, the Soviet counterstroke might well destroy much of Western Europe. NATO strategists eventually fixed on an alternative: if non-nuclear NATO forces could not stop the Soviets, then NATO would fire a nuclear "shot across the bows," a very few (perhaps only one) nuclear warheads intended to prove to the Soviets that much worse might happen. The hope was that the sobered-up Soviets would call a halt. Unfortunately even a single nuclear weapon exploded on land, necessarily within the prewar NATO borders, would be quite devastating to NATO territory. The "shot across the bows" would probably have been fired at sea.[2]

Alongside nuclear poker was another, subtler, game. One side might collapse without war, due to economic exhaustion or to ideological attack. For example, in the late 1940s there were very strong Communist parties in France and Italy. The Soviets confronted Western Europe with a large army, and it could be argued that unless the Western Europeans rearmed, they could be overrun at Stalin's whim. On the other hand, the economies of Western Europe had been ruined by World War II. Any massive rearmament would further depress living conditions. Voters might well prefer to elect Communist governments rather than accept that fate. Thus a central problem of early Western Cold War strategy was how to buy enough military force to deter the Soviets without buying so much that an economic collapse would occur, leading to a Soviet political victory. Stalin did not face the same dilemma because he could coerce his population. Ultimately it turned out that Stalin's successors could not manage the same degree of coercion. What seemed, about 1948, to be a prescription for the collapse of the West was actually the prescription, about four decades later, for a Soviet collapse: too much military might bought at the cost of a disastrous economic slide.

Both in peace and in a possible war, the West depended heavily on control of sea routes. The great question, as in World War I, was whether Western seapower could go any further to defeat the Soviets if war broke out. From the perspective of armed competition, this question translated into a questions of leverage. How much could Western seapower burden the Soviet economy by forcing the Soviets to maintain expensive kinds of forces, or to shift forces away from places in which they most threatened NATO territory? To what extent could NATO naval forces substitute for other more expensive NATO forces? Also, to what extent could Western seapower increase the degree of deterrence the Soviets might feel? The Soviets could ask the same questions in reverse. Just like the pre-1914 Germans, they could wonder whether it would be wise to buy ships instead of, for example, armored divisions.

As in the world wars, the United States fought the Cold War to prevent a hostile power, in this case the Soviet Union, from taking over so much of the world's productive capacity that it could menace the United States. At the end of World War II, the Soviets seized one of the main productive centers, Central Europe. The fear was that they would also seize Western Europe and, perhaps, Japan. Thus the Cold War was fought specifically to keep the Soviets out of Western Europe. Because this area was so valuable, and because it was still in friendly hands at the outset, in a strategic sense the Cold War was more like World War I than the Napoleonic wars or World War II.

Fought under largely peacetime rules, there could be no direct naval action between the principal combatants during the Cold War. In essence, however, NATO and the other major Western states formed a maritime alliance against a land power. The strategy for such action is that the maritime partner seeks coalition partners who, working together, exhaust the land power they border. Until the early 1970s there was only one vital front in the Cold War, in Europe, and the Soviets could concentrate their forces there. The European NATO states could never match the sheer strength of the Soviet army and associated air force facing them, and over time this threat demoralized them. Both in France and in Italy, Communists enjoyed substantial electoral success. There was a fear that initiatives like Germany's Ostpolitik would lead to the neutralization of Western Europe, a prelude to a gradual takeover that would ensure a Soviet victory in the Cold War. The presence of U.S. armed forces became less and less important, and in any case they were there by invitation, not by right of arms. If Western Europe slid into neutrality, U.S. forces would simply be ejected. The situation worsened in the early 1970s because the sheer cost of the war in Vietnam, a very peripheral part of the

Cold War, made it more and more difficult for the United States to retain strong forces in Western Europe, where they were thought to stiffen European resolve.

China and Taiwan

A second Cold War front was developing. The Sino-Soviet relationship had always been somewhat tense. The Chinese resented being junior to the Soviets, and they particularly resented Stalin's willingness, even eagerness, to bleed them during the Korean War he precipitated. In 1957 Mao Tse-tung broke with Stalin's successor, Nikita S. Khrushchev, ostensibly over Khrushchev's unwillingness to support Communist expansion via revolutionary war. In fact the main opportunities for revolution were in East Asia, and in effect Khrushchev was denying Mao the chance to form his own Communist empire there. The clear implication was that Khrushchev's ultimate goal was to subordinate China. Mao would have none of it. Initially the split between the two main Communist powers allowed smaller parties, such as that of North Vietnam, to deny Khrushchev's ban on revolutionary war; thus the Vietnam War itself can be blamed on the Sino-Soviet split. Ultimately, however, the Chinese had to find a coalition partner capable of dealing with the Soviets. Only the technologically advanced Americans filled the bill. Mao responded warmly in 1972 when President Richard Nixon proposed reopening relations.

This was coalition, not alliance. Nixon was feeling the after-effects of Vietnam. Anything that tied down the Soviets would reduce the pressure in Europe. For his part, Mao was beginning to see a massive Soviet buildup on his border. Anything applying pressure elsewhere (e.g., deterring a Western European slide into neutralism) would make it more difficult for the Soviets to threaten him. There was also a significant naval dimension. The U.S. Seventh Fleet, with its three or more carriers, was the strongest mobile striking force in the Far East. The Chinese themselves were poorly armed. Soviet forces could overrun them, leaving them only the option of a World War II–style guerilla warfare that they called a "people's war." If the Soviets had to take the Seventh Fleet into consideration, however, they could not begin a war unless they had transferred more sophisticated forces to the Far East and built up the infrastructure to support those forces. From a U.S. point of view, of course, the Soviet military was finite even though large; anything moved to the east was permanently removed from the threat to Western Europe. By the 1980s, the United States was actively promoting Chinese military modernization, in hopes of worsening the strain on the Soviets.

This type of coalition squeeze had often won in the past. The difference this time was that it was applied in very slow motion. The coalition with China exhibited the problems of other coalitions: the two partners had different objectives. The Chinese agreed with the Americans that it was vital to contain the Soviets. However, before becoming coalition partners they had been antagonists, in Korea and then in Vietnam. American seapower had helped prevent Mao from completing his Chinese Civil War victory by seizing Taiwan.[3] In 1958 it even prevented him from taking Quemoy and Matsu, which were much closer to the Chinese coast than Taiwan. The 1958 confrontation was notable because it showed the Chinese just how much of the Cold War was bluff. Their own coalition partner, the Soviet Union, initially threatened nuclear war over the islands, then quickly backed down under U.S. pressure. Mao interpreted the backdown as proof of Soviet duplicity. Had he possessed sufficient seapower of his own, presumably the United States might have backed down rather than risk war and potential escalation. In this case, U.S. seapower placed the onus on Mao and the Soviets.[4]

Mao may have imagined that the United States would sell out Taiwan to gain him as a coalition partner. By the time he was being courted, however, the United States had been allied with the Chinese Nationalist government on Taiwan for more than two decades. The shadowy Cold War confrontation with the Soviets presented the U.S. government with much less pressure than a fast-moving war, and any desertion of the old alliance would have been difficult to sell to the U.S. populace. Moreover, Taiwan was becoming a major trading partner. The U.S. solution was to drop recognition of the Chinese Nationalist government on Taiwan as the legitimate government of China, but to continue to supply that government with defensive weapons—and to tell the Chinese Communists that no violent solution of the "Taiwan problem" would be tolerated.

This policy was viable because of seapower. Taiwan is separated from the Chinese mainland by a wide strait. There was never any possibility that Communist troops could simply infiltrate across. The Communists would have had to mount a massive invasion. As Taiwan became wealthier, due to the economic advantages of sea transportation, the country could afford sufficient naval forces to preclude such an assault. As in other naval confrontations, much depended on whether the continental power, in this case Communist China, could concentrate on naval forces. In effect the Soviets were vital if unwitting coalition partners to Taiwan, because the Chinese had to maintain strong ground forces to resist a possible Soviet land attack. They also needed ground forces to maintain security in large parts of China, such as Sinkiang and Tibet. Another drain on Communist Chinese military resources was the need to build and maintain strategic nuclear forces to bluff the Soviets (and the United States) so China could maintain her freedom of action. Thus, even after the United States had dropped the mutual security treaty with Taiwan, she remained an important coalition partner, imposing on the Communist Chinese high costs that precluded development of the sort of seapower required to successfully overrun the island. Moreover, the United States was the source of much of the technology that Taiwan needed to maintain security against seaborne invasion. All these considerations continue to remain valid today.

For example, just as the Chinese built a strategic attack force to limit U.S. freedom of action, at the beginning of the twenty-first century Americans were considering erection of a national missile defense that would cancel out that advantage. Would the system work? This is poker, not chess. What matters more is how the Chinese Communists see it. When they speak of American reluctance to trade Los Angeles for Taipei, they mean that Americans will not enter a crisis for fear of their nuclear threat. If they destroy Los Angeles, the United States has the firepower to destroy a large part of China. They sense that Americans will not chance the loss of a major city, whereas they will be perceived as sufficiently cold-blooded to take exactly that chance. It may be that by devaluing the Chinese strategic threat, a U.S. defensive system will cancel out this perception. Its real effect, then, will be to reinforce the stated U.S. position, demonstrated in 1996, of rejecting any Chinese invasion of Taiwan. That position in turn is feasible because it can be enforced by mobile U.S. naval forces, without emplacing troops in Taiwan and thus intervening directly in the drawn-out continuation of the Chinese Civil War.

From a Taiwanese point of view, the U.S. ability to intervene is welcome, but U.S. ground troops would be a much stronger deterrent to Chinese action. Any Communist assault would probably cause U.S. casualties, hence the United States would be brought into the war. From an American point of view, no such commitment is possible. When the U.S. government decided to bring Communist China into the Cold War as a coalition partner, it necessarily abandoned any direct defense position on Taiwan. It also escaped any inevitable involvement in a future war in the Taiwan Straits. The situation is typical of coalitions. Assistance limited to aid plus possible naval involvement allows the U.S. government to control the level of commitment. However, it also sends a signal that the United States can be deterred altogether.

The situation still affects Russia. The current Chinese regime justifies its rule of China largely on its commitment to regain the territory wrested from it by various imperialists. Thus the return of Hong Kong and Macao were major triumphs. Taiwan is advertised as territory stolen first by the Japanese and then by the Americans. Much larger swaths of Chinese territory were taken by the Russian czars, however, beginning in the seventeenth century. If the Chinese interest in Taiwan ends, for example, in recovery, their eyes may turn north toward Siberia and its rich resources. A weak Russia presumably benefits as long as the Chinese government focuses on Taiwan, just as Taiwan benefits as long as the Chinese feel that they must maintain a large army to secure their border with the Russians, and possibly to threaten to extend that border.

U.S. seapower, then, helped maintain the economic strain the Cold War Soviets felt in the Far East. Given seapower, the United States could form a coalition with the Communist Chinese without selling out Taiwan, a course of action that would probably have been impossible for internal political reasons. U.S. seapower helped convince the Communist Chinese that they could fight and survive a war against the Soviets, as well as convincing the Soviets that the United States really would back the Chinese.

Afghanistan

U.S. seapower made it possible to support the Afghan guerillas, whose success helped destabilize the Soviet state. Afghanistan is land-locked, but the key to the guerillas' success was arms shipped via Pakistan and, to a lesser extent, China. Thus the war gained a maritime dimension. The Pakistanis in particular always had to fear retaliation; the Soviets were well aware of the source of the weapons frustrating them. They knew the United States could move powerful forces into Southwest Asia to support them. Indeed, the likelihood of such support made it improbable that the Soviets would intervene. In 1980 the United States established a maritime prepositioning force in the Indian Ocean specifically to help deal with any further Soviet thrust south. Reassuring the Pakistanis, initial air support would have come from a carrier newly assigned to the area. A historian might liken the situation to British support for Napoleon's "Spanish ulcer," although in this case no Western army was employed.

For that matter, the Chinese could afford to join a Western coalition because they enjoyed maritime access to the West, and because a strong Western force operating in their waters encouraged them. U.S. maritime access to

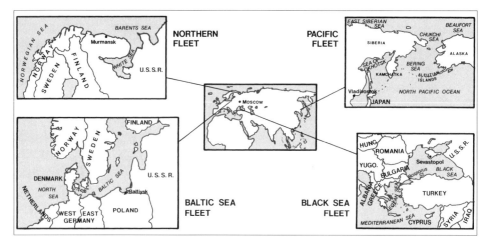

Soviet naval geography during the Cold War. Maps of Cold War Soviet naval bases show NATO's enormous geographic advantage. The four Soviet fleets (Baltic, Northern, Pacific, and Black Sea) were separated so widely that they could not unite tactically. In the 1970s some U.S. strategists argued that the Soviets would find it difficult to shift forces from the Pacific to Europe, thus in wartime the U.S. Pacific Fleet should unite with the Atlantic Fleet to provide sufficient combat power in the crucial theater of war. The counterargument was that the land-based bombers attached to the fleets could shift from fleet to fleet, and that Pacific Fleet submarines could transit the Soviet Arctic to join the Northern Fleet. It was important, even from a merely naval point of view, to retain a powerful Pacific force. The inability to unite the separated U.S. fleets in wartime in turn implied that overall U.S. naval strength was insufficient to fight the Soviets, and helped justify the buildup of the battle force during the Reagan administration. None of the Soviet fleets enjoyed unhindered access to the open sea. The Baltic Fleet bases were at Leningrad (now St. Petersburg), near Finland and Baltiysk (shown); the fleet had to pass through the Danish Straits to get to the North Sea. The Northern Fleet, based on the Kola Peninsula, near Murmansk, had to pass down the Norwegian Sea, through the Greenland–Iceland–United Kingdom gap into the North Atlantic. The Pacific Fleet had its main submarine base at Petropavlovsk on Kamchatka, near U.S. territory (the Aleutians). The main surface base, Vladivostok, is blocked by the Japanese home islands. A major shipbuilding plant, Komsomolsk on the Amur, was on the Chinese border, hence it was vulnerable to Chinese enmity. The Black Sea fleet was blocked by the Turkish Straits. During the Cold War, the United States provided minelayers to Denmark and Turkey specifically to enable them to seal in the Baltic and Black Sea fleets. For their part, the Soviets assigned Polish units specifically to overrun Denmark both to open the Danish Straits and to cover the seaward flank of their planned ground advance through West Germany. The U.S. Navy planned an amphibious counterattack in Denmark (Jutland). *U.S. Naval Institute*

Western Europe encouraged Europeans who might otherwise have felt entirely at Soviet mercy. The two U.S. carriers in the Mediterranean were the mainstay of NATO striking power for the southern European command.[5] Considered sovereign U.S. territory, these ships were rendered immune from certain kinds of political assault. For example, they did not have to be withdrawn when France quit the NATO military command structure in 1966. Similarly, NATO naval strike forces in the Atlantic provided the alliance with a military depth it would have lost altogether if all its theater striking forces had been at bases ashore.

Naval measures, however, did not solve all the problems. By the early 1960s there was a real fear that Soviet submarines would be able to cut off early reinforcement of NATO. The U.S. solution was to stockpile unit-configured equipment in Germany, to mate with troops flown in from the United States if or when necessary.[6] Because it was generally believed that West Germany was filled with spies and Soviet agents, many wondered whether the stockpiles had much chance of surviving sabotage.[7]

The Cuban Missile Crisis

Both the main Cold War combatants, the United States and the Soviet Union, were restrained by fear of nuclear war, so the battles of the war (e.g., the Korean and Vietnam wars) generally involved proxies on at least one side, if not both. There were, however, several naval confrontations that the governments may have been willing to risk on the theory that they could not escalate directly to nuclear war ashore. The best-known was the embargo the United States imposed against Cuba in 1962, at the height of the missile crisis. Embargo was useful to the U.S. government as an alternative to either a military assault on the island, which might risk Soviet use of nuclear weapons and further disastrous escalation, or humiliating surrender. Establishing a quarantine zone around Cuba proved that the U.S. government was doing something, but as long as it was not contested by the much weaker Soviet navy, it was unlikely to lead to war.

For his part, the creator of the modern Soviet navy, Adm. Sergei Gorshkov, claimed that he had protected the Soviet and Cuban operation in Angola from American intervention by interposing a Soviet surface group. He used the incident as proof that building up the Soviet navy would support Soviet state objectives abroad. The Angolan crisis erupted at just about the time the United States was finally being ejected from Vietnam. In a deeply anti-Vietnam mood, Congress cut off money for Angola for fear that it would develop into another Vietnam. The presence of the Soviet ships was virtually unremarked.

More recent embargoes, off Iraq from 1990 on and in the Adriatic against Serbia, have had similar content to the 1962 embargo against the Soviets in Cuba. Whether or not they are actually effective in weakening the target, they demonstrate action at a time when anything more aggressive may be unacceptable. In the case of Iraq, the advantage of an embargo was that it could be enforced while support was built for actual combat. If nothing at all had been done, it might appear to many that the West had backed off, then staged its own aggression against Iraq. On a small scale, then, the use of embargo recalls the basic rules of maritime warfare: while using the sea for very controlled action, build a coalition that has sufficient weight to win. In this case, too, the naval action bought time to put a large U.S. army force in place.

There were many other examples of the Cold War leverage offered by naval forces. For example, for the first few years of the Cold War, the U.S. carrier force in the Mediterranean was often more powerful than any of the air forces of the littoral powers. In 1948, when Yugoslavia's Josip Broz Tito bolted from Stalin, the latter imposed an arms embargo that soon crippled Tito's air force. The Soviets actively planned an invasion of Yugoslavia by their proxies. They would have needed the air superiority denied them by the presence of the Mediterranean carriers. Tito's defection was extremely important to the West. Among other things, it convinced Stalin that his allies were unreliable, and thus led him to order a crippling purge of senior East European Communists in 1951, at a time when he was contemplating war in Europe. Stalin clearly saw Mao as a possible second Tito, and the measures he took to bind Mao to him ultimately led to Mao's defection and to the creation of the devastating second front against the Soviets. Stalin was a deeply suspicious man, so perhaps he would have tried to cripple Mao whether or not he had the example of Tito before him. Tito's defection certainly crystallized his thinking, however.

The Mediterranean

The Mediterranean became the main venue for U.S.-Soviet naval confrontation. The prize was Egypt, the most populous country in the Arab world, through which the vital Suez Canal ran. Initially the Soviets courted the Egyptians with arms. The Israeli air force smashed most of the Egyptian air force at the outbreak of war in 1967. To save face, the Egyptians claimed that the damage had actually been done by the U.S. Sixth Fleet. After the Israeli victory, the Soviets established a Mediterranean fleet, the Fifth Eskadra. In theory the new fleet would protect the Egyptians and other Soviet clients from any repeat performance. The Soviets convinced the Egyptian dictator, Gamal Abdel Nasser, to allow them to base it at Alexandria, the old British base. At least in theory, that gave them a valuable foothold in Egypt. The price was continuing support for Nasser's ongoing fight with the Israelis, including risky direct Soviet engagement in the war of attrition along the Suez Canal in 1970–71.

To the extent that the main wartime mission of the Sixth Fleet was to strike the southern Soviet Union, maintaining the Fifth Eskadra in the Mediterranean was a way of protecting the southern Soviet flank in that event. Without any defensible base, the Eskadra would not have lasted long (just as the German overseas force did not last long in World War I), but even so it might have made a valuable contribution. As it was, in 1972 the Egyptians ejected the Soviets, leaving them with much less satisfactory bases in Syria and in Libya.

In October 1973 the Egyptians and the Syrians attacked Israel. When the Soviets learned what they planned to do, their first decision was not to become involved militarily. They would resupply their clients, but they would not risk anything more. They feared that, whatever the outcome, they would be ejected from the Middle East. If the Arabs lost, they would blame inferior Soviet equipment. If they won, they would feel so confident that they would no longer need Soviet support. Moreover, they might well feel that they had won through American restraint applied to Israel.

Using the Fifth Eskadra the Soviets could support the Arabs without risking open-ended costs. Through the war it trailed the Sixth Fleet, and there was a real fear in the U.S. formation that a battle would be fought. From the Soviet point of view, this was ideal. To the extent that the Arabs blamed the United States, and particularly the Sixth Fleet, for their problems, the Soviet fleet was neutralizing that threat. The Soviets were perfectly aware that the Sixth Fleet would have little to do with Israeli success on the ground, so the risks were minimal. Ultimately Soviet fears were realized, to the extent that the Egyptians turned toward the United States. Their naval operation, however, probably helped keep Syria and Libya as clients, and thus kept the Soviets in the Middle East.

The Korean War

The most famous case of naval intervention during the Cold War is undoubtedly Korea. In June 1950 the North Koreans crossed the border and the opposing South Korean army, with a few U.S. advisors, effectively collapsed. U.S. units fed into the war from the occupation army in Japan fared badly, so much so that analysts thought the Communists had found a new way of creating a first-class army from scratch. Within weeks the surviving U.S. and South Korean forces had been packed into a small area around Pusan, in the extreme south of the country. The bulk of the North Korean forces had followed. They could not easily be redeployed.

The United States and her allies, however, controlled the sea around Korea. In September, a powerful U.S. force landed at Inchon, well in the North Koreans' rear, and close to the South Korean capital of Seoul. The North Korean force besieging Pusan broke and ran; it took about a year to rebuild the North Korean army, and even then it was used only sparingly. The war did not end, however, because the Chinese entered on the North Koreans' side.

The question then was whether any sort of pressure, comparable to the Inchon landing, could be applied in the Chinese rear. Because the United States controlled the air and sea approaches to China, special forces could be (and were) inserted. The hope was that many Chinese, who had supported the losing side in the recently ended Chinese civil war, could be induced to rise, thus tying down Chinese ground forces that might otherwise have been sent to Korea. In fact the efforts turned out to be monuments mainly to the amateurism of the new U.S. Central Intelligence Agency (CIA), which promoted them, but no efforts could have been made at all without sea access to China.

Perhaps the most interesting lesson of the Korean War was that even a small involvement on the ground can grow into a commitment far beyond the intrinsic value of the place involved. As in World War II, U.S. Cold War policy made Europe the primary theater of operations. If the U.S. force had been defeated in Korea, however, the loss of prestige might well have depressed Western Europeans. At this time NATO forces appeared far weaker than their Soviet opponents; the equalizing tactical nuclear weapons had not yet been deployed. It did not help that the local commander, Gen. Douglas MacArthur, demanded that wherever he was fighting become the central theater of war. Even though the Truman administration resisted MacArthur's pleas, and ultimately fired him because he went public with them, it did funnel much of the small U.S. Army into a peripheral country. So much of the army was in Korea that there was a real fear that any military disaster there would cripple the army as a whole by destroying too much of its officer corps and its key force of noncommissioned officers.

The Korean experience probably helped demonstrate to Truman's successor, former Gen. Dwight D. Eisenhower, that the Soviets could manipulate their proxies to mount further peripheral ground wars that could tie down U.S. forces and suck up valuable U.S. resources. President Eisenhower's secretary of state, John Foster Dulles, announced what amounted to a parallel maritime-flavored strategy: the United States would respond to further aggression by the Soviets at places of its own choice. One translation was that using a proxy like Kim Il Sung would not necessarily shelter the Soviet Union itself from the resulting war. The forces involved would be American, and such peripheral attacks were practical only because the United States and the West in general enjoyed maritime supremacy, including the free use of the seas around the Soviet Eurasian empire. For Eisenhower, American strategic firepower, mainly air force nuclear-armed bombers, guaranteed that the Soviets would not lightly begin a major war, either by attacking the United States directly or by invading Western Europe. For the peripheral role, Eisenhower built up the U.S. Navy and the U.S. Marines.

For Eisenhower, Korea also demonstrated just how dangerous a ground commitment could be. His solution was to shrink the U.S. Army, stating that any future ground commitment ought to be a coalition operation, in which U.S. liability would be strictly limited. The army argued that its forces were needed in Europe, mainly to offer initial resistance to a Soviet attack as a way of limiting any need to escalate to nuclear warfare. The argument recalls the British army's statement made in 1911: a bit of a ground commitment would save the day. Eisenhower doubted that a few more U.S. divisions would make much impression on the 175 Soviet divisions. A large U.S. ground force would merely be a temptation for some future administration to become committed somewhere in the Third World, where the extra divisions could be expected to make a difference. The reconstruction of the U.S. Army under President John F. Kennedy certainly paralleled interest in intervention in South Vietnam.

The Vietnam War

One irony of Vietnam was that Kennedy, when he was asked why he was willing to fight there instead of in Laos, said that Vietnam was much closer to the

sea, hence much more subject to U.S. naval action. In fact a key line of communication to the Communist army in South Vietnam ran, not along the
coast, but through Laos, to the west. Sea-based forces could certainly strike
targets anywhere in North or South Vietnam, but one key to the war was surrendered when the United States failed to resist Communist control of key
parts of Laos. Eisenhower's administration had built up strong relations with
Thailand, which bordered Laos, presumably in the understanding of just
how important this geography could be. The Kennedy administration apparently missed this point; Thai forces were not called in to help stop the Communist advance in Laos. In effect, Eisenhower understood that U.S. seapower
had to be backed by a coalition partner in a strategic position. The United
States could supply Thailand from the sea, and the Thai army could help cut
the Ho Chi Minh Trail. From a political point of view, there was a vast difference between direct U.S. support for South Vietnam and support by a
wide coalition of local powers, all of whom actually did feel threatened by the
North Vietnamese. Kennedy did understand that seapower and sea-based airpower were the most deployable U.S. assets, but he did not understand that
they could not suffice, because the guerillas fighting in South Vietnam relied
heavily on land lines of communication; their materiel needs were not great
enough to necessitate sea transportation. The enclaves U.S. seapower could
maintain were unlike the enclave into which U.S. and Korean forces had
retreated early in the Korean War, because there was no analog to Inchon.

There was one pressure point, however. North Vietnam produced very
little of what it used in combat. Weapons had to come from the Soviet Union
and China. Modern equipment, which was needed to defend against U.S. air
attacks, came from the Soviet Union. By 1972 the Soviets were less and less
willing to ship materiel through China by rail, because the Chinese were seizing many of the weapons and copying them. By this time the Soviets feared
war with China. The North Vietnamese port of Haiphong became more and
more important. The United States was reluctant to attack the port for fear of
antagonizing the Soviets. However, in 1972 the Nixon administration wanted
to apply sufficient pressure to force the North Vietnamese to bargain, to end
the war. Haiphong was the obvious pressure point, and it was bombed and
mined. Meanwhile U.S. aircraft attacked North Vietnam. In the air battle, the
North Vietnamese expended most of their missiles on hand; the mining of
Haiphong cut them off from resupply. They were now almost completely open
to air attack. To avoid disaster, they negotiated. This outcome was acceptable
partly because the United States demanded only the limited concession of a

truce in South Vietnam. That would leave open the option of resuming the war later, after the United States withdrew entirely from South Vietnam, which is what happened. The 1972 attack was a textbook example of the value of seaborne interdiction when the enemy is forced to expend his materiel at a high rate.

During the war, U.S. dominance of the sea did offer another possibility. Through much of the Vietnam War, the United States maintained a powerful amphibious strike force in the Tonkin Gulf. At least in theory, it could have landed troops in North Vietnam itself, threatening the state; the North Vietnamese should have held powerful forces back against exactly that contingency. To what extent they did so is unclear. Certainly they feared a U.S. invasion during their own Tet offensive, and they made probing attacks to see whether the United States would react that way. Today it is known that as early as 1965 the United States secretly assured the Chinese that it would never invade North Vietnam, the object being to preclude something like the Chinese intervention in Korea. We also know that the North Vietnamese demanded and received assurances from the Chinese that they would intervene if the United States invaded. What is not yet clear is whether the Vietnamese were ever aware of the 1965 U.S. assurances. For that matter, they may well not have trusted any reports they received.

Vietnam was a peripheral conflict within a wider Cold War. Throughout the war, U.S. government spokesmen emphasized that they were fighting simply to guarantee the survival of a small country in the face of Communist aggression, that Vietnam had no intrinsic value to the West. In other words, the fight was entirely idealistic.[8] The war proved Eisenhower's assertion: U.S. commitment on the ground, with little coalition support, is virtually limitless. Once major ground forces had been committed, the outcome could be expected to have a disproportionate effect on U.S. prestige. The war would inevitably devour U.S. resources, no matter how peripheral it was. Whether or not the United States won, any such concentration would (and in this case, did) give the main enemy, the Soviet Union, an enormous opportunity to build forces threatening the United States while U.S. energies were focused on a local problem.[9]

Yet it can also be argued that the Western alliance could not easily have withstood a continuing series of territorial losses, even on the periphery, if it was not matched by any obvious gains. Too often the rule appeared to be that "what was theirs was theirs, but what was ours was negotiable." A student of the success of maritime strategy against Napoleon would conclude that the key

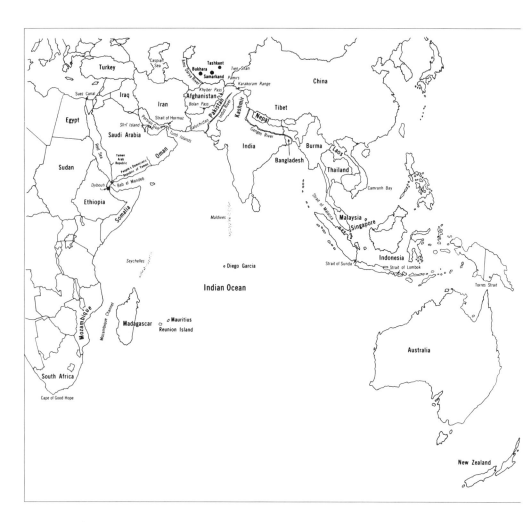

U.S. tasks were to preserve the coalition it led and to preserve public morale for the long run. In the early 1970s, just after the disaster in Vietnam, many people felt that the Soviets had the momentum and that the West, or at least the United States, was clearly on the defensive. Moreover, continuing U.S. concentration on Vietnam endangered the U.S.-led coalition, because the main allies, who were European, did not see it as a proper Cold War focus. In their view, the Cold War was about Europe. Cynics might say they had lost their global focus with their empires, or they secretly enjoyed watching the United States, which had thrown them out of their empires, embroiled in a colonial war.

Soviet threats to maritime routes during the Cold War. Through the 1970s the Soviets acquired control of territory beyond the NATO choke points, just as the Germans acquired colonies outside Europe before World War I. In each case, the new territory presented potential threats to vital maritime routes. When the Suez Canal was closed in 1967, the vital tanker traffic to Europe shifted from the Mediterranean to the route around Africa. Soviet influence in Mozambique and in the Seychelles became potentially threatening, although the Soviets never built naval bases in either country. The tanker route through the Red Sea passed between Soviet-leaning People's Republic of Yemen (Aden) and Soviet-leaning Ethiopia, which displaced Somalia as a client state. The Soviets established a base in Somalia, and their warships sometimes operated from Aden. American strategists feared that the Soviet assault on Afghanistan was a first step toward the Persian Gulf, the other tanker route, or toward Pakistan, which effectively blocks the mouth of the Persian Gulf. Further east, in the early 1960s the Soviets sought control of Indonesia, which lies athwart the tanker route to Japan through the Malacca Straits. Cam Ranh Bay, which the Soviets used as a base after the fall of South Vietnam, lies athwart the same route. The great question, never resolved, was whether the pattern of support to particular client states, including support of the revolutionaries who gained control for the Soviets, reflected a maritime strategy. For example, it now appears that the push into Afghanistan was done in defense of a Soviet-oriented revolution that was encountering serious trouble. Of course, if the Soviet-backed regime had gained full control of Afghanistan, its success might well have engendered revolutions farther south, and the Soviets would surely have been tempted to follow the old czarist path toward the Gulf.
U.S. Naval Institute

Navies in Wartime Strategy

The other aspect of the Cold War was the shadow war that would have been fought if deterrence had failed. Throughout, there were two quite divergent approaches. As in World War II, the U.S. Army argued that the key was to place a force in Western Europe strong enough to stop a mass Soviet assault; when no such force could be built, NATO came to rely on tactical nuclear weapons. In this view the role of maritime forces was mainly to maintain the sea communications keeping the army on the Central Front alive. In the late 1940s the U.S. Air Force espoused a variant, in which the point of the navy was to support the bases, mainly in Britain, from which it would mount a decisive strategic (i.e., nuclear) air offensive. On this basis, in 1948–49 both the U.S. Army and the new U.S. Air Force argued that the U.S. Navy should concentrate on sea control, specifically antisubmarine warfare.

The U.S. Navy espoused a radically different strategy, which foreshadowed the maritime strategy of the Reagan administration.[10] It argued that a small army enjoying seaborne mobility could effectively disrupt the flanks of any Soviet army advancing through Europe. Given their combination of mobility and sea-based security, carrier aircraft could strike at that army's supply lines, quite possibly slowing or stopping it. As for antisubmarine warfare, the new types of submarines might well make classical convoy operations difficult or impossible. It would be well worthwhile, however, to expend some of the scarce new atomic bombs against Soviet submarine bases, thus destroying the threat at source. To this end the U.S. Navy planned a new generation of heavy aircraft carriers. This latter argument exemplified the idea that sea control and power projection can be two sides of the same coin, rather than opposites. These arguments were rejected in 1948–49, but they show how a powerful navy sees the problem of war against a continental power. Harking back to the Napoleonic wars and to the Crimean War, the emphasis was on flanking attacks with a very mobile army.

Gen. Dwight D. Eisenhower became the first NATO supreme commander in 1950. His wartime experience, including the main European invasions, had taught him how valuable maritime mobility could be. In effect he accepted the navy's arguments espoused just a few years earlier. He saw Western Europe as a peninsula, and remarked that his forces were or could be in place on its flanks, in the United Kingdom and in the Mediterranean. The deeper the Soviets penetrated into that peninsula, the more vulnerable they would be to flanking attacks.

Naval Geography

Naval geography enormously favored the West. Almost all Soviet outlets to the wider oceans led to choke points under Western control: the Greenland–Iceland–United Kingdom (GIUK) gap from the northern fleet base on the Kola Peninsula, the Danish Straits leading out of the Baltic, the Dardanelles leading from the Black Sea, and the straits leading out of the Sea of Japan, which faces the main Pacific fleet base at Vladivostok. Because the outlet from the Baltic was so narrow, the Soviets put most of their offensive strength into the Northern Fleet; in wartime they did plan to overrun Denmark to open the straits, however. The situation in the Turkish Straits was so bad that the Soviets did not bother to run submarines through them from the Black Sea to the Mediterranean. Instead, they deployed submarines from the Northern Fleet, which thus had to pass through at least two NATO choke points, the GIUK gap and the Straits of Gibraltar. Those going to the Eastern Mediterranean had to pass through a third, the Sicilian Narrows. Only the submarine base at Petropavlovsk in Kamchatka on the Pacific was not directly blocked, but its exits lay near the U.S.-owned Aleutians. Thus, at the least, submarine traffic out of Petropavlovsk could be monitored and submarines trailed (or attacked) as they went to sea; the Aleutians, therefore, were nearly as good as a choke point.

The West never had as many submarines as the Soviets, but geography would place Western antisubmarine forces in just those choke points Soviet submarines would have to pass through en route to patrol stations in the open Atlantic and Pacific. Submarines carry limited numbers of weapons. Even if they are nuclear powered, then, they have to reach bases periodically in order to rearm. In a protracted naval war, any one Soviet submarine would presumably have to pass back and forth through a choke point dominated by the West; each time it would face a reasonable chance of being destroyed. The Soviets were aware of the problem, and several times during the Cold War they planned to build submarines specifically to supply their attack submarines at sea. Resources, however, were limited. The prototype supply submarine actually ordered was cancelled in favor of more vital strategic missile craft.

Western possession of the choke points was precisely analogous to the British position in the great wars leading up and through the Napoleonic wars, the wars that Mahan analyzed to form his theories of seapower. There was one major difference. The Western position was very much a consequence of alliance. Thus the collapse or dilution of the alliance could have crippled Western naval dominance.

For that matter, just as in 1940, successes on land could drastically tilt naval geography. From a Cold War naval perspective, land on either side of the choke points, particularly those of the GIUK gap, was terribly important. Because Norway and Iceland were NATO members, with NATO bases on their shores, the Soviet Northern Fleet could not run freely down the Norwegian Sea through the GIUK gap. Many in NATO considered territory such as Norway and Iceland peripheral; surely the issue was the defense of the aptly named Central Front in Germany. Soviet conquest of Norway and Iceland, however, would have freed the Northern Fleet to attack NATO shipping crossing the North Atlantic toward ports feeding an effort on the Central Front. Thus the defense of apparently peripheral territory might well determine the outcome of the land battle on the Central Front, because it might decide whether the army fighting there could receive the supplies it needed to survive. That Norway could decide Soviet access to the sea was hardly a new idea. In 1945 the Soviets tried unsuccessfully to gain bases there for exactly that reason.

In addition to submarines, the Soviets maintained a large land-based naval air arm. It was intended to attack enemy naval forces both in their bases and at sea. World War II experience, particularly in the Mediterranean and in the Norwegian Sea, showed that such aircraft could be quite effective. Just as in World War II, it would have taken carrier-borne aircraft to deal with the bombers in the air. The situation worsened as the Soviets adopted the longer-ranged jet Tu-16 "Badger" bomber in the 1950s. It could fly from bases in the Soviet arctic far down into the Norwegian Sea and from bases on the Black Sea coast far out into the Mediterranean. Initially these aircraft presented only a very limited threat, but in 1955 the Soviets introduced stand-off missiles that a bomber could fire from well beyond antiaircraft range.[11] The bombers were as much antishipping forces as Soviet submarines. One peculiarity of much NATO naval thinking during the Cold War was the identification of submarines but not maritime bombers as major threats to shipping.[12]

Beginning in 1953, NATO planned to form a Strike Fleet Atlantic in the event of war. At the outset, it would attack the Soviet north, running up the Norwegian Sea. Strike Fleet Atlantic would limit the growing threat posed by the Northern Fleet by incinerating it at source. Any submarines deployed at sea would inevitably try to attack the strike fleet, which would be far more heavily escorted than any convoy. Hence the fleet would have a much better chance of destroying them. Presumably the frequent strike fleet exercises helped convince the Soviets to deploy substantial forces to the north, away from the Central Front, and thus enforced an important degree of virtual attrition.

Another strike carrier force was already operating in the Mediterranean. As noted above, it provided the bulk of the tactical nuclear firepower available to the NATO southern command.

Overall, the carriers' nuclear firepower, to be delivered against land targets, was expected to be their main contribution in a NATO war. The Soviets began arming their naval bombers with stand-off missiles specifically to attack the carriers, and through the 1960s and 1970s the U.S. Navy labored to develop effective defenses. The problem was so difficult that all elements of the fleet's layered defense—its fighters, defensive missiles, and electronic countermeasures—were focused entirely on defeating the incoming missiles. Some bombers might be destroyed, but most of them would probably be able to attack from beyond the range of the defenses. The carriers' main contribution to the survival of other naval forces would be that the Soviets would have to concentrate on attacking them; therefore, as long as carriers could survive, Soviet assets could not be used to strike less survivable units, such as convoys.

The Decline of Forward Strategy

In 1970 Adm. Elmo Zumwalt became chief of naval operations. As a senior officer under Secretary of Defense Robert S. McNamara, he had learned the art of fitting military forces into well-defined categories to justify their composition. He readily accepted the idea that naval forces could be characterized as power projecting or sea controlling. Moreover, he was uncomfortably aware that in the wake of Vietnam, when the defense budget was cut to provide a peace dividend, interservice rivalry would be fierce. He therefore sought a naval mission the other services could not touch; he emphasized sea control rather than power projection. From his point of view, it was particularly advantageous to minimize power projection because many Americans identified it with the failed war in Vietnam.

Zumwalt was apparently the first post–World War II U.S. naval commander to express his strategy publicly. It was extremely appealing, because its central distinction appeared logical. The existing strategy, in which power projection and sea control were tightly integrated, was largely unexpressed, particularly in public. However, that Zumwalt went against the grain is evident in an unsigned contemporary critique of his strategy by a U.S. Navy captain at the Center for Naval Analyses. The captain argued that to abandon the naval offensive would be to lose the war. For example, in order to deal with Soviet air attacks against convoys, Zumwalt planned to assign one carrier to each convoy. His critic argued that any such policy would leave the fleet open to destruction in detail.

When Jimmy Carter became president in 1976, he ordered a major strategic review. His defense team clearly had no great use for a power-projection fleet; the navy ordered its own counter-review, titled Seaplan 2000.[13] This document argued, possibly for the first time, that a strike fleet could use new technology to seize sea control by destroying Soviet forces in place or, should they choose to fight, in decisive battle. The new Aegis antiaircraft system was expected to be so effective that, for the first time, the fighters could concentrate on the Soviet bombers as targets in an offensive battle. Seaplan 2000 envisaged the use of carrier fighters specifically to destroy the Soviet bomber force, which no other NATO asset could touch. It was expected that the decisive battle would be fought in the Norwegian Sea. The Soviets would be induced to attack because the strike fleet threatened the Soviet Union directly. Eventually American strategists concluded that it could threaten the one naval asset the Soviets valued, their strategic submarines, by threatening their own control of bastion areas such as the Barents Sea. If the Soviets refused to accept battle, the fleet's strike aircraft could, it was hoped, destroy much or all of the Soviet naval air arm on the ground. The stated goal was maritime air superiority, and the hoped-for decisive air-to-air battle consciously recalled the decisive Marianas "Turkey Shoot" of June 1944.

The Maritime Strategy

The Carter administration emphasized the European theater. Given the weakness of naval forces in the Atlantic, it suggested that in a crisis the Pacific fleet should "swing" to the Atlantic to reinforce them. After all, what could Soviet forces in the Pacific really do? Adm. Thomas Hayward, who commanded in the Pacific, thought otherwise. His fleet was very much in the virtual attrition business. It tied down submarines and bombers that might easily be transferred to the Northern Fleet. Without the threat posed by Pacific forces, the Soviets might even choose not to maintain so strong a ground force in the East. Much of the Soviet Far Eastern force faced the Chinese; it could be argued that in the run-up to a crisis the Soviets might make some deal with the Chinese. The latter would be much more amenable to such a deal if no American forces were present to back them up. With the Pacific fleet in place, the Soviets could never be sure that the Americans had not made their own deal for a concerted attack. This was flanking and coalition warfare with a vengeance. In 1979 Hayward came to Washington as chief of naval operations, and he assigned a special group at the Naval War College to rethink naval strategy in the event of war against the Soviets. The outcome naturally favored classic concepts such as flanking operations and gaining sea control through power projection.

This rather drastic shift in naval priorities went publicly unremarked.

After the Reagan administration entered office in 1981, however, Secretary of the Navy John Lehman decided, with the president's strong support, to rebuild U.S. naval strength. Lehman was unusually aware of naval issues (among other things, he was a naval reservist), and he had participated in Seaplan 2000. Familiar with Congress, Lehman wanted to present it with the logical reasons for the fleet he was building. He therefore asked his naval leadership to describe the type of war they had in mind, and the way the fleet would function in it. The result, reflecting Hayward's thinking as well as Seaplan 2000, was publicized as the "Maritime Strategy." Because it was so different from Zumwalt's public utterances, it was widely attacked as radical and provocative. Yet, it simply revived the pre-Zumwalt ideas, which in turn reflected practices at least as far back as the Napoleonic and Crimean wars.[14]

The strategy was, necessarily, sequential.[15] The first phase would be the fight for sea control, that is, the destruction of the main Soviet fleet through either strikes or through decisive battles in the Norwegian Sea. Success in these battles would require that NATO defend its northern flank, in places like Norway and Iceland. This phase had to be concluded rapidly; while it was under way the Soviets would presumably be pouring into Central Europe.

When sea control was secured, the fleet could turn its striking capacity against Soviet ground targets. In particular, it could do what the navy had proposed in the late 1940s, attack the flanks of the advancing Soviet force. The credible threat of such attacks could promote virtual attrition before any war. Moreover, by slowing any Soviet advance the fleet could buy time for NATO to mobilize its own force on the ground.

This was hardly an all-maritime strategy, as critics sometimes charged. It was an attempt to use overwhelming Western, particularly U.S., seapower to magnify the power of Western forces in general. There was never any question that NATO could or would raise, in Central Europe, a ground force equivalent to what the Soviets and their Warsaw Pact colonies could mobilize, or that NATO would necessarily begin to mobilize as soon as the Soviets began to plan an attack. Nor, by the 1980s, was there much expectation that NATO could use its nuclear weapons as an equalizer. By this time the Soviets had powerful tactical nuclear forces of their own. Few if any in Western Europe would have welcomed a two-sided nuclear war on land, and many studies suggested that, if the war escalated to nuclear use, NATO would only lose in a more devastated way. There was some hope that a new generation of Western deep-attack systems, heavily dependent on computers, could slow or even stop a Soviet armored thrust into Western Europe, but even with their advent

NATO hardly had the capacity on land to mount the sort of counterattack that would force the Soviets back. Thus even a successful NATO ground defense in Germany would lead to a stalemate, not too different from the World War I impasse.

The maritime strategy also offered a valuable degree of deterrence just as the NATO nuclear threat became far less credible. That is, for much of the Cold War, it was sufficient to convince the Soviets that a major ground attack in Western Europe would lead to a devastating nuclear confrontation. As the Soviets gained nuclear firepower, however, it occurred to them (and to the West) that deterrence might well be double-edged. What then? One response, "conventional deterrence," which the U.S. Army and U.S. Air Force supported, was to examine Soviet military doctrine, to work out just what the Soviets thought were the necessary preconditions for a successful non-nuclear ground war in Europe.[16] If these conditions could not be met, surely the Soviet leadership would hesitate to fight. If the Soviet leadership was constantly calculating the chance of success (and there is no reason to imagine that such calculations had much effect even if they were done), the basis of calculation might well have differed from that imagined by Western theorists. Most likely the leadership would not have gambled on war unless it felt forced into such a choice; in that case subtle calculations would have little or no impact. It is difficult to find a case in which a national leadership chooses war on the basis of a mathematical calculation, although it is much easier to find cases in which particular strategies are chosen on the basis of calculation.

The U.S. Navy argued that as long as the United States maintained any degree of sea control, the Soviets could not overrun our country. They could not, therefore, end a war without using nuclear weapons, which would be suicidal, largely because, however cleverly they attacked the continental United States, the Soviets would be unable to eliminate the seaborne portion of the U.S. nuclear deterrent, on board ballistic missile submarines. Moreover, as long as the United States could project forces onto the European mainland from the sea, the Soviets could never consider any victory there complete. Reaching the English Channel would not be enough. The United States might be able to build alternative coalitions, for example, with China. This idea, that even the greatest victory ashore could not end the problem, harked back to the Napoleonic wars. A powerful U.S. fleet thus became a valuable deterrent against any Soviet assault into Europe. This concept was not tested because the Soviets apparently never gained the impression that they could easily win even a ground war in Western Europe. Nevertheless, it is difficult to avoid the view that the Soviets would have paid more attention to something as blunt as denying them easy war termination than to a marginal decline in their expected rate of success.

Most of the NATO European navies saw matters quite differently. To their governments, the only legitimate wartime naval role was sea control, which meant antisubmarine warfare. U.S. emphasis on strike warfare appeared unduly provocative, likely to escalate a war limited to, for instance, the Central Front. Thus most NATO navies specialized in convoy protection (against submarines) and in mine countermeasures, the latter vital because mining NATO ports could end sea communication across the Atlantic quite as effectively as submarine attacks in mid-ocean. Many scholars described the U.S. strike force as a power-projection entity and the NATO antisubmarine force as a means of sea control, designed to maintain NATO's ability to use the sea freely. To these arguments the U.S. Navy would answer that once the Soviets had decided to risk war in Europe they would hardly expect NATO to limit itself to any one front. They themselves planned to strike on multiple axes, in hopes of outflanking the NATO defense. Provocation was thus a nonissue. Because the Soviets had invested in a massive, although ground-based, naval air arm, the threat to shipping and sea control was clearly multidimensional.

By backing the right side in revolutions and civil wars, the Soviets gained access to positions outside the choke points. Client states such as Cuba, Angola, Mozambique, Vietnam, and South Yemen were astride key sea routes. Cuba blocked the exit from the Gulf of Mexico, through which traffic out of the Mississippi River would flow. American Cold War strategists feared that Communist success in Nicaragua would ultimately lead to control over Panama and the Panama Canal, through which materiel from the U.S. Pacific coast would have flowed toward Europe. Angola and Mozambique lay astride the tanker route around Africa to Europe. Soviet forces operating from Vietnam could attack tankers carrying oil from the Persian Gulf to Japan. Forces in South Yemen (Aden) could block tankers exiting the Gulf en route to both Europe and the Far East. In earlier decades, Western strategists believed that Soviet attempts to curry favor with the Indonesians had a similar motivation; the Soviets supplying the Indonesians with considerable naval hardware appeared to prove the point. Despite the release of considerable Soviet Cold War documentation, we still do not know whether there was any maritime design behind Soviet cultivation of particular client states. There is some evidence that Vietnam was cultivated largely to provide bases for use against China, a particular Soviet enemy in the 1970s, rather than against Western tankers. Soviet interest in Africa—Angola, Mozambique, and South Africa—may have been motivated largely by hopes of controlling Western access to raw materials there. There is some evidence, however, that the Soviets were sometimes motivated mainly by a desire to counter Chinese influence.[17]

A Soviet Point of View

The question remains: Just what did the Soviet investment in seapower buy them? Stalin tried hard to build a big-ship blue-water navy both before and after World War II. He was interested partly in denying enemies the ability to assault his coast, but he probably also had a strong feeling that a powerful navy was essential to national prestige. Stalin's World War II experience also demonstrated that individual large surface warships could disproportionately disrupt convoy operations, so he sponsored a program to build large cruisers (Project 82). After Stalin died, his naval chief, Adm. Nikolai G. Kuznetzov, tried to build a modern Western-style fleet, including carriers. By that time it was becoming apparent that these projects were quite expensive; they competed with army modernization and with the new technologies of missiles and nuclear weapons. Khrushchev considered the fleet a poor investment, and brutally cut naval construction, particularly of surface warships. The carrier program was killed outright. As a rationale, Khrushchev cited the development of antiship missiles, arguing that they made surface warships obsolete. Thus he accepted a submarine-heavy program.

After Khrushchev was ousted, the navy did materially better, but the Soviet army was still clearly the premier service. The navy had to justify itself in terms of direct support for the army; one of its claims was that it could cut NATO supply lines. An attempt to justify an independent oceanic theater of operations, which would have belonged to the navy alone, failed. Nevertheless, the cost of the naval construction that did proceed was enormous. The navy was a leading consumer of scarce high-technology items such as electronics. Minister of Defense Marshal Dmitriy F. Ustinov began to describe the navy in Khrushchev's terms, as a "metal eater." To the Soviet army, this was not too different from the way in which Tirpitz had eaten into resources that would have been better used by the kaiser's army in 1914. It can certainly be argued that the well-publicized U.S. maritime strategy and the accompanying buildup made it much easier for the Soviet navy to make its case for continued expensive construction, including the first Soviet aircraft carrier, appropriately named after Kuznetzov. These expenses contributed to the strain on the Soviet economy, which ultimately proved fatal. The Soviet army and its strategic rocket force were even deeper sinks for resources. Blaming the ultimate economic disaster on naval construction may have been the army's way of avoiding its responsibility, just as after 1918 it was far easier for the kaiser's generals to blame Tirpitz than themselves.

Still, the question is open of just how much good the Soviet fleet would have done if the Cold War had turned hot. Clearly the deployed units, such as the Fifth Eskadra, could have done some damage, but by the 1980s Western fleets probably would have destroyed them fairly quickly. The choke point geography could not have been reversed unless the Soviets had devoted major ground forces for that purpose, and such diversion of wartime resources would have depleted any attack against the main NATO army units in Central Europe. There is no evidence that the Soviet army ever seriously contemplated such operations. Moreover, Soviet naval officers have recently argued that the antishipping forces were never powerful enough to break the NATO lines of communication across the North Atlantic; much of the naval buildup was self-aggrandizement.[18] Perhaps, then, Khrushchev was right: the Soviet Navy was a pack of "metal eaters."

10

Seapower in Continental Warfare

How can seapower influence a war conducted largely on land? Three cases will be examined: the 1971 war between India and Pakistan that created Bangladesh; the 1870–71 war between France and Prussia; and the 1973 Middle East war.

The 1971 India-Pakistan War

In 1971 India and Pakistan fought over what was then called East Pakistan, which became the independent country of Bangladesh as a result. Most of the action occurred on land, but both combatants had navies, and they fought a naval war. To what extent did that naval war affect what occurred ashore? Clearly there was some connection, because Pakistan was one country (East Pakistan and West Pakistan) enjoying only sea communication between its two halves. Pakistan did have two quasi-allies, the United States and China, with which the Indians had to reckon. Less than a decade earlier, China had fought India in a border war. The Indians negotiated a Treaty of Peace and Friendship with the Soviets, signed in August 1971, that partly neutralized the potential Chinese threat. Because China was a land threat, the Indian chiefs of staff demanded that the war be conducted in winter, when the Himalayan passes would be closed by snow. The Indians assumed that the Soviet navy would, in effect, contain any Chinese submarine threat. The Indians calculated that the United States was too involved in Vietnam to intervene. Overall, the Indians felt vulnerable to international pressure. They therefore planned on a short war, and the chiefs of staff demanded that the East Pakistan rebels be built into a credibly independent force that they would, in effect, be backing.[1]

Indian strategy was to isolate East Pakistan while protecting Indian ports and shipping from any Pakistani naval counterattack. Well before war broke out formally, the Indians were training a maritime arm of the East Pakistan rebels, the Mukhti Bahini, who attacked ports and shipping.

For its part, the Pakistan navy had recently received three new French-built submarines; it also operated the old ex-U.S. submarine *Ghazi*. The Pakistani surface force was quite obsolete, and was not expected to leave port. The Indians expected the three modern Pakistani submarines to operate in the Arabian Sea, protecting West Pakistan, the dominant part of the country, and its major port, Karachi. *Ghazi* would operate in the east. Given this expectation, in June the Indians decided to use their one carrier, *Vikrant,* in the east, where she would be reasonably safe from the Pakistani submarines, while the navy's modern missile boats operated in the Arabian Sea off West Pakistan. The boats could be considered reasonably immune from submarine attack. They would also deter the Pakistanis from sending their surface ships to sea.[2] As it turned out, the missile boats had to be towed at sea by frigates, so they could not be used effectively against ships in the open sea. They could, however, be used to bombard Karachi harbor.

The Indians lacked any forces to convoy essential shipping, but in November 1971 the Indian government passed legislation giving the navy's new Naval Control of Shipping organization control of shipping movements in and out of Indian ports. Its main tool was evasive routing, and its main concern was to ensure safety for tankers because both countries depended on foreign sources for their oil. To support evasive routing, the Indians activated a signals intelligence organization.[3] Pakistan had harbor attack craft ("chariots") and the Indians feared that they would be brought into harbors on board merchant ships; they therefore required that ships not proceed into harbors until they had been checked.

Overall, Pakistani doctrine held that the east could be defended only in the west; that is, that to preclude Indian conquest of East Pakistan, the main strength of the Pakistan military, which was located in West Pakistan, would be thrown against the nearby Indian frontier. As the Indians expected, the three new submarines operated in the west, but that was because they had much less than the advertised radius of action. There was some hope that the older but much longer-ranged *Ghazi* could catch the Indian carrier in the east. At the same time the limited Pakistan surface force, which included an old cruiser, was deployed to defend Karachi, the main port of West Pakistan. As in the case of India, covering oil shipments, in this case into Karachi, became a very high priority.

The Pakistan army was unable to achieve much in the west; the Indians had redeployed troops from the north, facing China, and were able to gain territory there. Indian carrier aircraft raided the main port of East Pakistan, Chittagong, sinking shipping in it; they also struck the airfield at Cox's Bazar. That in effect announced the isolation of East Pakistan; the Pakistan army already there could not fight for long. Pakistan lacked the naval wherewithal to relieve its army. The Pakistan submarine in the area was lost while laying mines around the main Indian east coast base.[4] Toward the end of the short war, the Indians blockaded East Pakistan to break Pakistani morale and accelerate surrender.

The Indians also attacked in West Pakistan, the remaining part of the country, and the only likely source of relief to the beleaguered force in the east. Indian missile boats attacked Karachi harbor, the largest in West Pakistan, sinking merchant ships inside.[5] They also destroyed fuel oil tanks. Presumably such large-scale raids helped convince the Pakistanis that they could not hope to ship troops east. One of the Pakistan submarines, however, sank an Indian frigate. The resulting Indian search precluded a third missile boat raid on Karachi.

Pakistan was a U.S. ally, and the Indians, though nominally neutralist, were widely thought to be very nearly a Soviet ally. The U.S. government was, understandably, anxious to demonstrate its support for its ally. A seaborne force offered just the right combination. At the end of the war, a group built around the nuclear carrier *Enterprise* was sent into the Bay of Bengal. By this time the war was all but over; presumably the carrier's presence was intended to deter the Indians from taking any of West Pakistan. The carrier offered a real threat, because the Indians could not be sure her aircraft would not intervene. Because she was nuclear powered, she needed no base, which the United States did not have in the area. If the Indians disregarded the threat, as in fact they did, then the damage to U.S. prestige was limited. The United States could, then, take as much or as little of the coming war as it pleased.

The Indians loudly protested the U.S. naval demonstration. Later they took it as yet another proof that they would not be secure until their fleet could keep all foreigners out of the Indian Ocean. Indeed, they proclaimed their own version of a retrospective Monroe Doctrine: East Asia would have been far better off if the Europeans had been kept out from the fifteenth century onwards. The Indian defense budget, however, still leans heavily toward ground forces.

In retrospect, it is not clear just what Pakistan could have done to save the situation in Bangladesh. A maritime approach would have been to threaten an amphibious operation against the Indian coast. If the threat were credible enough, presumably it might have tied down so large a part of the Indian army that the Indians would have been precluded from invading, let alone overrunning, East Pakistan. The Pakistan army tried a land-oriented version of this strategy, but the Indians clearly had no difficulty mobilizing sufficient troops to counter it. The difference between land-borne and seaborne threats is that the latter may compel defense over a much wider area. As it was, Pakistan never built up the sort of amphibious or maritime strike force required. Pakistan did build up an impressive submarine force, which might have neutralized the Indian navy, and that in turn might have made it possible for the Pakistanis to have reinforced East Pakistan by sea. However, the province would probably have been lost before any such relief could have been effective.

The Franco-Prussian War

To some extent the Pakistan situation recalls France's situation during the Franco-Prussian War of 1870–71: Can naval action retrieve a disaster suffered on land, in a war prosecuted mainly by ground forces? In 1870 France had a powerful fleet, and the Prussians had almost no navy at all. Both countries had powerful armies, but the French army proved ineffective, and it was quickly crushed. In the event of war against Prussia, the French navy planned both a blockade and the landing of an army corps in the Prussian rear. It also planned to destroy the two incomplete Prussian naval bases, Wilhelmshaven and Kiel.[6] The French had hoped that Denmark, which Prussia had defeated six years earlier, would join them. The French planned to land an army corps in Schleswig, on the German border, to fight alongside a Danish army.[7] The Germans advanced so quickly into France, however, that the troops earmarked for the expeditionary force had to be used instead in France. Even so, the threat of an attack from the sea caused the Prussians to hold back a substantial force both in Schleswig and along the Baltic coast. When the French failed to attack, these troops were quickly sent into action in France.[8] Counting time for German troops to regroup and get to the front, the diversion due to a French seaborne threat lasted only about a month. The fleet did mount a futile blockade off the Prussian coast, but its ships were not suited to attack the German ports.

Overall, the approaches to the German coast were too shallow for large warships. The Germans compounded the problem by removing buoys and by extensive mining. They could afford to do so because they had no substantial fleet of their own to inconvenience. For all the navies of this period, steaming endurance was short, so nearby bases were extremely important. The French lacked anything suitable. Their northernmost port, Dunkirk, was over three hundred miles from the mouth of the Elbe, the main target of a North Sea blockade. The British refused to allow the French to coal at Heligoland, which they then owned (the French did coal at sea in the lee of the island). Despite French hopes, the Danes remained neutral, thus denying the French base facilities on the Baltic. Even so, the French did mount blockades of both the German North Sea and Baltic coasts. They could not be sustained for long, mainly because the disaster ashore was so bad; when ships returned to France to fuel and provision, they were laid up and their crews sent to fight ashore, although they had little effect because their numbers were so small.

The French blue-water armored ships were not powerful enough to force the fortifications at Kiel, the main German fleet base. The French did have a specialized coast attack fleet comparable to what had been developed fifteen years earlier for the Crimean War, but it was useless without an advanced base, which the Danes denied the French.[9] The small French Baltic force was left with a choice between continuing to contain the smaller German fleet or attacking the German coast. The force was ordered to attack the coast, although not any open town. Its commander selected two targets: Kolberg and Danzig. To approach them he had to uncover Kiel. He received erroneous intelligence informing him that three German armored ships had left Kiel and threatened his line of communications back to France via the Danish Straits. The squadron commander saw no alternative but to withdraw to the Danish Straits. Once there, he found that the Germans were still in Kiel, so he enforced a blockade of the German Baltic coast until he ran short of coal a few weeks later, and withdrew for good.

Neither geography nor technology favored the French. Because the Germans had two coasts, each with a naval base, the French felt compelled to blockade each. Contemporary armored ships had very limited endurance. Even though the French managed to coal at sea (a considerable achievement), they still had to bring ships back to base for repairs. The squadrons managed to spend only twenty-five days off the German North Sea coast and only thirty-six days off the Baltic coast. To maintain continuous coverage, the French needed at least two ships for every one on station. At the outbreak of war they appeared to have enormous naval superiority, because their fleet included thirty-five armored ships. Only half could be on station at any one time, however, thus eight were in the North Sea and seven were in the Baltic. The Germans had only five armored ships, which might seem pathetic in comparison to the French, but they could choose their moment to emerge from port. The French could never afford to split either squadron; they could only choose either to mask even the very weak German fleet in Kiel or bombard towns on the German coast. The only solutions to this dilemma would have been to concentrate a powerful fleet to destroy a German base and the fleet within, and thus avoid any need to maintain an armored squadron offshore, or to concentrate on one German coast or the other. French hopes of landing on the Germans' strategic flank in the Baltic precluded abandoning that sea in order to concentrate on the North Sea. Given the speed with which the French army was defeated, no blockade could have been very effective; only a successful landing might have diverted enough German troops to reduce pressure on the French army.

The French did keep the German navy from interfering with the vital flow of arms from the United States. That was an unglamorous achievement, however; to the public it appeared that the navy had done nothing at all to justify its high cost. Only the service of naval personnel ashore, where they formed the core of a reforming army, and where they organized the defense of Paris, gained the navy any prestige. On a longer-term basis, the failure of the French navy to affect the outcome of the war presumably taught French politicians that naval power was virtually worthless, hence the British were welcome as coalition partners only if they contributed substantial numbers of troops. That perception had gruesome consequences for the British, four decades after the end of the Franco-Prussian War.

For the time being, the French concluded that they needed a better amphibious capability. They continued to build coast defense (actually coast attack) ships specifically to attack the German Baltic coast.[10] If the French fleet had been able to capture a valuable port or, better yet, a larger piece of territory, presumably they might have acquired a valuable bargaining chip. When the army collapsed, however, the French had no bargaining power. The Prussians exacted a huge indemnity, including compensation for ships seized by the French blockaders. For their part the Prussians drew the lesson that they needed a more powerful fleet.

The 1973 Middle East War

The 1973 Middle East war offers some other lessons. Both Israel and her Arab enemies concentrated on land forces, but in important ways their wars were maritime. From the point of view of supply, for many years Israel was effectively an island because none of the countries on her borders would trade with her. The sea route through the Mediterranean was open, but it passed Egypt, the largest of the hostile Arab powers. The main Israeli port, Haifa, was on the Mediterranean, and its access to Asia was through the blocked Suez Canal. Israel did have a Red Sea port, Eilat, but its access to Asia was through two narrow straits, the mouth of the Gulf of Aqaba and the mouth of the Red Sea itself. Both could be blocked in wartime. Israel produced virtually no oil until Israeli forces captured a small Egyptian field during the 1967 war, so maritime access was absolutely vital.

On the other hand, before 1973 the Israeli navy was of little significance within the Israeli military.[11] It had performed poorly during the 1967 war. As a consequence, although the navy was able to obtain resources to build a fleet of missile boats, it was never integrated with other elements of the military, such as the air force. Nor did the Israeli high command appreciate the potential of seapower. The assumption was that any war would necessarily be quick, leaving no time for naval measures such as blockade to take effect. Moreover, from its formation the navy was split into two opposing factions. One recalled the considerable success of naval special forces during the 1948 War of Independence. Such forces were used during the 1967 and 1973 wars, and extensively during the war of attrition centered on the Suez Canal. The other faction pressed for creation of a sea denial or even a sea control fleet, on the ground that otherwise Egypt and perhaps other Arab countries might eventually impose an effective blockade of the Mediterranean coast. The fleet of Sa'ar 3–type missile boats that fought in 1973 exemplified the latter view.[12] In 1956 and again in 1967 the Israelis went to war because the Egyptians shut off their main source of oil, the tanker route through the Red Sea from Iran. The tankers had to pass an Egyptian position, Sharm-el-Sheikh, at the mouth of the Gulf of Aqaba. In both wars the Israelis captured Sharm-el-Sheikh, and after 1967 they retained it. With Sharm-el-Sheikh in their hands, the Israelis now wanted to safeguard the sea route through the Red Sea; they had to gain the ability to keep the Straits of Bab-el-Mandeb, at the far end of the Red Sea, open.[13] One of the Israeli goals in the 1956 war was free passage through the Suez Canal, and by winning its right bank in 1967 they closed the waterway altogether.

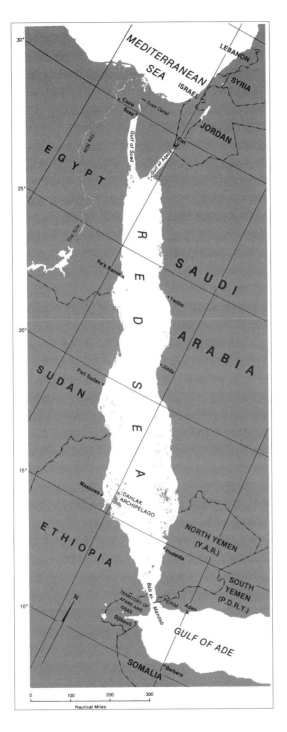

Middle East, 1950s–1970s.
Israel fought three wars, mostly on land, largely to maintain maritime access to overseas resources. In 1956 and again in 1967 the Israelis considered it intolerable that the Egyptians closed the mouth of the Gulf of Aqaba, using their coastal guns at Sharm-el-Sheikh, at the southern tip of the Sinai Peninsula, between the Gulfs of Suez and Aqaba. In 1956 Israeli forces racing across the Sinai reached the Suez Canal, helping to close it. The Israelis withdrew on condition that a United Nations force occupy the Sinai, neutralizing the canal and also ensuring free passage down the Gulf of Aqaba. War broke out in 1967 when Egypt's President Gamal Abdel Nasser asked the United Nations force to withdraw (to his surprise, it agreed to do so) and reoccupied the Sinai. In 1973 Egyptian block- age of the southern end of the Red Sea, at the Bab-el- Mandeb, interdicted the tanker route from Iran. This map shows why the Bab-el- Mandeb was a maritime war zone for both Israel and Egypt; it was well beyond normal tactical air range of their bases. Only ships could loiter long enough to have much impact. *U.S. Naval Institute*

Between 1962 and 1967 the Egyptians obtained missile boats from the Soviet Union, and on 21 October 1967, in the world's first missile engagement, they sank the Israeli destroyer *Eilat* off Alexandria.[14] At the same time the Soviets provided Syria, Egypt's ally, with missile boats of her own. The Israelis built up their own force of *Sa'ar*-class missile boats, which they considered technologically superior to those being transferred to the Egyptians and the Syrians.[15]

In effect each navy could imagine its missile boats as a kind of miniature main fleet, protecting its own base and denying the sea to enemy shipping within its limited range. By the time war broke out, neither Israel nor Syria had any large oceangoing warships left; they had concentrated on missile boats. Egypt retained a considerable surface fleet, mainly destroyers, as well as twelve submarines (two Israeli submarines were laid up). Egypt also had bases at both ends of the Suez Canal. The base at the southern end could support surface operations not just in the Gulf of Aqaba but also at the mouth of the Red Sea, a choke point called the Bab-el-Mandeb. It lay outside the effective range of Israeli strike aircraft. At the outbreak of war, the Egyptians had two destroyers, two missile boats, and two submarines in the Red Sea.[16] With the Suez Canal closed, the Israelis could not easily transfer missile boats between their main theater of operations, the Mediterranean, and the Red Sea to challenge Egyptian sea control there. For that matter, the Egyptians could, at least in theory, interdict merchant shipping en route to Israel at the Mediterranean narrows between Sicily and North Africa, well beyond the range of Israeli aircraft. At the outbreak of war, one of their destroyers was in position at Tripoli in Libya, a friendly port.

Apart from oil, Israel depended heavily on foreign trade, which came mainly through the Mediterranean. When war began, equipment and ammunition were quickly expended. Without resupply, the Israelis could not have executed their war-winning assault across the Suez Canal into Egypt. Given the sheer mass required, much of it had to come by sea. Thus Israeli control of the Eastern Mediterranean was a crucial condition for continuing and winning the war. Both the Israelis and their Syrian and Egyptian enemies were well aware of this fact. Early in the 1973 war the Israeli missile boats managed to sink many of the Syrian and Egyptian craft at no cost to themselves. They established sea control by destroying the enemy's main fleet.[17] Once the Israeli missile boats had achieved sea control, they were free to attack shore targets such as the main Syrian ports. These attacks were initially intended to lure the remaining enemy missile boats into combat, but they were also considered a useful contribution to the ground war. It was claimed that the Syrians detached substantial forces for coast defense. Although not achieving substantial damage, the boats demonstrated Israeli success to the Syrian civil population. They thus posed a direct threat to the Syrian regime, much as deep-penetration air strikes did. Strikes against Syrian harbors sank or damaged several cargo ships, including at least one Soviet ship, and may have been intended to block cargo shipments to Syria.[18] In addition to these main fleet operations, Israeli patrol boats operating out of a base seized by the Israeli army on the Gulf of Suez helped complete the encirclement of the Egyptian Third Army in the Sinai by denying it seaborne supplies.

The two more distant choke points remained, however. The destroyer deployed to Tripoli began hunting Israel-bound merchant ships, but fled when two Israeli missile boats headed in its direction. An Egyptian submarine sank a Greek merchant ship in the Mediterranean. It is not clear whether these threats to shipping had much impact. The Egyptians later claimed that only twenty-three merchant ships entered Israeli ports during the three-week war, whereas the Israelis claimed that the shipping lanes had been kept open, with more than a hundred ships entering during that period.[19] The oil route was at least as important. It was also much more vulnerable, because the Israelis had concentrated all their missile boats in the Mediterranean. The Israelis did have two patrol boats in the area, and they sank an Egyptian gunboat. They had little chance of sinking a missile boat, however. The Egyptians had missile boats at the southern end of the closed Suez Canal that were capable of striking at the Israeli outpost at Sharm-el-Sheikh.[20] At the outbreak of war their aircraft destroyed several Israeli radar stations nearby, making it possible to mine the Straits of Jubal, leading into the Gulf of Suez, a few nights later. These mines interdicted the route from the sole Israeli oil field at Abu Rodeis, to the Israeli Red Sea port of Aqaba.[21] Egyptian destroyers at the far end of the Red Sea (the Bab-el-Mandeb) conducted a successful blockade.[22] Indeed, it has been claimed that the Israelis made lifting the oil blockade a precondition for relaxing the encirclement of the Egyptian Third Army, at the northern end of the canal, at the end of the war.[23]

Seapower entered the situation on another vital level. In 1973 U.S. European allies disapproved of U.S. support for the Israelis. Support included flying crucial aircraft directly to Israel, and that in turn required refueling.[24] Except for Portugal, which allowed use of the Azores, and Germany, bases in Europe were all denied to U.S. combat aircraft en route to Israel to replace losses. That illustrated an important aspect of coalition war: governments allied with the

United States to fight the Cold War against the Soviets had quite different views of the Arab-Israeli conflict.

The carriers of the Sixth Fleet had, among their aircraft, aerial refuelers that allowed extension of the carriers' strike range. During the 1973 war, these aircraft refueled F-4 Phantom fighters flying from the United States.[25] The carriers were U.S. sovereign territory, so they were not affected by the veto the Europeans were trying to impose. Perhaps significantly, the Soviet Fifth Eskadra made no attempt to interfere with these activities.

From a European perspective, the war involved another vital waterway, the Suez Canal. Prior to the Anglo-French-Israeli-Egyptian war of 1956, it had been the main route for tankers carrying oil from the Middle East to Europe. The earlier Arab-Israeli war of 1948 had cut vital oil pipelines between the oil fields and the Mediterranean, hence the need for tankers to go all the way around the Arabian peninsula. The war cut this flow; the tankers had to steam all the way around Africa, greatly lengthening their voyages. This was virtual attrition of tankers, and it had dire consequences for Western European economies. The experience, however, helped convince the French to concentrate on nuclear power. The canal was cut again in 1967, when the Israelis captured Sinai and, with it, the eastern bank of the waterway. One consequence this time was the construction of much larger tankers suited to the trip around Africa.

Even so, the canal remained valuable. It finally reopened when the Israelis and Egyptians reached a peace settlement in 1978. The canal was then dredged sufficiently to take the new tankers and, incidentally, large aircraft carriers. As a consequence, when the United States became more interested in the Indian Ocean in 1979, it was possible to support operations there from both the Mediterranean and from the Pacific, drastically reducing the cost (in carriers) of maintaining one on station in the Arabian Sea, within striking range of Iran and Pakistan. Access via the canal became particularly vital during the Gulf War buildup of 1990–91. Conversely, after the attack on the destroyer *Cole* in October 2000 the U.S. Navy was loath to use a constricted waterway in which further attack might be easy to mount. That choice added enormously to the voyage the damaged ship underwent en route home. Seapower and geography are still closely linked.

11

A New Strategy

THE U.S. NAVY achieved success during the Cold War by making its central strategy explicit. Inevitably it needed a post–Cold War equivalent. The new strategy was outlined in a 1992 U.S. Navy paper titled ". . . From the Sea." It was followed by "Forward . . . From the Sea" in 1995.[1] Both are necessarily general. In contrast to the situation during the Cold War, the United States now has no single obvious enemy, hence a strategy tailored to a particular place, let alone a particular scenario, cannot be designed. Instead, the emphasis in both papers is on explaining why the navy remains relevant, and in laying out the principles on which a post–Cold War navy should be developed.

". . . From the Sea" was concerned largely with explaining how seapower remained relevant to the United States. In the wake of the Cold War, some Americans imagined that isolationism might be attractive, or that it might be possible to avoid any armed conflict abroad. Studies showed just how deeply the American economy was interlocked with those of overseas countries, and also just how seriously instability abroad could affect Americans. There was some hope, which was ultimately disappointed, that the navy's role of maintaining security could be equated to particular economic advantages, so that investment in the navy could be shown conclusively to be cost-effective. Obviously Americans and other Westerners benefit when U.S. military power, including its naval component, maintains security in the Gulf and thus holds down the price of oil, but that is only one of many cases that need to be considered. Costs and benefits will vary wildly from case to case.

The central conclusion was that seapower remains important because so much of the world's population and wealth is concentrated along the world's shorelines. The sea remains the preeminent means of transporting heavy cargoes. It is no accident that almost all large cities are located either on seashores or on rivers affording transportation to the sea. The sea bottom is increasingly a source of vital raw materials, including oil. That is why, for example, sovereignty over the South China Sea is so delicate an issue. In addition, much of the world's population is fed by fisheries, competition for which is increasing.[2]

In ". . . From the Sea" the U.S. Navy argued that a key area of future naval operations would be the littoral, which it defined as a strip of sea backed by a strip of shore. The land portion of the littoral is the area affected by events at the shoreline. The seaward portion is the area that affects events on and inland of the shore. Thus the littoral is distinguished from the blue-water area in which navies fight for sea control. It is also distinguished from a much narrower coastal strip. Littoral waters include most of those from which resources are regularly extracted. The landward part of the littoral includes most of the world's population and most of the major cities. As an indication of the seaward extent of a littoral area, the United Nations treaty on Law of the Sea allocates to each country a two-hundred-mile exclusive economic zone offshore, which goes far beyond the old three-mile or twelve-mile limit of territorial waters.

With the end of the Cold War, the U.S. Navy faces no blue-water challengers, at least for the present. With ". . . From the Sea" it announced that, given free use of blue water, its mission would be to affect events ashore, including both attacks on shore targets and the projection of U.S. troops ashore. Initially navy analysts hoped to define a limited number of scenarios or potentially hostile countries against which the navy of the future could be designed. No such definition was possible. It was not difficult to define classes of potential future enemies, but that was not nearly enough. Crises are unpredictable in every way. Compared to other military forces, the navy offers flexibility and mobility. A relatively small naval force can deal with crises spread around the world.

All the U.S. armed services had to define their roles and their appropriate forms in a post–Cold War world. As the Soviet Union collapsed, it seemed that existing forces were obsolescent. The army and the air force announced major restructuring. The navy was in an ironic position. For years it had dealt with exactly the sort of low-level crises that would probably characterize the new situation. It was already well adapted to a post–Cold War world. Unlike other NATO navies, the U.S. Navy had never divorced power projection, which is the major theme of ". . . From the Sea," from sea control, which was vital in a Cold War context. Thus the navy did not really need radical restructuring, although it had to explain that to the public, including defense policy decision makers. ". . . From the Sea" was part of the U.S. Navy's attempt to defines its roles and appropriate forms. Post–Cold War cuts included all types of naval forces, but they fell most heavily on forces developed to deal with Soviet open-ocean attacks: frigates, maritime patrol aircraft, and attack submarines.[3] Unfortunately the navy's critics reversed this argument, saying that alone of the three services the navy had failed to reinvent itself for the new situation.

The U.S. Navy has four ways of using force to affect events ashore. One way is traditional: control of offshore shipping, as is done in an embargo. Embargoes have been imposed on Iraq and Serbia, and the drug war in the Caribbean is a type of embargo. A second way is discrete strikes against particular targets ashore, either by aircraft or missiles. Examples include the air raid on Tripoli in 1986 and the missile strike against a terrorist base in Afghanistan in 1998. A third way is sustained air attacks, generally in support of other operations, as was done in the Kosovo war and in Iraq. A fourth way is landing marines. The last mission may include support during and after a landing. This mission may be extended to supporting troops on the ground who have not arrived by sea. Except for landings and troop support, missions can be carried out from outside the littoral, using aircraft and stand-off missiles.

Missing from this list is any emphasis on antiship warfare, except as it is needed to shield forces carrying out their main missions. Most countries' navies cannot contest the use of the sea more than a few hundred miles offshore. They can certainly oppose landings in their waters, and the U.S. Navy still needs the means to deal with them in their home waters. Much of the time, however, attacks can and will be mounted from a sanctuary area farther out to sea. If U.S. units do have to pass onto the coast itself, it will be increasingly important to overcome an enemy's defensive mining, as was done in the Gulf War.

Littoral warfare is not inshore warfare, because the combat zone extends a few hundred miles out to sea or farther if longer-range weapons are used. It is not coastal warfare, because some important actions will occur well inland. It was also distinguished from Cold War plans to land marines on the Soviet periphery. This new kind of warfare, called littoral warfare, was sometimes described as "naval expeditionary warfare."

The realities, however, did not change after the Cold War. Access, flexibility, and the ability to land and withdraw forces at will, what is essentially the ability to limit or control a commitment, are key considerations. The concept of a phased strategy also made excellent sense.

Access was no longer likely to be gained by a decisive blue-water battle, but it would still be essential to be able to deal with an enemy's navy. That would include dealing with mines and coastal missiles. The emphasis in antisubmarine warfare would shift from nuclear submarines in deep water to diesel-electric submarines in much shallower water. The best tactics might well involve some sort of blockade of an enemy's base, rather than, for instance, escort. Attack at source might well be impossible given the rules of engagement of a limited operation.

There might be situations, as in Iraq and Yugoslavia, in which it would be essential to mount an embargo on the seaward side of the littoral. In such cases rules of engagement might prohibit attacking the enemy's navy. Instead, it might be contained in some less violent way. A continuous U.S. naval presence in the offshore part of the littoral would be needed, with sufficient firepower to make it impossible to remove even if the enemy retained its naval forces.

Once the enemy's navy had been swept aside, the U.S. force would be free to operate against its real target, on the shoreward side of the enemy's littoral. Even before that had been done, the U.S. Navy would be able to mount its usual deep strikes, using both aircraft and missiles. That was nothing new.

The next paper in the series, "Forward . . . From the Sea," announced a new approach to supporting land operations. The navy had always emphasized its ability to insert—and withdraw—forces from the sea. In a new world of frequent crises, quick withdrawal would be increasingly important, because the same force might be needed to deal with a new problem in a very distant place. The smaller the footprint of the force going ashore, the more easily it could be moved in and out. Yet what normally gave a force its punch —heavy armor and artillery—also added enormously to its footprint.

"Forward . . . From the Sea" offered a solution. Some or all of the heavy support, which the force usually took with it, could be kept offshore on board ships. With good communications, the force ashore could call the ships for support that otherwise might have come from its own artillery.[4] This was very different from past practice. In classic World War II landings, the fleet put down very heavy artillery fire at and near the shoreline, and only around the time of the landing. In modern parlance this is termed "kicking the door in," defeating the enemy's beach defenses. In the past, once the door was open, heavy equipment would be landed. The troops heading inshore would take their artillery with them.

"Forward . . . From the Sea" posited that the fleet of the future would still kick the door in, if need be, but that it would remain in place offshore to provide support over a depth of fifty or even a hundred miles, over a sustained period, perhaps as long as a month. Few operations would extend much deeper or last much longer. If they did, heavy equipment would still have to come ashore. Overall, the ability of a small ground unit to land, overrun its objective, and quickly withdraw for a second operation would greatly magnify its power. The new vision is reflected in new technology; both the long-range version of the 5-inch gun and the new 155-mm gun fire extended-range guided projectiles.

"Forward . . . From the Sea" fit some new and uncomfortable realities. The navy can no longer supply the sort of firepower that supported the big amphibious operations of the past. Thus frontal attacks against enemy fortifications, even hasty ones, are extremely dangerous. In addition, as the Gulf War proved once again, it is almost impossible to clear minefields very quickly. Protracted mine clearance operations tip off an enemy to the location of the landing, probably in time for him to concentrate troops and build simple fortifications against it. On the other hand, it is possible to conduct covert mine reconnaissance, and thus to find areas that have not been mined.

"Forward . . . From the Sea" dovetails with a new Marine Corps concept, operational maneuver from the sea (OMFTS), and the related ship to objective maneuver (STOM). "Operational maneuver" is a standard phrase in land warfare; it refers to the phase of operations out of contact with the enemy. By way of contrast, tactical maneuver is in contact with the enemy, as part of a battle. Examples include frontal or flanking assaults. An operational maneuver might be a landing in the enemy's rear, to cut his line of communications.

It is far easier to maneuver at sea than on land. So much of naval warfare might be considered operational maneuver that the term is never used for naval operations. As the quantity of naval fire support declined, the Marines asked whether they could use operational maneuver as a way of avoiding frontal assaults, which had required so much fire support. At sea, they could move heavier masses than an army could easily move along a beach. They might well be able to outflank a defending force. The first approach to such maneuver was a Cold War concept, termed "over the horizon assault."

In the 1980s the Marines adopted fast landing craft, air cushion (LCACs) to replace existing slow beaching craft, and they tried to buy fast amphibious vehicles to accompany the LCACs. Given higher speed, the new vehicles could approach a beach from much farther offshore. Besides their speed, LCACs could land over a much wider variety of beaches than their predecessors. The combination of reach and flexibility in choice of beach offered the Marines a valuable element of surprise. An enemy might detect an amphibious force well offshore, but forces could land anywhere along a coast.[5]

Over the horizon assault still contemplated a massed landing somewhere to create a beachhead. The Marines needed the beachhead both to assemble their mountain of supplies and to regroup before moving inland. After regrouping, the Marines would become a conventional ground force capable of operational and tactical maneuvers. The beachhead itself was absolutely essential, despite being an inviting air or missile target. The landing force creating the beachhead was vulnerable to mines, and any protracted attempt to clear mines before landing would ruin the element of surprise.

Thus over the horizon assault offered a degree of operational maneuver, but not after the assault force had been committed. The beachhead itself was the problem. The Marines asked whether the mountain of supplies ever had to be assembled ashore, or whether it could be maintained offshore. Perhaps units could come ashore in fighting formations, with helicopters supplying them from the ships as they advanced. If that could be done, the Marines would not be tied to any particular place on the beach. Nor would an enemy be able to predict the path of advance from the beach, because there would be no single landing place. The objective of any landing operation was not the beach itself, but something farther inland. In the new concept of operations, Marine units would go directly from ships to objectives, without pausing at the beach.

This kind of operation in turn would be effective only if the units were small and did not need mountains of supplies to support them as they advanced. Small-unit operations were also attractive because they could infiltrate enemy defenses instead of making the traditional frontal assault. A shift to infiltration might make up for the decline in the navy's shore bombardment firepower. In the past, small-unit landings were pointless because viable units had to carry enough fire support to survive attacks by enemy ground units inland, beyond the reach of naval supporting fire. However, "Forward . . . From the Sea" posited that the ships offshore would continue to provide fire as the unit moved inland. For that matter, the guns would also be needed to support troops that had landed ashore without facing any direct opposition. Not only would the landing force gain mobility by reducing its overall footprint, it could split into smaller units capable of infiltrating their way in. It would still be important to clear minefields so that heavy equipment could eventually get ashore, but the month of offshore support offered in "Forward . . . From the Sea" would allow considerable time for mine clearance.

Accepting the concept that a force's landing footprint must be minimized, other new ideas become attractive. For example, the headquarters element of a landing force carries a considerable footprint, because it requires a sizeable staff and defense. Modern communications enable much of the staff to be relocated to sea, on board a specialized flagship. Such concepts apply not only to the marines but also to army forces operating near the shoreline.

Clearly ". . . From the Sea" encompasses many kinds of operations beyond the assaults contemplated in "Forward . . . From the Sea." Since 1950 the United States has never had to land troops in the face of enemy fire, although it can be argued that the ability to threaten such assault has been quite valuable.[6] It is not clear to what extent the naval investment required by concepts such as STOM will be forthcoming. For example, the new *Zumwalt* class (DD 21) has been advertised as a land attack destroyer; its special offensive feature is the 155-mm gun required for STOM support. In the past, the U.S. Navy has generally eschewed special-purpose ships for fear that they will not be useable in actual crises, which may not be suitable for their special capabilities.

For the next few decades ". . . From the Sea" seems to describe the U.S. Navy's place in national security quite well. It will surely be some time before a challenger comparable to the Soviet Union reappears. Ships last a long time, however. The more that are needed, to cover wider-spread emergencies, the longer they must be made to last. The U.S. Navy succeeded at the end of the Cold War, where many of its allies failed, because it deliberately built a fleet that could shift between Cold War and post–Cold War priorities, between sea control and power projection. Just as it was easy to imagine a Cold War fleet of antisubmarine frigates and attack submarines, it is easy to imagine a power projection fleet of single-purpose land attack ships and amphibious assault units. Single-purpose ships are generally less expensive than general-purpose alternatives. It is also easier to evaluate their effectiveness, because they are rated in a narrow range of roles. The great strategic challenge is to remember that roles are transitory, that ". . . From the Sea" rather than "Forward . . . From the Sea" is the dominant reality—and that not even it encompasses the possible return to another Cold War situation.

12

Using Seapower

MUCH OF WHAT we do, and what we hope to do, requires that U.S. military influence be projected abroad on a sustained basis. This book describes a maritime approach. It is not a U.S. Navy or a U.S. Marine Corps approach. Rather, it seeks to make the best possible use of the mobility naval forces offer. In distinct contrast to the Cold War, crises now may be simultaneous and randomly distributed. We need agility to deter war if possible, to fight it when we must, and to withdraw when expedient. The American people must not find U.S. actions onerous. Deterrence in particular requires credible U.S. forces that can loiter as long as necessary in a crisis area, yet withdraw without loss of face. Nineteenth century Britain is probably the closest analogy to our current situation. The British government of that century did not have a patented solution to all its problems, but the Royal Navy came very close. If anything, we need a more maritime solution. Unlike the nineteenth century British, however, we cannot build an empire to provide us with bases near every potential crisis area. Nor can we hope to maintain a global coalition to deal with every crisis we face.

The only alternative to a roving presence is garrisons of ground-based forces. Each would have to be powerful enough to deal with local ground forces. Because we can no longer predict exactly where we will fight, garrisons would have to be spread over much of the world. In many places they might be welcomed, but only because their presence would necessarily embroil the United States in local conflicts, whether or not we were willing. The objective of our policy should be a combination of impact (otherwise, why bother?) and controllability. The decision to engage should be ours, not manipulated by a foreign host. To retain ownership of our decisions, our forces abroad should overwhelmingly be on U.S. soil or property, which generally means on board ships.

In recent years our emphasis has been on the need for agility, because U.S. forces must be able to deal with a wide range of possible conflicts. The solution proposed combines dominant information and dominant maneuver— the ability to outmaneuver an enemy because our maneuver is based on a much better idea of the tactical situation. A seapower or maritime strategy bases its dominant maneuver on the sea, because it is far easier to move anything heavy by sea than by land or air. Moving a complete air base several thousand miles at thirty miles per hour is what a carrier does routinely.

Much of the world's population, its wealth, and even the sources of that wealth are so close to the sea that maritime forces can deal with the initial stages of almost all confrontations. There are, of course, exceptions. Some countries have inland borders, and in some cases we have guaranteed their security. In those cases ground forces may have to be introduced at the outset. Even then, those forces cannot sustain operations for long unless they have ready access to the sea, which is the route for heavy supplies.

To make dominant maneuver possible, the force maneuvering has to be able to secure the space in which it maneuvers. Ideally it denies that space to its enemy. At sea, this combination of freedom to maneuver and denial of enemy countermaneuver is sea control. Securing sea control requires that we be able to deny enemies the ability to block us at sea. Depending on circumstances, that may involve the use of blocking forces or simply defensive measures on our part.

To make dominant maneuver meaningful, the force maneuvering must be able to exert pressure on something the enemy values. U.S. warships can attack land targets in a world in which most of what is valuable is near or on the sea. In some situations attack may be by missile or even gun; in others, it is by troops projected ashore and supported from the sea. The ability to sustain such support becomes more important as the troops carry less with them in order to preserve their own agility.

What makes seapower so crucial in current conditions is that it can exert its influence without resorting to force. It can be present without another country's permission. What is offshore is sovereign U.S. territory, only loosely subject to the desires of those ashore. No base ashore offers anything like the same degree of political security; no base ashore can always be used as the U.S. government chooses. Any base ashore carries with it commitments that may prove open-ended. Throughout this book are examples of what appeared, at the outset, to be small commitments on the ground that grew out of all proportion to their intrinsic importance.

Seapower offers mobility, both to engage where we wish and to disengage as we must, in both cases at minimum cost. Our freedom to act—assuming our seapower is effective—will often attract the coalition partners we need to become more effective, as in the case of the Gulf War. Conversely, our freedom includes the freedom to withdraw, to limit our commitment to partners. That is, we should always be attractive to them, but we devise our policy to achieve U.S., not foreign, interests.[1]

History shows that seapower in itself is rarely decisive. In the post–Cold War age, however, we are not fighting for our lives; we rarely seek decisive ends. Almost always we seek some limited outcome, which reduces dangers to ourselves. We cannot afford unlimited investment in each conflict to achieve the most favorable decisive resolution. Agile, mobile, seapower is well suited to such a world. We can gain a satisfactory outcome, and then leave when we want or when we must. History also shows that seapower generally requires a land-oriented coalition partner in order to achieve decisive results. Applied at will, our seapower can attract coalition partners. These partners may provide the land access needed to deploy heavy forces, or indeed to do the job of some of those heavy forces themselves. They may also provide indispensable basing for sustained naval operations.

This is quite aside from current interest in attracting coalition partners for political reasons. If the main purpose of our foreign policy is to maintain peace that fosters economic development, then coalitions become vehicles for gaining important political consensus. A navy is valuable in building a coalition because if offers valuable military support without the cost inherent in granting rights for basing ashore.

Finally, we cannot accept a force posture that is adapted only to the current post–Cold War world, with its geographically and materially limited threats. Forces last a long time, and over decades something similar to the Cold War may develop. Agile seapower, well attuned to the needs of the current situation, can deter a potential great-power enemy while we rebuild the forces needed for larger-scale war or, hopefully, further deterrence. Again, it is seapower's ability to strike at targets of great value ashore that gives it deterring power. Seapower's mobility allows a limited force, of limited cost, to cover a wide variety of such targets for as long as it can survive. No fixed tactical force can do as well. Conversely, the need for a limited naval force to be usable in a future cold war or even a hot war should shape decisions about the sort of ships the United States should be buying and the weapons needed to arm them.

These ideas apply to any government that wants to use seapower. One prerequisite for a maritime-oriented national strategy is that a country be free of major overland threats, so that it can concentrate on using the sea. Such countries still face threats, but in their case mortal threats can come only by sea (or by nuclear-tipped missile). They can choose between coast defense and a more oceanic strategy in which offensive action may preclude invasion. The longer the coast, the more coast defense is needed. A maritime solution substitutes a few concentrated naval formations; mobility multiplies their effectiveness.

The maritime solution may also be a better way to leverage national advantages in high technology or in a well-educated population. Indeed, a well-educated population is probably a prerequisite for maritime power, simply because a navy embodies so much technology. When Admiral Mahan wrote about the prerequisites for seapower in the 1880s and 1890s, he pointed out that a vibrant seagoing community produced the sailors needed to operate a wartime fleet. Without that reservoir of manpower, how could a navy expand? In his day, technology was limited enough that merchant seamen could, at least in theory, man ships with little additional training. In a modern navy, seamanship is a limited part of a much larger training curriculum. Education prepares personnel to learn about specialized technology. It may be that much of what separates advanced from developing countries is that the latter have very limited pools of sophisticated people. Functions that can be assigned to noncommissioned officers in advanced countries fall instead to elite officers. The Cold War Soviets were famous for exactly this sort of personnel policy; they could never trust their draftees with technical jobs. Officers did the jobs that petty officers did in the West. The Soviet practice was generally ascribed to paranoia, but it seems fairer to say that potential petty officers were in such short supply that they had to be returned to the Soviet economy. Thus Soviet military personnel and associated repair practices reflected, among other things, the less developed character of Soviet society.[2] In an advanced society technically competent individuals become commonplace, so they can support a higher-technology military as well as a higher-technology economy. The question is not absolute numbers of individuals of various levels of accomplishment, but rather their distribution within the wider society. It would be crippling, for example, for the military routinely to siphon off half of the technicians in a country.

The contingency against which a navy is built may not be overtly military. In many cases the main perceived threat to national security may be uncontrolled immigration by sea. The analog to preemptive assault would be an attempt to affect conditions in the country from which immigrants are likely to come, as opposed to coast defense, which would mean tighter controls exercised over the length of a coast. In their present role, naval forces may offer useful backing to any peaceful attempt to intervene overseas. Coast Guard units can be interposed between the sources of immigrants and their destination, as happened in the U.S. responses to Cuban and Haitian refugees. For example, some European governments currently see uncontrolled seaborne immigration from Algeria, due to local problems, as a major threat. Aid to, or assisted reform of, the Algerian economy might drastically reduce the incentive to chance passage across the Mediterranean. It also might be easier to implement than closure of the Mediterranean coast of Europe. The aid solution corresponds to a maritime outlook, while the coast closure solution is a more traditional ground defense outlook.

Islands are obvious candidates for maritime national strategies: Australia, Japan, Taiwan. In each case, it can be argued further that each is vulnerable to attack on seaborne trade. A future unified Korea at peace with the countries on its remaining border might also become a primarily maritime power. Now that the Russian threat has faded, the case can be made that if the European Union evolves into some sort of national entity, it may adopt a more maritime outlook. In the latter two cases, security on land buys the potential for maritime power, although not necessarily the realization of that potential. In fact, remarkably often the potential for maritime power has been rejected in favor of land power. For example, the northern Italian frontier is so mountainous that the country is easy to defend against most overland attacks. Italy therefore had the potential to concentrate on seapower; indeed, Italy could potentially dominate the Mediterranean. Italy did build an impressive fleet, but in World War I she concentrated more intently on a costly ground war against the Austrians. Would naval power have been better? Would it have come closer to achieving and defending Italian national aspirations? The question probably was never asked.

History shows that governments find it difficult to abandon traditional land-oriented outlooks in the face of drastically changed strategic circumstances. People live on land, and it is natural for them to value only the territory they occupy. The maritime orientation demands a considerable level of abstraction. It goes against intuition. Thus, even when they do build expensive navies, land-oriented governments often seem to misunderstand what seapower can and cannot do for them. Armies, for example, typically associate navies with coast defense. Thus the author of a recent history of European armaments before World War I asked why Austria-Hungary, with only one-eighth the coastline, needed as many warships as Italy.[3] The answer was that the Austrians could not feel secure unless their fleet could neutralize the Italian fleet. It would have been the same if Austria had only 5 percent as long a coast as Italy. If the issue had been border defense on land, with relatively immobile army units, the length of the border, or at least of the part of the border that could be crossed, would have determined the appropriate defensive force. It is up to navies to explain just how much difference the inherent mobility of seapower makes. Fifty aircraft on board a highly mobile aircraft carrier are very different from fifty aircraft at a fixed air base; the mobility the latter might achieve by hopping from base to base is also very different from what the carrier offers.

Before and during World War I the British were much affected by the land orientation of France, their prospective coalition partner. The French cared about nothing except territory, particularly the territory they had lost to the Germans in the Franco-Prussian War a generation earlier. They professed no interest in a coalition unless the British supplied troops; they had no confidence in the value of British maritime power. The British government of the day considered the coalition so important that it gradually abandoned its classic maritime strategy, although it is not clear that the ministers involved realized just what was happening.

Another important issue is the character of maritime coalitions. Ships have long, but hardly infinite, endurance. Sustained operations require bases. Although the U.S. Navy of World War II developed seaborne logistics that permitted lengthy operations thousands of miles from its base, no navy currently has a comparable capability. Thus sustained U.S. operations will generally require coalition partners, quite apart from any desire for political cover. Conversely, the ability to host such operations can make a country attractive as a partner. From that country's point of view, membership in a coalition is an opportunity to shift the overall coalition goals in its direction, for example, toward protecting its interests. This possibility makes it attractive for navies to seek a considerable degree of interoperability with the U.S. Navy. That will carry increasing costs. Interoperability is largely a matter of communications, and the U.S. Navy is rapidly changing its communications and command systems to exploit evolving computer technology and, incidentally, to cut operating costs. Conversely, to the extent that the U.S. Navy will want to continue to operate with coalition partners, it is in the navy's interest to maintain an ability to use existing widespread communications channels. The issue of interoperability is technical, but its resolution has enormous strategic implications.[4]

The effect of new operational concepts such as "Forward . . . From the Sea" is to connect the U.S. Navy much more closely to evolving ground forces command and control systems. Most Western navies share at least the U.S. command network evolved during the Cold War. In the past, armies have not had comparable automated command and control systems. With the advent of the "Revolution in Military Affairs," the U.S. Army is adopting a navy-style automated command system. Among other things, the automated system connects offshore ships to units ashore requiring deep fire support. Thus it is crucial to the new kind of amphibious war the U.S. Marines envisage. How would such a system be used to support coalition troops whose armies had never adopted comparable, let alone interoperable, technology? To what extent should alternatives suited to other armies be retained, even though they would affect the savings to be achieved by adopting the new automated command systems?[5]

The issue is always the same. Is the sea a barrier or a highway? If seapower makes the sea a barrier, then it is a tool to promote isolationism. The argument against isolation is that some weapons, both military (missiles and aircraft) and economic, can leap any barrier. It is better to use the sea as a highway, and engage potential threats as close to source as possible. That is the ultimate character of maritime strategy—for the United States, and for any other country contemplating such a strategy.

Appendix A: Naval Technology

Technology helps determine how well a particular force fits a chosen strategy. Conversely, buying technology without reference to how it is likely to be used can be very counterproductive. Often a new ship or weapon seems attractive, but fails to fit strategic requirements. For example, U.S. coasts are at least three thousand miles from likely theaters of operation. Traditionally the U.S. Navy has built large warships specifically because they must spend so much of their time in transit to distant operating areas. Even if overseas bases are available, the gross uncertainties of the post–Cold War world would seem to demand strategic mobility that, in turn, is best satisfied by large ships. A navy forced to concentrate on limited numbers of long-range ships may well feel itself forced to favor a main fleet strategy. This logic clearly is far from universal. A navy operating within a few hundred miles of its base hardly needs long range, so it may choose to emphasize much smaller ships. Even so, it may have good reasons to favor large ships over smaller ones.

The purpose of our fleet is to influence events abroad. To do that, our ships should be able to impose meaningful damage on land targets. They should be able to interdict foreign shipping and, more generally, deny the sea to an enemy. These capabilities apply to the presence mission as much as to actual combat; navies probably influence events more often by tacit threats than by actual combat.

Ships, particularly large ones capable of operating far from home, are necessarily few, yet there are many naval roles. Moreover, naval roles are likely to change over a ship's lengthy lifetime. Therefore it is very important that ships be as flexible as possible. Single-purpose ships are always less expensive than multipurpose ones, but that economy becomes waste if their single mission becomes obsolete.

233

Our ships must be robust in the face of the many threats the post–Cold War world may impose. Rules of engagement may often preclude counterattack. Some attacks, for example, the USS *Cole* incident, may be complete surprises. The ideal is probably that our ships should be able to take the first shot from an enemy and fire the last shot, which destroys that enemy.

We must be able to maintain enough ships, despite high unit costs. Over the long run in peacetime, the total available number of ships of a given type is the number affordable each year multiplied by ship lifetime. The longer the unit lifetime, the larger the number in service. For example, in the 1980s the U.S. Navy tried to build to a six-hundred-ship fleet, a size that seemed sustainable on the ground that Congress could be expected to provide about twenty ships each year; each ship could be expected to last about thirty years.[1] The number in service through the early 1970s was much larger, because so many ships had been built during World War II. It was not sustainable once those ships had reached the end of their lives, however. The size of the fleet declined precipitously in the early 1970s as World War II–built ships were retired. Given the sheer size of the war-built fleet, the rate of new construction through the 1960s had been quite low.

The number of ships actually available at any one time depends on the reliability of each ship and on how much of a ship's lifetime is spent being maintained and modernized. A design that limits the maintenance and modernization time each requires makes a limited number of hulls more effective. Similarly, ship design determines the extent to which ships are subject to operational problems, such as weather damage. The situation is complicated because a design perfectly acceptable in one operating area may perform very poorly in another. U.S. destroyers designed for service in the Pacific during World War II proved quite wet in the northern waters that were of greater interest during the Cold War. Conversely, a ship designed on the same tonnage for rough northern weather would not have been heavily enough armed to stand off Japanese kamikazes during World War II.

Our navy must be interoperable so that its forces can be integrated with coalition forces, and also so that they can be effective in joint operations. This is largely a matter of command/control capacity, both physical (size of command space) and electronic (including computer capacity).

Our requirements are consistent. They point to the same general characteristics in ships, thus large ships are favored over smaller ones. Larger ships are more survivable in the face of battle damage and more adaptable in the face of radical technological change, because they are easier to modify. Conversely, this set of requirements argues against building relatively inexpensive point solution ships, such as the Cold War NATO frigates.

Cost, Lifetime, and Obsolescence

Quite aside from issues of sheer durability, a ship's useful lifetime depends both on whether she can be upgraded to continue to accomplish her designed mission and on whether that mission itself remains relevant. As ships become more expensive, the number built each year or each decade inevitably falls, yet geography demands that a global power maintain sufficient numbers. The only real solution is to extend ships' effective lifetimes.

During the Cold War, the modernization aspect seemed dominant, because missions and even overall national strategy changed slowly. For example, antisubmarine frigates became obsolete when they could no longer accommodate large new sonars that were needed to detect and track quieter or faster new submarines. Mission obsolescence was an important issue immediately after World War II, and it is a phenomenon of the post–Cold War world. Perfectly adequate NATO frigates are obsolescent because they cannot carry out the major current naval mission of attacking land targets. Even some ships not yet built may be conceptually obsolescent because they correspond more to Cold War than to post–Cold War missions. Given the instability of the post–Cold War period, it would seem particularly unwise to assume that point solutions to current perceived problems will necessarily be relevant when ships designed now are completed or when they reach mid-life. The gap between conception and completion is now about a decade; ships last thirty years, and probably will soon be required to last forty or more years. Past history shows just how much can happen in the thirty years between conception and mid-life.

Sheer size makes it much easier to adapt a ship to new roles. For example, most U.S. World War II warships were substantially larger than their British counterparts. During the war the British director of naval construction argued that they were quite uneconomical to build as well as operate. Then both missions and naval technology changed dramatically. The massive U.S. fleet in existence in 1945, most of it newly built, suddenly became largely obsolete. Yet, given the youth of the fleet, Congress was not about to buy another fleet. Fortunately, size bought valuable flexibility. It proved relatively easy to rebuild U.S. ships to accommodate new weapons such as guided missiles and jet aircraft; many ships built during World War II were not retired until the 1960s or even the 1970s. The Royal Navy, which had designed its ships far more tightly, was much less fortunate. It, too, tried to modernize its fleet, but with much less satisfactory results. For example, only one of the six existing fleet carriers could be rebuilt; some, still under construction, were modified more successfully. Attempts to modify cruisers to take guided missiles failed. Although existing destroyers were rebuilt as fast antisubmarine frigates, they could not accommodate the larger sensors and weapons of the 1960s, as U.S. ships could.[2]

The U.S. Navy's later *Spruance*-class destroyers were so roomy that they were easy to modify to respond to radical changes both in technology and in mission requirements. Size bought good performance, and over time equipment was augmented considerably.[3] For example, it was possible to install a large vertical missile launcher forward, accommodating long-range Tomahawk land attack missiles. This weapon, unimagined when the ships were designed, transformed their capabilities.[4] Smaller frigates, such as the *Knox* class, which started with much the same weapons and sensors as a *Spruance,* could never be rearmed.

The *Spruance* class also showed that larger did not have to be more expensive: they did not cost much more than frigates half their size, with similar armament. It may even be less expensive, on a ton-for-ton basis, to build a larger ship because access is easier in a larger hull; a larger hull also may be more durable, because it faces lower stresses at sea. The larger the ship, however, the greater the temptation to fill it with weapons and sensors, in which case it really is much more expensive.

For a large sophisticated warship, the weapon system costs about as much as the rest of the ship. For a ship with a relatively limited weapon system on a large hull, as in the *Spruance* class, the weapon system represents a much smaller fraction of total cost. Many navies cut the first cost of ships by making provision for systems but not installing them, a practice sometimes called "fitting for but not with." A version of this practice might be to install a large number of vertical missile launcher cells, which are inexpensive, but not initially to buy the missiles to fill them.

During the Cold War, European NATO navies, such as those of Britain, Germany, and the Netherlands, specialized in antisubmarine warfare, on the theory that the bulk of the Soviet threat to NATO shipping would be from submarines. They built efficient antisubmarine frigates, in effect point solutions to a military problem. Because they were specialized, these ships could be made relatively small, which policy makers equated to low cost. Their navies, or perhaps their civilian overlords, apparently never understood that bigger did not need to be much more expensive. When the Cold War ended, the naval situation changed radically. Recently built frigates, much too small to rebuild or rearm, became largely obsolete because the world had changed radically, thus facing obsolescence just as the U.S. and British fleets did in 1945.

The lesson is that ships should be designed with an open architecture. Aircraft carriers come closest, with their capacious hangars and large flight decks. It is relatively easy to modify a carrier to accommodate new aircraft. A U.S. *Midway*-class carrier, for example, was designed in 1942 to launch small piston-engine fighters and attack aircraft. By about 1950, little modified, she could launch a large piston-engine bomber capable of carrying a nuclear bomb deep into the Soviet Union. She lasted, with some reconstruction, through at least four generations of jet fighters (subsonic, transonic, supersonic day only, and supersonic all-weather). To the extent that the small NATO frigates remain viable, it is thanks largely to their helicopters, which can be modified or replaced to carry out alternative missions. The key to continued usefulness, then, was the open architecture—the carrier-like—aspect of the frigates' designs.

For the U.S. Navy, the vertical missile launcher provides large surface combatants with a valuable degree of open architecture. The launcher can fire any missile that fits into its cells. Earlier kinds of launchers (e.g., those using trainable rails) were generally limited to one or two types of missile, which had been selected at the time of launcher design. Initially the vertical launcher was favored because it fired faster and was more reliable mechanically; a missile did not have to be up on a rail before firing. It was decided, however, to make the cell long enough to take the then-new Tomahawk cruise missile. That was possible only because the ships planned for the vertical launcher were so large that the extra length imposed no great burden. At the time, Tomahawk was planned as a nuclear missile for land attack, with a possible extension to antiship capability. The main rationale for fielding it on board surface ships was to complicate the Soviet navy's task of dealing with the U.S. fleet. Instead of merely tracking carriers, the Soviets would now have to track every U.S. surface combatant capable of firing a Tomahawk. In time, however, Tomahawk changed into the conventionally armed land attack missile now used widely. Ships that had been conceived mainly as antiaircraft platforms, to deal with mass Soviet missile raids, became long-range land attack shooters. Also, they could shift back to their antiaircraft capability, or to a future theater missile defense capacity, simply by changing the load in the vertical launchers.

Combat Direction

The combat effectiveness of a modern warship is determined by the way her weapons and sensors are tied together by her combat direction system, which is built around an array of computers. Data from the ship's sensors, and any available offboard information, are fed into her combat information center (CIC) or combat direction center (CDC), the center of the combat direction system, and the data are merged into an intelligible tactical picture of what is happening around the ship. The ship's commander makes tactical decisions on the basis of this picture, and he commands the ship's weapons through the combat direction system. For example, an antiaircraft system is ordered to engage a target displayed on a computer screen; without the display on that screen, no engagement is possible. Ships' combat direction systems vary radically, for example, in the number of objects (some of which may become targets) they can display and track and even in the degree of precision with which data are carried. Operationally, much depends on the number of operators, who help form the tactical picture, and even on the quality of the display available to the command.

As in other computer applications, the controlling cost is now software. Just as a large hull makes it relatively easy to install new equipment, maximum computer capacity makes it easier to build and operate modular software that is easiest to modify to handle new weapons and sensors. Ships are designed to last for decades, and it may be more than a decade between conception and completion. One great challenge, then, is to design a command system so that it can be upgraded throughout that period. For decades, computers have doubled in power every eighteen months; the rate may accelerate more than this in the near future. This Moore's Law suggests strongly that any ship conceived for thirty or forty years' service should accept several radically differing generations of controlling computers, as well as weapons exploiting new computer capability, including some not currently imagined. This idea was central to the design of the command system of the new U.S. *Virginia*-class attack submarine.[5]

The more complex the tactical situation, the more important computer power and good programming become. For example, the Royal Australian Navy rejected the computer-driven combat system on board its new *Collins*-class submarines when the computer's picture noticeably lagged the raw sonar data being fed into it. Like other modern combat systems, this one could fire only on the basis of the displayed tactical picture. Usually that was quite acceptable, but in one crucial case it was not; the submarine had to be able to fire instantly back along the line of approach of a nearby torpedo, in hopes of forcing the firing submarine to evade and thus to break the torpedo's guidance wire. In such a case the lag in displaying a tactical picture could be fatal.

The British Type 23 ("Duke" class) frigates illustrate the importance of computer combat direction. The system being developed for these ships proved inadequate, so eight were completed with no central computer system at all. While they were being built, the system was put out to tender, a new one was selected, and it was developed—but not in time for the first eight ships. Externally, these ships were quite as complete as their later sisters, but the Royal Navy was uncomfortably aware that they had little combat capability, particularly against air attack. They could not be deployed anywhere ships faced serious air threats, which meant most of the places in which the Royal Navy operated in any numbers (e.g., the Gulf). Unfortunately the British treasury had placed a stiff upper limit on the total number of destroyers and frigates the Royal Navy could operate; therefore, perfectly adequate ships had to be retired without being replaced by fully operational Type 23s. The increased load on the remaining effective ships was quite painful. Ultimately the first eight ships were refitted with the required systems, and the Royal Navy was quite lucky that it faced no major combat before that had been done.

Command Style and Data Links

In Western navies at least, the basic tactical units of seapower are not individual ships or aircraft, but rather organic, mutually supporting combinations: carrier battle groups, surface action groups, escort groups, underway replenishment groups, amphibious ready groups. Submarines are an important exception, at least at present. This reality may be obscured in peacetime when ships intended to operate in formations have to operate independently.

Tactical communication within a group of combatant ships is largely based on radio data links connecting ships' computer combat direction systems, using stereotyped messages. By this means, at least in theory, the group builds a common tactical picture as a common basis for tactical decisions. For example, the data link identifies friendly forces, and thus helps prevent "blue on blue" attacks. Conversely, without some sort of data link, cooperation becomes difficult. Thus, it is difficult, at least at present, for submarines to support surface forces directly because they cannot easily communicate with those forces on a continuous basis. Much effort has gone into providing submarines with limited access to the common tactical picture, generally through link reception schemes, but that is not the same type of communication most surface ships have with each other.

Through the Cold War the NATO ship-to-ship standard became Link 11, which will soon be replaced with Link 16/22.[6] Like any other form of communication, Link 11 has a vocabulary, which is limited by the message format. All targets are identified as either enemy, friendly, or unknown (presumed enemy). The system, then, is ill-adapted to large numbers of neutrals likely to be met in a post–Cold War situation. They can hardly be described as presumed enemies, and the system cannot reflect the shades of friendliness that must be discerned. The *Stark* incident is a case in point: the Iraqi airplane that attacked had to be identified as a friendly, because it was clearly neither enemy nor unidentified. When the picture based on the link data is the basis for instant decisions, it is hardly satisfactory for the officer using it to have to step back and reinterpret it each time he sees it. The newer Link 16 (joint tactical information distribution system) offers a better vocabulary, as well as more precision in its data. NATO navies may adopt Link 22 (i.e., double-11), which uses modified Link 11 media to transmit Link 16 messages.[7]

Many Western-built export warships have a simpler, incompatible, Link Y. For such ships, real tactical cooperation with NATO units requires a gateway of some kind, to translate between link messages. Similar considerations apply to a NATO force containing some Link 11 and some Link 16 ships.

The Soviets operated quite differently. Reflecting their army-type command structure, their standard naval link sent tactical data up to a flagship or command post ashore, and received orders in return. In the future it may be important politically for Western navies to be able to work with navies raised on Soviet lines. It is not clear how the difference in philosophy and practice, as exemplified by the difference in data link practice, can be bridged. This is not a trivial issue. At present the main striking element of a naval formation is often a force of naval aircraft. Other aircraft are often the main threat to surface ships. Moreover, ships are generally fragile enough that their main defense is to shoot down aircraft before they attack. What happens as a mass of aircraft approaches a fleet? If they are returning strike aircraft, shooting them down disarms the fleet. If they are unfriendly, not firing sacrifices the fleet. The shared tactical picture—the fruit of the links and the computers—should say which is which. What happens to ships that cannot share the same picture, or whose weapons systems are not connected to the computers displaying it?

At present the U.S. Navy supplements its formatted data links with a type of internet, the hardware and software of which are called IT-21 (Information Technology-21). IT-21 has become a vital command aid. For example, officers within a battle group can exchange views via the equivalent of an internet chat room. A force relieving another on station can receive a detailed package of data via e-mail. At present U.S. ships and other forces receive a variety of formatted broadcasts that, among other things, provide them with a valuable over-the-horizon picture of shipping and of the situation ashore. Plans call for these broadcasts to be folded into the military classified internet (SIPRNET).

Allied navies generally have not followed a similar path. Relatively few ships can participate in the IT-21. That is probably nearly as bad as lacking Link 11, and in the future it may make it almost impossible for them to cooperate tactically with the U.S. Navy. The embargo against Iraq, for example, depended heavily on a shipping picture disseminated by satellite broadcast, one of the special formatted U.S. broadcasts.

IT-21 was adopted partly to support a new network-centric form of naval warfare. Beginning in the 1970s, the U.S. Navy merged data about Soviet naval movements at shore data fusion centers. The resulting picture was transmitted to ships, providing their officers with information extending far beyond their own horizons. As a consequence, they could use the antiship version of Tomahawk against Soviet warships. The system employed a variety of sensors, many of them in space. In effect a ship receiving this data was provided with external sensors. The result was called network-centric because sensing was dispersed to a net of external sensors rather than being centered on any one ship. Conversely, multiple ships or groups of ships sharing a common tactical picture could be netted together to attack the same targets. The idea of network-centric warfare was extended further; for example, data for attacks against land targets by distant ships relying on requests for fire were inserted into a computer network. Many other applications have been developed. To some extent network-centric warfare is an extension of existing practice using data links to maintain a common tactical picture within a tactical force.[8] Its dramatic extension of a ship's horizon made possible the use of long-range ship-launched missiles, and its advent has led to a wide variety of new tactics. To use external sensors a ship and her weapons must know exactly where they are; network-centric operations demand the precise navigation now possible through the use of satellites.

Networking has definite limitations, however. Most of the distant sensors see the world on an intermittent basis. The picture constructed from their outputs is inevitably a mixture of somewhat dated, or "time-late," information projected ahead on a statistical basis. It is good enough to support firing weapons at a distance against targets with estimated courses, because failure is not likely to be fatal. On the other hand, the distant sensors are unlikely to warn a ship in time to ward off attack. To survive, the ship still requires her own sensors to support her defensive weapons.

One important question for the future is whether networking makes it possible or desirable for a dispersed group of smaller ships to replace smaller numbers of larger ones. The dispersed ships can hit a common target, thanks to networking. Any single attack is unlikely to destroy all ships, thanks to their dispersion. On the other hand, the cost per weapon deployed is likely to be far higher, because each of the dispersed ships requires many of the ship and defensive systems that a single larger ship would have. More important, naval functions extend well beyond simply firing weapons at a target. Small missile ships may not be effective in roles such as shipping protection, embargo enforcement, or presence. As for vulnerability, in the usual circumstance short of actual war, the destruction of a single inexpensive ship may be quite as unacceptable to the government and to the public as the destruction of a single larger one.

The concept of a networked flotilla of smaller missile ships recalls Soviet naval tactics during the Cold War. The Soviets largely eschewed naval missions other than attacks against major U.S. warships, particularly carriers, and offensive antisubmarine warfare. They consciously rejected the typical Western naval model, which is designed for much more than sea denial. For example, the Soviets had only a very limited ability to attack shore targets. Even so, by the 1980s they found themselves building large expensive ships as predicated by the demands of evolving naval technology. Thus it is by no means clear that limiting missions and relying on networked data can always cut the unit size or cost of warships.

For the U.S. Navy, network-centric practices gave Tomahawks launched by surface ships and submarines the long range that makes them so valuable. Planning long-range strikes requires detailed current knowledge of activity, particularly air defense, around a target, not merely a set of target coordinates. Current data are provided by remote reconnaissance devices, such as satellites and unmanned aircraft, fused into usable form, and provided on the network tapped by the ship. Conversely, a navy lacking an over the horizon sensor and communications network lacks weapon reach, even if it buys a missile with extraordinary aerodynamic range.

Littoral Conditions

Many would say that the near-term future of naval warfare is littoral. Littoral areas differ significantly from the open sea. In some parts of the world conditions just above the sea, often near a coast, can drastically modify radar performance. Evaporation off the surface creates ducts, which act as waveguides, projecting signals vast distances, but reflecting away signals from outside the duct. Other ducts appear as bands in the air. This effect is felt mainly at X(I)-band, although a somewhat analogous effect, scattering from the troposphere, often extends the range of L(C/D)-band radars. Unless the extended ranges are taken into account, the radar picture can be disastrously confused. During the Cold War, the Soviets became interested in both types of extended propagation, and they designed many of their missile targeting radars specifically to exploit them. Although such propagation is called anomalous, in some places, such as the Eastern Baltic, the Eastern Mediterranean, the Gulf, the Indian Ocean, and the South China Sea, it is the rule. Local navies may exploit such conditions; outside navies neglect them to their peril. For example, the Indian navy deliberately adjusted its Soviet-made surface search (missile targeting) radars to exploit ducting.

Close inshore, electromagnetic signals can reflect off a jagged coastline, confusing analysis. Ducts, however, may trap important signals created onshore, so that airborne receivers cannot capture them. Seaborne receivers, such as those aboard submarines, may become far more important.

Shallow water enormously modifies sonar performance, generally for the worse. If the water is warm and calm, a shallow surface layer, which traps sound, will form, and hull sonars may become useless. Generally, signals will be repeatedly reflected from both the bottom and the surface, confusing a receiver. The usual methods of extending sonar range, by using convergence zones or long-range bottom bounce, become irrelevant.[9] There are still ways of extending sonar range, using carefully shaped beams, but they require sonar configurations quite different from those common in the world's warships.[10] Usually the criterion for shallow water is the continental shelf, defined as the line at which the sea is only one hundred fathoms (six hundred feet) deep. Moreover, if the water is less than about a thousand feet deep, a diesel non-nuclear submarine being pursued may well choose to sit on the bottom, where a sonar is distracted by complex terrain features and possibly even wrecked ships. Water depth also determines which kinds of mines can be used.

Thus naval technology well suited to inshore or littoral operations may be strikingly different from that best suited to deep water. Yet a navy most likely has to transit considerable deep ("blue") water en route to any littoral ("brown water") operation. Moreover, in the course of time its emphasis may swing back to blue water.

Trade-Offs in Warship Design

Ship size is characterized in several ways: tonnage, internal volume, deck area, and linear dimensions. They are not at all equivalent. The classic ships of the past—battleships and cruisers—were weight critical because they carried dense objects such as gun turrets, armor belts, and machinery. The ship's hull was chosen to provide enough buoyancy to carry these weights; it always had much more volume than required. One visual clue to this situation is that many battleships had small superstructures projecting above their hulls. They did not need the volume that a big superstructure would have offered. Conversely, weights had to be calculated carefully because once a hull had been chosen, it could carry only so much. The basic design documents for warships of this kind are lists of weights, which must add up to the displacement offered by the hull.

In the missile age, however, most of the key elements of ships are bulky but relatively light: control spaces, computer rooms, missile magazines. Ships have become volume critical. It is easy to provide enough buoyancy to carry their weights, but sufficient volume is another question. Thus modern warships generally have bulky superstructures, because their hulls just cannot house everything. In many cases the issue is sufficient deck area, rather than simply volume. There is a vast difference between a large deck space with just enough height to admit system operators, and a tall narrow space with the same volume, which is virtually useless. The first clearly volume-critical warships were aircraft carriers. Modern warships cannot be armored in the old sense because the areas to be covered are too large; useful thicknesses of armor spread over the areas would be far too heavy.

A key issue is how well the ship can adapt to changes during its life. If the ship is weight critical, any major change is likely to add weight. A conventional (i.e., displacement) hull simply sinks slightly deeper in the water as weight is added. If a ship has enough freeboard (i.e., enough hull above water), she is viable over a wide range of tonnage. All of this is apart from any loss of stability due to the added weight. The larger the ship's waterplane, the area of hull at the waterline, the less the ship sinks for every ton added. The waterplane also generates waves as the ship moves, so the larger the waterplane, the more power it takes to attain a given speed.

Larger also means that less of the ship's hull must be devoted to the powerplant. At high speed a surface ship uses most of her power to overcome wave-making resistance. A good measure of this resistance is the ratio of the ship's speed (in knots) to the square root of her length (in feet); for a fast ship the ratio is greater than one. It is relatively easy to power a four-hundred-foot ship at twenty knots, or a nine-hundred-foot ship at thirty knots. The higher the ratio, the higher the power needed per ton of ship. That is why longer ships sometimes need less power to reach a given speed than short ones, and why small ships, such as motorboats, always need exotic hull forms, such as planing hulls, and high-powered engines to reach high speeds. Thus, with twice the power on something more than twice the displacement (i.e., with fewer horsepower per ton) a *Spruance*-class destroyer is several knots faster than a *Perry*-class frigate. A nuclear carrier, which displaces more than ten times as much as a *Spruance,* is somewhat faster on only about seven times as much power. In a rough sea, the larger the ship, the better she can maintain her speed.

At least for a conventional hull, seakeeping depends on size. Explained simply, to ride well, a ship should be large compared to the waves she encounters. It takes more wave energy to overcome the inertia of a larger, heavier hull.

Several proposed alternative hull forms minimize waterplane area. The ship can be supported by submerged bodies, which are connected to the above-water structure by the narrowest possible struts. A small waterplane twin-hull (the SWATH) is an example: typically two bodies support a large flat above-water structure. Such an arrangement offers drastically reduced resistance and far better seakeeping because of drastically reduced response to surface waves. On the other hand, because the waterplane is so small, the ship may sink quite deep into the water with any addition of weight. The underwater bodies may be made larger than necessary and ballasted to provide the ship with a wider range of tonnage, but that adds structural weight and resistance, thus it requires more power. The underwater bodies, which can be quite far apart, offer steadiness and stability; because they are well under water, they are less affected by wave action. Moreover, SWATH offers a much larger, and more usefully shaped, deck than a conventional ship of the same displacement. Much the same can be said of the *Sea Knife,* which is a single-hull SWATH.[11]

The new British *Trimaran* uses another approach. The slimmer the hull, the less it is affected by waves. Normally the need to keep a ship stable limits how slim her hull can be. As the Polynesians learned centuries ago, outriggers can stabilize the slimmest hull. Connecting the outriggers can be a broad deck. As an added advantage, the wave trains from the main hull and the out-riggers can interact in such a way that the ship's overall resistance, and thus her need for power, over some critical speed range can be drastically reduced. The *Trimaran* may be unable to offer the sort of range of ship weight that a SWATH or even a *Sea Knife* can handle. On the other hand, during their careers modern warships tend to require more deck area or volume rather than more weight capacity, and deck area is just what *Trimaran*, SWATH, and *Sea Knife* offer.[12]

Another alternative type of hull, now less popular than in previous decades, is the surface effect or air cushion ship. Whereas other types are supported by buoyancy, that is, by the water itself, a surface effect ship rides a bubble of air. It achieves high speed because the bubble has minimum friction. For example, only by adopting an air cushion hull could the U.S. Navy exceed forty knots in a small landing craft, the LCAC, capable of carrying heavy tanks over a beach. The bubble is generated by one or more fans. In a surface effect ship it is captured between surface-penetrating sidewalls and flexible bow and stern skirts. An air cushion craft uses flexible skirts that ride the surface; therefore, the craft has virtually zero draft and can ride up on the shore. On the other hand, because it rides the surface, the air cushion craft is more subject to wave action. Besides offering high speed, cushions or air bubbles offer a degree of shock absorption, which may be quite useful for mine countermeasures craft. Examples include the Russian "Sivuch" class surface effect fast attack craft, the Norwegian air cushion mine countermeasures craft, and the U.S. air cushion landing craft (LCAC). Such craft generally have rectangular decks, thereby offering more usable deck area for a given overall size than do conventional hulls with sharply pointed bows and tapered sterns. It is unlikely that this type of hull can be expanded to several thousand tons, thus precluding its use in major warships.

Missile Weapons

Missiles are relatively inefficient in terms of explosive content. The two-ton Tomahawk, a widely used cruise missile, carries about half a ton of warhead, so one hundred such weapons, a full load for a destroyer or cruiser, offer about fifty tons of warhead in a ship displacing about nine thousand tons. A ninety-thousand-ton carrier has magazine stowage, which is much denser than vertical missile stowage, for about twenty-five hundred tons of warheads, equivalent to five thousand Tomahawks. The sheer size of the carrier makes it possible to wrap considerable protective material around that magazine, far more than in a ten-thousand-ton surface combatant. Moreover, the missile is expended each time it is fired, whereas the carrier's aircraft, which are in a sense equivalent to the missile engine, airframe, and guidance package, are reusable—as long as they can survive in the face of enemy air defenses.[13]

On the other hand, precisely because the missile carries everything with it, it can be launched by an inexpensive ship. Thus the first major Western antiship missile, the French Exocet, was designed specifically so that it could be carried aboard a coastal attack boat. The Russians squeezed two of their much larger Styx missiles into a modified torpedo boat. To the extent that such weapons are effective in small numbers, they can be seen as useful equalizers against large-ship navies.

That is not a new idea. Classical big-gun warships were large partly because their hulls had to absorb the force of heavy recoiling guns. The gun represents a trade-off. Its structure is reusable, so only a small fraction of total armament weight is fired off with each shot. A big ship can accommodate numerous shots—but at the cost of a heavy reusable structure, and a heavy hull to support it. Self-propelled weapons, the first of which were torpedoes, do not need heavy launchers, hence they can be carried in small numbers by small hulls. By the end of the nineteenth century it was widely accepted that even a few torpedo hits could sink a large expensive battleship. Thus a small warship armed mainly with torpedoes might well offer a small country, which has limited resources, the ability to fend off an expensive navy. The French in particular became very interested in this option, and they built hundreds of torpedo boats, both surface craft and submarines. Many small countries also bought torpedo boats. There was, however, a flaw in the argument. To be effective, torpedo craft had to be built in large numbers, because the overall kill probability per torpedo, taking aiming errors and reliability into account, was quite small. To be affordable, the craft had to be quite small, thus limiting their seaworthiness.[14] Simply remaining well off-shore afforded conventional battle fleets much of the protection they needed. That did not kill off the torpedo as a ship killer; it merely qualified its value: to be effective, a torpedo often had to be on board a substantial warship.

It takes a large surface ship to accommodate significant numbers of missiles, either offensive or defensive. Generally they are stowed vertically, and only rarely can they be stowed one atop the other. Thus a ship's missile capacity is generally proportional to her deck area. As a ship grows, deck area increases more slowly than displacement. Doubling dimensions increases deck area by a factor of four, but displacement by a factor of eight. To double the number of missiles on board a ship requires about a 40 percent increase in her length and beam—for nearly three times the displacement.

Alternatively, a ship can carry a modest number of guns but numerous shells for them. Thus the shift has been from many projectiles, of which only a small percentage could hit a given target, to a small number of very accurate projectiles. That is a considerable improvement if the target is small, and if direct hits are what counts. Examples would be other ships and aircraft. However, there are also area targets, such as concentrations of troops and tanks, that can be engaged only by large numbers of projectiles. Several current missiles carry submunitions to solve this problem, and new submunitions are self-guided. It is not clear whether the numbers will suffice to handle large but widely dispersed enemy formations.

In the past, guns were multipurpose weapons. The same launcher (a gun) could engage ships, sometimes aircraft, and also shore targets, albeit how flexible it really was depended on its ammunition and its fire-control system. That is why, during World War II, a U.S. battle line built to sink enemy battleships could be used to smash the defenses of Normandy and Japanese-held islands in the Pacific. Then this flexibility evaporated; unguided shells could not deal with the new fast aircraft. Moreover, carrier aircraft could reach far beyond gun range, and so were more effective against many surface targets. Ships armed mainly with heavy guns were now useful mainly against shore targets. Navies buy multipurpose ships because special-purpose ones are too expensive to maintain. Although they were still quite important in one kind of naval warfare, amphibious assault, the battleships and the gun-armed cruisers gradually, inevitably, disappeared. With them the navy's ability to deliver massed fire passed from surface warships to carriers, which were the only ships left armed with large numbers of weapons.

This story has an odd twist. By the late twentieth century, it was possible to provide gun projectiles with a degree of guidance, to give them some of the advantages previously enjoyed by missiles. These munitions were still compact, like earlier unguided shells. They could be provided with postfiring propulsion, to give them the desired reach. A gun, then, could once again be a multipurpose launcher, with the advantage over missiles that a ship of a given size could carry larger numbers of projectiles. It remains to be seen whether the potential of the gun as multipurpose missile launcher is realized in the next few years.

Survivability

In the past, ships were designed to keep fighting until the water closed over them. Anyone visiting a preserved World War II ship will be impressed by the number of alternative command and fire-control centers, the theory being that control would shift as any of them was put out of action. With the advent of elaborate electronic weapon systems, however, the shock of even minor damage might be fatal. Computer systems had to be centralized, and radars were relatively fragile. Electronics is now much more robust, however, as anyone with a home computer knows. Computer systems can be decentralized, thus no single hit will knock out a ship's combat capability. Ships can go back to that earlier standard, and there is every reason to expect that to happen.

The October 2000 attack on the missile destroyer USS *Cole* illustrates how important damage resistance can be to a ship on a presence mission. She had put into the port of Aden to fuel, but more importantly to demonstrate friendly U.S. seapower. Two individuals ran a small boat alongside and detonated a large onboard charge. *Cole* was badly damaged, but she survived, thanks both to her sturdy design and construction and to the ability of her crew. No proactive measures, such as jammers, guns, missiles, or decoys, could have affected the outcome. Nor did it matter whether *Cole* had signature-reduction (stealth) features. Presence is about visibility and, for that matter, accessibility. If U.S. ships visiting foreign ports have to hide behind protective screens, much of the value of their presence is lost. Moreover, the vast majority of small boats in such ports, many of which will inevitably come alongside, are quite innocent. Measures to deal with the few dangerous ones would be horrifically counterproductive. Ship survivability becomes an important means of ensuring that incidents, if they do occur, have limited consequences.

In a presence situation, an enemy can usually fire the first shot, but ships should be so designed that they can fire the last. Unless our ships can survive surprise attacks, such attacks can be used to turn U.S. policy. *Stark*, discussed above, is a case in point. It is sometimes argued that smaller warships, though inherently less survivable, can act as lightning rods. Will the public willingly accept the loss of a relatively inexpensive ship, whereas the loss of a major unit is an unacceptable catastrophe? That seems unlikely; the issue is whether a U.S. ship has been attacked, rather than whether the ship is large or small. For example, early in December 1941 the U.S. Navy was ordered to set up a picket line of small ships off the Philippines.[15] It was believed that the Japanese were bent on invasion. If they were allowed to land the first blow in a manner of their own choice, however, they might be able to make an effective surprise attack. The hope, then, was that en route to the invasion, the Japanese would feel compelled to sink one or more of the pickets barring their way. This act in turn would justify a U.S. declaration of war. Given a hostile Japanese act, the United States could legitimately carry out spoiling attacks on the invasion force. That such an expedient was considered credible shows that the government considered the sinking of anything flying the U.S. flag a full-fledged act of war. As it happened, the Japanese acted first, with full-scale attacks on both the Philippines and Hawaii, so the pickets never did their job. Another illustration of this point is the furor that accompanied the sinking, by the Japanese, of the small Yangtze River gunboat *Panay* in 1937. There was a real fear at the time that the incident might lead to war, despite reluctance on the part of the U.S. government. In the event, the Japanese apologized and paid an indemnity; no one said that the incident could be ignored because the ship was so small or that, because she was so minor, the loss of the ship did not damage U.S. prestige in China.

Against missiles, the emphasis is on either destroying the weapon in flight or diverting it from its target into a decoy. The larger the ship, the greater her capacity for active defense, all other things being equal. For example, she can carry a longer-range sensor, a better defensive fire-control system, and more defensive weapons that are more powerful. She can also support a more powerful jammer, and more decoys. Against this, it may be argued that the ship has a larger intrinsic signature, offering an incoming weapon a better chance of distinguishing her from a decoy. This potential disadvantage of sheer size, however, has largely been overcome by modifying the shape of surface ships and by covering parts of them in radar-absorbing material.[16]

A major current question is the extent to which ships should be designed specifically to reduce their radar and other signatures. Up to a point, such design is relatively easy and inexpensive. For example, to eliminate corner reflectors a ship's sides can be sloped. Because the insides of a compartment also form a corner reflector, gold mesh is placed in portholes to keep radar beams out. Outside details of ships, such as lifelines, are scrutinized for their radar-reflecting properties. Radar-absorbing material can be applied to vertical surfaces. Radar antennas themselves can be tuned so that they reflect only over the narrow range of frequencies the radar uses, rather than over a wider range an enemy may use. Such measures may reduce radar cross-section below that of decoys the ship can fire. To go further requires radical design steps, as evidenced in the proposals for the new DD 21 destroyer class, which may affect other aspects of ship performance. For example, conventional ships have flared bows. As the bow goes down in a seaway (when the ship pitches), its buoyancy increases due to the flare, and a force is generated that brings the bow up out of the water. The flared bow does not reflect radar signals as intensely as a vertical hull section, but it is inferior to a section angled away from the radar beam. To form a ship's hull of such sections would be to adopt tumble home reminiscent of some late nineteenth century warships. Without flare, the ship cannot bring her bow up out of the water; she is described as a wave-piercer (in the nineteenth century such ships were simply described as very wet). If there is little need for access to the deck in a seaway, such wetness may be entirely acceptable. Wave-piercing may also preserve other aspects of radar cross-section reduction, which might be ruined as a ship pitched.

Missiles typically produce localized damage, which ship designers characterize by the length of expected damage. The larger the ship, the smaller proportion of her hull any given weapon is likely to destroy. Moreover, the larger the ship, the easier it is to duplicate vital equipment and to distribute it over the ship so that many hits are needed to disable her. Hits above the waterline (i.e., most missile hits) may *never* directly sink a large ship. Yet sinking is the only unambiguous indication that a ship has been knocked out. It is not clear how well a ship beyond the horizon can gauge that her missile fire has knocked out a target. For example, if electronic emissions appear to cease, has the ship been damaged, or is her commander playing possum—or has he switched to some waveform that is inherently difficult to detect? There is evidence that senior commanders tend to pour on fire until ships sink. For example, in 1986 the U.S. Navy attacked a pair of Iranian frigates in Operation Praying Mantis. When one of them appeared ready to fire, she was hit in succession by antiaircraft missiles, which were fast enough to knock out her own antiship missile system before it could fire; Harpoons; Rockeyes, which saturated the ship with bomblets; and guided bombs. The frigate sank, but surely she had been disabled long before the fatal blows were struck. The scale of attack was acceptable because there were few potential targets, so whatever ordnance that was on hand could safely be expended. War gaming reportedly shows the same tendency to keep firing despite estimates that small numbers of weapons will produce "mission kills."[17] At present not only is the number of weapons shrinking, but it also appears acceptable to use smaller warheads that depend more on precision for lethality. As weapon effects inevitably become more subtle, battle damage assessment (BDA) becomes much more crucial.

There is no hope of keeping any antiship missile out of a ship by armoring. Small Western antiship missiles are physically roughly equivalent to the heavy artillery shells of an earlier era. The armor needed to keep such shells out was so heavy that it could be applied only over limited areas of ships' hulls. The big Soviet missiles and their Chinese equivalents had massive shaped charges quite capable of piercing any existing armor, even on board the battleships that survived into the missile age. It is possible to protect a limited portion of a ship using voluminous, but not necessarily very heavy, armor, and this technique is used around the magazines of current U.S. aircraft carriers. Smaller ships, even missile cruisers, lack the necessary volume. Their vitals can, however, be protected against the fragments (splinters) the missile creates when its warhead explodes. That may be quite enough. Of the two Exocets that hit the frigate USS *Stark*, one exploded near her missile magazine. The ship was saved largely by the thin armor, which was covered in Kevlar, surrounding the magazine and by the crewmen who kept the explosion from starting a fire hot enough to cook off the magazine. In the current *Arleigh Burke* class, armored bulkheads limit the lengthwise extent of damage due to fragments.

Attempts to armor ships are complicated by the sheer variety of antiship missiles. A system of protection that will defeat a particular kind of warhead, such as a shaped charge, may well fail to defeat others, such as pure blast or semi–armor-piercing warheads. All three types are well represented among the world's antiship missiles. The key strategic reality of the post–Cold War period is that it is impossible to say with any certainty which countries will be friends or enemies, hence which kinds of weapons a U.S. warship is likely to face around the world. As the arms trade opens, moreover, weapons that in the past were always associated with friends may find their way into hostile hands. As in the *Stark* incident, friends may inadvertently fire at U.S. ships. In the past, at least in theory, the situation was simpler: U.S. experts concentrated on the threat presented by big Soviet and Chinese weapons. Future missiles will probably be able to select their aim points along a ship's hull. In that case any uniquely important part of a ship, such as a combat information center, will be targeted if a potential enemy knows where it is, and as long as it is above water. Probably the best defense will be to disperse vital functions around the largest possible hull, on the theory that the number of hits can be held down by shipboard defenses, and that the extent of damage from any one hit can be limited by appropriately heavy construction. New technologies make it possible to disperse computer systems, possibly even to place dispersed system operators in a virtual combat direction center.

When they work properly, underwater weapons are inherently far more lethal than their above-water counterparts, because they can flood and thus sink a ship. Many modern torpedoes (and all bottom mines) explode under a ship rather than in her side, which, paradoxically, is much more effective. The explosion forms a gas sphere, which rises and pulses. It is so buoyant that it literally lifts the ship out of the water before it contracts to let the ship down again. Given sufficient explosive power, two such lifts often snap a ship in half. The best defense is probably to design a ship so that the initial pulse breaks through her soft keel, while the ship's sides provide enough strength to hold the hull together. In that case the gas bubble will probably destroy only the compartment under which it forms. To do that requires a large hull. Probably current U.S. aircraft carriers, which have considerable strength in the side protection designed to deal with earlier contact torpedoes, would survive in this way, but few if any other warships enjoy the same degree of security.[18]

The torpedoes' great drawback is relatively low speed. The fastest conventional torpedoes are capable of about sixty knots, whereas quite average missiles make six hundred. The only current exception to slow torpedo speed is Shkval (Squall), a Russian rocket torpedo that runs in its own gas bubble, thus overcoming the usual water resistance. It achieves two hundred knots, running in a more or less straight line for about six miles.[19]

To strike their targets from sufficient range, torpedoes generally home on them. Most Western antiship torpedoes home passively on the noise a ship's engines and propellers generate. Antisubmarine torpedoes, however, are active homers, because submarines are quiet. To counter these weapons, ships may tow or fire noisemakers. Many antiship torpedoes, particularly those exported with Russian "Kilo"-class submarines, are wake followers. Their small upward-looking sonars register when they enter and leave a ship's wake as they cross it. The torpedo is set to turn back as it leaves the wake, causing it to ladder up the wake. The wake is so huge a signature that it is by no means clear that any decoy can be effective. The torpedo can also detect the difference between the wake and the bottom of a ship's hull, thus allowing it to explode under the ship. The main drawback of wake crossing is that the net speed of the torpedo along the ship's wake is far less than its forward speed (it takes up much of its time simply crossing the wake), so it may never connect with a fast ship. Some torpedoes simply detect the edge of the wake, however, then follow it; they suffer no such disadvantage.

The alternative to decoying is simply to destroy the incoming torpedo. Unfortunately that is more difficult than destroying an incoming missile. For years the major navies have tried in vain to devise effective torpedo killers to protect both surface ships and submarines.

The Electric Ship

Electric drive is an interesting twist on the idea of survivability through dispersal. Current prime movers—diesels or gas turbines—drive propeller shafts through gearing. It is physically difficult to disperse them widely, although for many decades warship designers have divided them among multiple compartments, so that one hit will not disable them altogether. The propeller shaft itself remains a vulnerability. Shock from a hit nearby may bend it, perhaps to the point where it opens up the hull as it turns; that actually happened to the battleship HMS *Prince of Wales,* off Malaya in December 1941.

What if the propeller is turned by an electric motor? The engines driving the generators, which power the motor, can be anywhere in the ship. Immediately after World War I the U.S. Navy placed turbogenerators along the centerline of five battleships and two aircraft carriers, where they were farthest from possible torpedo damage (the boilers were outboard of the turbines, and well inboard of the ship's side). The concept was deemed successful, but it added substantial weight.[20] The postwar naval arms control treaty limited the tonnage of individual battleships, so electric drive was abandoned. It was revived during World War II for some smaller ships, including destroyer escorts, when gear-cutting capacity was insufficient.

In the 1980s the idea was revived. Not only did it offer much better survivability, it also added space in a ship's hull by eliminating long propeller shafts.[21] There was also a strong feeling that electric weapons, such as lasers and rail guns, would soon enter service; ships would then need much more electric power. Thus, plans called for unifying the prime mover and the generators normally supplying auxiliary power. The key technological requirement was a computer-driven switchboard capable of handling large amounts of power, thereby shifting the power between the main motors and the auxiliaries at will. Development proved difficult, and the U.S. Navy recalled the rather painful experience it had recently had with the turbo-electric submarine *Glennard P. Libscomb.* The electric drive program was killed, only to be revived in the late 1990s. Currently, virtually all new U.S. warships, from carriers down, are expected to use electric drive.

The new kind of propulsion offers some incidental advantages. If all hydraulic power is replaced by electric power, then computer control is considerably easier, because electric circuits are easily controlled by electronics. If future warships can be more highly automated, crew size and hence operating cost can be drastically reduced, a vital issue for any large navy. Replacing small numbers of large gas turbines with larger numbers of much smaller ones makes it possible to run much more economically at low speed, simply by running only a fraction of the total powerplant. It may even be possible to build spare capacity into a ship, giving her a reserve against mechanical failure during a long deployment. In that case fewer maintainers might be needed. Moreover, separating the prime movers from the propellers might make it practical to switch prime movers, for example, to replace gas turbines with fuel cells if the latter became more efficient.

Replenishment

The larger the ship, the less dependent she is on local support, and the less burden she imposes on underway support, which may itself be quite expensive. Sustained operations inevitably require some logistical support. Typically a U.S. carrier battle group steams with a fast support ship (AOE), which periodically fuels the ships and carries ammunition for the carrier aircraft. This "station ship" is periodically replenished by ships shuttling from a distant base or port. In wartime the shuttle ships would form underway replenishment groups (URGs) screened by frigates. In peacetime they generally operate alone, and they may replenish combatant ships at sea. They in turn are supported by point-to-point ships that bring materiel to the base or port for transfer to the specialist underway replenishment ships. This system breaks down if ships have to operate on a dispersed basis, for example, when the navy has to provide a degree of presence with a smaller number of ships. There cannot be enough station ships or even shuttle tankers to fuel every individual ship. This problem helps explain why the destroyer Cole was in Aden for a fueling stop when she was attacked.

Ships intended for sustained operation, that is, for underway replenishment, have to be designed so that they can efficiently accept ammunition, stores, and fuel over the side while steaming. For example, U.S. warships typically have wide passages down their sides specifically to make it easier to move stores. Many are designed so that helicopters can bring important stores aboard, a process called vertical replenishment (VERTREP). Such features drive up the size of a ship, and they help explain why U.S. Cold War ships of a given size always seemed far less heavily armed than Soviet counterparts. Another factor was that Soviet missiles tended to be larger, often for much the same performance.

Some important items are quite difficult to transfer at sea. For example, large missiles cannot easily be passed from ship to ship (necessarily horizontally, if at all) and then swung down into the current standard vertical launcher. That was not always obvious; many vertical launchers have special strike-down cranes, which are now being eliminated. Sustained missile strikes require either a port at which to rearm or else a stream of newly rearmed ships, the latter tactic becoming more difficult as the fleet shrinks in the aftermath of the Cold War.[22] It is relatively easy to transfer missiles, however, onto the elevators of aircraft carriers. Thus a carrier can sustain combat much longer than a surface missile shooter. There is current U.S. Navy interest in techniques to transfer large missiles at sea, using specialized rigs that would be landed on a ship (together with the necessary personnel) by helicopter, before replenishment begins. Tests of the necessary equipment at a land site at Port Hueneme have begun. Unless the tests succeed, the only ammunition that easily can be transferred to surface ships at sea is a shell. That considerably increases the potential importance of naval guns firing guided shells.

Aircraft Carriers and Carrier Battle Groups

At present the most powerful naval formations are carrier battle groups, comprising a carrier, escorts (generally including a pair of missile cruisers), and a station (replenishment) ship fast enough to steam with them. The escorts often include one or more nuclear submarines operating in support, to sanitize the area ahead of the battle group. The submarines are also armed with Tomahawk land attack missiles. For maximum integration, the same surface combatants are always assigned to the same carrier, and the group as a whole deploys together. Due to rapid changes in command and control, each battle group has a unique command configuration, thus it requires more work-up prior to deployment than in earlier, more standardized, days.

The carrier battle group uniquely offers heavy sustained offensive and defensive firepower. Its units are mutually supportive. Thus carrier aircraft can sustain their attacks as long as the enemy's air defenses are suppressed. The Tomahawks aboard the submarines and surface escorts are well suited to exactly that task. Submarines are particularly useful, because a potential enemy cannot generally know where they are and thus cannot focus air defenses on any threat axis they may define. In antiair warfare, carrier aircraft can more easily concentrate on destroying enemy aircraft because the surface ships provide backup against any missiles those aircraft may fire; otherwise the carrier fighters would have to try to shoot down the missiles. Thus the surface escorts free the carrier's aircraft to seize air control by destroying the enemy's air force, both on the ground, via strikes, and in the air. The carrier uniquely offers long tactical reach, because she supports aloft sensors, usually by using onboard E-2C radar early warning aircraft.

A carrier can accommodate eighty to one hundred aircraft. During the Cold War, the typical carrier air group included two F-14 squadrons, two squadrons of light attack bombers (A-7 Corsair IIs), and a medium attack squadron (A-6 Intruders). As aircraft costs have risen, however, purchases have fallen; carrier air wings are noticeably shrinking. The current standard is four rather than five squadrons of combat aircraft, and the squadrons are smaller (twelve rather than fourteen aircraft), for a typical total of only forty-eight combat aircraft plus supporting aircraft.[23] However, all forty-eight are dual-purpose fighter/attack bombers, mainly F/A-18 Hornets, usually with a squadron of modified F-14 Tomcats. Because electronic advances allow the aircraft to function either as fighters or bombers, the current air group can offer twice as many fighter or bomber squadrons as the earlier air group, although not at the same time. Compared to Cold War bombers, the F/A-18 is much easier to maintain than its predecessors; as long as it can survive in combat, it is much more available. Thus the decline in numbers may be overstated.

As long as airplanes can easily penetrate enemy air defenses, as was done in Iraq, they are in effect flying dump trucks. The carrier's striking power is set more by her magazine capacity than by the number of dump trucks in the air at any one time, because turnaround can be quite fast. Currently an all–F/A-18 air wing is considered capable of delivering 125 to 140 sorties per day, about 2.6 to 2.9 per airplane. Late in 1997 the carrier *Nimitz* experimented with measures to boost that to two hundred per day, by adding twenty pilots and one hundred maintenance personnel. It can also be argued that new precision weapons can make each sortie considerably more effective. For example, in the past an airplane could deliver only one laser-guided bomb at a time, and time had to be allowed for debris to settle before the target was reattacked. With the new Global Positioning System (GPS)–guided bombs (JDAMS), however, an airplane can deliver everything on board to whatever targets are preset. Similarly, it can be argued that greater precision makes up for the reduced bomb capacity of the F/A-18. Numbers of sorties certainly matter. One of the abiding lessons of Kosovo was that the Serbs proved quite adept at deception, inflicting what one might call virtual attrition on NATO air capacity (i.e., nullifying a percentage of the sorties conducted).

The F/A-18 exemplifies the basic problem that the number of aircraft is quite limited on board even a large carrier. In the past, the U.S. Navy preferred specialized aircraft, partly because different roles required different kinds of performance: there is a real difference between supersonic fighter combat and long-range bombing. However, aircraft were also specialized because for years radars and aircraft computers were quite specialized. The F-14 radar did have a surface attack mode, but the airplane as a whole was hardly optimized for such work. The radars on A-6s and A-7s could not support air-to-air combat. By the late 1970s, however, computers and radars had changed; a truly multipurpose weapon system could be built. The appearance of such avionics explains the fighter/attack designation of the Hornet.

Other navies, with smaller carrier capacity, have long felt intense pressure to field multirole aircraft, whatever the sacrifice in capability in one area or the other. Thus the French are replacing their Crusader fighters and Super Etendard strike bombers with a single type, Rafale-M. On the other hand, the British Sea Harrier was conceived as a multirole fighter/attack aircraft, but British carriers currently operate RAF Harriers alongside it for ground attack.[24]

The carrier's aircraft capacity depends on how she operates. For example, U.S. practice is to stow about a third of the aircraft in the hangar, which is used mainly for maintenance; most aircraft permanently ride on the flight deck. Thus the dimensions of the flight deck, more than anything else, determine the maximum number of aircraft the ship can accommodate. They are largely set by the requirements of particular aircraft taking off (a sufficiently long catapult to bring the aircraft to flying speed at a survivable acceleration) and landing (enough space to stop the airplane, again at a survivable deceleration). By way of contrast, beginning in World War I, and extending through the Falklands War, British practice was usually to stow all aircraft in the hangar when not in use (the British reluctantly adopted U.S.-style deck parks during World War II).[25] Thus the hangar dimensions and configuration of *Invincible*-class light carriers set the number of aircraft they could operate. That number roughly doubled when the British adopted a U.S.-style deck park. On the other hand, carrier capacity also depends on aviation fuel capacity. The ship can replenish her fuel supply only so often, and her aircraft burn a set amount each day. Since aircraft burn much the same fuel as do a ship's gas turbines, the *Invincible* class could trade off ship endurance for air group endurance. Most U.S. carriers are nuclear powered, so no such trade-off is possible for them.

Since World War II carriers have often operated in conjunction with land-based air forces. In the Gulf War the two air arms were particularly closely linked because all aircraft in theater followed a single unified air tasking order (ATO). In addition, land-based tankers fueled many of the carrier-based aircraft. The carrier's independent operation, however, is vital at the outset of an operation when land bases either may not be available (as in Korea, where they had been overrun) or where sufficient assets had not yet been built up ashore to sustain land-based operations (as in the Gulf).

Tomahawk and Surface Action Groups

Carrier groups are expensive to operate, yet they were the only U.S. naval force with any substantial land attack capability until the advent of the Tomahawk cruise missile. With Tomahawk missiles, a carrier-less group of surface ships could present a credible threat against land targets. Aegis, an effective antiair system, allowed a group to survive in the face of an enemy's air and missile forces, although not as well as a carrier battle group. A surface action group (SAG) using these two systems is not equivalent to a carrier battle group, however, because it lacks sustained firepower and it does not have the presence that is created by carrier aircraft. Also, it cannot gain air superiority by destroying an enemy air force in the air; the war against Iraq showed that strikes against airfields can require enormous numbers of weapons. Yet, during the Cold War, when the U.S. carrier force was stretched, SAGs built around Tomahawk-armed battleships were created as a way of covering areas of naval responsibility.

The combination of Tomahawk (or future land attack missiles) and the highly effective Aegis antiair system makes it possible to envisage a single-ship surface action unit. Missiles and perhaps a future gun would provide her with a quite credible ability to attack shore targets. Aegis and effective anti-submarine armament would offer the ship viability in the face of many potential Third World threats. The single ship would hardly match the firepower offered by a carrier battle group, or even by a surface action group, but on the other hand she would offer credible naval presence at a low cost in personnel, which is an attractive possibility. To make her truly effective, she would have to be nuclear powered; otherwise she would be subject to the availability of fueling resources either ashore or afloat. The U.S. Navy actually considered such a ship, which was called a strike cruiser (CSGN), in the 1970s, but dropped the project because of its high cost. At that time the ship would not have had credible striking power, because Tomahawk was not yet in service; she would have been limited to an 8-inch gun then under development. A quarter century later the situation has changed. Perhaps it is time to revive nuclear power for some surface combatants.

The great divide in surface combatants is between ships capable of attacking land targets and specialized escorts, primarily antisubmarine or antiaircraft. Until the advent of Tomahawk, U.S. surface combatants were all conceived as escorts. Other navies still operate ships that were designed primarily as Cold War convoy escorts. Because numbers were important, they were conceived as the smallest ships with adequate seakeeping and endurance, with self-defense against submarine-launched missiles, that could accommodate the necessary antisubmarine sensors (mainly sonar) and the means of attacking submarines when they were detected (usually helicopters armed with homing torpedoes). Considerable attention went into silencing, both to avoid revealing positions to submarines and to enhance sonar performance. None of these qualities makes the ships terribly useful if the naval mission shifts to land attack. These ships cannot accommodate anything as large as a Tomahawk, and their helicopters carry only small antiship missiles. There was no real point, during the Cold War, in providing any such capacity, which would have imposed an enormous cost in ship size. Now, however, navies are concerned mainly with directly influencing events ashore. Cold War frigates do retain a valuable capacity to enforce embargo, by stopping and searching merchant ships, but otherwise they have quite limited value. As has been argued, the antisubmarine escort mission itself may be less valid for a naval force projecting power. Moreover, the main threat to such a force is probably not enemy submarines so much as enemy aircraft and enemy coast defense missiles. Finally, the small size that was economical in the context of Cold War convoy escort may well make ships far less survivable than they should be in the face of missile fire.

Submarines

Western nuclear submarines offer an unequaled combination of stealth, endurance in a target area, and long reach. On the other hand, the physical barriers that make them so hard to detect also make communication with or between them, at least covert communication, difficult. As a consequence, submarines cannot easily combine closely with other naval units, or with each other. Just how submarine qualities will be used in the aftermath of the Cold War is still being debated, but some points are clear.

Reconnaissance was a vital, albeit extremely secret, Cold War role. The sheer variety of potential crises makes it more important than ever before. In this role covertness is an important virtue; in many potential crisis situations the mere appearance of a surveillance platform may exacerbate the situation. Most airborne platforms are quite observable, therefore emitters can be turned off in their presence, and satellite passes are predictable. It used to be said that satellites and aircraft could collect about 97 percent of what was wanted, but that the remaining 3 percent could be obtained only by a covert platform loitering near a coast, which only a submarine can provide. This ratio is now changing—in favor of the submarine. It is questionable whether important but very weak signals, such as those from cell phones, can be detected from space or even from the air. For many countries cell phones are becoming a dominant means of communication, however. Because they are often at radar frequencies, many cell phone signals may even be subject to ducting, that is, they may not be detectable from above.[26] Yet a country's telephone traffic, probably detectable by an offshore submarine, is likely to be an extremely valuable source of information. A submarine can also send special operations teams (SEALs, in the U.S. Navy) ashore, retrieving them when they have completed their mission.

Another important new role is missile strikes against land targets. Compared to a surface platform, an attack submarine carries many fewer missiles, but it can operate entirely alone; therefore the cost per missile in terms of men is much smaller. The submarine can transit to its station at higher sustained speed, as long as it need not fear detection during transit, which is the rule with the demise of the Soviet Union. Moreover, because it is a covert platform, it cannot exacerbate a crisis when it gets into position to fire. Conversely, it offers little or no presence until it acts.[27]

There is also the post–Cold War extension of the classic overt Cold War submarine mission of countering enemy submarines by operating in forward areas inaccessible to Western surface units. Even though there may be few enemy submarines, their potential for disrupting a limited Western naval operation is huge.

For the U.S. Navy, the reconnaissance mission apparently currently predominates. It and the strike mission explain why the U.S. Navy finds its submarines almost always assigned to "national" rather than to purely naval missions. The submarine force, which was sharply drawn down at the end of the Cold War, is likely to grow to meet such needs. As of the year 2000, for example, the Joint Chiefs of Staff had approved an increase from an authorized level of fifty-five to sixty-eight submarines, to be achieved by refueling existing units.

Submarines are both weight *and* volume critical. When they submerge, their volumes (actually, the weight of water that would fill their volumes) must exactly match their weights, because they must be neutrally buoyant. For a surface ship, the underwater part of the hull (whose volume, in terms of weight of water must match the ship's weight) is only about a third of the ship's total volume (the rest is reserve buoyancy, in effect insurance against sinking by flooding). Thus a submarine has about a third of the internal volume of a surface ship of the same tonnage. She carries many fewer weapons. For example, an *Arleigh Burke*–class missile destroyer has ninety vertical launchers (each of which can accommodate a Tomahawk), plus eight Harpoons in canisters, a 5-inch gun (with six hundred rounds), and six ASW torpedo tubes (with reloads). A *Los Angeles*–class submarine, which has about 20 percent smaller displacement, carries fewer than forty Tomahawk-sized weapons, which she cannot launch as rapidly as the destroyer.

Moreover, the submarine cannot add volume simply by adding superstructure, or by moving equipment onto her decks. She can carry some equipment outboard, if it is pressure proof, and she may be able to tow a capsule, but both solutions to insufficient internal volume are less than completely satisfactory. For example, submarines have sometimes been provided with additional armament in the form of external tubes. A recent example is the U.S. improved *Los Angeles* class, in which twelve vertical missile tubes were added in the forward ballast tank, outside the pressure hull. The only current example of adding equipment by towing is the towed (acoustic) array, which in some navies is simply clipped onto the submarine as she leaves port. Others, such as the U.S. Navy, reel it onboard when not in use; it is stowed externally, outside the pressure hull. Overall, a submarine's potential for growth beyond her designed equipment is limited. More effort must go into modernizing the submarine—intended to last a long time—by replacing existing equipment.[28]

Most navies operate diesel-electric submarines. When they have access to the air, that is, when operating on the surface or running at shallow depth while snorkeling, they run on diesel power. Submerged, they run on their batteries, which are topped up when they run on diesel. Batteries have only a limited energy capacity; no matter how little power they use, submarines cannot run for very long while submerged. Submerged endurance also depends on the submarine's air capacity. Nuclear submarines, however, generate their own air by breaking down water electrically. The submarine is inherently quiet when on batteries (although this can be exaggerated), but must be specially silenced when running on diesel. Because she is completely submerged when snorkeling, she is actually loudest at that time, because more of the sound of her diesels goes into the water.

By way of contrast, a nuclear submarine creates noise simply by running her reactor. The powerplant requires pumps and piping that can whistle and gurgle and, usually, gearing that can whine. In U.S., British, and Russian submarines such plants are silenced largely by sound isolating them from the outside of the submarine, on a rigid raft or comparable supporting structure. This type of construction makes for a large submarine. The French managed to build smaller nuclear submarines, partly by adopting turbo-electric propulsion, and partly by limiting silencing. Such measures are not entirely satisfactory, evidenced by French statements that their next-generation nuclear attack submarine, code-named Barracuda, will be more than a third larger than the current type.

The inherent noisiness of nuclear plants shaped Western Cold War submarine-detection technology. Effort was eventually concentrated on passive (listening) sonars. The theory was that, no matter how well the submarine had been silenced, she still created a steady signal that a sufficiently powerful signal processor could pick up against the randomness of sea noise. A diesel submarine, however, is inherently quiet. The natural means of detection is active (pinging) sonar. It generally lacks the range of passive systems, and its use alerts the target. A diesel submarine, however, is likely to be less able to do much about an alert than her nuclear cousin. Examples of active sonar include units in the bows of ships and submarines, and also explosive echo ranging, which combines small explosive charges with passive sonobuoys.

Apart from the fact that they can submerge, diesel-electric submarines have little in common with nuclear craft. Nuclear submarine speeds run from twenty-five to about thirty-five knots, although tactical (quiet) speeds are lower. The fastest diesel submarines have maximum speeds of about twenty-four knots, but this speed cannot be sustained for more than an hour, and sometimes for no more than fifteen minutes. Moreover, once the submarine has exhausted her battery in this way, she needs considerable time to replenish it. On the other hand, in water shallower than her test depth, typically about one thousand feet, a diesel-electric submarine can sit on the bottom, where she may be difficult to distinguish from other bottom features, including sunken ships. A nuclear submarine bottoms at her peril, because her steam plant relies on cooling (condenser) water sucked in from outside. On the bottom, mud can easily be sucked into a condenser, thus ruining it and effectively immobilizing the submarine. Attempts to overcome this limit, for example, by placing condenser inlets in the submarine's tail fins, are unlikely to be very successful. A diesel submarine does need cooling water, but only under some circumstances (e.g., when running diesel), so she can shut down any inlets when she bottoms. For example, during the Falklands War the Argentine *San Luis* escaped from British attacks by bottoming. Although a British frigate overhead had a sonar capable of distinguishing her, the frigate's anti-submarine weapons (homing torpedoes) could not do so. Only if the submarine rose off the bottom was she in danger. *San Luis* had to stay down as long as the frigate was overhead; after about twelve hours the frigate left, and the submarine rose off the bottom and got away.[29]

The vast difference between the two types of submarine is illustrated by their tactics in attacking surface ships. A nuclear submarine is at least as fast as a surface ship, particularly if the latter is slowed by waves. Soon after fast nuclear submarines entered service, their commanders learned to exploit their speed. Early experiments with *Nautilus,* the first U.S. unit, showed that she could generally escape any pursuit (the surface ships could not use their sonars at full speed), but that she was slightly too slow to double back and destroy surface units. That experience led to the construction of the much faster *Skipjack* class. One commander made a specialty of exposing himself to screening ships, then making a "knuckle" in the water to present them with a sonar target on which they could concentrate. He then ran back around the screen to hit the carrier they were protecting. Even if nominally faster than the submarine, a surface ship cannot use her sonar at full speed, because she is deafened by the flow of water. The usual solution is a helicopter, which hovers to dip its sonar, pings, and then hops to dip again or to attack. Alternatives include a helicopter laying a field of sonobuoys, or an airplane doing the same.

Diesel attack tactics generally require that the slow submarine place herself ahead of the much faster target, in an area defined by limiting lines of approach, the opening angle of which depends on the relative speeds of submarine and target. The faster the submarine, the wider the area from which she can attack. As the target formation approaches, the submarine works patiently through the screen. Once she strikes, she has revealed herself, and the escorts pursue her. This is when her hour or quarter-hour of high underwater speed counts. She tries to run beyond the effective sonar range of the escorts. If she fails, she is essentially immobilized. The standard escort tactic is simply to hold her down until she runs out of battery charge or air.

In recent years several builders have offered supplementary air-independent propulsion (AIP). At least in theory, the AIP combination of oxidant and fuel offers more stored energy density than a battery. Current AIP engines are low powered; they allow a submarine to loiter for an extended period, perhaps two weeks, without making noise by snorkeling and also without running down the battery. Thus she retains full underwater power for combat. It is possible that one of the AIP alternatives, the fuel cell, may eventually be developed to the point where it can become a sole powerplant, offering a submarine significant underwater speed (for instance, about fifteen to twenty knots) for several weeks on end.

The main arguments against AIP are that it adds complexity and, possibly, vulnerability to a small submarine whose crew is already fully occupied in running a conventional powerplant. Nor is it clear that most submarines will ever encounter the degree of surveillance that AIP can counter. For example, in a crowded coastal area a submarine should often be able to surface at night to recharge batteries, in effect posing as a civilian surface ship. In the Falklands, the Argentine submarine *San Luis* snorkeled under the cover of the sound of the surf. For years, standard NATO antisubmarine torpedoes were ineffective against anything on the surface, which is probably why the Soviets preferred to recharge there even though they fitted their diesel submarines with snorkels.[30] Hence Russian-built "Kilo"-class submarines have a special air defense platform in their sails, to be occupied by a sailor armed with a handheld antiaircraft missile, usable only on the surface.

The Amphibious Force

Marines who can be launched from the sea are increasingly part of U.S. power projection. Parallel to the twelve carriers are twelve amphibious ready groups (ARGs), each built around a large-deck amphibious carrier (for helicopters and Marine attack aircraft) and supported by other amphibious ships carrying more marines and their heavy equipment. Each group supports a marine amphibious unit (MAU) or marine expeditionary unit (MEU), an air-ground force including what used to be called a battalion landing team (BLT). Such units can be added together to form larger ones, up through divisional size (a marine amphibious force or marine expeditionary force). The MEU is the smallest fully capable Marine unit, comprising troops and all supporting arms. Organizing the Marine Corps into such units expresses the current reality: we face many more or less simultaneous crises of limited scope.

Like a surface action group, an ARG can be used to project U.S. presence. It has severe limits, however. The large-deck amphibious ship (an LHA or LHD) looks like a carrier, but it is not one. The Marines' attack aircraft (AV-8B Harriers) are not quite fighters. Most important, they are not supported by airborne early warning aircraft, at least not at present. As a consequence, the Harriers cannot be expected to destroy an enemy's air arm, although Aegis ships operating with the amphibious ships ought to be able to provide them with a useful degree of self-defense.

Marines come ashore either via helicopters (in the near future, VTOL aircraft, the MV-22 Osprey) or amphibious vehicles, which were once known as amtracs. The initial objective is to seize a beach, onto which materiel can be brought. The force on the beach then regroups to press inland against its main objective. Using helicopters, the Marines land in the rear of any defenders already on the beach, or else interdict any enemy thrust toward a beach. Like other airmobile troops, the marines landed by helicopter are lightly equipped, and cannot hold their ground for long unless they receive support, thus requiring the heavier force to arrive over the beach. Mobility, once ashore, is provided by the same amphibious vehicles that bring marines over the beach. Typical plans call for two-thirds of the marines to land by air and the other third over the beach. Heavy equipment comes ashore mainly via air cushion landing craft (LCACs), supplemented by slower landing craft during the buildup phase after the beach has been secured.

Prepositioning

Often governments may be quite willing to accept U.S. forces. Troops can be flown in, but airplanes cannot easily accommodate tanks and other heavy loads. In 1979, when the Soviets invaded Afghanistan, the U.S. government was faced with the possibility that they would drive further south. If, in extremis, the Pakistani or Iranian government asked for help, what could the United States do? It could not maintain garrisons in the area, nor would any local government allow it to stockpile materiel against the distant possibility of attack. The sea offered an answer. Troops could remain in the United States, because they could quickly fly into the area. Their heavy equipment could be maintained on board ships, which could, in effect, orbit offshore.[31] As sovereign U.S. territory, the ships would not be subject to the objections that stocks ashore would create; they would be, in effect, U.S. bases without entailing many of the problems inherent in bases. Moreover, one set of ships could transit quickly to many different places, whereas it would take enormous effort to move stockpiles emplaced on land. The floating stockpiles became maritime prepositioning squadrons. Each of the three could equip a full marine amphibious brigade, which is equivalent to three ARGs. The army and air force also stockpiled floating ammunition, but on the whole the army preferred fast sealift ships held at readiness in U.S. ports. That made sense. The Marines' role was to provide initial armed presence, the army following up with heavier forces. For its part, the army maintains a unique capability to airlift light units capable of seizing and securing an airport needed for any troops, including marines, who are to mate up with the equipment.

The Soviets never drove south from Afghanistan. However, when Iraq invaded Kuwait in 1990, marines, using their prepositioned equipment, provided an invaluable initial barrier to further Iraqi attack, while a much heavier ground force was built up—using materiel moved mainly by sea.[32]

Mine Warfare

At least for the U.S. Navy, mine countermeasures are usually associated with amphibious assault. Moreover, it can be argued that if the chosen beach has to be cleared before it can be used, the act of clearance, which is likely to last some days or even some weeks, will surely reveal it, destroying the element of surprise. Neither the U.S. Navy nor any other navy has sufficient mine countermeasures craft to clear several feint beaches in parallel with the real one.

The great problem is that mines on the bottom are difficult to distinguish from other objects, including the industrial rubbish likely to be encountered off a Third World coast. At one time mines were swept: moored mines were dealt with by cutting their chains and then sinking them when they floated to the surface. Bottom mines use sensors to decide when a ship passes overhead, and the simpler versions could be triggered by special influence sweeps (in effect, decoys). Sweepers were simple, and they could easily be mass produced. Late in World War II, however, mines existed that could not be swept, that is, they could not be fooled into thinking that a decoy was a real ship.[33]

Given such complications, navies turned to mine hunting. Using a high-definition sonar, a small ship examines the bottom foot by foot. Suspicious objects are checked in greater detail. If they appear to be mines, they are dealt with one by one. Unfortunately, the charges laid by mine hunters usually do not completely destroy a mine; they merely neutralize its mechanism. To the next mine hunter along, the neutralized mine will probably look like an active mine. Hunting thus requires each craft to precisely mark the position of each neutralized mine, which is usually now done on an electronic chart. This process is necessarily tedious. On the other hand, it should be able to deal with any mine, no matter how clever its combination of sensors.

Hunting and neutralization systems are sophisticated and expensive. Because they operate in mine fields, the hunters themselves become expensive; their own acoustic and magnetic signatures must be controlled. Because they are so small (to limit their signatures), mine hunters and other countermeasures craft are inherently slow, with limited seagoing endurance.[34] They cannot, therefore, be part of a high-speed fleet intended to operate independently. In recent years they have often been transported to the scene of operations on board a flo-flo merchant ship, a semisubmersible that takes them on board while flooded down, then pumps out tanks to bring them out of the water. A flo-flo may run at speeds up to twenty knots, and thus can drastically cut transit time. It cannot, however, deploy the mine countermeasures units until they reach an objective area. Thus it cannot solve the fleet's problem that it may have to pass through a possibly mined strategic strait, or that it may have to pass through shallows. Also, the flo-flo cannot deploy the minecraft under fire.

In recent years Western navies have tried to limit the cost of mine hunting by using self-propelled mine hunting sonars, which can run ahead of a ship; thus the signature does not need not be controlled as well as that of a mine hunter. The most extreme version of this "dog on a leash" technique is the U.S. remote mine hunting system that is actually a mine reconnaissance system using a self-propelled semisubmersible craft linked by radio to the controlling ship, usually a destroyer. It has the additional advantage that it can be deployed at the fleet's speed, although it does its hunting at reduced speed.

During the Cold War the U.S. Navy developed an alternative to the minecraft. A helicopter could tow a contact, influence sweep, or mine hunting sonar. Despite early hopes, however, helicopters did not entirely replace surface minecraft. They were limited to precursor sweeping, the attempt to trigger (hence eliminate) any mines set sensitively enough destroy mine hunters. Helicopter mine hunting was impractical; a helicopter could tow a precision sonar, but the analysis needed to decide whether a particular contact was or was not a mine had to be done aboard a ship. Without precise navigation, a second (killer) helicopter could not find a mine detected by the hunter. With GPS, however, the killer can drop a weapon where the hunter found the mine. Moreover, helicopters can hunt through an area much quicker than surface craft. A surface hunter must stop and deal with each mine it encounters before going on to the next. Because none of the mines directly threatens a helicopter, multiple helicopters can search in parallel. The killers can also go out in parallel.

Perhaps the greatest problem in mine countermeasures is that it is so difficult to be certain that a field has been cleared. For example, in 1984 a Libyan merchant ship laid a string of influence mines in the Red Sea, the object being to disrupt the ships carrying pilgrims to Mecca in Saudi Arabia and thus discredit the Saudi government, which is the guardian of Mecca. After an explosion, the main Western navies tried to neutralize the field. Weeks later they declared the Red Sea safe. Shortly thereafter a merchant ship reported an explosion. Because the hunters could never be sure that they had caught all the mines, they had to go back and reexamine the bottom of the Red Sea. Eventually they found nothing. The master of the apparently mined ship ultimately admitted that the explosion had been a fraud perpetrated to collect insurance money.

It is far better, then, to avoid a mined area altogether, rather than bet on clearing it in time for some operation. The coalition tried to use this mine reconnaissance technique during the Gulf War. Iraqi naval traffic was observed, both from the air and probably from space. On that basis it was assumed that the limits of possible minefields could be deduced. Unfortunately, the observers had also assumed that the Iraqis would use their only two specially built minelayers to lay their fields. Sorties by numerous smaller craft were taken to be the looting of Kuwait. Many of them were, but unfortunately others were minelaying. The two U.S. ships that set off mines, the missile cruiser *Princeton* and the helicopter carrier *Tripoli,* which was actually a mine countermeasures flagship, hit these unexpected fields.

Yet mine reconnaissance still makes excellent sense. To be effective, it has to be covert; otherwise the miner knows exactly where to lay unexpected mines. The current U.S. incarnation uses the most covert available platform, a submarine. It launches an unmanned underwater vehicle, resembling a low-speed torpedo, into a suspected field. The device can pick up suspicious objects, which may be mines. That suffices because there is no intent to destroy them one by one. The submarine can quietly transmit the position of a suspected minefield back to the approaching surface force, obviating lengthy mine clearance.

That is not to say that hunting and sweeping can be abandoned altogether. For example, ships must pass through some particular places, such as harbors and straits; all the reconnaissance in the world cannot change that geography. The situation is further complicated by the advent of rising mines, which fire a projectile or torpedo up at a ship, which may be quite some distance from the mine. In the face of such weapons it may no longer be possible simply to clear and mark a narrow channel.[35]

Appendix B: The Shape of the Fleet

Strategy does not determine the size of a fleet, but it does shape the configuration of the fleet that finances permit. For example, the U.S. Navy of the Reagan years numbered about six hundred ships, predicated on economics, but its shape was determined by the maritime strategy. It was very much a "main fleet" strategy, so it concentrated on carrier battle groups and, as surrogates, surface action groups, backed by a powerful amphibious force. Critics of this maritime strategy would presumably have spent their money instead on a large escort force, perhaps backed by more submarines to close off choke points such as the Greenland–Iceland–United Kingdom gap. Similar tensions are discernable in other navies. For example, the Royal Navy has always fought hard to maintain a core main fleet capability, despite attempts by its political masters to force it to concentrate on the antisubmarine aspects of sea control.

In the aftermath of the Cold War, the U.S. fleet, like other elements of the armed forces, shrank. The main fleet orientation, however, survived and even intensified. As of early 2000, the U.S. Navy operated 12 aircraft carriers (down from 15 during the Cold War), 18 ballistic missile submarines (of which 4 are either to be discarded or converted into special forces and cruise missile units), 56 attack submarines (including 1 special forces transport), 27 missile cruisers, 31 missile destroyers, 24 destroyers (with vertical Tomahawk launchers), 27 frigates, 13 patrol craft, 27 mine countermeasures craft, 4 command ships, 11 amphibious carriers, 26 other active amphibious ships, 8 combat support ships (AOE), and 2 submarine tenders. With a total of 286 battle force ships, the fleet is about half the size of the Reagan-era fleet. A few ships are inactive, in reserve. The comparison with the 1980s is slightly misleading because other ships, some of them of types formerly operated by the combatant navy, are operated by the Military Sealift Command.

The following comments explore the alternatives we currently face. In one way they are deeply misleading. The overwhelming advantage of naval forces is their flexibility; they can be mixed and matched in many different ways. To imagine, for instance, that a missile destroyer is always an integral part of a carrier battle group is misleading, because the same ship might be used in a surface action group, for individual presence duty (for instance, to enforce an embargo), or to support an amphibious operation. Thus the distribution of ships suggested here is illustrative only.

For the U.S. Navy, the main fleet elements are the carrier battle group, still backed by surface action groups and the amphibious ready group. During the Cold War, the navy also expected to maintain underway replenishment groups (URGs), which required escorts, and to provide escorts for a limited number of vital convoys. With the end of the Cold War, and thus with the passing of a major open-ocean threat, both the convoy and the URG escort tasks disappeared. On the other hand, it can be argued that the surface warships that in the past would have been assigned to these roles are now needed for presence in an increasingly unstable world. If, as expected, the U.S. Navy develops a navy theater-wide (NTW) ballistic missile defense capability, then it will probably be necessary to deploy special surface action groups (missile defender plus screen) to provide it abroad. Because missile defense may well be needed at the same time as other capabilities, presumably ships providing it should be in separate groups.

During the Cold War, the U.S. Navy tried to maintain two carriers in the Mediterranean at all times, although they rarely operated together. The Far East was much larger. Until the mid-1970s, the fleet there had to cover Soviet, Chinese, and Korean targets, not to mention the needs of the Vietnam War. Even after the rapprochement with China, the range of Far Eastern requirements was wide. Ideally, there would have been two groups of carriers in the Far East, north and south, for a total of four ships. That was never affordable, so the choice was to provide a two-carrier force backed by a third "swing" carrier.

There was a rule of thumb that it took three carriers to maintain one forward-deployed carrier: one actually deployed, one returning from or steaming out to the overseas station, and one under overhaul. Thus the ideal total Cold War carrier force, which often seemed unaffordable, was fifteen deployable carriers, which might equate to as many as sixteen or seventeen, counting ships under overhaul or major refit. For example, a nuclear carrier has to be refueled periodically, a process that may take more than two and a half years, including modifications made at the time of refueling. Up to the end of the 1960s, the backlog of surviving World War II carriers offered sufficient numbers. When most of those ships were retired, by about 1972, the situation quickly became critical. The stopgap solution was to forward base a carrier, so that she would not spend so much of her time in transit. The U.S. Navy homeports a carrier in Yokosuka; an attempt to use Athens was abortive. This arrangement survived the end of the Cold War. It may not last much longer. Japanese public sentiment currently precludes the basing of any nuclear-powered ship in a Japanese port. It is U.S. naval policy, however, to build only nuclear-powered carriers, because they offer such enormous operational advantages. Given current plans, the last U.S. oil-powered carrier will be retired about 2015–18.

Even under Cold War conditions, it sometimes took more than three carriers to maintain one on a forward station. For years, for example, the U.S. carrier assigned to the Arabian Sea always had to be within a set number of hours of the position from which she could launch a strike at a particular place, specified by U.S. national strategy. The requirement was set at the National Security Council (presidential) level, not at the service level. Unless the carrier was within the box that requirement implied, she was not on station. Distances were such that to keep one actually on station the navy had to have about 7.8 carriers. This requirement has never formally been retracted, but the presence in the Arabian Sea has been gapped to provide presence elsewhere.

Ultimately deployments are limited by the stress felt by ships' crews. During the 1970s, when the carrier fleet contracted dramatically but commitments did not, ships were deployed for longer and longer periods. Many sailors reacted by refusing to reenlist, which drastically cut the level of skills within the fleet. The outcome, about 1986, was a firm pledge to limit deployments to six months, at whatever cost. Shorter deployments are considered inefficient. That is why, for example, USS *Eisenhower* returned to the United States during the buildup to the Gulf War; she had exhausted her 180-day deployment time. To concentrate carriers in the Gulf in December 1990, Adm. Frank Kelso, then chief of naval operations, decided specifically to break the deployment limit. There is also a pledge that ships will spend at least a year at their home ports. Carriers are currently committed to three commands: European (i.e., Mediterranean), Pacific, and Central (in effect, Arabian Sea). The Pacific carrier is homeported in Japan, which means that in theory it is locally based. The six-month rule does not apply, and the ship is serviced at Yokosuka.

The situation is complicated by the rapid changes in command and control technology. Each carrier battle group deploys with an essentially unique command system, because the technology is changing too fast for the choice to be made to fix and standardize it. That is why the entire battle group must work up together and must be kept together; in the past battle groups were more ad hoc collections of ships. Work-up time is longer because the new systems must be tested and learned. Presumably the situation will eventually stabilize, work-ups will shorten, and it will become easier to deploy battle groups. It is by no means clear when that time will come.

A carrier goes through four distinct phases between deployments: a stand-by period as a ready carrier in home waters, a refit, work-up, and then a short stand-down before redeployment. The usual refit period lasts six months, but every third period involves drydocking, which lasts about ten and a half months. Nuclear carriers have to refuel. The first of the current class, USS *Nimitz,* was completed with a thirteen-year core; current cores are designed to last about twenty-four years. Nuclear refueling takes about thirty-two months.

For the Mediterranean, under the current rules it takes six carriers to keep one continuously forward based. Transit back and forth plus a three-day carrier qualification period subtracts three-quarters of a month from the six-month deployment period, so each carrier spends about five and one-quarter months on station. The next carrier must be on station before the last one leaves, so deployments overlap. Six carriers offer a cycle lasting twenty-six and one-quarter months between deployments. That includes a two-month ready-carrier stand-down period and about a year of work-up, leaving something less than twelve months for refits. The average refit period is only seven and a half months. Each nuclear carrier, however, needs a much more extended period for refueling. A nuclear carrier deploying every thirty months refits twenty-three times in her fifty-year lifetime; at least one of those refits lasts thirty-two months, necessary for refueling. That raises the average refit time from seven and a half to about eight and a half months. With five carriers, cycle time between deployments would be twenty-one months, leaving only six and three-quarter months for refits. The twelve-month work-up time is presumably tied to the requirement that a carrier remain home for at least a year at a time, but it is also advantageous if basic command systems change as rapidly as they now do. It is not clear just how drastically it could be cut.

During the stand-down and work-up periods the carrier is available for operations in the Western Hemisphere, including fleet battle experiments used to develop the new command and control systems and concepts. At present there is no Western Hemisphere military threat. However, there are hints that the United States may find itself involved in, for example, Colombia. In such a case carrier deployment schedules might be badly deranged; work-up might turn into six months of operations off South America.

Changing the rules would make it possible to make do with fewer carriers. For example, if deployments averaged seven months, the time between deployments for three carriers would be twelve and a half months, which would allow enough time for each to have a refit but not a lengthy work-up. During times of more static technology, which will presumably return, this would be more satisfactory. In the past, typical Mediterranean deployments did run about seven months, and typical Pacific deployments lasted eight, because of the longer transit time to the Far East. Under the old rules it was one-in-three *deployable* carriers, that is, not counting those in major refits such as refueling.

These estimates are all predicated on steady operations spread over many years; carrier lifetime is currently given as fifty years. Experience with existing ships suggests that they need not only a half-life refueling but probably also a major reconstruction after thirty to forty years of service. In that case the average refit times quoted above are overly optimistic, and the excess in the six-carrier example is somewhat deceptive.

On current estimates similar to those for the Mediterranean, it takes eight to maintain one carrier continuously in the Arabian Sea. Atlantic and Pacific fleet carriers rotate this duty, with access via the Suez Canal and the Straits of Malacca. On this basis, as of the year 2000, the U.S. Navy's estimate is that a total of fifteen are required to maintain three forward carriers, with the forward basing at Yokosuka. At any one time, most of the force is in U.S. waters, available to reinforce the forward-deployed ships. Ships in U.S. waters are available for Western Hemisphere duty.

Our navy currently has only twelve active carriers. A thirteenth is under construction, for delivery at the end of 2002, and two others are in reserve. One of the reserve ships, USS *Independence,* is reported in excellent condition; the other, USS *Ranger,* might be somewhat more difficult to reactivate. A third carrier, USS *America,* a newer ship, was laid up in 1996 and in 1998 was stricken and ordered scrapped. As of late 2000, however, she still exists and thus may be considered a candidate for revival. Thus a fifteen-carrier force could be created by about 2003, if no carrier is deactivated when the new one is completed, and if the two laid up carriers are reactivated. Provision of sufficient aircraft might be a more serious problem, but less so if only three forward-deployed carriers had full air wings. It is also possible that air wing numbers will be reduced below the roughly fifty combat aircraft currently required, on the theory that new precision weapons magnify the effectiveness of each airplane.

What happens, though, if the current level of twelve carriers persists? In the past, a twelve-carrier force sufficed only for two forward carriers in each ocean. Therefore, either the Mediterranean or the Arabian Sea deployment would have to be discontinuous. Over the past decade, gaps have been accepted in the coverage of both stations. With the Cold War over, the Arabian Sea appears to be the more urgent of the two. When the Kosovo crisis escalated in 1999, the Mediterranean was gapped, and the Arabian Sea carrier (*Roosevelt*) had to move through the Suez Canal to that sea. Her station in turn was filled by the carrier *Kitty Hawk*, which was forward homeported at Yokosuka. It may be argued that in at least some cases land-based aircraft can cover for a carrier. For example, the air force in Saudi Arabia can make up for the absence of the Arabian Sea ship. The counterargument is that U.S. national requirements may conflict with the views of the host country, as happened when the United States and Britain decided to raid Iraq in 1998 despite a Saudi veto. In the case of Bosnia, although the Italians certainly allowed free use of the base at Aviano, weather conditions often precluded flights, whereas the carrier in the Adriatic could find appropriate flying weather. That, incidentally, applied as much to the small British carrier as to the large U.S. one, and at times the small British carrier generated more sorties than the land base. If these arguments are persuasive, then the best way to fill gaps in carrier coverage would be by one or more surface action groups. They could not match carrier capabilities, for example, in sustained strike operations, but they would be something. Perhaps the worst of their defects would be an inability to demonstrate presence by flying aircraft near local shores, or, if war began, to place a hostile air force at risk.

Of course, the situation could be rectified if one or more carriers could be forward homeported in Europe, preferably in the Mediterranean. Homeporting entails basing an entire battle group abroad, and supporting all the dependents of the eight to ten thousand service personnel there. Whatever agreements a host government may sign, those dependents can become hostages to local nationalism. It is unlikely that any European Union country other than Britain would agree to such basing now, given increasing interest in Europe in establishing a fully independent military posture. The British do host U.S. air bases, which may serve as a precedent. The Israelis have offered homeporting in the past, probably as a way of gaining leverage over U.S. policy makers. Egypt might be considered an alternative, but local reactions to the fall 2000 explosion in Israel suggest that it would be impractical at best and extremely dangerous at worst. In Japan the homeporting arrangement is, in a sense, a holdover from World War II and the security treaties ending it; Yokosuka hosts not only a carrier battle group but also a three ship ARG, and nearby Atsugi hosts the associated air wing. The air wing in particular gives rise to increasingly vocal complaints, because pilots continue flying to remain proficient even when the group is home.

The suggestion has been made that the carrier force should be cut to nine ships. All would then be nuclear, with the ship now on order replacing the elderly *Enterprise*. Nuclear carriers can transit at higher speeds, but the reduction in time lost in a deployment would be marginal; the figures above assume a fourteen-knot transit speed. This force would just cover the Arabian Sea, plus one forward-homeported carrier in the Pacific. Arguments favoring uncovering the Mediterranean would include the disappearance of the Soviet threat. If Japan refused homeporting, cutting the force to nine ships would have a drastic effect, because it would remove a visible element of U.S. naval power from Northeast Asia at just the time when tensions in that region may be growing. Surface action groups cannot provide anything like the same impact. Certainly it would be necessary to find an alternative homeport. Alternatives discussed publicly are Australia, Guam, Korea, and Singapore. Guam offers advantages because it is a U.S. territory, but also a disadvantage due to its lack of infrastructure. As of late 2000, arrangements were nearly complete to homeport four to six submarines in Guam within two to three years.

These alternatives highlight another point, which is political. The United States maintains forward military commands around the world. Their areas of responsibility mirror the strategy the United States would have adopted if the Cold War had become hot. In the absence of a Soviet threat, U.S. *geographic* interests are already changing. Central Command responsibility has increased because its area of responsibility includes the newly independent states that were formerly part of Soviet Central Asia: Kazakhstan, Uzbekistan, Turkmenistan, Tajikistan, Kyrgzstan. Some are likely to become important U.S. trading partners, particularly after the discovery and exploitation of major oil and natural gas reserves. Closer to home, Southern Command is now more important. It has taken over responsibility for operations on both South American coasts. Presumably Southern Command is responsible for the naval side of the war on drugs, which may extend into armed support for the

Colombian government. Geography itself demands that the United States split forces between the Atlantic and the Pacific, but not necessarily that they be split evenly between, for instance, Europe, the Middle East, and the Far East. During the 1980s U.S. defense was reorganized so that operational commanders, the commanders in chief (CinCs), gained considerable power. The CinCs command those geographically defined theaters. The decision as to which CinC is more important than the others, or as to which CinC's primary concerns are less important than another CinC's secondary concerns is made at the presidential or national security advisor level.

The carrier battle group is now a fixed entity, typically including two missile cruisers and four other surface combatants (missile destroyers, destroyers, and sometimes frigates). It trains together and deploys together. This integration is probably necessary given the unique command and control configuration of each deploying battle group. There are currently twelve carriers, thus seventy-two surface combatants are required. Enlarging the fleet to fifteen would raise the number to ninety. Cutting the carrier fleet would not cut the surface force proportionately, because it is likely that surface action groups, in effect battle groups without carriers, would be needed to make up for the absence of the carrier. They would not provide the same capability, but that might be unavoidable, given financial limits. Probably at least two surface action groups would be needed to substitute for a carrier.

There are also currently twelve amphibious ready groups (ARGs). In theory an ARG requires three surface escorts, although often these ships are not available because they are otherwise employed. The requirement to screen ARGs, then, adds another thirty-six surface combatants.

Experience suggests that one carrier battle group barely suffices in each main theater. During the Cold War, the Soviets controlled most of the minor states that fought wars against us or our allies. In retrospect it is fairly clear that they often feared that the United States would escalate such crises into full-blown war. They tended to concentrate on one area at a time. Now, however, there is no controlling force whatever. Crises really can occur in tandem. During the Gulf War, governments, such as North Korea and India, sympathetic to Saddam Hussein fomented crises in their own areas, which may have been designed specifically to tie down nearby forces that might otherwise have gone to the Gulf.[1] Ideally, then, there should be at least two independent naval intervention groups in each major theater. That might not apply to the Gulf, however, because one of two Mediterranean forces could presumably "swing" through the Suez Canal in an emergency; the Pacific is too far away for quick redeployment. At least at present, it is much easier to maintain forces in the Mediterranean than in the Arabian Sea.

A surface action group might be substituted for the second carrier battle group. Surface action groups have already been used to mount strikes against Iraq from the Arabian Sea. Given the long range of Tomahawk land attack missiles, a single group can attack widely spaced targets. In 1998, for example, the ships of one battle group struck targets on two continents, in Afghanistan and the Sudan, simultaneously.

In cost terms, a surface action group is a carrier battle group without the carrier; it does not have a carrier's over-the-horizon air capability and its sustained hitting capability. Because the surface action group cannot currently replenish its land attack missiles at sea, it may be argued that it takes several to approach the value of a single carrier battle group. For example, when the surface groups were used against Iraq, first one fired its Tomahawks, and then another entire surface action group moved into place to relieve it. As of the last Quadrennial Defense Review (1997), the navy wanted 128 surface combatants; presumably the twenty not required for carriers and ARGs were counted in four surface action groups. Clearly this is not an ideal figure, and most likely it is based on the Reagan administration's creation of four such groups, each built around a battleship. Presumably four surface action groups can maintain one forward-deployed group. If it takes four surface action groups to keep one forward deployed, then one might imagine a need for two forward-deployed groups in each of the Mediterranean and the Pacific areas, for a total of sixteen groups. This would require eighty surface combatants, which is sixty more than are currently planned to be available for such units. In reality, many more separate units are needed to provide presence around the world. Some of them are simply detached from forward-deployed groups; in effect, *Cole* was on detached presence duty when she was attacked.

There also are new demands. If the U.S. Marines take their current doctrine seriously, then each ARG needs fire support ships (DD 21s) literally to replace the howitzer batteries marines currently take ashore. Although in theory a single DD 21 can replace a howitzer battery, her ammunition supply is limited. In practice one ship would offer support while another replenished ammunition. Because the ammunition ship would remain outside the battle area, time would also have to be allowed for transit back and forth. The prudent allowance would presumably be three DD 21s or equivalent per ARG. Some of these ships would likely be more sophisticated cruiser versions, adding missile defense for the amphibious force. As currently conceived, DD 21 has limited antisubmarine capability. It is questionable, therefore, whether the three DD 21s per ARG would actually replace the three escorts currently envisaged per ARG.

There is also missile defense. The surface combatants involved might be part of the increased number of surface action groups suggested above, or NTW may be considered so unique a role that it demands its own specialized groups. An NTW ship might be tied down to a particular place for a long time, whereas other naval forces hit and leave as required. The ship would have to operate in a group because it would be a prime target, demanding significant cover against underwater and missile threats.

There is also an attack submarine force. Carrier battle groups typically operate with a pair of submarines in detached support. Like carriers, submarines deploy for 180 days at a time, replenishing in a friendly port. It follows that the three forward-deployed carriers would require a total of six. Submarine operating cycles are probably faster than those for carriers, but at least four are probably needed to maintain one forward. Thus the carrier force would need at least twenty-four attack submarines in service.

Submarines, however, are needed for intelligence/surveillance/reconnaissance (ISR) and as Tomahawk shooters. The rationale for the current desired force level of sixty-eight submarines is classified because it would reveal how many separate sustained ISR stations the United States wishes to maintain. The fact that all submarine assignments are "national" rather than "naval" suggests that in practice few if any submarines can be spared for their nominal battle group assignments. In the past, the number of submarines was generally set by what could be afforded rather than by wartime or Cold War missions, because there was always a demand for more. Submarine availability is being improved by the current generation of "one-shot" reactors, which eliminate the need for refueling, thus restoring perhaps two years over the thirty-year life of a submarine.

Nuclear submarines are clearly expensive. It can be argued that a sophisticated non-nuclear submarine, which would be less expensive both to build and to maintain, can be an effective ISR collector. It would, however, have some important deficiencies. It would have only about half the transit speed of a nuclear submarine. It would be considerably less comfortable, and as a consequence it could not deploy for as long a period; many more submarines would be needed for the same coverage. For example, as long as a nuclear submarine need not fear detection, it can transit at high speed, about thirty knots. If the surveillance target is six thousand miles away, it takes the submarine about 8.3 days to get there. Out of a total period at sea of about ninety days, the submarine loses 18.4 percent of its time. Even a large non-nuclear submarine would have a shorter endurance, for instance, seventy-five days. Transit alone would consume about half of its time. The submarine could be transported to the vicinity of the target on a flo-flo merchant ship, leaving nearly all of its endurance for surveillance, but the flo-flo would hardly be covert. Long range is important because it is most unlikely that the United States can count on forward basing for surveillance absent some crisis. Nor does forward basing contribute to the covertness of surveillance.

Cold War experience of ISR off the Soviet coast suggests, moreover, that a nuclear submarine has an infinitely better chance of escape in the event the surveillance target notices its presence. A nuclear submarine has far more electric power at its disposal, allowing it to operate a wider variety of devices, including large unmanned underwater vehicles (UUVs). Diesel-electric submarines have performed ISR tasks quite effectively in the past, and the new Australian *Collins* class is intended largely for this role. It is quite clear, however, that nuclear power would have been preferable.

In theory, if ARGs are likely to operate fully independently, each ARG needs its own mine countermeasures capability. That is clearly unaffordable, unless the capability is organic; such a system is being developed. An older demand is for the mine force to be able to mount a major operation in each ocean simultaneously. That, too, appears unaffordable. We currently maintain enough capacity for a single major countermeasures operation. For example, there is a single mine countermeasures flagship (MCS), a converted amphibious carrier.

Behind the combatants is a support force. For example, a carrier battle group typically operates with a station ship (AOE). Without the AOE, the carrier air wing enjoys only limited endurance, set by the ship's aviation fuel capacity. Typically that is a few days to a week. Clearly the AOE is not fully integrated within the battle group, so it operates on a less stringent schedule. Still, it is reasonable to imagine that the ratio of forward-deployed to total AOEs should be one to three. If two carrier battle groups are always forward deployed, they need about six AOEs; presumably another can be homeported with the Yokosuka carrier. In fact, as of 2000, the United States has eight AOEs, four of which are due for early retirement due to their length of hard service. Construction of additional ships has been deferred. Clearly, other naval tankers, not intended for the forward combat support role, can act as station ships, but they are significantly slower than AOEs and thus constrain the battle group.

The afloat support force is down to two submarine tenders homeported at Maddalena, Sardinia, and Guam. Presumably each could help support for-ward-homeported submarines. Two destroyer tenders and one submarine tender are in reserve; all other destroyer tenders and repair ships have been discarded. In the past, the availability of tenders determined to what extent destroyers and submarines could be forward based. However, tenders become less important as individual ships become larger and more self-sufficient. At one time the central distinction between a cruiser and a destroyer was that the destroyer required a tender for periodic assistance. Now, however, destroy-ers like *Spruance* and *Arleigh Burke* are hardly distinguishable from cruisers in their need for assistance; only frigates probably need tender-level support. Modern large nuclear submarines can also operate without much tender assistance abroad.

Conversely, if the U.S. Navy should adopt proposed small surface com-batants, it would have to provide appropriate supporting forces. In some proposals the small littoral warfare combatants, displacing about a thousand tons, are transported to the combat zone aboard flo-flo mother ships. Presum-ably they would need separate tenders for afloat support; that was certainly the case with destroyers and frigates in the past. A group of eight littoral com-batant ships would probably require at least two mother ships and a separate tender, as well as a protected forward base for the tender and probably the mother ships. Although the small agile littoral combatants themselves might be quite survivable, their endurance would be limited, and the destruction of their base would probably be fatal. Thus at least a fraction of the forward-deployed littoral combatant force would probably be absorbed in protecting the base from enemy submarine and special forces attack, and a high-capacity air defense ship might also be needed to protect the base.

Besides all the ships, the U.S. Navy maintains an impressive shore-based or shore-centered establishment including maritime patrol squadrons and largely space-based maritime surveillance. The two are, to some extent, linked. Space-based sensors pick up signatures. Aircraft overflying ships can associate a particular ship with a particular signature. Repeated detections of the sig-nature make it possible to track the ship. The United States has a strong inter-est in controlling the spread of weapons of mass destruction; often weapons or their components or manufacturing technology go by ship. It follows that the United States benefits from maintaining and improving the ship-tracking sea surveillance system devised during the Cold War. At present surveillance can be conducted by a combination of shore-based P-3s and carrier-based S-3s. The S-3s on board carriers have already lost their antisubmarine function and are to be retired by 2004–5. When that happens, carrier-based area ship-ping surveillance will effectively end, unless some UAV replaces the S-3. It is not clear just how many P-3 squadrons and bases are required and, more important, to what extent allies or friendly governments will accept the pres-ence of such aircraft in future. In the past, it was easier to estimate the need for P-3s: they were used primarily to intercept and track submarines detected by SOSUS and similar systems. The base structure was designed to place a P-3 over a SOSUS detection spot quickly enough for the aircraft to have a good chance of reacquiring the submarine using its sonobuoys, which became more difficult when the Soviets silenced their submarines in the 1980s. Each base needed its own squadron, to provide ready aircraft. With the demise of the Soviet submarine force, the P-3 force, too, has contracted, but it is diffi-cult to say just what a sufficient P-3 force would be.

With the advent of really long-range unmanned air vehicles (UAVs), it is also possible to imagine a shift of surveillance roles to such craft, which might be based far from a combat zone. They might or might not be under naval control; this decision will determine if they are included in naval budg-ets. However, the United States is unifying its military intelligence/informa-tion network, so if these craft report into the universal network now being constructed their output will be available in some form to naval command-ers. It is much too soon to say whether advances in UAVs will make for further contraction in the P-3 force. In the past, the P-3 was valued not for its ability to find or even to track a submarine, but for its ability to destroy that sub-marine. Now the P-3 is clearly mainly a surveillance platform, and under some circumstances its crew may not be necessary for that mission. UAVs may be seen as a reasonable and less expensive alternative.

The P-3 fleet is aging, and despite efforts at life extension the aircraft will soon need replacement. This requirement coincides roughly with two other expensive aircraft programs: the new joint strike fighter (JSF), and a replace-ment for special-mission carrier aircraft (the E-2 airborne surveillance air-craft and the EA-6B escort jammer; probably the S-3 will not be replaced at all). Aircraft programs differ from shipbuilding ones because any new airplane imposes a considerable development cost, whether or not it is produced in any quantity. To develop three or four new aircraft simultaneously may be prohibitively expensive. Cutting production of new aircraft over several years to compensate might be unacceptable because it might become impossible to make up operating losses and retirements due to overage. It is also possible to trade off some aircraft sophistication against missile sophistication. It may be possible to limit aircraft development cost if much of the airplane's capability is inherent in the weapons it carries. On the other hand, as in the case of ships, naval aircraft are valuable not only for their combat roles but also for presence. They must be able to survive in potentially hostile air space without enemy defenses destroyed in advance, and without the luxury of operating far from potential threats (using stand-off weapons). All aircraft and missile costs can be traded off against new shipbuilding efforts, and vice versa.

Typically the cost of air programs roughly equals the cost of shipbuilding programs; weapons are about half of either.[2] The size of the aircraft bill reflects the extent to which the U.S. Navy relies on aircraft as its main offensive arm. No other navy in the world shows a similar balance in investment. Conversely, some would now argue that missiles are displacing aircraft, thus the missile bill should rise at the cost of the aircraft or the shipbuilding bills. For example, when it retired the A-6 Intruder bomber, the U.S. Navy explicitly accepted the loss of the aircraft deep strike mission. At least for the time being, that mission fell to Tomahawks. It may be resurrected if the new JSF, a true A-6 replacement, enters service.

Remarkably, programs setting the size of the fleet in numbers of ships do not include corresponding numbers of aircraft. It should because it can help decision makers decide whether the sustained shipbuilding program implicit in the numbers is affordable. That is perfectly reasonable in the case of carrier or surface ship aircraft, for which numbers are clearly tied to the strength of the fleet. The P-3 situation is radically different, yet clearly there is a fiscal trade-off between P-3 numbers (and basing costs) and procurement and operation of shipboard aircraft. To the extent that land-based aircraft perform duties that would otherwise fall to shipboard aircraft, there is an implicit trade-off between P-3 and carrier (and possibly helicopter-equipped destroyer) numbers.[3]

The chief driver toward radical change in the shape of the U.S. Navy is that total resources seem insufficient even to maintain the current force structure. Can enough ships be built to keep up the size of the fleet, even to half the strength of the Reagan years? Can enough aircraft be built to keep the carriers equipped, even at the current low levels per ship? Can enough weapons be produced to make up for expenditures? From a budgetary point of view, perhaps the most striking difference between the post–Cold War and the Cold War situations is that combat is more, not less, likely. During the Cold War weapon stockpiles could be built up and then maintained at relatively low cost, because few weapons were expended each year. Since 1990 the United States has expended about a quarter of all the Tomahawks it ever made.

The strategic arguments developed in this book imply that the main value of the U.S. Navy is that its ships can operate in forward areas for long periods. On that basis it would be difficult either to cut the more expensive parts of the fleet or to replace large long-endurance ships with small low-endurance ones. It would certainly be possible to imagine cuts at the margins, for example, a reduction in the number of surface warships per carrier battle group. The carrier and her aircraft, however, account for so large a proportion of the total cost of the group that such cuts would have only limited impact. Cuts in the total number of carrier groups would save more money, but they would also carry enormous and probably unacceptable strategic costs. Whatever Americans might say, a carrier and her aircraft exert more influence than a surface action group armed with a few hundred Tomahawks. It may be possible to limit investment in new combat aircraft themselves by placing greater emphasis on missile and electronics performance that can be applied to upgrade programs for existing aircraft. Because the U.S. Marine Corps budget is part of the U.S. Navy budget, there may also be some discussion of the relative impacts of carrier battle groups, surface action groups, and ARGs in various situations.

It is also possible to imagine efforts to cut ship procurement costs by stretching ships' lives. Ships' hulls are quite durable, and capabilities can be improved considerably by changing weapons and electronics. The justification for buying a completely new type of ship and, by implication, downgrading existing ones, is that improvements in hull and machinery offer such advantages that existing hulls are not worth retaining in production. Much this sort of argument is used to justify new stealthy supersonic-cruise aircraft such as the air force's F-22 and the new JSF. In the case of ships, the hull argument is that a new class of wave-piercing hulls offers such advantages in stealthiness that it is well worth adopting, even at a high cost. The machinery argument is that the all-electric ship is a step improvement in propulsion, perhaps to be compared to atomic power.

Overall, strategy dictates the reasons why ships matter, as well as how far ships should be able to steam and how long they should be able to remain off a foreign shore. In this sense the airplanes the ships carry are part of their armament; shore-based patrol aircraft are something like ships.[4] Finances dictate whether the navy can buy enough of a particular kind of technology to carry out national objectives. National politics determine whether the navy can make the case for enough resources to buy enough ships, of the appropriate kind, to survive not only the enemy but also the onslaught of technology over their lifetimes.

Notes

Chapter 1. National Strategy

1. For a current review of projections, see Sam J. Tangredi, *All Possible Wars? Toward a Consensus View of the Future Security Environment, 2001–2005*, McNair Paper 25 (Washington, D.C.: National Defense University, 2000).

2. Ideology is not logical; it is not susceptible to tests. The claim that democracy makes the world safer is questionable. It can be proven only if the rules are carefully set. In 1914, for example, both France and Germany were reasonably democratic countries, with elected legislatures; indeed, throughout Europe some measure of parliamentary democracy was accepted. The elected German Reichstag enthusiastically supported the kaiser's call to arms. Both the French *and* the German populations understood the war as defensive. Thus World War I does not test claims that democracies do not fight aggressive wars. The general popularity of the war at its outset in 1914 is well known; only later did people realize just how foolish they had been. More recently, much of the Greek population appears to have backed war against Turkey quite enthusiastically, and President Vladimir Vladimirovich Putin won the most recent Russian election largely on the basis of a vastly popular attack against Chechnya.

3. This is not a novel problem. Consider the parallel to U.S. entry into World War I. President Woodrow Wilson presented the war as a crusade for democracy. He never explained that backing the Allies was in the U.S. national interest (for balance-of-power reasons). After the war, Americans became disillusioned (was the kaiser really the devil?) and decided that the war had somehow been promoted by bankers in debt to the Allies. Consequences included an extremely destructive brand of isolationism, which probably helped cause World War II. Wilson's ideological approach led him to proclaim "peace without victory" as a goal. When the Allies imposed real penalties on the Germans, Wilson's proclamations made it possible for Germans to claim they had been cheated—again, opening the way for a new war. Wilson was also directly responsible for the breakup of the Austro-Hungarian empire, on ideological pro-nationalist grounds, which may have left a power vacuum Adolf Hitler was all too ready to fill.

4. This planning, programming, and budgeting system (PPBS) was put in place in the 1960s by Secretary of Defense Robert S. McNamara as a way of limiting the cost of defense. McNamara claimed to examine alternative forces to achieve each specified mission. Unfortunately, missions often are complementary, as in the case of some forms of power projection and sea control. It may have been significant that McNamara had been an air force officer during World War II; air force aircraft tend to be fairly specialized. Any such top-down process is inevitably risky because the choice made at the top may well be wrong. The chance of error is much greater in a confused post–Cold War world than in the relatively simple Cold War environment, and even then serious errors were made. McNamara's detractors much preferred military judgment, which had far more respect for the way forces actually function.

5. The Treaty of Paris, which the United States did not sign, also outlawed privateering. It set the rule that a blockader had to board a suspected contraband carrier, and that if the blockader sank the ship, provision had to be made for the safety of her passengers and crew. These were the rules the German U-boats broke so flagrantly during World War I. On the other hand, items for civilians, such as food, were not supposed to be subject to blockade. In their attempt to squeeze the Germans during World War I, the British expanded the list of contraband to include just such items, and the Germans claimed this expansion into a "hunger blockade" justified their unrestricted U-boat warfare.

6. On the outbreak of war in August 1914 the British seized all warships being built in their yards. The Turkish navy was apparently particularly furious that this included two new battleships, the crews for which had already arrived in Britain; they became HMS *Agincourt* and HMS *Erin*. Supposedly the seizures helped propel the Turkish government into the arms of the Germans, with the devastating consequence that the Dardanelles were closed to traffic with Russia, a major British ally. Perhaps recalling this consequence, in World War II the British delivered to Turkey part of a prewar order for destroyers, despite the Royal Navy's severe shortage of such ships. For examples of British warship construction for export, see Peter Brook, *Warships for Export: Armstrong Warships, 1867–1927* (Kendal, England: World Ship Society, 1999).

7. The French post–World War II arms industry notoriously depended on exports, mainly to the Third World, for financing. Until the 1980s, when the French decided to switch to the NATO market, French forces received weapons, such as the lightly protected AMX 30 tank, its specifications set to meet Third World rather than European requirements.

8. Although the Dutch had a land border, for a time during the seventeenth century they felt secure enough, due to the geography of rivers and the ability to flood key areas, to concentrate on maritime trade and seapower. The British shifted between alliance with the Dutch and attempts to destroy their seapower. Generally attempts to destroy Dutch seapower were through alliances with the French, which presented the Dutch with both maritime and land threats.

9. See Norman J. W. Goda, *Tomorrow The World: Hitler, Northwest Africa, and the Path toward America* (College Station, Texas: Texas A&M Press, 1998).

10. One crippling British strategic problem was that they had no coalition partner to exert pressure over U.S. land borders, complementing the mobile pressure offered by seapower. Canada offered a long land border, but insufficient population or infrastructure to support any sustained invasion. It was far more likely that U.S. forces would seize Canada in the event of war. After World War I, when British war planners examined possible strategies against the United States, they concluded that at best they could blockade the United States and make continued war so unpleasant that the Americans would seek some settlement. They estimated that U.S. forces could blockade and thus starve Britain, perhaps due to overestimates of the effect of trade warfare during World War I. We now know that defense-minded American planners never contemplated the forward strategy the British feared. The British seem not to have discussed the problem with the Canadians. The single Canadian war planner, an army colonel, proposed an initial offensive in the entirely false expectation that the British would send a large army to back up the Canadians. Worse, he assumed that the Americans would initially strike for the larger Canadian cities of Montreal and Toronto, probably because these were the points of greatest value to a Canadian. In fact American planners concentrated on ports like Halifax, through which any British empire reinforcements would have come. Thus the Canadian planner exemplified a decidedly non-naval outlook in a war that would necessarily have been maritime in character. See Christopher M. Bell, "Thinking the Unthinkable: British and American Naval Strategies for an Anglo-American War, 1918–1931," *International History Review* 19 (November 1997), 757–1008.

11. This strategy is laid out in detail by Andrew D. Lambert in *The Last Sailing Battlefleet: Maintaining Naval Mastery, 1815–1850* (London: Conway Maritime Press, 1991).

12. For an account, see William Roger Louis, *Imperialism at Bay: The United States and the Decolonization of the British Empire, 1941–1945* (Oxford: Clarendon Press, 1977). Much of the effort was through secret services; a recent account appears in Richard J. Aldrich's *Intelligence and the War Against Japan: Britain, America, and the Politics of Secret Service* (Cambridge: Cambridge University Press, 2000).

13. During the Cold War, President Dwight D. Eisenhower particularly represented this point of view. He was under constant heavy pressure to invest more in current military forces, particularly strategic bombers (later missiles) and the army. His rejoinder was that the United States had to be able to maintain Cold War forces for as long as forty years (a prophetic guess, as it turned out); extravagance now would mean disastrous economic weakness later. On this basis Eisenhower was particularly furious when John F. Kennedy made specious claims of a missile gap during the 1960 election.

14. Open architecture helps. The *Arleigh Burke*–class destroyer was designed primarily as an antiaircraft platform to support operations in the teeth of Soviet naval air power. Her vertical launchers are now filled largely with land attack Tomahawks. This open-architecture solution minimizes change in platforms in favor of weapons development. Platforms are inherently expensive, so only a limited number can be bought at any one time. The more open the architecture, the less vulnerable they are to obsolescence, hence the longer they can last. Numbers in service, the numbers that count, are the product of the number bought each year and the lifetime of the platform. On the

other hand, technology can make the platform itself obsolete. That is what happened to the British sailing battlefleet.

15. This incident is celebrated as the first time a moving warship fired a torpedo at a moving target; the torpedo was so slow that it missed.

16. Hence the British Empire defeats by the Japanese in 1941–42 had devastating effects. Often the prestige issue was cast in racial terms; the British Empire was based on the perception that white men would always defeat all others. When the Japanese won, the myth was exploded.

17. According to Anthony Clayton, *The British Empire as a Superpower, 1919–1939* (Athens: University of Georgia Press, 1986), 33, in the wake of World War I Indian units were used to garrison places like Iraq and Hong Kong, but such deployments met with political opposition within India. Indian units also deployed during the 1920s to Aden, Ceylon, Malaya, Hong Kong, and North China, but these were all small commitments, and they were gradually run down. Given limits on what India could provide, in the 1920s the British seriously considered raising a second imperial army from East or West Africa or from the Middle East, but it was considered prohibitively expensive. In the 1930s, as the supposed threat from the Russians via Afghanistan receded, and as the Japanese threat loomed, India was again seen as a reservoir of manpower for imperial defense (Ibid., 294–98). When Italy threatened, Indian units were also earmarked for Middle East defense.

18. The problem was that in an even moderately healthy economy the British could not man their forces with volunteers. Despite the Depression, at best they had enlisted only 207,000 men in one year, whereas by 1946 it seemed that 275,000 per year would be needed postwar. A much-enlarged Royal Air Force would place an especially severe strain on recruiting for the other services. In 1939 the British army strength was 176,000, including 47,000 Indian troops and 9,500 colonial troops; in 1945 it seemed that an army of 500,000 would be needed. At a 24 October 1946 cabinet meeting, Minister Without Portfolio A. V. Alexander said that India "had hitherto provided not only trained forces ready for immediate use in war, but also an immense reservoir of recruits" (British Public Record Office, Cabinet Minutes for 24 October 1946, document CAB 128/6). A more recent study by L. V. Scott, *Conscription and the Attlee Governments: The Politics and Policy of National Service, 1945–1951* (Oxford: Clarendon Press, 1993), gives a more complex explanation of the British decision to continue the draft postwar. Prime Minister Winston Churchill decided, on the advice of the chief of the Imperial General Staff, to consider a postwar draft as early as October 1944, when he was by no means certain that India would be abandoned. Foreign Secretary Ernest Bevin of the postwar Labour government remarked in 1947 that he accepted the case for permanent conscription, which was foreign to British tradition, as a quid pro quo for Indian independence. In a letter to Prime Minister Clement Attlee he described India as the empire's strategic reserve. Neither the War Office nor the Armistice and Post War Planning Committee (within the British government) linked the two issues. Also, Bevin had not earlier tried to use conscription to convince Churchill, when the latter was prime minister, to accept change in India. Nor was the Indian issue used to convince senior

Labour leaders to favor conscription. Scott suggests that Bevin's remarks were hindsight, developed when Attlee attacked British Middle East strategy in 1947. Much of the drive for large forces was to carry out the Middle East strategy of the time. For that matter, by 1947 India was a net liability. If the British had stayed in India, they would have needed about 50,000 troops simply to maintain order.

19. The war in the Sudan is graphically illustrated by the famous 1939 movie *Four Feathers,* which also gives a sense of how the 1885 failure had damaged British prestige. The 1898 war brought Lord Horatio Herbert Kitchener, who commanded the British land effort in 1914–16, to prominence.

20. See David Stevenson, *Armaments and the Coming of War: Europe, 1904–1914* (Oxford: Clarendon Press, 1996), 98. The Germans immediately began developing war plans against Britain. The kaiser accepted a secret memorandum from Adm. Alfred von Tirpitz advocating a battle fleet rather than a commerce-raiding navy, and the legislation to build this fleet was passed by the Reichstag in 1898.

21. See Peter Hopkirk, *On Secret Service East of Constantinople: The Plot to Bring Down the British Empire* (London: John Murray, 1994).

22. For example, in 1986 the French refused overflight rights for F-111s flying from Britain to attack Libya in conjunction with carrier aircraft. Flying all the way around France added considerably to the length of the flight, and may have led to a system failure that downed one of the bombers. The use of British airfields apparently was intended as a demonstration that an ally backed the U.S. action. Because the British had not been consulted beforehand, they were not pleased; they demanded that any future use of British airfields be subject to their veto.

23. During the war, there was a real attempt to unseat Saddam. The deep ground forces thrust, the "Hail Mary" maneuver, was aimed specifically against the Republican Guard, which was seen as the key prop of the regime. The troops were to get between the guard divisions and their refuge deeper in Iraq, destroying them and thus opening a real possibility of successful rebellion against the regime. Some ground units stepped off early, probably because the strategic objective, to destroy the regime by destroying the guard, was not made explicit enough. The guard units began to withdraw earlier than expected, and the opportunity was lost. Those on the scene equated success simply to ejecting the Iraqis from Kuwait, and reported that success to Washington, which was clearly anxious to complete the war as quickly as possible. Later, several tactical commanders said that when operations were suspended they had been within a day of destroying key guard units. All this story proves is that it is more and more important to clarify war aims implicit in subtle tactics.

24. There is a long-standing rivalry between Iraq and Egypt, the two most populous Arab states, for leadership of the Arab world. This rivalry has not always been appreciated in the West. In the mid-1950s British attempts to form a Middle Eastern defense alliance foundered because neither country would join an alliance in which the other was a partner, even though both had been British allies.

25. The maritime causes of the war, the Orders-in-Council governing the blockade and the impressment of seamen, seem in retrospect to have been pretexts for American

action. In 1812 the British hoped that once the Americans found out that the Orders-in-Council had been revoked, they would cease hostilities. Continued British insistence on impressment made it possible for the U.S. government to stay at war. See Adm. Sir Herbert Richmond, *Statesmen and Sea Power* (Oxford: Clarendon Press, 1946), 253. The British soon concluded that the war was actually over Canada.

26. The defense of Canada included an attempt to dominate the Great Lakes, and both sides began large building programs to help achieve that end. The Americans gained effective control of Lakes Erie, Huron, and Superior in the spring of 1814. By that time, however, the defeat of Napoleon had released substantial British ground forces, thus precluding any fresh American assault on Canada. As for the open sea, large forces were needed, partly because the British could not spare troops (from those required to defend Canada) to seize American bases and hopefully stop the American naval threat at source. At the outset the Royal Navy deployed seventy ships in the western Atlantic; by February 1813 the force had been increased to ninety-eight (eleven ships of the line, seventy-five frigates and sloops, and twelve smaller units), backed by forty (ten ships of the line, ten frigates and sloops, and twenty smaller units) in the eastern Atlantic and on detached duty. The total force involved required more seamen than had been lost through desertion. They would have to be recovered by the impressment at sea, which the Americans considered the cause of the war. Richmond, *Statesmen and Sea Power,* 252. As a measure of the effectiveness of the British blockade, according to Donald R. Hickey, *The War of 1812: A Forgotten Conflict* (Urbana: University of Illinois Press, 1989), 215, American export trade fell from $61.3 million in 1811 to $6.9 million in 1814, and imports fell from $53.4 million in 1811 to $6 million in 1814.

27. By the fall of 1814 dissaffection for the war had reached the point where the Russian ambassador wrote that in any European country similar conditions would have been considered a prelude to revolution (Hickey, *The War of 1812,* 231). The Republicans, who favored the war, suffered in the 1814 elections.

28. According to Hickey, *The War of 1812,* 196, the Americans regarded Baltimore as having far more strategic value than Washington, hence they could not believe that the British would waste resources on the capital. Baltimore was a major port and thus a privateering center.

29. Hickey, *The War of 1812,* 205. According to Robin Reilly, *The British at the Gates: The New Orleans Campaign in the War of 1812* (New York: Putnam, 1974), 181, the 1800 treaty ceding Louisiana to France (in exchange for Tuscany) included the stipulation that the French not sell the territory without first offering it back to Spain. For his part, Napoleon abandoned the territory after his forces suffered disaster in Haiti. The Spanish vigorously protested the transfer to the United States. In 1812 the Spanish still controlled Florida, and they cooperated with the British, allowing them to use Pensacola as a base. From it the British issued a proclamation to the natives of Louisiana "to assist in liberating from a faithless and imbecile government, your paternal soil," on 29 August 1814. The Americans then attacked the city, which its Spanish governor surrendered. The severity of Andrew Jackson's rule of New Orleans, during its defense, suggests that he had real doubts of the loyalty of its citizens; in December, just before the British

attack, there was a rumor that the local legislature had voted to surrender. The British seem to have been preparing for a spring campaign when the peace treaty was ratified.

30. The proposed area amounted to about a third of Ohio, half of Minnesota, and most of Indiana, Illinois, Michigan, and Wisconsin. The 100,000 whites located there would have had to move out, and the United States would have pledged not to acquire land in the area by purchase "or otherwise," meaning by military action.

31. Reilly, *The British at the Gates,* 250–51, quoting Wellington's comments on the situation as in fall 1814, when it seemed that New Orleans would soon be in British hands.

32. Reilly, *The British at the Gates,* 254; he comments that the Americans seem not to have grasped this possibility fully. Reilly, ibid., 343, makes it clear that the British cabinet considered it a definite option to retain Louisiana in the event their forces managed to capture New Orleans. The British strongly resisted any attempt during the peace treaty negotiations to force them into agreeing that the Louisiana Purchase had been legitimate. The evidence that the British hoped to annex Louisiana at the end of the war is limited but suggestive.

33. Andrew D. Lambert, *The Crimean War: British Grand Strategy, 1853–1856* (Manchester: Manchester University Press, 1990), 342.

Chapter 2. The Flavor of Seapower

1. The advent of bombers appeared to change matters, but during the Battle of Britain they were proven ineffective. Only with the appearance of ballistic missiles, V-2s, at the end of World War II, did the British government feel that the protection of the English Channel had been negated. Because there was no direct defense against missiles (as there was against aircraft), the British view was that safety required that a hostile power be kept beyond missile-launching range. In this sense British control of West Germany contributed directly to the defense of the British Isles. This logic helped propel Britain into a continental commitment of troops in 1948–49, at the birth of NATO.

2. During World War I, at least in the Mediterranean, the Allies operated a system of secret patrolled routes, port commanders assigning them to ships before they left. At one point the British employed random routing, while the French retained the patrolled routes. Patrols failed because surface ships on patrol could not detect a U-boat at any distance; the U-boat could often dive before it was spotted. The odds against engaging a U-boat were far too great. Contrast this concept with convoy, in which the antisubmarine craft travel with the potential targets, so that any U-boat that intercepts the targets automatically encounters them. During the Cold War, the U.S. Navy considered using antisubmarine aircraft to detect submarines entering designated shipping lanes. These "sterilized lanes" would be moved periodically to avoid offering other Soviet forces lucrative targets.

3. Peter Padfield, *Maritime Supremacy and the Opening of the Western Mind: Naval Campaigns That Shaped the Modern World, 1588–1783* (London: John Murray, 1999).

4. For example, in Kosovo, Slobodan Milosevich used paramilitaries to enforce

ethnic cleansing. The same units maintained him in power at home. Normally they operated in small sections, hence they could not easily be attacked, certainly not from the air. Late in the war, however, they began to concentrate to fight the Kosovo Liberation Army (KLA). In at least one case, such a concentration was hit from the air. It is at least arguable that Milosevich decided to withdraw for fear that such tactics would destroy the force maintaining him in power in Serbia. In this case the KLA was the coalition force, creating targets for network-centric attack. After the war, however, the U.S. officer in charge of information warfare claimed that the war would have ended much earlier if his unit had been allowed to operate freely. One interpretation would be that U.S. spoofers, not the KLA, caused the fatal paramilitary concentration, that is, turned the dispersed Serbian force into an attractive air target.

5. This is the position taken by Richard B. Frank, *Downfall: The End of the Imperial Japanese Empire* (New York: Random House, 1999).

6. By 1914 the German government was very heavily in debt, partly because the Reichstag was unwilling to levy taxes on the various fragmented principalities that made up the German empire. The major source of tax revenue, customs duties, was grossly insufficient. Victory in World War I would have solved the problem, because the losers would have paid off the government debt in the form of an indemnity. Defeat meant national bankruptcy, which helped cause the ruinous inflation of the early 1920s. This theme of using war to finance government spending, apparent in the Franco-Prussian War, is explicit in A.J.P. Taylor, *The Course of German History: A Survey of the Development of Germany Since 1815* (New York: Capricorn, 1962; reprint of 1946 edition with a new introduction).

7. The board's report appeared in the March 1890 issue of the *Proceedings* of the U.S. Naval Institute, replete with drawings of the ships it suggested.

8. The U.S. interest in Southeast Asia, which was connected to requirements to fight a possible European War, is described by Jonathan Marshall in *To Have and Have Not: Southeast Asian Raw Materials and the Origins of the Pacific War* (Berkeley: University of California Press, 1995).

9. Aircraft on board a carrier are an intermediate case. Because they operate en masse, at least near the carrier, they are necessarily subject to rigid control and to standardized procedures. As extensions of the carrier's (or the group's) weapon system, moreover, many of them are tightly controlled. That is certainly true of carrier-based interceptors. On the other hand, because the ship is subject to local weather conditions, it is difficult to imagine fitting her into the sort of rigid plan that might be attractive at an airfield ashore. That is one reason the carriers in the Gulf War were ill-equipped to work with the air force's tight air tasking order (ATO).

Chapter 3. The Geopolitics of Seapower

1. For a good account of such a battle, see Jurgen Rohwer, *The Critical Convoy Battles of March 1943: The Battle for HX.229/SC.122* (London: Ian Allan, 1977).

2. The islands were taken in 1770 specifically to interdict the trade route from Spanish colonies on the Pacific coast of South America, particularly wealthy Peru, via

the Straits of Magellan to the Atlantic and home. Trade winds set this route. For the Spanish, the alternative was to transship across Panama or Mexico, then reembark cargo in the Caribbean—from which it could be interdicted in the West Indies.

3. Brest was not blocked by British territory, and the winds were favorable for French ships to sail from it into the Atlantic. When Napoleon planned to invade Britain, he built up his force at Boulogne, on the English Channel, which is about the closest point to British soil. The force at Ushant was too far south to cover Boulogne; on the other hand the French fleet was at Brest because that was a fully equipped base, while Boulogne was a minor harbor. British base structure changed to reflect changing likely enemies. In the seventeenth century, when the Dutch were the enemy, the main naval bases were on the Thames and on the Medway, close to the center of the British economy at London, and well placed to interdict any Dutch fleet coming down from the north. Unfortunately these bases were to windward of Brest; a British fleet sailing from them would find it difficult to reach the vicinity of the French port. To deal with the French the British modernized the base at Portsmouth and built a new one at Plymouth. Both were ill-placed to face the Germans in the twentieth century, when the Admiralty had to trade off the cost of a new east coast base, Rosyth, against the cost of new ships. When strategy against the Germans shifted toward distant blockade, the key operating area became the gap between Scotland and Norway, and an operating base had to be established at Scapa Flow. Far from British industrial infrastructure, it could not become a full-fledged fleet base; Rosyth filled that role.

4. Although ships carried sufficient provisions for months at sea, a nearby base made provisioning much easier, and helped maintain the health of the seamen. The British maintained blockading fleets at sea for months during the wars of the French revolution and empire by having fresh supplies sent out. A fleet supply ship, distinguished by a bullock painted on her mainsail, is shown in Robert Gardiner, ed., *The Campaign of Trafalgar 1803–1805* (London: Chatham, 1997), 98.

5. This point was made by Jon Tetsuro Sumida in *Defending Naval Supremacy: Finance, Technology, and British Naval Policy, 1889–1914* (London: Routledge, 1989). Only once did the battlecruisers carry out their trade defense role, when two of them, HMS *Invincible* and HMS *Inflexible,* went to the South Atlantic to destroy von Spee's armored cruiser squadron. Battlecruisers were generally derided because of the vulnerability they showed at Jutland, but Nicholas Lambert has pointed out that the losses there were the consequence of a British decision, made well after the ships had been designed, to take a calculated risk and stow more ammunition in each turret. That in turn could be traced to developments in gunnery and fire control, and to the perception that the sort of deliberate fire envisaged when the ships were designed, which would have been appropriate for long ranges, was not wanted; effective ranges were shorter than expected. Lambert's data explain why, in 1916, the chief of the U.S. Navy's Bureau of Ordnance told the U.S. General Board that the battlecruiser concept was valid despite what had happened at Jutland, *because he understood exactly why the British ships had exploded* (he was defending the new U.S. battlecruisers, as lightly protected as their British counterparts). See Andrew D. Lambert's "'Our Bloody Ships' or 'Our Bloody System'? Jutland and the Loss of the Battle Cruisers, 1916," *Journal of Military History,*

Vol. 62, No. 1 (January 1998), 29–55. Sumida had previously pointed out that a new fire-control system might well have offered a fast, maneuverable ship considerable protection. Nevertheless, it was not adopted for most British battleships.

6. To some extent, too, the battlecruiser concept was connected to the Franco-Russian threat; it was less important if the main threat were German.

7. The submarines and the battlecruisers never lived up to expectations. The failure of Fisher's radical technology seems to have contributed to a determination, in the post–World War I Royal Navy, not to adopt further innovation until existing technology could be made to work. This conservatism proved costly in areas such as naval machinery and antiaircraft fire control.

8. A few cruisers intended as commerce raiders were intended to operate without putting in to friendly bases. They were built around extraordinarily capacious coal bunkers, which considerably distorted their designs.

9. For the Royal Navy this was déjà vu. During the age of sail, it depended on foreign sources of vital naval stores, such as pitch and turpentine. Masts and spars also came from abroad, particularly from the Baltic. Hence sea access to the Baltic was vital to the British during the age of sail much as access to Middle Eastern and American oil was vital during World War II. The British tried to develop alternative sources of vital shipbuilding and ship repairing material in their empire, even at higher cost than material from the Baltic; sources included Australia, Canada, India, and New Zealand. Without them, French blockage of the Baltic during the Napoleonic wars would have been fatal. With the shift to iron or steel and coal-fired steam engines, the British had what they needed within the British Isles. The later shift to oil fuel brought back dependence on foreign suppliers. The situation was even worse because much more than the Royal Navy depended on oil.

10. Richmond, *Statesmen and Sea Power,* 131–32, describes the British decision on the eve of the Seven Years' War (1756–63) to seek a coalition partner specifically to divert French strength.

11. For details, see Nicholas Tracy, *Navies, Deterrence, and American Independence: Britain and Seapower in the 1760s and 1770s* (Vancouver: University of British Columbia Press, 1988). In the fall of 1770 the British partly mobilized their reserve fleet to demonstrate what they could do; fifty-five ships of the line were brought forward, including the squadron of twenty "guardships" maintained partly manned and with stores on board for particularly quick mobilization. By January 1771 the first forty ships were 61.5 percent manned, and twenty-four ships could have been fully manned.

12. G. J. Marcus, *A Naval History of England: The Formative Centuries* (Boston: Little, Brown, 1961), 417. Masts were normally replaced every ten years, and in 1775 Royal Dockyards had a nominal three-year supply. No substitutes for American mast timber were found for some time, and Marcus claims that this shortage in itself crippled many ships. Often ships were fitted with old masts that had lost their natural strength and resilience. Ultimately masts were obtained from Riga and from New Brunswick.

13. Marcus, *A Naval History of England,* 416. According to R. Gardiner, ed., *Navies and the American Revolution, 1775–1783* (London: Chatham Publishing, 1996), 10, at the

outbreak of the Seven Years' War the Royal Navy had 25,824 seamen, sufficient to man thirty-nine ships of the line; at the end of the war personnel strength was 84,770.

14. Gardiner, ed., *Navies and the American Revolution,* 9.

15. According to Gardiner, ed., *Navies and the American Revolution,* 18, in June 1776 there were twenty guardships in European waters, but all usable frigates, as well as some small ships of the line, were either in American waters or earmarked for American service. American service accounted for about eighteen thousand seamen, compared to only eight thousand in home waters and seven thousand abroad.

16. In 1779 and in 1781 the British fleet was more powerful than the French fleet, but not the combined French and Spanish fleets. In 1780, for example, the British had 103 ships of the line, the Spanish and French a total of 126. In 1785, however, the totals were 121 and 118, respectively. Richard Harding, *Seapower and Naval Warfare, 1650–1830* (London: UCL Press, 1999), 244. So important was the Spanish naval contribution, at least in French eyes, that the French handed over their main surviving New World possession, Louisiana, to Spain; Napoleon got it back in 1800, in time to sell it to the United States.

17. The standard fleet unit also included six destroyers and three submarines, presumably for local defense. Admiral Fisher argued that thanks to improved radio communications and efficient intelligence a fleet unit at sea could be vectored against enemy raiders. There is also evidence that he favored a modular fleet consisting of fleet units maneuvering more or less independently, on the ground that a conventional battle line would make too good a target for enemy torpedoes. Much of the evolution of battleships, at least in the Royal Navy before 1914, was driven by the need to engage outside torpedo range, because ships were so vulnerable to underwater damage.

18. The fleet unit concept could not be revived after World War I, when Japan really was perceived as a threat, because all British empire capital ships were counted together under the 1922 Washington Treaty. Any dominion units would have come out of British tonnage, and thus would have weakened the British battle fleet. Australia alone was willing to buy major units (heavy cruisers) after 1922, and the British could not help underwrite a comparable New Zealand squadron. Canada showed no interest in buying ships, and the Royal Indian Navy never bought anything more powerful than escort vessels (sloops).

19. See Nicholas A. Lambert, "Economy or Empire: The Fleet Unit Concept and the Quest for Collective Defence in the Pacific, 1909–1914" in Keith Neilson and Greg Kennedy, eds., *Far-Flung Lines: Studies in Imperial Defence in Honour of Donald Mackenzie Schurman* (London: Frank Cass, 1996). According to Lambert, the Pacific situation relaxed after the Japanese victory over Russia; both of the other Pacific powers, France and the United States, brought their modern battleships home. The British also controlled the situation to some extent because only they maintained large enough coal stocks (300,000 tons) to support major fleet movements. However, by 1909 there was fear of ultimate attack by Japan, despite the Anglo-Japanese Treaty. A review of Pacific empire defense began in January 1909, prompted by a complaint by the commander at Hong Kong that his own shore defenses were too weak. At this time the concept was to send the Mediterranean Fleet to the Far East in the event of an emergency, but there was

some feeling that sending powerful reinforcements could actually exacerbate a crisis. The review coincided with a European naval crisis; in March Canada and Australia offered to buy capital ships to support Britain. These offers evaporated as the crisis receded, the Canadians being particularly reluctant to buy major warships. However, they showed that the major dominions could afford capital ships. On 30 April 1909 all colonial heads of government were invited to a conference in London, which opened on 28 July. Australia actually bought a fleet unit, and the agreement with New Zealand was that the Royal Navy would pay maintenance and buy everything beyond a capital ship. The British planned to station a unit of their own, built around the battlecruiser *Indomitable* (sister to the Australian and New Zealand ships), at Hong Kong. By the time that was being considered, however, the situation in home waters was far more critical. As First Lord of the Admiralty (equivalent to a U.S. Secretary of the Navy), Winston Churchill found it impossible to ask for expensive new ships while stationing a major modern unit in the Pacific. Not only did *Indomitable* stay home, but the Australian and New Zealand ships were brought to British waters early in World War I. The fleet unit idea died.

20. Winston Churchill ordered the two capital ships to the east on the ground that the Japanese would be unable to risk sending invasion convoys toward Malaya and the East Indies as long as they were loose. It had long been assumed that Japan would not risk attacking Australia and New Zealand if a powerful British fleet lay athwart the prospective invasion route; that was the basis for prewar British plans to send a fleet built around seven capital ships to Singapore in the event of war with Japan. Through 1940–41 the Australians pressed hard for at least some capital ships to be sent out, asking whether the improved situation after the strike at Taranto did not justify denuding the Mediterranean. Because Australia supplied ground forces vital to the defense of Egypt, such demands could not be taken lightly. The dilemma was that the British considered the Middle East far more important than the Far East. Churchill said that "nothing that could happen in Malaya could amount to a fifth part of the loss of Egypt, the Suez Canal, and the Middle East." The British considered, moreover, that even if they did attack, the Japanese probably would not try to invade Australia, because nearer territories, such as Malaya, were far more attractive. The Australians saw matters rather differently. By the spring of 1941 the British felt badly stretched, and they faced the prospect of two new German battleships (*Bismarck* and *Tirpitz*). In August the Australian premier, Sir Stewart Menzies, asked urgently for a deterrent against Japan. The U.S. Atlantic Fleet had been reinforced, and the Germans were down to a single battleship, *Tirpitz*. The British could tentatively plan a substantial Far Eastern fleet, but Prime Minister Churchill wanted something impressive done at once to deter the Japanese. He was painfully aware of the disproportionate influence the single German battleship exerted on the British, and concluded that a small squadron should have similar effects on the Japanese, particularly because they also had to take the U.S. fleet into consideration. In his words, *Tirpitz* "exercises a vague, general fear and menaces all points at once. It appears, and disappears, causing immediate reactions and perturbations on the other side." That is, the force sent out would threaten the Japanese as a raiding unit. See

Arthur J. Marder, *Old Fiends, New Enemies: The Royal Navy and the Imperial Japanese Navy, Vol I: Strategic Illusions, 1936–1941* (Oxford: Clarendon Press, 1981), 213–41. Marder does not draw the parallel with the pre-1914 fleet unit, but Churchill presumably remembered it. The fleet unit was seen as a raider-killing unit rather than as a raiding unit, but both functions were presumably inherent in it. The Admiralty resisted sending the *Prince of Wales* and *Repulse* east, on the ground that they constituted too weak a force to survive, particularly without the carrier accompanying them.

21. The sense of betrayal—Australia backed the home country in 1939 and two years later got vulnerability in return—is still strong more than half a century later; it accounts for the Australian tilt toward the United States not only during World War II but afterwards.

Chapter 4. Using Naval Forces

1. Radar normally gives few or no clues to identification; it merely indicates a target at a particular position. The best long-range radar ship identifier technique is inverse synthetic aperture radar (ISAR), which can be applied to surface search radars. Antiradar materials probably drastically reduce its efficacy. Nor is it likely to be effective at very long ranges. Because the visual content of the ISAR image is limited, ship identification by ISAR requires an electronic library of ISAR images of all likely targets, which may be impossible to assemble. A more recent alternative, which might be less susceptible to radar camouflage, is spotlight synthetic aperture radar (SAR), which can form a more detailed image of a target. Compared to ISAR, spotlight SAR requires far more computing power to form its image, but image interpretation is much simpler. In both cases maximum range is likely to be much less than a hundred miles. Wide-area reconnaissance is possible only if the target identifies itself by producing characteristic electronic emissions. As a countermeasure, the U.S. Navy deliberately standardized long-range (two-dimensional) air search radars among all its major units, from frigates up through carriers, so that at a distance all offer the same electronic signature.

2. For accounts of British sea surveillance in World War I, see Patrick Beesly, *Room 40: British Naval Intelligence, 1914–1918* (London: Hamish Hamilton, 1982); for World War II, see Patrick Beesly, *Very Special Intelligence,* rev. ed., introduction by Jock Gardner (London: Greenhill Books, 2000).

3. The Operational Intelligence Centre collated all available intelligence, including that derived from code-breaking, to produce a picture of enemy naval movements and, where possible, intentions. Many of the problems of World War I exploitation of radio intelligence had been due to an unwillingness to allow code-breakers to draw the operational implications of the data they collected. For example, until 1917 they were not permitted to maintain a plot of enemy positions, nor to see the main Admiralty plot. In the most famous British code-breaking blunder, on the eve of the battle of Jutland a captain in the Admiralty, wanting to seem sophisticated, asked the code-breakers not "where is the German fleet?" but "where is the call sign of the German flagship?" He was told, correctly, that it was at the mouth of Wilhelmshaven harbor. The code-breaker

did not care to add that it was standard practice for the call sign to be transferred to the lighthouse there when the German fleet sortied, or that the code-breakers had intercepted numerous signals indicating a sortie some hours earlier. The captain then told Adm. Sir John Jellicoe, commanding the British Grand Fleet, that the Germans, who were about to go to sea, were not yet out of port, and Jellicoe shaped his course accordingly. When he sighted the German fleet much earlier than expected, his confidence in the code-breakers suffered badly. On the night of Jutland, the German commander sent an elaborate signal indicating his planned course back to base. The British instantly deciphered it, and the results were passed to Jellicoe—who preferred his own guess as to their course, because he had been failed so badly the previous day. At daybreak he found himself on an empty sea, rather than, as he had hoped, between the Germans and their base. The lesson, so often ignored since, was that those not used to handling raw intelligence (the location of the call sign) ought to defer to those better aware of the implications of what they obtain.

4. For an account of SOSUS, see Norman Friedman, *The Naval Institute Guide to World Naval Weapons Systems,* 1991–92 edition (Annapolis, Md.: Naval Institute Press, 1991).

5. For an account of U.S. and Soviet Cold War sea surveillance systems, see Norman Friedman, *Seapower and Space: From the Dawn of the Missile Age to Net-Centric Warfare* (Annapolis, Md.: Naval Institute Press, 2000).

6. According to recent Russian publications, research on silencing was a specific theme of the 1971–80 ten-year shipbuilding plan (presumably drawn up in the late 1960s). The specifications for the "Sierra" class (Project 945) were approved in March 1972. The "Akula" class (Project 971) was a parallel project with similar silencing but with a less expensive steel (vice titanium) hull. In 1975 a project for a silenced version of the existing "Victor" class, "Victor III" (Project 671RTM), was approved. At about the same time the Soviets also bought computer-controlled machining equipment illegally in the West specifically to produce quiet propellers for existing submarines.

7. Because JOTS amounted to software running on a standard commercial computer, it was easy to install on board the many ships involved, a striking difference from other major naval systems.

8. For an account of convoy history, see John Winton, *Convoy: The Defence of Sea Trade, 1890–1990* (London: Michael Joseph, 1983).

9. This strategy was embodied in the "Z [target, or *ziel*] plan" adopted in January 1939 as the result of studies begun the previous May to prepare for war against Britain. The German staff planner, Comdr. Helmuth Heye, argued that to contest British sea lanes Germany would need not only new ships but also forward bases along the French Atlantic coast and probably in Denmark, the Netherlands, and Norway. Adm. Erich Raeder was reportedly furious; he wanted only good news to report to the führer. Raeder then ordered development of what turned out to be the Z plan. It would have provided four task forces for oceanic operations, each comprising a carrier, a battleship or pocket battleship, and a heavy cruiser. The home fleet would comprise the four capital ships already under construction, the two *Scharnhorst*s and the two *Bismarck*s. Crit-

ics have pointed out that the planners assumed that the British would not build up to match it, and that a smaller German shipbuilding industry could outbuild the much larger British one.

10. First Sea Lord Sir John Jellicoe later wrote that one important reason for delaying the introduction of convoys was that there were no suitable ports on the American coast at which they could assemble. Also, the destroyers that would be needed as escorts were also needed by the British Grand Fleet, which had to contain the German fleet-in-being. See Jellicoe, *The Crisis of the Naval War* (London and New York: Cassell, 1920). American entry into the war provided the ports. To a limited extent the destroyer problem was solved by building specialized lower-performance convoy escorts; the same thing was done in World War II. Fortunately the U.S. Navy of the time was destroyer heavy, and it did not deploy a battle fleet, which would have required U.S. destroyers as escorts, to European waters. Convoying became effective, however, well before many U.S. destroyers arrived in European waters.

11. He expected to be intercepted, if at all, when he penetrated the screen on the way out. A screen of escorts surrounds the ships being protected. Because the area protected grows much faster than the perimeter, it takes fewer escorts per ship as a convoy is made larger. On the other hand, a large convoy does not cover so much more water than a smaller one that it is easier for submarines to detect. Hence the "law of large convoys" discovered in the middle of World War II: it is much better to dispatch smaller numbers of larger convoys, each of which can be strongly escorted. There is a catch. A fast submarine with long underwater endurance can get under a convoy and fire up at the ships, while being covered by the convoy's noise. To counter it, escorts would have to be interspersed with the merchant ships, and the latter dispersed to limit the noisy sanctuary any submarine would enjoy. The situation of a fast long-endurance submarine is analogous to that of a submarine attacking on the surface at night prior to the advent of effective surface search radar, as U-boats did, very effectively, in the first years of World War II.

12. Described in Cross Associates, *History of Airborne Anti-Submarine Warfare 1941–1977*, a secret 1978 report declassified in 1990 (copy in the U.S. Navy Operational Archives).

13. For example, it may become more important to provide ships with some form of antitorpedo weapon. Many ships have decoys to attract homing torpedoes, but the ideal would be a hard-kill weapon that would destroy an incoming torpedo.

14. Admiral of the Fleet S. G. Gorshkov argued on the basis of numbers of personnel employed directly in submarine and in antisubmarine warfare (100 to 1) or numbers of ships and aircraft. See, for example, S. G. Gorshkov, *The Sea Power of the State* (Annapolis, Md.: Naval Institute Press, 1979), 120. He thus avoided issues of production cost, for example, of the special steels used in submarines, or of the submarines themselves. That may have been natural given the unreality of Soviet economics. Philip Pugh, in *The Cost of Seapower: The Influence of Money on Naval Affairs from 1815 to the Present Day* (London: Conway Maritime Press, 1986), 245, argues that total British and Canadian spending on escorts, representing the great bulk of those involved in the most

critical period of the Battle of the Atlantic, was substantially less than German expenditure on U-boats, due to the high cost per ton of a submarine. Tracy, *Navies, Deterrence, and American Independence,* 206–7 and 212, quotes Pugh's more elaborate 1988 analysis of total costs on both sides between October 1942 and June 1943; he claims that the Germans spent about £10.72 million each month (in 1938 figures) compared to £9.99 million for the Allies. These figures are only approximate, but they suggest that Gorshkov's gross disparity was an illusion. Tracy points out that the Germans spent so heavily because they were pursuing submarine warfare as a potentially decisive instrument; if they had merely tried to contain the Allies, they might have enjoyed much better economics. On the other hand, the effects of submarine warfare, such as limiting the Allied ability to conduct an offensive during 1943, may have been worth the money spent.

15. For a sense of how this was done, see J. H. Holmes, *Double-Edged Secrets* (Annapolis, Md.: Naval Institute Press, 1977).

16. Thus according to Samuel Eliot Morison, who interviewed all the senior American commanders, the post-battle mood in the American fleet, Task Force 58, was one of letdown rather than exhilaration, because the commanders sensed that the opportunity to destroy the enemy fleet, which had come out for the first time in two years, had been lost. Eight years later Admiral Spruance, the U.S. commander, still saw the Philippine Sea as a lost opportunity. Samuel Eliot Morison, *U.S. Naval Operations in World War II, Vol. VIII: New Guinea and the Marianas* (Boston: Little, Brown, 1953), 313–19. The Japanese lost 92 percent of their carrier aircraft during the battle. Morison points out (ibid., 235) that training was part of the reason for the Japanese disaster. The U.S. Navy did not allow pilots to enter combat until they had had two years of training. That was acceptable because of the sheer number of aviators available, although earlier in the war the U.S. Navy had accepted considerably lower training standards. The best of the Japanese pilots had trained for only six months, and they had been unable to fly while their fleet lay at its base at Tawi Tawi, largely because the Japanese carriers could not steam freely for fear of being sunk by American submarines. It was impossible to train new Japanese aviators in time to fight at Leyte Gulf, only four months after the Philippine Sea battle. The low standard of Japanese training in 1944 was a direct result of earlier practices. The prewar Japanese fleet air arm was a highly trained elite force. There was very little margin for losses; the Japanese believed that high individual quality would make up for the greater weight of American industry. Thus losses at Midway and in the Solomons were crippling. The Japanese were unwilling or unable to change their training system to provide greater numbers. A year or more after the disasters Japan only had small numbers of pilots who had partially completed the standard training. Losses of elite pilots was not a unique problem of the Japanese. The unpublished British official history of the Fleet Air Arm at war blames the low quality of pilots and aircrew in 1941 (as evidenced, for example, in an erroneous attack on a British cruiser during the *Bismarck* chase) on the loss of too much of the small elite Fleet Air Arm cadre in 1940, both in Norway and in the Mediterranean.

17. They were based in Montenegro, part of the Federal Republic of Yugoslavia, but increasingly estranged from Slobodan Milosevich, and thus largely immune from attack. Also, they made no threatening moves.

18. For example, in 1914 the British ratio of superiority over the German High Seas Fleet was seriously reduced when the battleship HMS *Audacious* was mined and sunk. Some British capital ships were always unavailable due to refits and repairs. Therefore, if the Germans picked their moment exactly right they might actually win a battle. Worse, Americans not subject to British censorship witnessed the sinking from the decks of the liner *Olympic*.

19. The first modern Soviet strategic submarines, the "Yankee" class (Project 667A), could not attack from within bastions. Some of them patrolled off the U.S. coast, but the Soviets assumed that the U.S. Navy could and probably would detect and track them. Earlier Soviet strategic submarines had even shorter-range missiles. At least initially, the Soviets apparently saw the "Yankees" mainly as a reserve force, for use after long-range land-based missiles had been expended. In 1972, however, the Soviets introduced the "Delta" (Project 667B) class, which could fire from a bastion. Once these submarines were in service, defense of the bastions was considered defense of a primary strategic weapon, usable at the outset of a war. According to E. M. Kutovoy, P. M. Serebrov, and V. P. Kolpakov (in "Submarine-Launched Ballistic Missiles" in the May 1999 issue of the Russian-language journal *Taifun,* pp. 22–29), the impetus for the "Delta" was an attempt by a Soviet missile designer, V. N. Chelomey, to take over submarine-launched missile development by placing his "universal" UR-100 (NATO designation SS-11) intercontinental ballistic missile (ICBM) on board submarines as well as at land sites. The design bureau already developing Soviet naval missiles made the countersuggestion that produced the missile (approved in 1964) on board the "Delta"-class submarines.

20. Nicholas Tracy has tried, in *Attack on Maritime Trade* (Toronto: University of Toronto Press, 1991).

21. Adm. Sir Herbert Richmond, *Sea Power in the Modern World* (London: G. Bell and Sons, 1934), 64. Lambert, *The Crimean War,* 334, argues that the Paris declaration was actually a victory. Without merchant auxiliaries (privateers), in the mid-nineteenth century neither France, Russia, nor the United States could damage British shipping. If privateering was revived, the British could drop the restraints imposed by the treaty. Moreover, the declaration included no definition of contraband, which would be quite flexibly defined during World War I.

22. These points were made by a French naval officer, Lt. Louis Guichard, in *The Naval Blockade, 1914–1918* (New York: D. Appleton and Co., 1930).

23. Tracy, *Attack on Maritime Trade,* 144–46.

24. The German navy sold unrestricted submarine warfare by claiming that by sinking enough shipping it could knock Britain out of the war in six months, based on an analysis of the British economy and its import needs. The Germans sank as much tonnage as they hoped in the first six months of the campaign, before either convoy or a policy of increased British food production could have much impact. Effective rationing apparently saved the country (Tracy, *Attack on Maritime Trade,* 141). The situation was so serious that First Sea Lord Admiral Jellicoe proposed withdrawing from eastern operations specifically to limit the use of scarce merchant shipping there. He urged a land attack on the U-boat bases in Flanders. In this sense the submarine blockade helped cause the third Ypres campaign. According to Tracy, ibid., 139, by early 1917

the Entente already suffered from a serious shipping shortage, partly because ships were assigned to the long run from Australia to make up for an expected shortfall in the North American harvest. The North American harvest turned out better than expected, so the Australian runs were not needed. On the other hand, attempts to build more merchant ships than the Germans were sinking failed. When U-boat attacks began, shipowners panicked, and it was particularly difficult to convince neutrals to go to sea. Because Germany was still benefiting from cargoes carried by neutrals, this effect actually tightened the blockade of Germany. Ship losses rose from 171 from all causes in January 1917 to 234 in February, the first month of unrestricted submarine warfare, to peak at 373 in April 1917. Convoying began at the end of April, and monthly losses began to fall in May (to 287). By July 1917 the Germans realized that the U-boat campaign was not succeeding. In November 1917 only 128 ships were lost. Even so, many ships were out of service due to damage repairs. In June 1917 the merchant fleet was down 10 percent compared to February. Convoying itself may have reduced effective carrying capacity by 30 percent. Tracy points out that this latter figure is misleading: ships sailing independently often put into harbors to avoid U-boats, thus losing considerable time.

25. Not only did Japan depend heavily on imports, but in 1941–42 her newly conquered empire required nearly all existing shipping. Japanese calculations assumed that most shipping required to support the assault on Southeast Asia (the Southern Operation) would soon be returned to civilian use, to bring home the resources thus obtained. Three million tons of civilian shipping were required. On the eve of war Japan had 6.6 million tons of shipping, of which 2.1 million tons was reserved for the army and 1.8 million tons for the navy, the latter to be increased to 2.8 million tons (at army expense) after the first four months of war. The Japanese estimated that they would lose 800,000 to 1,000,000 tons per year, and that they could build 600,000 tons per year (400,000 tons were produced annually in peacetime). Japan captured very little additional shipping during the conquest of Southeast Asia, and the longer shipping routes to the new territories increased losses beyond prewar estimates. Even in 1942, despite defects in their torpedoes, U.S. submarines managed to sink about as much tonnage as the Japanese added. Given the continued demands by the Japanese military, after August 1942 the three million tons needed for imports was never available. See Atsushi Oi, "Why Japan's Antisubmarine Warfare Failed," in *The Japanese Navy in World War II in the Words of Former Japanese Naval Officers,* 2d ed., ed. David C. Evans (Annapolis, Md.: Naval Institute Press, 1986). According to Oi, Japanese victories on the Asian mainland in the 1930s led to a dangerous misperception that Japan was now a continental power less dependent on sea transportation, even though communication with the mainland part of the empire was necessarily by sea, and far too little attention was paid to the security of sea communications with the newly seized territories, such as Indonesia, in the south. Marder, *Old Friends, New Enemies,* 322, quotes Oi as having been told in the fall of 1940 by a strategist in the Navy Ministry that the navy would secure oil in Borneo and Sumatra soon after the outbreak of war. The strategist rejected his argument that it would be nearly impossible to prevent submarines from sinking tankers trying to bring that oil to Japan through the South China Sea: "to occupy the land and

produce petroleum there was one thing, but to transport the product from there to Japan would be quite another." Oi also thought that the Japanese downgraded shipping protection because they had not faced any threat to sea communications in earlier wars.

26. For a summary of the tanker war in the Gulf, see Martin S. Navias and E. R. Hooton, *Tanker Wars: The Assault on Merchant Shipping during the Iran-Iraq Conflict, 1980–1988* (London: I. B. Tauris, 1996). Navias and Hooton point out that it took the Western powers six years to intervene to limit damage to their vital oil supplies via the Gulf.

27. For an account, including the Iranian offer, see Jeffrey L. Levinson and Randy L. Edwards, *Missile Inbound: The Attack on the Stark in the Persian Gulf* (Annapolis, Md.: Naval Institute Press, 1997). The guess as to just how the Iranians were involved is my speculation.

28. During the Cold War, the United States abandoned ballistic missile defense largely on the theory that for every dollar the Soviets spent to overcome it the United States would have to spend about three dollars to maintain the defense. Later it emerged that the Soviet economy was probably less than a third the size of the U.S. economy, therefore the Soviets would have spent a larger fraction of their own defense budget to overcome the U.S. defense.

Chapter 5. The Rise and Fall of Mass Forces

1. The land-based tactical air arm was not yet effective, but Saddam appeared to have been unaware of the limitations imposed by logistics. According to Edward J. Marolda and Robert J. Schneller Jr., *Shield and Sword: The United States Navy in the Persian Gulf War* (Washington, D.C.: Naval Historical Center, 1998), 73, U.S. Army officers also overrated the sustained capabilities of the tactical aircraft in the Gulf, before they had received backup spares and ammunition.

2. U.S. participation in the ground phase of the Vietnam War appears to have been bound up with the abandonment of Eisenhower's essentially maritime way of fighting peripheral conflicts during the Cold War, and in particular with the U.S. Army's fight for greater prominence in the Kennedy administration. A parallel can be drawn with the British army's fight for greater prominence in the years leading up to 1914, and with the consequent abandonment of the earlier British maritime strategy in favor of a continental one. See Norman Friedman's *The Fifty-Year War* (Annapolis, Md.: Naval Institute Press, 1999) for details of the change in U.S. strategy.

3. Napoleon created the first modern mass armies by drafting large numbers of citizens. However, like earlier European armies, his lived off the land. Their greater scale tended to starve out districts in which they operated, and thus probably helped incite resistance. In 1812 Napoleon led 400,000 men into Russia, leaving another 250,000 elsewhere, including Spain; this did not count allied Prussians and Austrians. Previously, typical armies had numbered 50,000, and the British felt strained to maintain armies of about 40,000 on Walcheren and in the Peninsula.

4. The basic assumption appears to have been that an army detached from the population could more easily meddle in politics; certainly France has had its share of coups. Also, the French used army service as a way of indoctrinating draftees into national virtues, as did the Soviets.

5. Even in this case economics had a decisive impact. The size of the U.S. Army, hence the demand of the draft, was set by cost. As the baby-boomers reached draft age, the army needed only a small fraction of those subject to the draft. Inevitably many were allowed out of the draft, and there was a strong feeling of inequity. The fury of those who were nonetheless drafted to fight made the war even more unpopular. It became clear that using draftees drastically limited the U.S. government's freedom of action. Earlier Cold War history suggests that there was less difficulty when virtually everyone of draft age was called up.

6. For example, some years ago the Chinese government decided to prohibit the manufacture and sale of satellite television dishes, for fear that the wrong messages were getting into Chinese heads. The effort collapsed when the General Staff pointed out that the military was the main producer of such equipment; it had no interest in abandoning the profits it was making. A later, apparently abortive, Chinese government attempt to force its military out of commercial enterprises may reflect this experience.

7. In January 1945 Adm. William F. Halsey raided Tokyo using large numbers of carrier aircraft. The operation is generally rated a failure; bomb loads were far too small. A B-29 Superfortress could carry up to ten tons of bombs, compared with one ton for each of up to thirty attack aircraft on board a carrier. Thus a task group of four carriers could deliver, per sortie, only the bomb loads of twelve B-29s, at a time when hundreds of Superfortresses were attacking every night.

8. This issue was discussed when the Israeli-made Harpy antiradar drone was proposed for service during the Kosovo war. Although its effective range is short, the drone can loiter for hours over a radar, so its point-to-point endurance is considerable. The U.S. solution to the legal problem was to order development of a ship-launched Harpy. Armed unmanned vehicles have actually been used in the past, important examples being the U.S. Navy's DASH antisubmarine drone and bomb-carrying versions of the Firebee drone used in Vietnam.

9. During the buildup to the Gulf War, the U.S. Air Force's chief of staff suggested that the best U.S. policy would be to say that we knew where Saddam, his family, and his mistress were, and that all had been targeted. He was immediately dismissed for proposing an illegal plot against a foreign head of state; yet he had named the only worthwhile deterrent targets in Iraq. During the 1980s some U.S. strategists suggested that the only important deterrent, as opposed to war-fighting, target in the Soviet Union was the leadership itself. That probably explains why later editions of the official *Soviet Military Power* booklet showed diagrams of the leadership's shelter system under Moscow, conveying the message that it was a target.

10. As a case in point, consider the B-2 that attacked Belgrade during the Kosovo war. It took about thirty hours for the round trip between its base in Missouri and the target area. To maintain a single bomber loitering for an hour over one battle area, then,

would have required thirty B-2s in the air at all times. Since no airplane is always ready for flight, at least fifty or sixty would be needed. Even then unpredictable events at the distant base or en route, such as weather, might leave the target area uncovered for hours at a time.

11. The hope appeared to have been that attacks on the personal assets of those supporting Milosevich would cause them to topple him, in hopes of saving remaining assets. This tactic failed. There were also attacks on the headquarters of organizations, such as his political party, which supported Milosevich, and on state television and radio stations that presumably helped transmit his orders both to the population and to the paramilitary units in Kosovo.

Chapter 6. Seapower versus Land Power

1. Two other possibilities were explored at the outset. One was direct military support for allies fighting in Flanders, to keep the French out of the Low Countries, from which Britain could most easily be invaded. A second was to support counterrevolution in the Vendee. One perceived advantage of supporting the Vendee was leverage: a relatively small British force, transported and supplied by sea, could encourage a large counterrevolutionary movement and tie down a powerful French force, to an extent impossible in Flanders (where the allies might be quite unreliable). The British also tried to support a rising in Toulon, but found that the allied army required was not forthcoming. Spain was Britain's coalition partner, but the Spanish admiral in charge refused to destroy the warships in the harbor when Toulon was seized. He decided that was not in the interest of Spain, which might soon find herself allied with France, as was the case in 1796. Throughout the war, the British found that their coalition partners often had, and pursued, conflicting interests. The British operation in the West Indies proved costly, largely because so many troops died of tropical diseases. Nor did it have any decisive effect on the French. Richmond, *Statesmen and Sea Power*, 177, points out a central problem of war aims. Was the objective the defeat of France or of the Jacobin revolutionaries? If the latter, then the physical target was the heart of Jacobinism, Paris, which might be reached either through Flanders or through the Vendee. Exhausting France as a country would not necessarily destroy Jacobinism, and it would be difficult to demand a change of government as a condition of peace. As for the Low Countries, in the winter of 1794 the Netherlands joined the French. She presented three distinct threats: she had a considerable fleet; she was a potential invasion base; and she possessed both the Cape of Good Hope, a base dominating the route around Africa to India, and Ceylon (Sri Lanka), which dominated the sea route around India farther east, to what is now Indonesia. The British seized both, and retained them after the war. Richmond, ibid., 182, points out that neither the Cape of Good Hope or Ceylon was considered a source of wealth in itself; each was valued only for its contribution to British seapower.

2. For example, in July 1804 Spain seemed to be on the verge of joining France in war against Britain. To cripple her, the British preemptively seized the treasure convoy,

carrying a cargo worth 6.5 million Spanish dollars, from Montevideo. They assumed that the Spanish planned to declare war when the convoy reached them. The Spanish could not declare war before the convoy arrived, because they could not ensure safe wartime sea communications with the New World colonies in the face of British seapower. The situation was similar to a 1761 event, when the British had sought to forestall a Spanish declaration of war by seizing a treasure convoy.

3. The great mutiny at Spithead and the Nore ran from April through May 1797. French preparations for invasion were ordered in October 1797, and a forty-five thousand man army assembled; the project was abandoned in February 1798. As for Ireland, a French fleet carrying thirteen thousand troops appeared off Bantry Bay in December 1796, but did not land the troops. The successful landing of a small force at Fishguard in Wales caused a run on the Bank of England; the troops were, however, soon rounded up. After a rebellion began in Ireland in 1798, the French landed about 1,150 troops at Killkila Bay; they, too, were soon rounded up.

4. The French plan is described by G. J. Marcus, *The Age of Nelson: The Royal Navy 1793–1815* (New York: Viking, 1971), 249–51. The French already had a squadron in the West Indies, and Napoleon may have considered it much safer to concentrate his Franco-Spanish force there than in any European port under British watch. Napoleon rejected a request by the Brest force to attack a temporarily inferior British blocking squadron on the ground that it was more important to break out intact in support of his larger plan.

5. The French did have an extensive semaphore system to transmit messages rapidly over land. When ships left port, however, they could not communicate over any distance except by sending dispatches on board other vessels. The British had a similar semaphore, and such devices were called telegraphs (which is why the successor was initially called the electric telegraph). For a description of such devices, see Stephen E. Maffeo, *Most Secret and Confidential: Intelligence in the Age of Nelson* (Annapolis, Md.: Naval Institute Press, 2000), 68–73.

6. Napoleon's overt threat of invasion ended on 30 August 1805 when the invasion flotilla was demobilized. The Grande Armee assembled for the invasion had begun a march from Boulogne, the invasion port, to the Danube on 27 August. Adm. Pierre de Villeneuve's long run into the Atlantic, however, had certainly been a feint intended to uncover the British coast, and as long as the Franco-Spanish fleet survived, so did the potential for invasion. As late as 1808 the British seriously considered an assault against Boulogne, as a way of precluding its use as an invasion base.

7. According to Richmond, *Statesmen and Sea Power*, 239–40, at the beginning of 1809 France had nearly 60 capital ships built and 30 more under construction, plus another 104 in allied hands: 16 Danish, 17 Dutch, 60 Russian, and 11 Swedish. Against them the British had 127 capital ships either in commission or ready to commission. The French ships were spread among numerous ports, and the Russians were considered inefficient, but the British could not afford to take many risks.

8. The British reaction to Napoleon's invasion of Egypt is discussed in Edward Ingram, *Commitment to Empire: Prophecies of the Great Game in Asia, 1797–1800* (Oxford: Clarendon Press, 1981). At this time British India was only one of numerous Indian

states, depending on a balance of power for its security. While Napoleon headed to Alexandria, the French in Mauritius opened negotiations with Tipu Sultan of Mysore, in hopes of forging an anti-British coalition. The great fear was not so much that the French would invade, as that the presence of a few French troops would cause the various Indian princes to join together against the British. Against this threat, numerous British troops were sent to India. Nelson was sent to the Mediterranean specifically to deal with Napoleon, and he did so at Aboukir on 1 August 1798.

9. Maffeo, *Most Secret and Confidential,* 223–78, uses the campaign culminating in the Battle of the Nile as an example of the practice of naval intelligence at the time. The French could not hide the concentration of forces at Toulon, but they quite successfully maintained operational security. As a cover, Napoleon was appointed to a command at Brest, not Toulon, as commander of an army to invade England. Cover stories included claims that the fleet at Toulon was destined for Ireland or for Portugal; both were plausible targets. Security was easier to maintain because the expedition to Egypt was Napoleon's own idea. It was not developed within the French government of the time, which might have had security leaks, or within any sort of staff. Writing to the French foreign minister on 13 September 1797 Napoleon called for French mastery of the Mediterranean by taking Malta, among other islands. An attack on Egypt would follow, to "make the British tremble for the safety of India," after which he would return to Paris to give the British their "death-blow," presumably by invasion (ibid., 229). France had long had hopes of dominating the Mediterranean, and a French officer had reconnoitered Suez in 1777 with much the same aim as Napoleon. Given French security and the mobility inherent in the French fleet, Nelson could not be sure of the fleet's destination. Ideally frigates would help him keep in touch with it as it sailed east from Toulon. Frigates, however, were scarce because of the overall demands of global naval warfare, including trade protection. Nelson had a powerful fleet of capital ships, but the absence of frigates rendered them almost blind. The French fleet left Toulon in a gale, thus precluding close blockade by Nelson's fleet, and the lack of frigates made it impossible for Nelson to regain contact.

10. Napoleon's opportunity arose when the Spanish added their fleet to the two French fleets (at Brest and at Toulon); the French could now achieve local superiority in either the Mediterranean or the English Channel. British naval resources were insufficient to provide a superior force in both places at about the same time, and the Spanish ships could quickly "swing" from one to the other via the Straits of Gibraltar. The British did not decide to blockade the Cadiz fleet or, even better, destroy it in place before the Spanish declared war. In the Mediterranean, the Cadiz fleet plus the Toulon fleet so outnumbered the British that they had to withdraw their inferior force to Gibraltar, thus in effect ceding the Mediterranean to the French. The British found themselves compelled to evacuate Corsica, from which they had supported the fleet outside Toulon. Then the Cadiz fleet swung to the north, to join a French fleet at Brest; the combination should have been powerful enough to gain control of the channel long enough for an invasion. Instead the Cadiz fleet was badly mauled at the Battle of Cape St. Vincent (14 February 1797). The immediate invasion threat had ended, but the British were still out of the

Mediterranean. By the winter of 1796, according to Richmond, *Statesmen and Sea Power*, 191, Napoleon was planning to invade Egypt. French victory in Italy, which was partly a consequence of the withdrawal of the British, denied the British bases for a potential return to the central Mediterranean. In April 1797 Austria, the main remaining British continental ally, made peace with the French, blaming the British for having withdrawn from the Mediterranean. Austria controlled Belgium, so the French gained the Flanders ports from which Britain could most easily be invaded. Only Portugal remained allied with the British, who depended on a base there to support the fleet watching the Spanish base at Cadiz. French peace with Austria, however, did not last; by the spring of 1798 the Austrians were seeking both a British subsidy and a fleet to support them in the Mediterranean. They retained enough territory in Italy to give the British a base, and warned that without a fleet the French would soon control not only all of Italy but also the Middle East (then called the Levant). By this time a large fleet and numerous troops were mobilizing in Toulon, destination unknown. Likely targets were Sicily (the remaining potential base in the central Mediterranean), Portugal, and Ireland. All of these targets were critical locations for the British. It was impossible to defend all three; the only possible solution was to deal with the fleet at Toulon. Nelson was sent to the Mediterranean with a fleet, even though that drastically reduced British naval strength guarding the channel against invasion. Richmond, *Statesmen and Sea Power*, 196, considers this decision both correct and remarkably courageous, as the enemy fleets at Brest and Cadiz still threatened England with invasion. In fact the fleet was destined for Egypt.

11. Quite apart from saving British India, Nelson's victory impressed governments in the area. Naples, Russia, and Turkey joined the anti-French coalition and a Russo-Turkish fleet entered the Mediterranean and ejected the French from Corfu and from some Venetian territory. Anglo-Turkish trade revived because the Mediterranean was now largely safe from French attack. Presumably governments in the region concluded that Napoleon could not soon replace the army marooned in Egypt. As long as the French fleet survived, and France had effective control of the Mediterranean, the marooned army could easily be redeployed anywhere in southern Europe. With the fleet and control lost, however, it was almost entirely cut off from combat in Europe.

12. The British reasons for war were maritime. Under the treaty signed in 1801, Napoleon had agreed to evacuate Holland and the British would evacuate Malta in return. The British wanted Holland neutralized to eliminate the worst invasion threat. Holland still owned the Cape of Good Hope (restored by the 1801 treaty), so French control of one was control of the other—the sea route to India. A Mediterranean fleet based at Malta would preclude French control of the Mediterranean, and thus would make another French expedition to Egypt too risky. Napoleon refused to give up control of Holland, so the British refused to evacuate Malta, particularly given French statements about a new attack on Egypt. According to Richmond, *Statesmen and Sea Power*, 217, the parliamentary debate over war was concerned mainly with Malta and with possible, although unsatisfactory, alternative fleet bases in the Mediterranean. The British opted for war because it was clear that Napoleon was rebuilding his own fleet and that he would strike as soon as he was ready. Britain enjoyed only a very narrow margin over

her enemies: 115 capital ships (75 in commission, 40 in reserve, not including ships fit only for harbor service), against 112 in the enemy fleets (33 French, 63 Spanish, and 16 Dutch). The margin was actually narrower because a blockading force would always have some of its ships in harbor refitting, and it would be subject to accident at sea, whereas the blockaded fleet could pick its time to attack. Given the narrowness of the margin, the British badly needed an ally. They approached the Russians, but they wanted Malta, which the British refused to relinquish because of its naval significance.

13. British manufacturers initially thought that access to Spanish colonies would help make up for the losses due to the French blockade, but that did not happen. In 1810–12 the effect of Napoleon's blockade caused serious problems, and representatives of several British manufacturing towns called for peace.

14. According to Christopher D. Hall, *British Strategy in the Napoleonic War, 1803–1815* (Manchester: Manchester University Press, 1992), 89–90, the British depended on Russia for medium-size masting, on Baltic oak for underwater planking, on Russian fir for decking, and on Russia for most tallow and for half of British pitch, tar, and iron; Sweden also supplied much of the pitch, tar, and iron. Most Baltic timber was loaded at Memel and Danzig in Prussia. Russia alone accounted for 90 percent of Baltic timber, and there was no alternative source of this quality. Britain accounted for about half the ships going though the sound (i.e., out of the Baltic) in 1805, but shipping roughly halved by 1807.

15. In December 1813 Wellington told the czar that his 30,000 men, supported by 40,000 Spaniards, were tying down 200,000 French troops. The czar was asking that Wellington's army be moved to the main theater of war, in the Netherlands, and Wellington's answer was that nowhere except in Spain could a small British army exert such leverage (Richmond, *Statesmen and Sea Power*, 177). By this time French manpower was so tight that troops had to be withdrawn from the Baltic to fight in Spain, thus reducing French control of key ports needed to enforce the continental system.

16. Because the colonies sent Spain so much cash each year, the British considered seizing them, thus breaking Spanish seapower by bankrupting the country. Presumably they feared that cash from the Spanish colonies would make Napoleon even more powerful. On the eve of the Spanish revolt, the British were preparing an expedition to South America in hopes of supporting rebellion by the inhabitants; once Spain became an ally, they had to damp down talk of insurrection.

17. Lambert, *The Crimean War*, 1, argues that the traditional view that the war was fought to maintain Turkish control of the Dardanelles and thus to keep Russia out of the Mediterranean, is misleading.

18. Even before construction of the Suez Canal, the overland route between Suez and the Red Sea was considered a shortcut around Africa, en route to India. When Napoleon took Egypt, the British sent a squadron to the Red Sea. Later troops were sent from India to Upper Egypt (the Sudan) to tie down French troops in Egypt. In 1839, well before the Suez Canal had been dug, the British seized Aden to control the mouth of the Red Sea. Later the British made special attempts to protect the small states along the Red Sea from Turkish or French control. On the other hand, in 1880–81 the British were

unable to keep the Italians out of Eritrea, on the Red Sea coast. A few years later they saw Italian colonization as a valuable counterweight to the French. Once the French had Indo-China and Madagascar, off the African coast not far from the Red Sea, they seemed bound to expand onto the shore of the Red Sea. Not all British statesmen considered the Red Sea vital. In 1887 Prime Minister William E. Gladstone pointed out that if the route through the Mediterranean was blocked the trip to India would be lengthened by only three weeks, which he felt would hardly be disastrous. See Richmond, *Statesmen and Sea Power*, 269.

19. Lambert, *The Crimean War*, 85–86.

20. The key issue was whether, as many governments demanded, "free ships mean free goods"—in other words, whether or not blockaders could interfere with neutral ships. Not only did the British concede the point during the war, they accepted it at the peace conference. Richmond, *Statesmen and Sea Power*, 266, regarded this acceptance as a cardinal error. He also doubted the efficacy of any blockade against a largely self-sufficient Russia, whereas Lambert, *Crimean War*, claims that the Russian economy was badly damaged by the war, and that the czar's advisors wanted a settlement so that the economy could be reformed.

21. Richmond, *Statesmen and Sea Power*, 265.

22. Lambert, *The Crimean War*, 5.

23. A more conventional view is that the 1856 settlement was a peace of exhaustion, because the czar was broke. By early 1856, Russian exports had declined 80 percent since 1853 due to the wartime blockade. Imports were down by only a third, so Russian cash was running out. Customs revenue, the main source of government money, was sharply down, and could not pay for wartime spending. By early 1855 it appeared that two of the important states on the Russian land border, Austria and Sweden, were about to join the Anglo-French-Turkish coalition, presumably because they were encouraged by the fall of Sevastopol and the successful British bombardment of the fortress of Sveaborg in the Baltic. They would have added a land coalition aspect to the naval expeditionary character of the war. Austria held the central position in the Balkans and was considered the leader of the German states. Her declaration of neutrality at the outset limited the war to the Russian maritime frontiers, in the Baltic and in the Black Sea. Conversely, if she joined the coalition she would impose intolerable pressures on the Russian land frontier in the Balkans. The allies courted the Swedes for their position in the Baltic, and by 1855 the Swedish king was willing to enter the war. He feared it would end before he could claim any benefits from an allied victory. Across the Baltic from Sweden, Prussia was neutral, but leaned toward Russia. The king of Prussia urged the czar to settle. He feared the victorious French and Austrians would take the opportunity of the war to settle scores, thus in 1856 he might see the French cross the Rhine and the Austrians entering Silesia. Lambert, *The Crimean War*, 298.

24. The emphasis on the preparations for the 1856 campaign has developed only recently in British naval history; previously the verdict was that the Royal Navy accomplished little or nothing in the Baltic. For example, Stephen Roskill, *The Strategy of Sea Power: Its Development and Application* (1962; reprint, Aylesbury: John Goodchild, 1986),

91, recounts a contemporary satiric riddle from *Punch:* "What is the difference between the fleet in the Baltic and the fleet in the Black Sea?" Answer: "The fleet in the Baltic was expected to do everything and did nothing; the fleet in the Black Sea was expected to do nothing and did it." Andrew D. Lambert has vociferously disagreed, concentrating on the effect of British preparations for the Baltic campaign aborted by the 1856 peace conference. He prefers to call the conflict the Russian rather than the Crimean War for this reason. See Lambert's *The Crimean War,* and his chapter "The Shield of Empire, 1815–1895" in *The Oxford Illustrated History of the Royal Navy,* ed. J. R. Hill (Oxford: Oxford University Press, 1995). For the preparations themselves, see Antony Preston, "Creating an Inshore Navy: Royal Navy Littoral Warfare Forces in the Russian War, 1854–1856" in *Warship 1999–2000* (London: Conway Maritime Press, 1999). See also D. K. Brown, *Before the Ironclad: Development of Ship Design, Propulsion, and Armament in the Royal Navy, 1815–1860* (London: Conway Maritime Press, 1990), including a chapter on the Russian War and Appendix 13 on preparations for the 1856 assault against Kronstadt.

25. Lambert, "The Shield of Empire," 190, points out that during the war scare of 1877–78 a fleet of coast assault ships and ironclads formed at Spithead for service in the Baltic, to complement a Mediterranean Fleet sent to Istanbul; Indian troops were concentrated at Malta. When the Russians threatened India by attacking Afghanistan in 1885, the British again chose to form a fleet for the Baltic. It was likely to be far more effective than troops sent to northern India. Many of the same personalities were involved in both crises. In 1878 the Baltic fleet commander was Rear Adm. Cooper Key; his flag captain was John Fisher, the navy's leading mine expert. The Mediterranean commander was Vice Adm. Sir Geoffrey Phipps Hornby. For an account of Admiral Hornby's 1878 operations, see Richard Humble, *Before the Dreadnought: The Royal Navy from Nelson to Fisher* (London: Macdonald and Jane's, 1976), 141–44. In 1885 Key was First Sea Lord (CNO), Hornby was Baltic commander, and Fisher was once again flag captain. Each time the Russians backed down.

26. Lambert, *The Crimean War,* 347.

27. This plan originated with Lt. Gen. Winfield Scott, the senior Union military commander. He urged it at a special Cabinet meeting on 29 June 1861, cautioning it might take two or three years to defeat the Confederacy. At the same meeting Brig. Gen. Irwin McDowell urged a much quicker option, a direct attack toward the Confederate capital of Richmond (via Manassas). On the theory that the Northern public would be unwilling to wait, the Manassas attack was approved, with unfortunate consequences. The name of the strategy, initially intended as ridicule, was later widely adopted. Herman Hattaway and Archer Jones, *How the North Won: A Military History of the Civil War* (Urbana: University of Illinois Press, 1983), 35.

28. For example, see Richard E. Beringer, Herman Hattaway, Archer Jones, and William N. Still Jr., *Why the South Lost the Civil War* (Athens: University of Georgia Press, 1986), 53–64. They reported that 87 percent of blockade runners from the Gulf Coast succeeded in 1864; in 1865 the figure was 94 percent.

29. According to Tracy, *Attack on Maritime Trade,* 94, of 6.8 million bales of cotton produced during the war, 600,000 went to Europe and 900,000 to the North; exports to

Europe paid for 600,000 stand of arms, which were run through the blockade. The South was also able to buy some arms from Northern suppliers. This type of evasion is typical of embargoes and blockades.

30. Beringer et al., *Why the South Lost the Civil War,* 57.

31. Tracy, *Attack on Maritime Trade,* 91.

32. Hattaway and Jones, *How the North Won,* 127.

33. Tracy, *Attack on Maritime Trade,* 94.

34. Ibid., 91; in 1861–64 Union shipowners transferred 609 ships to British registry. Many more ships were built in Canada for the U.S. trade.

35. Beringer et al., *Why the South Lost the Civil War,* 191–92.

Chapter 7. War with Limited Sea Control: Britain and World War I

1. See, for example, Daniel A. Baugh, "British Strategy during the First World War in the Context of Four Centuries: Blue-Water versus Continental Commitment," in *Naval History: The Sixth Symposium at the U.S. Naval Academy,* ed. Daniel M. Masterson (Wilmington, Del.: Scholarly Resources, 1987).

2. For part of the book, see I. F. Clarke, ed., *The Tale of the Next Great War, 1871–1914: Fictions of Future Warfare and of Battles Still-to-Come* (Liverpool: Liverpool University Press, 1995). The Dorking Gap is the cut in the range of hills between the southern British coast and London, hence a focus for invasion.

3. Paul M. Kennedy, *The Rise and Fall of British Naval Mastery* (New York: Scribner, 1976), 232.

4. According to Holger Herwig, *"Luxury" Fleet: The Imperial German Navy 1888–1918* (London: Allen and Unwin, 1980), 95, the Prussian army regained first place in German defense spending in 1912, when the Balkan War made it painfully clear that the Imperial Navy could not defend Germany against French and Russian armies. By this time the German government was in deep financial difficulties. In April 1914 Tirpitz was unable to sell the kaiser plans requiring major new spending. Herwig also points out that the German confederation was badly strained. Many within the imperial government thought that gains on land, which only an army could bring, might improve the situation. No defensive effort by the navy could have that effect. The added funds paid for the much-enlarged army, which came close to victory in 1914. For the kaiser's rather hysterical reaction to the Russians, as expressed at a key December 1912 meeting, see Ernest R. May, "Cabinet, Tsar, Kaiser," in Ernest R. May, ed., *Knowing One's Enemies: Intelligence Assessment Before the Two World Wars* (Princeton, N.J.: Princeton University Press, 1984).

5. The Germans had to choose between defending the Baltic and defending the North Sea coast. Until 1905 the German navy planned to emphasize cruiser warfare (against enemy trade) in the event of war. As Tirpitz built a battle fleet, he elaborated the "risk theory." His fleet would defend the Baltic against an expected British attack. The exposed German coast would be protected by fixed defenses. To this end work began in 1906 on coast defenses at places like Cuxhaven and Heligoland. Late in 1912,

after losing the political fight against the army, Tirpitz chose the Heligoland Bight rather than the Baltic as the focal area for the battle fleet. This seems to have been a political rather than a strategic choice: Tirpitz argued that merely defending the Baltic would deprive the fleet of offensive capability in the eyes of the German people and of the world. See Ruddock F. Mackay, "Historical Reinterpretations of the Anglo-German Naval Rivalry 1897–1914," in Gerald Jordan, ed., *Naval Warfare in the Twentieth Century, 1900–1945: Essays in Honour of Arthur Marder* (London: Croom Helm, 1977).

6. See Wolfgang Wegener's *The Naval Strategy of the World War*, reprinted by Naval Institute Press in the Classics of Sea Power series in 1989, with an introduction by Holger Herwig. Wegener first published his book in 1929 (a version for internal circulation within the German navy dates from 1925), and the Naval Institute Press version includes some of his wartime writing. Due to his strong criticism of the Tirpitz concept, he was ostracized, being forcibly retired in 1926. Herwig argues that Adm. Erich Raeder, the architect and commander of the German World War II fleet, cribbed Wegener's ideas of seizing Norway and Denmark in a 1937 presentation for Hitler. In 1940 Raeder justified the Norwegian occupation as defensive: to secure the ore port of Narvik, to preclude a new British mine barrage between the Shetlands and Norway, and to deny Britain an operating base in Norway. Arguably, however, Raeder found it easier to describe the chancy Norwegian operation as necessary defense than as a way of giving naval forces (as Wegener would have liked) a better offensive posture, at the possible expense of ground forces with much stronger political backing. This is an example of how offense and defense mix in naval warfare.

7. Stevenson, *Armaments and the Coming of War*, 102.

8. This scare had a maritime origin. In 1904 Britain was allied with Japan, and France was allied with Russia. Despite the defensive character of the Anglo-Japanese and Franco-Russian treaties, there was some fear that the war between Russia and Japan might spill over into Europe. As the Russian Baltic Fleet passed through the Dogger Bank in the North Sea, it ran into a fleet of British trawlers at night. The Russians panicked, thinking that the trawlers were Japanese torpedo boats waiting in ambush. They fired on the trawlers. Briefly it seemed that the British would fight the Russians, in which case they would face the French navy. To Germans it seemed that Tirpitz's idea, that the British would have to reckon with the German fleet because it held the balance of power, was relevant. If the British had to face the Russians and their French partners, how could they tolerate the presence of a third, potentially hostile, fleet in northern Europe? In 1807 they had destroyed the Danish fleet at Copenhagen in order to keep it out of Napoleon's hands. Now, in the winter of 1904, the Germans feared that the British would "Copenhagen" their own fleet to ensure that they held the balance of maritime power. In retrospect the "Copenhagen complex" seems bizarre, given that at the same time the British were courting the French. The Germans apparently did not envisage the possibility that the British would solve the problem of the maritime balance of power by befriending two of their three possible rivals and thus freeing themselves to face Germany, the third rival.

9. According to Mackay, "Historical Reinterpretations of the Anglo-German Naval Rivalry," the British began to consider Baltic operations as early as 1903. The

imperial navy understood the danger, and demanded that troops be assigned to threaten or invade Denmark in the event of war. The army objected that any such assignment would fatally weaken the assault against France. In November 1904 the kaiser personally ordered two army corps held for this purpose, but the following February his order was reversed. In August–September 1905 the British directorate of military operations considered a plan to land troops in the Baltic, and it concluded that it was too easy for the Germans to concentrate against a landing. As there were 850,000 reservists available, the Germans could surely deal with 120,000 troops, so any force would have to be much larger to be effective. This evaluation coincided roughly with early British discussions of assistance to France. For both the Admiralty and the war office, the point of a Baltic landing, as understood in 1905–6, was to relieve pressure on the French; if the Germans had enough reservists, they would not have to divert any of their first-line troops from the French front. As of March 1908 the German general staff expected the British to land troops on the German and Danish coasts but considered army reserves sufficient to contain them. First Sea Lord Admiral Sir John Fisher stated at a 23 March 1909 meeting of the British Committee of Imperial Defence that it was not essential for the Royal Navy to regain access to the Baltic in wartime. At the outbreak of war in 1914, however, the Germans did concentrate troops in Schleswig-Holstein, on the Danish border, so perhaps they took the threat seriously. The German army had expanded considerably in 1912–13; this assignment presumably was no longer seen as a fatal weakening of the attack against France.

10. In private conversation, Andrew Lambert has suggested that Fisher saw an attack on or toward the Baltic as the best way of drawing the German fleet to action and thus destroying it. Quite aside from German sensitivity to a threat against East Prussia, it was thought that the Germans would have found it difficult to tolerate the loss of iron ore from Sweden.

11. As evidence, the classic pre-1914 British novel of surprise attack, Erskine Childers' *The Riddle of the Sands* (London: Smith, Elder, 1903), does not involve the German fleet at all. German aggressiveness and predominance on land were frightening enough. Childers' classic has been reprinted frequently since 1903.

12. Kennedy, *The Rise and Fall of British Naval Mastery*, 233. Kennedy was apparently quoting Chancellor of the Exchequer Austen Chamberlain. The key demand was that the British offset a German advantage of 200,000 men. The French clearly considered naval assistance irrelevant.

13. Richmond, *Sea Power in the Modern World*, complained in his preface that "before the war of 1914–18 a British general believed that a navy was worth less than five hundred bayonets to a common cause, while French generals contemptuously dismissed its value as less than that of a single soldier."

14. This meeting in Whitehall Gardens is described in Ernest R. May, *Knowing One's Enemies*. According to Samuel R. Williamson Jr., *The Politics of Grand Strategy: Britain and France Prepare for War, 1904–1914* (Harvard Press, 1969; reprint, London: Ashfield Press, 1990), 169, Wilson's estimate was based on his belief that the Germans would take a particular route through southern Belgium into France. It had seventeen

roads, each of which could accommodate three German divisions. That limited the attack to fifty-one divisions, against which the French could field about forty. In such circumstances a six-division British force could literally save France. This was actually a revision of an earlier, far more accurate, estimate Wilson had made, in which the Germans would attack farther north, and it is possible that it was intended primarily to justify the expeditionary force.

15. Mackinder published in the journal of the Royal Geographical Society, an organization long identified with the "great game" against Russia—the heartland power —for control of the land approaches to India. In January 1904 he commented that the support of a Russian army in Manchuria was as strong an indication of land mobility as the support of a British army in South Africa had been for sea-based mobility. For a recent discussion of his thinking, see Geoffrey Sloan, "Sir Halford Mackinder: The Heartland Theory Then and Now," in *Geopolitics: Geography and Strategy*, ed. Colin S. Gray and Geoffrey Sloan (London: Frank Cass, 1999).

16. For prewar British blockade planning, see Paul G. Halpern, *A Naval History of World War I* (Annapolis, Md.: Naval Institute Press, 1994), 21–23.

17. The secret role of submarines in British pre-1914 naval thinking is laid out by Nicholas A. Lambert, *Sir John Fisher's Naval Revolution* (Columbia: University of South Carolina Press, 1999). Lambert, ibid., 52–54, describes the depressing secret tests conducted in 1902–3.

18. See Norman Friedman, *British Carrier Aviation: The Evolution of the Ships and Their Aircraft* (London: Conway Maritime Press, 1988). This idea persisted through the war, leading to the development of true aircraft carriers. Between wars a special committee convened to develop means of attacking enemy fleets in defended harbors. Among other things, it developed a semisubmersible that was radio controlled by a carrier airplane. This line of development led to special battle orders for the Mediterranean Fleet in 1936 describing an attack against the Italian fleet at Taranto, which was executed in November 1940.

19. William James Philpott, *Anglo-French Relations and Strategy on the Western Front, 1914–1918* (London: MacMillan, 1996), 23.

20. Ibid., 53–55.

21. David French, *The British Way in Warfare, 1688–2000* (London: Unwin Hyman, 1990), 169. Kitchener's phrase supporting premature use of the mass army was that "we make war as we must, not as we like." According to Philpott, *Anglo-French Relations,* 75, Kitchener's view was that no decision was possible until the British had created a mass army and converted their economic strength into munitions, and the Russians had fully developed their own strength. Until then the best strategy would be a limited offensive in the west, to tie down the Germans, coupled with peripheral operations.

22. Philpott, *Anglo-French Relations,* 71, points out that in 1914 the French political leadership, expecting a short war, surrendered control of strategy to the army. French support of the Salonika initiative came from the politicians, not from the army; the army argued through 1917 that with more resources it could break through on the Western Front to achieve a quick victory.

23. However, British plans for the Somme offensive did include an amphibious thrust onto the Belgian coast to capture Ostend. Later it was reduced to an adjunct to the land attack. Philpott, *Anglo-French Relations*, 121.

24. French, *The British Way in Warfare*, 171.

25. David French, "The Empire and the USA in British Strategy in the Spring of 1917," in Keith Neilson and Greg Kennedy, eds., *Far Flung Lines: Studies in Imperial Defence in Honour of Donald Mackenzie Schurman* (London: Frank Cass, 1996). The issue was raised by Chancellor of the Exchequer Reginald McKenna and President of the Board of Trade Walter Runciman in the fall of 1915, in the context of a debate about conscription. Without conscription, which the prime minister resisted, recruiting took the most productive men out of the economy. Removing more men from civilian production might bankrupt Britain.

26. Philpott, *Anglo-French Relations*, 129–30. According to Lt. Comdr. J. M. Kenworthy (later Baron Strabolgi), *Sailors, Statesmen—and Others: An Autobiography* (London: Rich and Cowan, 1933), 109, tank-delivering ships, which would beach to unload their vehicles, were proposed in 1917 for this operation. Tank-led forces would have outflanked the German defenses. Philpott, 144–45, notes that Admiralty support for the attack on the Belgian ports predated the German U-boat offensive. It is often suggested that the ports were important mainly because they supported U-boats, but Philpott argues that the issue was more general naval security in the narrow part of the North Sea, leading into the English Channel. The Germans mounted destroyer raids into the channel in February and April 1917. The naval-minded British interpreted these raids as probes to test the possibility of landing behind the Allied lines, and thus turning the Allies' seaward flank. Vice Adm. Sir Reginald Bacon, commanding the Dover Patrol and thus responsible for naval security in the area, told the war cabinet that only a lack of initiative and maritime thinking had kept the Germans from seizing command of the southern North Sea in 1916. The Germans do not seem to have considered any such option. In June 1917 German bombers based in Belgium raided London, and the case to attack into Flanders expanded to include countering air raids by forcing the Germans to fly over more friendly territory en route to England.

27. Ian Buxton, *Big-Gun Monitors* (Tynemouth: World Ship Society, 1978), 53–54, describes Admiral Bacon's plan for a landing at Middelkerke in Belgium to outflank the Germans, linking up with an advance from Ypres. Troops would have been landed from floating pontoons pushed into place by 12-inch gun monitors. One of three 540-foot pontoons is illustrated on page 54 of Buxton's book. The first was completed in March 1917. Each of the three would land a third of a division. The operation was canceled because the army at Ypres by 20 September was able to advance only two of the required ten miles; the idea had been that the troops coming from the sea would link up with those advancing overland. The monitors and pontoons were dispersed on 2 October. See also R. H. Bacon, *The Dover Patrol, 1915–1917* (London: Hutchinson, 1919).

28. The key, according to Halpern, *A Naval History of World War I*, 140, was that the Entente could offer Italy Austrian territory it wanted, whereas the Germans could offer only whatever Austria would willingly give up. The Italians, however, presumably also

wanted French territory (Savoy and Nice) that the Germans might have provided had they won; the Italians seized Savoy and Nice during World War II. Paul G. Halpern, "French and Italian Naval Policy in the Mediterranean 1898–1945," in *Naval Strategy and Policy in the Mediterranean: Past, Present, and Future*, ed. John B. Hattendorf (London: Frank Cass, 2000), describes the Austrian-Italian naval plan developed in 1913, which envisaged joining the two fleets, destroying the French fleet, and then landing an army in southern France to take the French army in the rear.

29. In 1900 the British rejected a German alliance because the Germans demanded that Britain join their Triple Alliance. Williamson, *The Politics of Grand Strategy*, 3.

30. Richmond, *Statesmen and Sea Power*, 284, referring to German statements published in 1916. At that time, looking forward to the fruits of victory, German writers predicted the establishment of bases in colonies regained in Africa, from which, in a future war, cruisers and submarines could attack trade in the South Atlantic and in the Indian Ocean. Richmond points out that another motive for colonial seizure, to deny the enemy financial support, did not apply. In the eighteenth century French colonies accounted for as much as a third of French foreign trade, but German colonial trade was no more than 1 percent of total German trade. After the war, according to Richmond, the British retained the colonies in East Africa to preclude a threat to trade routes around Africa, and New Guinea and Samoa to preclude a threat to Australasia. Other German bases in China and in the Pacific went to Japan, whose forces had captured them.

31. Halpern, *A Naval History of World War I* 267–70, describes the considerable potential for a Danube operation, although he doubts that it would have succeeded. Once Gallipoli had failed, any units for river operations had to be moved through neutral Greece to be assembled at Belgrade, and facilities were limited. Had Gallipoli succeeded, oceangoing ships could have steamed directly into the Danube, which is navigable up to Galatz in Romania, and riverine craft could have gone farther up. Halpern considers the Danube a major German and Austrian trade artery, comparable to the North Atlantic seaway used by the Allies; at the least, blocking it would have been a major victory for the blockade against Germany.

32. See Keith Neilson, "For Diplomatic, Economic, Strategic, and Telegraphic Reasons: British Imperial Defence in the Middle East and India, 1914–18," in Keith Neilson and Greg Kennedy, eds., *Far Flung Lines: Studies in Imperial Defence in Honour of Donald Mackenzie Schurman* (London: Frank Cass, 1996).

33. Halpern, *A Naval History of World War I,* 404 points out that Adm. Sir David Beatty, who commanded the Grand Fleet in 1917, considered British capital ships individually quite inferior to German ships, presumably as the result of the shock administered when three of his battlecruisers blew up at Jutland. He therefore did not consider his numerical edge over the Germans sufficient to take chances. Even when American battleships considerably boosted his numerical advantage, he was not inclined to take chances, because initially the American ships were not up to British standards of gunnery and signaling. Gunnery problems were particularly evident in official testimony before the American General Board in 1917. Arthur Marder, *From the Dreadnought to Scapa Flow, Vol 4: 1917: Year of Crisis* (London: Oxford University Press, 1969), 241–44,

describes alternative Baltic offensive schemes proposed in the fall of 1917, and explains why all of them were too hazardous. In particular the British feared that once their fleet was in the Baltic it could be trapped by the Germans. A proposed minelaying offensive might be costly in destroyers, which were essential for the new convoy strategy. When the Russian government fell in November 1917, British fears increased. Not only could the Germans now turn their full attention to the North Sea, but the four Russian dreadnought battleships might be added to their fleet. The fear was that the Germans could come out at a time of their choice, at full strength, whereas the usual repairs and refits would whittle down British strength at that moment. Younger officers on the Admiralty war staff, according to Kenworthy, *Sailors, Statesmen—and Others,* 125–33, were clearly more optimistic. Kenworthy's calculation of gross Allied superiority contrasts with senior officers' fear that the British fleet might lose control of the North Sea. The difference was that Kenworthy counted Allied battleships far from the North Sea (e.g., on the U.S. east coast or in the Adriatic) as part of the Allied margin of superiority. Ships are inherently mobile, but not to that extent.

34. Richmond, *Statesmen and Sea Power,* 282–83, points out that at the outset the British blockade was badly hampered by restrictions adopted during the mid-nineteenth century, and claims (ibid., 286) that had these rights not been abandoned the Germans would have been forced to abandon the war much sooner. The key issue was whether the British would stop neutral ships carrying goods destined ultimately for Germany. In retrospect it seems that they were reluctant to pressure the key neutral, the United States, for fear of precluding eventual U.S. entry into the war on their side.

35. Guichard, *The Naval Blockade,* 305.

36. Before 1914 U.S. strategists considered Germany ("Black") the most likely future opponent; it was assumed that German colonial expansion would lead it to seek New World territory in contravention of the Monroe Doctrine. Much later German archives disclosed a real interest in war planning against the United States. See Holger H. Herwig, *Politics of Frustration: The United States in German Naval Planning, 1889–1941* (Boston: Little, Brown, 1976).

37. Through the period before 1914, German naval spending amounted to a fifth to a quarter of total military spending. In 1912 German army spending increased dramatically compared to naval spending because the Russian army had revived more quickly than expected after its defeat by Japan in 1904–5. Kaiser Wilhelm II was apparently convinced that the rate of Russian industrial expansion would give that country supremacy by 1916. In his rather distorted view, he faced an attack by Russia, against which his army would have to strike preemptively. Although the kaiser favored naval expansion, the German army pointed to the Balkan War as proof that only an army could protect Germany.

38. See, for example, a revealing 12–13 February 1919 letter by Lt. H. W. Koehler, USN, a submarine officer serving as an armistice commissioner in Berlin, in the Submarine Warfare Division papers of the Office of the Chief of Naval Operations in the U.S. Navy's Operational Archives. Koehler predicted that the Germans would try again, because they did not blame themselves for their defeat.

39. The 1919 decision appears in Admiralty Board papers. However, the British cer-

tainly feared being relegated to second or third place. Several key Admiralty papers appear in B. McL. Ranft, ed., *The Beatty Papers: Selections from the Private and Official Correspondence of Admiral of the Fleet Earl Beatty, Vol. II: 1916–1927* (Aldershot, England: Scholar Press for the Navy Records Society, 1993). A 12 August 1919 memorandum by First Lord Walter Long (equivalent to a U.S. secretary of the navy) asked the war cabinet its policy with respect to the United States, citing a narrowing margin of superiority (ibid., 51–57). A 24 October 1919 Admiralty memorandum for the war cabinet (ibid., 61–64) pointed out that the only real rival to British seapower was the United States. Given the size of the ongoing program authorized in 1916, by 1923 the U.S. battle fleet would be larger than the British, unless the British began a program of new construction. In personnel strength the U.S. Navy already exceeded the Royal Navy. The memorandum noted that the U.S. Navy had not been taken into account in pre-1914 calculations of British naval strength because the United States showed little interest in European politics, but that World War I had thrust the country into Europe. Japan was also building, and by 1923–25 her own fleet of modern capital ships (eight battleships and eight battlecruisers) would exceed the Royal Navy's modern fleet. In July 1920 First Sea Lord Beatty (equivalent to a U.S. CNO), called for a one-power standard, with the Royal Navy at least matching the United States. Given the advance of technology, older capital ships would have to be replaced after fifteen years, but post-1914 capital ships could be replaced after twenty years. On this basis he wanted four new battleships and four new battlecruisers. The British government approved the program, but was clearly willing to abandon it if the United States abandoned the bulk of the 1916 program. Parity between the two navies was formalized in the Washington Treaty of 1922.

40. Richmond, *Statesmen and Sea Power*, 288, points out that Japan was hardly considered a close ally even in 1919; in effect she had ceased supporting the British as soon as she gained control of the German colonies in China and in the Pacific. The Japanese did send twelve destroyers to support convoy operations in the Mediterranean in 1917, but they specifically refused a British request that the four *Kongo*-class battlecruisers join the Grand Fleet (as U.S. battleships did). In 1919 Jellicoe proposed creating an eastern fleet of sixteen capital ships, to be financed by Britain, Australia, and New Zealand and based (as in the earlier empire fleet concept) at Singapore. The proposal for the base was accepted, but the fleet was rejected. In its place the British developed the concept of "swinging" their Mediterranean fleet east in the event of a Pacific crisis, Singapore being fortified to hold out until the fleet arrived. For Jellicoe's report, actually a series of reports, see *The Jellicoe Papers: Selections from the Private and Official Correspondence of Admiral of the Fleet Earl Jellicoe of Scapa, Vol. II, 1916–1935*, ed. A. Temple Patterson (Shortlands, Kent: Navy Records Society), 294–394. Jellicoe's proposal for the sixteen capital ship fleet (eight battleships, eight battlecruisers) is on p. 326. See pp. 185–89 for the *Kongo* saga, which began with an unrealistic panic about the loss of battlecruiser superiority in the North Sea in 1917. That in turn was presumably an echo of the failure at Jutland.

41. See Clayton, *The British Empire as a Superpower*, 21–25, for a summary of the Singapore plan as it was slowly implemented. The alternatives, Hong Kong and Sydney,

were rejected: Hong Kong was too difficult to defend because it was too close to Japan, and lacked any hinterland; Sydney was too far away. The dominions (Australia, New Zealand, Canada, South Africa) and the Indian government all strongly pressed for the base, but British governments feared the affront to Japan and balked at the cost. The initial estimate that it would take seventy days to bring the fleet east was later cut to forty and then to twenty-eight days. To support the concentration of the fleet in the East, supplies and fuel were to be gathered at Aden, Addu Atoll, Colombo, Trincomalee, and the Nicobar Islands. The distances between these places set the required steaming endurance of British warships designed during the interwar period. For more complete accounts of Singapore and the associated strategy, see Paul Haggie, *Brittania at Bay: The Defence of the British Empire against Japan, 1931–1941* (Oxford: Clarendon Press, 1981) and W. David McIntyre, *The Rise and Fall of the Singapore Naval Base, 1919–1942* (London: Macmillan, 1979).

42. For the prewar British concept of submarine operations in the Far East, see the Appendix to Alastair Mars, *British Submarines at War, 1939–1945* (London: Kimber, 1971).

Chapter 8. World War II as a Maritime Campaign

1. Walter Ansel, *Hitler and the Middle Sea* (Durham, N.C.: Duke University Press, 1972), 16–17. However, Hitler had also already told his military leaders that he needed Russia for its resources. By mid-1940 planning for an invasion was already under way.

2. Allied seapower made it possible to suggest to the Germans that an attack might be made in Greece rather than in Sicily. This was the first example of Allied wartime deception to be revealed. This operation is described in Ewen Montagu, *The Man Who Never Was* (London: Evans Bros., 1953). This was a unique case; virtually all wartime deception operations depended on knowledge gained by reading German codes. Because such code-breaking was a very closely held secret, they could not be disclosed for many years. For example, it could not be admitted that the British, thanks to code-breaking, had caught all spies the Germans tried to infiltrate into England, and was able to turn many of them. That made for an ironic situation. Ladislas Farago, *The Game of the Foxes: The Untold Story of German Espionage in the United States and Great Britain during World War II* (New York: McKay, 1972), had happened upon a trunk in the National Archives. It contained the German records of what seemed to have been a spectacularly successful espionage operation in England; some of the German spies had transmitted messages even as the Allied armies overran the German cities from which they were controlled. Shortly after Farago's book appeared, the British permitted publication of J. C. Masterman's *The Double-Cross System in the War of 1939 to 1945* (New Haven, Conn.: Yale University Press, 1972). Masterman, who had run the British agent control system, explained Farago's book: the German agents had survived because they had actually been working under British control. Code-breaking was an essential element of the deception because it enabled the British to be certain that there were no free German agents capable of contradicting the messages their controlled agents sent, and also

because it provided information on what the Germans wanted and on how they handled the bogus material the British provided. In another irony, Farago had been a wartime U.S. Navy intelligence officer, hence he undoubtedly had been privy to Allied code-breaking, although in a context other than counterespionage and deception.

3. Frank, *Downfall,* 191 describes the failure of one deception plan. Frank also points out that through the summer of 1945 U.S. radio intelligence discovered that Japanese forces on Kyushu were far stronger than had been imagined during the planning of the invasion, reflecting the failure of deception and the Japanese expectation that the battle for Kyushu would be decisive (ibid., 198–211).

4. Arthur J. Marder, *Old Friends, New Enemies,* 36, 40–41. The "swing" strategy became particularly difficult given the hostility of Italy after the Ethiopian war of 1935–36 and new security treaties with countries in the Eastern Mediterranean: Egypt in 1936 and Greece, Romania, and Turkey in 1939. By mid-1939 war in Europe seemed certain, and the British expected that Japan would fight once Britain was tied down there. The Admiralty position was that any such war would delay, rather than preclude, dispatch of the fleet to Singapore, because early in the war British naval forces would be dispersed to hunt down surface raiders. Italy would have to be knocked out before the fleet could be sent east (ibid., 50). There was some sentiment favoring sending a powerful fleet east while retaining a much smaller one in European waters, backed by the French, on the theory that even an inferior fleet could neutralize a stronger one, as the German High Seas Fleet had tied down the British during World War I. Unless the fleet was sent east, the empire there would surely be lost by default.

5. The fleet maintained on the China Station was quite small. The 1922 Washington Treaty lumped the dominion navies with the Royal Navy and so precluded any revival of the earlier concept of a separate Pacific fleet supported by the dominions. As for new construction, the five battleships begun in the late 1930s, the *King George V* class, were intended merely to replace the five elderly and unmodernized "R" class. The battle fleet would not have begun to grow until completion of the next new class, the *Lions. Lion* construction was stopped by the war. The slow rate of battleship construction can be traced to the Admiralty's insistence on building aircraft carriers, of which it had more under construction in 1939 than any other country. The treaties left Britain with a total of fifteen gun capital ships (including three battlecruisers), compared to ten Japanese (four battlecruisers), with two more under construction. In 1935 the Italians had four battleships, all being modernized, with two much larger ones planned. In 1941 nineteen British capital ships (HMS *Royal Oak* was sunk in 1939) were faced by ten Japanese plus six Italian plus four German battleships.

6. When the British fleet concentrated at Alexandria it switched to wartime codes. The Germans and Italians intercepted enough traffic to break those codes, with devastating effect on World War II operations. The League of Nations imposed sanctions on the Italians, but the British helped preclude oil embargo, the one economic sanction that would have been effective, specifically because they wanted to avoid any complete break with the Italians.

7. In 1942 Churchill justified the Allied assault on North Africa partly on the ground

that regaining control of the Mediterranean would save a million tons of shipping. By way of comparison, in 1941, 4.5 million tons of shipping were sunk. According to Tracy, *Attack on Maritime Trade,* 193, the indirect effects of U-boat warfare (for example, inefficiencies in ports and the inability of the British rail net to handle cargo from ports to which ships were being diverted) cost 2.3 to 3 million tons of cargo per year in 1940–41.

8. Michael Simpson, "Superhighway to the World Wide Web: The Mediterranean in British Imperial Strategy, 1900–1945," in *Naval Strategy and Policy in the Mediterranean: Past, Present, and Future,* ed. John B. Hattendorf (London: Frank Cass, 2000).

9. Attacks were mounted partly because Churchill hoped to impress President Franklin D. Roosevelt, who understood naval issues, with his determination. See Arthur J. Marder, *From the Dardanelles to Oran: Studies of the Royal Navy in War and Peace, 1915–1940* (London: Oxford University Press, 1974), 216–17. Churchill also apparently considered decisive action an important way of boosting British morale on the eve of a possible German invasion.

10. For example, at the end of World War II in 1945 the U.S. Navy operated thirty-one fleet carriers, with a total of about eighteen hundred fighters on board. The U.S. Navy maintained a replacement squadron for each front-line unit, so there were fewer than four thousand fighters in combat service. Yet production of one of two principal types of fleet fighter, the Grumman Hellcat, totaled over twelve thousand. The U.S. Navy did not buy replacement Hellcat engines because the probable lifetime of a Hellcat fighter was shorter than that of its engine.

11. The Marianas "Turkey Shoot" is a case in point. Having failed to sink the Japanese carriers, U.S. commanders thought that the Japanese naval air arm remained viable; in fact, with its trained pilots gone, it was spent. As a consequence, when Japanese carriers, without very many aircraft, appeared at the next major battle at Leyte Gulf, those carriers became key targets. The fleet assigned to cover the landing at Leyte Gulf steamed away to deal with the carriers, leaving the invasion beach open to a Japanese surface force that nearly disrupted the landing; the Japanese force was beaten off by the heroic resistance of the small U.S. escort carrier force assigned to support troops at the beaches. Airmen may have had a better understanding of the fragility of air forces. Thus the U.S. Army Air Force claimed that the air battles of the spring of 1944, in which U.S. fighters escorting U.S. bombers over Germany destroyed many German fighters, destroyed enough of the Luftwaffe to preclude effective air opposition to the Normandy landing a few months later. In some cases, too, specialized aircraft could not easily be replaced. In 1943 the Germans began using guided bombs against Allied warships. Their neutralization is usually credited to jamming. The key, however, may have been an air raid that destroyed most of the specially equipped German bombers on the ground. For bureaucratic and industrial reasons they were never replaced.

12. The British did use small escort carriers successfully to maintain air superiority in the face of German land-based bombers attacking convoys to Russia as they passed through the Norwegian Sea and around the North Cape. Presumably this success demonstrates what a carrier force in the Mediterranean, where the main threat was air attack, could have achieved. The carriers in question, however, did not become available in any numbers until after the Allies had gained control of North Africa, thus pro-

viding them with a chain of air bases from which they could resist any German air raids against ships in the Mediterranean.

13. There were also technical problems. When the British began designing new carriers in 1935, radar did not yet exist. Without it, enemy attackers could not necessarily be spotted until they were quite close to the carrier. It was unlikely that carrier fighters could deploy quickly enough to intercept and destroy enemy bombers. Carrying them therefore appeared pointless. The new carriers were therefore designed to carry only strike aircraft; they had armored hangars in which the strike aircraft could shelter when enemy aircraft attacked. Ironically, radar was invented as the ships were being designed. It made possible a new style of carrier operations in which enemy aircraft could be detected and then intercepted far from a ship. Prior to the advent of radar, the only way to seize maritime air superiority was to destroy the enemy's carriers. Because it was impossible to destroy a ground-based air force on the ground, that option seemingly was closed to the British. Consequences of this perception included limited procurement of naval fighters before 1941. The British were painfully aware of how few naval pilots they had, but they seem not to have realized how limited were the resources of land-based air arms. For a discussion of British carrier development, see Friedman, *British Carrier Aviation.*

14. British and U.S. code-breakers discovered in mid-1941 that Hitler promised the Japanese that he would join them if they attacked the United States. When Churchill was shown the decrypt he personally asked that Roosevelt be told. However, it seems unlikely that either was sure that Hitler would keep his word, and for a few nervous days in December it appeared that U.S. concentration on Japan would actually be at the expense of aid to Britain for the European war. Michael Smith, *The Emperor's Codes: Bletchley Park and the Breaking of Japan's Secret Ciphers* (London: Bantam Press, 2000), 90–91, quoting a decrypted Japanese message now in the Public Record Office, with Winston Churchill's annotation.

15. Due to the way the British fought World War I, they ran up enormous debts in the United States. Once the Depression began, they were unable to service those debts, and the U.S. government refused to forgive them. The British view was that the arms bought with the money involved had helped protect the United States, so that U.S. refusal was, to put it mildly, churlish. By this time many in Congress blamed U.S. intervention on Eastern financiers who had lent too much money to the Allies; the old saw being that anyone who owes a bank an enormous sum in effect owns the bank. To avoid any repetition, they banned arms purchases on credit. During the opening phase of the war, British industrial mobilization was limited because it was necessary to keep producing some luxury goods simply to earn the foreign exchange to pay for weapons. Even so, by the spring of 1941 the British were nearly bankrupt; they were saved only by the Lend-Lease Agreement. When Lend-Lease was abruptly withdrawn in 1945, bankruptcy was again apparent.

16. This invasion can be seen as an inevitable consequence of the lessons the Germans drew from the World War I blockade, hence a consequence of the application of seapower in both wars. Hitler said as much in September 1939, when he told his generals that he would have to gain the resources of Russia.

17. Ansel, *Hitler and the Middle Sea*, 9, quoting a 30 June 1940 memo, heavily influenced by Hitler's remarks, by Gen. Alfred Jodl.

18. In 1941–42 neither side enjoyed control of the Mediterranean. British attempts to resupply Malta were met by powerful attacks, but British submarines and other craft based on Malta often destroyed Axis convoys running to North Africa. It was later suggested that the Germans had made a fatal error in expending their elite paratroopers, in May 1941, in seizing Crete rather than Malta. Crete may have been chosen because of its position at the entrance to the Aegean Sea, which leads toward Russia. It was also seen as a danger to the supply line to German-Italian forces operating in Libya against the British in Egypt, that is, against the Suez Canal. Airfields on Crete did support antishipping aircraft that made it virtually impossible to reinforce Malta from Egypt, hence the epic battles of reinforcement via Gibraltar during 1942.

19. According to Ansel, *Hitler and the Middle Sea*, 19–20, the German drive into the Balkans began with a 30 August 1940 directive to secure and occupy the Rumanian oil fields. Other than the Soviet Union, Rumania was the only German source of oil, given the difficulties of getting through the British blockade. Greece became a target because of the World War I experience of Allied occupation of Salonika, beginning in 1916, as a beachhead into the Balkans. Ansel, ibid., 75–76, citing German directives, debunks the usual claim that Hitler invaded Greece to save the Italians from defeat there.

20. The British decision to use troops from North Africa in Greece, where it was acknowledged that there was little chance of success, coincided with near success in North Africa; removing the troops prevented the British from winning in North Africa and provided the Germans with the opportunity to insert Rommel and his Afrika Korps. Churchill presumably thought that, as in the past, the British had to show that they were willing to fight on the Continent, and he apparently grossly underestimated the difficulty of withdrawing those troops by sea if they failed ashore. The difference was German antishipping airpower, which was a kind of main fleet that blocked British sea access.

21. Churchill was not alone. During the interwar period B. H. Liddell Hart, *Strategy* (New York: Praeger, 1954), became famous as a proponent of the "indirect approach" in war.

22. The Soviets did much better than they had expected. Their prewar defense planning had been based on the assumption that they could not produce new weapons quickly enough in wartime, so they built up very large stocks prewar that were largely destroyed in the initial German attack. On the other hand, by the mid-1930s they were contemplating a possible war against Germany. They assumed that much would hinge on regeneration; thus they would need to depend on wartime production. This reasoning led them to plan for the mass evacuation of industry from the western Soviet Union, particularly the areas around Moscow and Leningrad (St. Petersburg), to beyond the Urals. Successful evacuation preserved the industrial base without which regeneration would have been impossible. The Germans may have doubted that any such evacuation was possible, in which case occupying the western part of the country would also have precluded regeneration.

23. W. N. Medlicott, *The Economic Blockade,* British Official History Series (London: HMSO, 1959). Blockade was one of three elements of economic warfare, as understood by the British; the others were the physical destruction of industry and domestic sources of supply, such as synthetic oil plants, and the occupation of key industrial or mining areas (or of intervening territory). Strategic bombing falls under the destruction element. The Allied advance cut off German access to some key materials, such as tungsten, in 1944–45. As the British saw it, the effect of economic warfare depended on just how seriously military operations stressed sources of supply. Medlicott, in *The Economic Blockade,* pointed out that it was difficult to disentangle the effects of the three types of economic warfare. At the outset, the British view was that Britain and her French ally were only strong enough to maintain a defensive. Because the British, and not the Germans, enjoyed access to world resources, they could build decisive strength over the next two or three years. "At no stage of the war was Germany decisively weakened by shortages due to the blockade alone. That it was not a negligible factor in the Allied war effort is equally certain. That is at once apparent if we consider what would have been Germany's position with full immunity from economic pressure" (ibid., 631). Medlicott points out that blockade (encirclement) had profound psychological effects on Germany, that the cry for *Lebensraum* was in effect a confession of vulnerability to economic pressure (ibid., 641). Hitler had justified the decision to fight at the earliest opportunity using blitzkrieg tactics precisely because he doubted any ability to sustain warfare as in World War I. For example, Hitler rejected "armament in depth" on the ground that peacetime rearmament would leave Germany at a disadvantage by 1943 or 1944. In a lengthy discussion of the projected war, quoted by Medlicott, on 23 May 1939 Hitler stated explicitly that only in the east (i.e., in Russia) could Germany secure her food supplies. Colonies could not suffice because they would be cut off by blockade. Medlicott notes that this attitude was in large part a reaction to the 1914–18 experience of blockade, as described in German internal propaganda; in the early part of the war the Germans were particularly insistent (in internal propaganda) that they were suffering no food shortages. Overall, a major achievement of the blockade was the creation of an encirclement neurosis "with marked effect on German political and military strategy" (ibid., 659).

24. Marshall, *To Have and Have Not,* points out that both the United States and Britain supported China in its war against Japan largely in hopes of tying it down and thus protecting their own Far Eastern possessions and interests. Marshall's resource analysis is compelling because it explains why the United States was willing to risk war against Japan; the usual explanation, that the crisis was over China, is difficult to accept. The same generation of government officials who saw Southeast Asia as crucial in 1940 also decided that it mattered during the early Cold War period.

25. See Marshall, *To Have and Have Not.*

26. The two views were not inconsistent. Presumably Japan had already decided to strike south at Malaya and the Dutch East Indies, and the imperial conference ratified a simultaneous strike against the United States.

27. For Japanese strategy, see David C. Evans and Mark R. Peattie, *Kaigun: Strategy,*

Tactics, and Technology in the Imperial Japanese Navy, 1887–1941 (Annapolis, Md.: Naval Institute Press, 1997). U.S. war planning against Japan is described in great detail by Edward S. Miller, *War Plan Orange: The U.S. Strategy to Defeat Japan, 1897–1945* (Annapolis, Md.: Naval Institute Press, 1991).

28. Using a base in the Philippines, as part of a strategy called the "through ticket to Manila," promised a short war. Much then depended on the security of the base. Initially the favored base was at Subic Bay, but then it had to be moved south for fear that Japanese aircraft based on Taiwan would destroy it. Miller, *War Plan Orange,* points out that Singapore was for the British much as Manila or any other Philippine base would have been for the U.S. Navy; its loss essentially ejected the Royal Navy from the Far East. Without a mobile base organization similar to the U.S. fleet train, the British could not take advantage of any islands they might have seized. Miller also points out that the Russian naval disaster in 1905 exemplified the perils of the "through ticket"; in that case the main fleet base, Port Arthur, fell while the relieving fleet was en route.

29. Miller, *War Plan Orange,* 36, points out that Japanese occupation actually simplified U.S. planning, because bases required en route to the Western Pacific could now be seized as enemy territory. Before the Japanese acquired the islands, the United States would have had either to negotiate with the Germans or to accept war with Germany as the price of success against Japan.

30. It turned out to be possible to isolate particular Japanese bases, such as Truk, without having to seize them, so the advance was less stepwise than had been imagined. The Japanese appreciation of the value of the islands roughly matched that of the U.S. Navy. They planned to use forces based in the islands to whittle down the U.S. fleet to manageable proportions as it passed through en route to the decisive battle.

31. These issues are clear in lectures on submarine warfare that then Capt. Thomas C. Hart, the navy's senior submariner, delivered at the Naval War College in the 1920s. His lectures are preserved in the Archives of the Naval War College.

32. For details of different approaches, see Norman Friedman, *U.S. Amphibious Force: An Illustrated Design History* (Annapolis, Md.: Naval Institute Press, forthcoming).

33. That conclusion, drawn from prewar fleet problems, explains why U.S. carriers had separate scout squadrons alongside dive-bomber squadrons flying the same type of aircraft. U.S. dive-bombers were designated SB, Scout Bombers.

34. For example, the consumer-oriented U.S. plastics industry created the basis for U.S. solid rocket propellants the Soviets could not match. The U.S. computer industry, created initially to meet military requirements, but later fueled by the civilian economy, was also unmatched by the Soviets. For elaborations on these points, see Friedman's *The Fifty-Year War.*

35. Ironically, kamikaze was one tactic that actually did oppose U.S. technological superiority, because the sheer number of separate kamikaze attacks on each ship threatened to overwhelm the combat information centers (CICs), which had made it possible for U.S. warships to direct their fire and their defensive aircraft.

36. Yamamoto's phrase was used in wartime as proof that Japan intended to invade

the United States and thus dictate peace terms *to the Americans* in the White House. Later it became clear that he meant that the occupant of the White House would dictate terms *to the Japanese.*

Chapter 9. The Cold War as a Maritime War

1. See Friedman, *The Fifty-Year War.* For example, most Cuban troops were transported to Africa by sea, aboard liners. The Cubans armed the liners for fear of attack by Western proxies.

2. This mission was not relished by the Western navies. Their surface ships were far more vulnerable to nuclear attack than were the submarines that made up the bulk of the Soviet fleet. The Soviets, moreover, had invested heavily in nuclear antiship weapons. To deter their use, American declaratory policy was to mount a nuclear strike against the bases, in Soviet territory, from which any nuclear attack was mounted against U.S. carrier battle groups, the most likely targets. For their part, after the end of the Cold War retired senior Soviet officers told American counterparts that they regarded their nuclear antiship missiles as unusable, precisely because they feared such an escalation, which would soon lead to general nuclear war. In their view, carrying the nuclear weapons merely cut into their rather limited supply of non-nuclear (hence usable) weapons. To make matters more complicated, for a period in the 1980s at least the Royal Navy claimed that its only counter to certain classes of Soviet submarines was a nuclear depth bomb. It is not clear how much thought had gone into the question of whether using such weapons would be permitted in wartime.

3. The Taiwan story is complicated. After winning on the mainland, Mao negotiated with the Soviets for sufficient naval materiel to invade Taiwan in 1951 or 1952. The Korean War intervened. Recent accounts of that war, based on Soviet and Chinese archives, suggest that Stalin feared that the Mao would behave like Marshal Josip Tito of Yugoslavia, bolting from his own camp to that of the Americans. Stalin saw the independence of Taiwan, which Mao would attribute to American intervention, as a constant reminder, to Mao, of American hostility, and thus as insurance of continued support for himself. On this basis it is suggested that Stalin precipitated the Korean War in hopes that it would preclude any Chinese seizure of Taiwan and at the same time bring China into direct conflict with the United States.

4. There was a twist to the story, however. Mao later told a confidante, the Australian Communist reporter Edgar Snow, that he preferred to leave Taiwan and the islands in Western hands, on the theory that tension over them strengthened his hand in China.

5. Gen. John Vogt, USAF, who commanded Allied Forces South, often attested to this during the late 1970s and early 1980s. The reference is to General Vogt's comments during seminars hosted by the then Hudson Institute in Croton-on-Hudson.

6. Under a 1950 congressional mandate, the United States could not station more than six army divisions in Europe; in any crisis additional troops had to be brought in.

7. This is an important point. Fixed installations, even when they are in nominally friendly territory, are subject to unconventional attack. For example, the U.S. Air

Force in Vietnam suffered numerous aircraft casualties to Viet Cong sappers. The problem is exemplified by the devastating attacks on the U.S. Marine barracks in Beirut in 1982 and by the destruction of the U.S. Air Force housing in Saudi Arabia in 1996. In each case, peacetime rules of engagement inevitably made it easier for the attackers; adopting wartime rules would have been unacceptable. Much the same can be said of the *Cole* incident.

8. When the first commitments were made, however, it was clear that the U.S. government feared that a Communist victory in Vietnam would lead to victories in parts of Southeast Asia that did produce vital raw materials, such as Malaya and Thailand. Mao's Chinese politburo statements about the war carry much the same message; he wanted to run south specifically to gain resources for use against the Soviets.

9. Ironically, the experience in Vietnam caused the United States to begin development of "smart" bombs and of what the Soviets would later call reconnaissance-strike complexes. By the late 1970s, senior Soviet officers were writing that the descendants of these weapons could be decisive in a non-nuclear war in Europe. To maintain its military posture the Soviet Union had to develop equivalents. The Soviet generals did not realize just how wrenching such a demand could be. Mikhail Gorbachev came to power on a pledge to expand the Soviet economy so that it could produce the computerized weapon systems involved, and just this attempt at expansion may have led him into the fatal relaxation of the coercion that had kept the Soviet Union together.

10. This connection is developed in Michael A. Palmer, *Origins of the Maritime Strategy: American Naval Strategy in the First Postwar Decade* (Washington, D.C.: Naval Historical Center, 1988).

11. Although big torpedo bombers could be effective, their weapons had to be launched dangerously close to their targets. Aware of this problem, the Soviets developed torpedoes that could be launched at considerable altitude and thus at a considerable slant range from their targets. They were quite inaccurate, however, so large numbers had to be fired to gain a few hits. Stand-off missiles, beginning with KS-1 (NATO AS-1 "Kennel") were a very different proposition. They could be launched from a considerable distance (fifty-five nautical miles for AS-1) and guided themselves into the target. Much of U.S. antiaircraft development beginning in the late 1950s was intended primarily to deal with this threat.

12. As long as there was no need to reinforce Norway, it could be argued that NATO shipping across the Atlantic could be routed far enough south to be outside bomber range. In that case the main threat presented by the bombers was mine attacks on key NATO ports. This argument certainly did not apply in the Mediterranean. As for Norway, the loss of that ally would have made it far easier for Soviet submarines to reach the open Atlantic. NATO thinking on air versus submarine threats is evident in NATO navies' concentration on building antisubmarine escorts.

13. President Carter thought the East-West confrontation had been overemphasized, and that much more attention should be paid the North-South confrontation, between the developed and undeveloped worlds. If the main point of U.S. naval power projection was to assault Third World countries like Vietnam, it clearly exacerbated the North-South problem. The president's attempts to heal the North-South divide included

the decision to hand the Panama Canal over to Panama in 1999. President Carter certainly recognized the East-West problem, but he seems to have believed that its naval aspect was antisubmarine warfare rather than a combination of antisubmarine, antiair, and even antisurface operations.

14. Capt. Peter Swartz, USN, who was involved in the formulation of the 1980s maritime strategy, and who developed a bibliography of it, often said that the strategy matched that proposed by Alfred Thayer Mahan in an obscure book, *The Problem of Asia and Its Effect upon International Policies* (Boston: Little, Brown, 1900). Clearly those who developed the strategy were unaware of the book; that they duplicated its content showed that they were following the basic logic of seapower.

15. For an account of the U.S. strategy, see Norman Friedman, *The U.S. Maritime Strategy* (London: Jane's Information Group, 1989).

16. See John J. Mearshimer, *Conventional Deterrence* (Ithaca, N.Y.: Cornell University Press, 1983).

17. Quite aside from any military threat on the border, the Chinese threatened a major source of Soviet national power, the leadership of the world revolutionary movement, beginning about 1960. The movement was the main mechanism for Soviet expansion into the Third World, and the Soviets probably saw it as an important lever to gain ultimate power in Europe, using national Communist parties. When Mao split from the Soviets, each national party had to choose whether to follow him or to remain with the Soviets. At the least, the split offered individual parties far more independence than in the past. For example, the North Vietnamese played off the Chinese against the Soviets to force the Soviets to provide them with materiel to fight the war in South Vietnam, despite Soviet reluctance to chance a violent American reaction. In the sense that the revolutionary movement defied geographical limitation, in strategic terms it resembled global seapower.

18. V. P. Kuzin and V. I. Nikol'skiy, *Voenno-Morskoi Flot SSSR 1945–1991 (The Soviet Navy 1945–1991: The History of the Creation of the Post-War Soviet Navy and the Possible Outlook of the Russian Navy)* (St. Petersburg: Historical Naval Society, 1996). According to the authors, who were Soviet navy captains, when Khrushchev's first defense minister, Marshal G. K. Zhukov, demanded a reformulation of the fleet in 1957–58, it would have taken enough submarines to sink two million tons of NATO shipping each month to win a new Battle of the Atlantic: one thousand submarines and at least fifteen thousand torpedoes each month, far beyond Soviet capability. Moreover, given the speed with which the Soviet General Staff hoped to conquer Western Europe, an antishipping campaign would probably be pointless. Even so, through the 1960s Zhukov's logic drove Soviet naval development. Kuzin and Nikol'skiy credit Gorshkov with formulating a consistent naval strategy. They claim further that Soviet naval forces contained a variety of Cold War crises, preventing the United States from using nuclear weapons in Vietnam and from intervening in the Arab-Israeli wars, and that the Soviet navy achieved effective parity with the NATO navies (at an enormous cost to the Soviet Union) at the end of the 1970s. None of these claims would be accepted in the West. At the end of the 1970s, again according to the authors, the Soviet navy had developed to the point where simply assisting the ground forces was secondary. The primary naval mission was to

destroy enemy ships approaching the Soviet Union to attack it, followed by attacks on the enemy's sea lines of communication, and then by army support.

Chapter 10. Seapower in Continental Warfare

1. James Goldrick, *No Easy Answers: The Development of the Navies of India, Pakistan, Bangladesh, and Sri Lanka, 1947–1996,* Papers in Australian Maritime Affairs, No. 2 (New Dehli: Lancer, 1997), 70.

2. Pakistani destroyers had raided the Indian coastal town of Dwarka on 8–9 September 1965, during the previous Indo-Pakistani war (ibid., 60).

3. Normally submarines merely receive a fleet broadcast. The Indians planned to jam the Pakistani fleet HF (high-frequency) broadcast in hopes that the submarines would break radio silence to request retransmissions (ibid., 78).

4. According to Goldrick, ibid., 83, the Indians managed to convince the Pakistanis that the carrier was not yet at sea, so the submarine laid a mine field to keep her in port. She had successfully evaded ships patrolling outside the harbor.

5. According to Rear Adm. Raja Menon, *Maritime Strategy and Continental Wars* (London: Frank Cass, 1998), 55, the dramatic effect of an attack on the enemy's main base so captured the imagination of the Indian government that the navy never had to explain its role. That was in stark contrast to the situation after the 1965 war, when the Indian navy, which had conducted no dramatic actions, was unable to sell concepts like sea control and commerce protection to a disbelieving government. According to Goldrick, *No Easy Answers,* 88, the Indian missile boats sank a Pakistani destroyer, *Khaibar* (with two hits), a minesweeper, and a Liberian merchant ship at sea before attacking Karachi.

6. Theodore Ropp, *The Development of a Modern Navy: French Naval Policy, 1871–1904,* ed. Stephen S. Roberts (Annapolis, Md.: Naval Institute Press, 1987), 22. By 1870, neither ships for coastal warfare nor preparation for amphibious operations was complete. Nor had plans been completed. Ropp traces French interest in assaults on maritime fortresses to successes during the Crimean War. Menon, *Maritime Strategy and Continental Wars,* 58, points out that the French should have seen the crisis coming, and that they should have made the necessary diplomatic arrangements to place their fleet in the Baltic before its outbreak.

7. Prewar French studies showed that any landing would have to be made in the Baltic. Given limited fuel endurance, French ships could not operate on a protracted basis in the Baltic without an advanced base in Danish territory, hence without a Danish alliance.

8. The French corps would have numbered 30,000, to fight alongside a 40,000-man Danish army. Against these troops and any others attacking from the sea, the Germans held back over 80,000 first-line troops amounting to two and a half army corps, plus 100,000 reservists (*landwehr*). H. W. Wilson, *Battleships in Action* (1926; reprint, London: Conway Maritime Press, 1995), 1:58–59.

9. The French ships were assembled into what they called a coast-defense siege-train. Ropp, *The Development of a Modern Navy,* 16.

10. Ibid., 35.

11. Moshe Tzalel, *From Icebreaker to Missile Boat: The Evolution of Israel's Naval Strategy* (Westport, Conn.: Greenwood, 2000). The title recalls that the first Israeli warship was an ex–U.S. Coast Guard icebreaker, *Northland,* renamed *Eilat.* For example, during a 6 March 1968 meeting then Israel Defence Force Chief of Staff Chaim bar-Lev accused the navy, which was then buying missile boats, of "living on the moon" and stated that according to the Israeli general staff its mission should be limited to coast defense and limited support for the army. Bar-Lev also said that the air force could handle all problems of attack and defense at sea (ibid., 37–38). Ironically, because its prestige was so low, and because it was virtually invisible to senior Israeli defense decision makers, the navy could evade limits placed on its mission. Thus, according to Tzalel, Defense Minister Moshe Dayan was surprised to learn that the navy's view of its mission—the rationale for buying a fleet of missile boats—was very different from his own idea that it was intended entirely for coast defense. Possibly as a way of overcoming the prejudices of the two other services, the 1968–72 Israeli naval chief, Rear Adm. Avraham Botzer, announced that naval personnel should be considered floating soldiers rather than seamen. The earlier Royal Navy–based uniform was discarded in favor of an army-style uniform with army ranks (ibid., 46). Botzer may have taken his army style of thinking from his origins in the Israeli naval special forces.

12. During the War of Independence the small conventional Israeli fleet achieved very little. However, a small marine sabotage unit, trained partly by Italian veterans of World War II special operations, sank the Egyptian flagship *El-Emir Farouk* and intercepted an arms shipment intended for Syria. Tzalel, *From Icebreaker to Missile Boat,* claims that the Israeli surface navy performed little better in either the 1956 or the 1967 wars, despite having obtained modern warships such as two ex-British destroyers and three ex-Canadian frigates. Tzalel ascribes the one major triumph, the seizure of an Egyptian frigate bombarding Haifa harbor in 1956, mainly to the French destroyer *Kersaint* (ibid., 92–95). The Egyptians showed little offensive spirit of their own; two destroyers headed for Haifa in 1967, but turned back well short of the location of a prepared maritime ambush by torpedo boats and special units. Ultimately the special unit became Flotilla 13 of the Israel navy. It embraced Italian-style explosive motor boats and diver delivery vehicles; its requirements accounted in large part for the Israeli decision to obtain submarines.

13. According to Tzalel, *From Icebreaker to Missile Boat,* 43, after the 1967 war Defense Minister Moshe Dayan levied this task on the Israel navy, adding it to the existing coast defense role. The Bab-el-Mandeb was too far away for the air force, so the navy received the job. Its response was to build a new generation of longer-range *Sa'ar 4*–class missile boats. The first two were available in time for the 1973 war, but had not yet deployed to the Red Sea.

14. Tzalel, *From Icebreaker to Missile Boat,* 143, speculates that the Egyptians wanted these boats mainly to deter gunboat diplomacy, such as occurred during the 1956 Anglo-French attack. Certainly the U.S. view of the proliferation of such craft in the early 1960s was that they were directed specifically against U.S. seapower.

15. According to Tzalel, *From Icebreaker to Missile Boat,* 40, the Israelis, as early as

1954, became interested in an antiship missile to overcome the perceived superiority of Egyptian shipboard firepower. If that is true, it predates the origin of the Soviet program that produced the "Styx" (NATO designation; Soviet designation P-15) missile that armed the Arab boats. Work on the Israeli Gabriel missile began rather later. Tzalel does not give the year that procurement of the missile and boat was approved, however; he states only that it was well before the 1967 war. The boats (not the missiles) were of German design, but plans to build them in Germany were aborted when the larger covert German military assistance program to Israel, agreed in 1960, was blown in 1965. Initially the Israelis wanted six large torpedo boats, to deal first with Egyptian *Skory*-class destroyers (ibid., 78). It is not clear when the Israelis became aware of the threat presented by Egyptian missile boats. They were apparently concerned about their coast-attack potential, which was demonstrated in 1971 when the Indians used Soviet-built missile boats to raid Karachi. When the arms deal was disclosed, the Germans retreated under both internal pressure and pressure from Egypt; they were still willing to finance construction, however. In 1966 the Israelis turned to a French yard, Constructions Mécaniques de Normandie (CMN), because they knew that it had built minesweepers to a German design. To the original order for six boats a second order, originally to have been let to a shipyard in Haifa, was added, to save time. Aware that the Soviet missile was designed specifically to destroy large Western warships, the Israelis believed that it could not lock onto a small missile boat. On 13 May 1970, however, an Egyptian missile boat sank the small wooden trawler *Orith,* thus proving that Styx could attack a small target. It also proved that the Israeli boats needed electronic countermeasures (and, it turned out, radar-absorbing material) to survive in combat.

16. Frank Uhlig Jr., *How Navies Fight: The U.S. Navy and Its Allies* (Annapolis, Md.: Naval Institute Press, 1994), 356.

17. The naval commandos were still an important element of Israeli seapower. For example, on the night of 16–17 October they raided Port Said, damaging, among other things, an *Osa*-class missile boat. Tzalel, *From Icebreaker to Missile Boats,* 54–55.

18. Because the distance from the Black Sea was short, the Soviets relied heavily on ships to resupply the Egyptians and Syrians. Because they covered the ships for much of their journey, attacks at sea would have brought the Israelis into direct confrontation with the Soviets. Attacks on ships in port were denounced, but they did not carry the same risks.

19. Uhlig, *How Navies Fight,* 357–58. See also Tzalel, *From Icebreaker to Missile Boats,* 137–41. Although U.S. seaborne shipments arrived only after the end of the war, the Israelis claimed that their own merchant ships carried significant quantities during the war. Mobilization of civilian trucks significantly hampered distribution from the ports. There was an attempt, apparently abortive, to route merchant shipping evasively.

20. Even though this force was within air attack range, the Israeli air force had no night attack capability against naval targets. Israeli naval commandos therefore mounted repeated attacks against the missile boats at Ghardaka, Egypt. For their part, the Egyptian missile boats tried to attack Israeli shipping on the first night of the war; the Israelis escaped by hugging the shore. The Egyptian missile boats were also considered a threat

to a planned Israeli naval attack against Egyptian territory across the Gulf of Suez, to gain a bargaining chip for use during the expected cease-fire negotiations.

21. According to Tzalel, *From Icebreaker to Missile Boat,* 136, Abu Rodeis, captured in 1967, provided most of Israel's crude oil. That contradicts the more widely held view that oil from Iran was essential to the Israeli economy. The Jubal field had only one victim, the tanker *Siris,* which was sunk on 26 October, a day before the cease-fire, while bound for Abu Rodeis. She was the only major Israeli merchant ship lost to enemy action. The mines were a serious problem because the Israel navy had no mine countermeasures capability.

22. On the first day of the war, according to Tzalel, *From Icebreaker to Missile Boat,* 135, an Egyptian submarine fired a three-torpedo spread at the tanker *Samson* after she had passed through the Bab-el-Mandeb. The torpedoes missed, and the submarine did not reattack, but the Israelis suspended all shipments through the Bab-el-Mandeb. On the other hand, they took the failure of the attack as proof that Egyptian submarines offered no threat, and therefore reversed their previous wartime policy and continued to operate their merchant fleet throughout the war.

23. Uhlig, *How Navies Fight,* 358–59.

24. Airlift delivered twenty-two thousand tons of material, beginning on 10 October (the war began on 6 October). The first freighter from the United States did not arrive until 2 November, after the war was over; ultimately sealift exceeded airlift by a ratio of three to one. Ibid., 360. It is not clear whether airlift tonnage includes combat aircraft flown directly to Israel.

25. The big c-5 transports also required fuel, which was provided by U.S. Air Force tankers based in the Azores. Carrier-based tankers had neither the fuel capacity nor the fueling system they needed.

Chapter 11. A New Strategy

1. For the origins of the new explicit doctrine, see Capt. Edward A. Smith Jr., "What '. . . From the Sea' Didn't Say," *Naval War College Review* (winter 1995), 9–33.

2. Fishery competition is a major current source of controversy within the European Union. Poaching is widespread. A few years ago a Malaysian national security expert objected to the word, in the context of the waters off his country, preferring the phrase "stealing our food." Thai poachers were increasingly well armed so that they could fight off Malaysian fishery patrol craft.

3. The inclusion of submarines in this list proved ironic. Throughout the Cold War period they were probably employed more on intelligence gathering than on antisubmarine missions, but those operations were classified so highly that few realized their scope. Because antisubmarine warfare was a much lower post–Cold War priority, it seemed safe to run down the attack submarine force. A decade later it is clear that intelligence gathering is more important than ever, and that the number of attack submarines is insufficient. With the end of the Cold War, battle force (power projection) forces certainly suffered; the carrier force was cut from sixteen or seventeen (to keep

fifteen deployable) to a total of twelve. The discarded missile destroyers were reaching the end of their service lives, but newer missile cruisers had recently undergone the "new threat upgrade" modernization, and they had service life left. One benefit of the wholesale elimination of these ships was the virtual elimination of steam powerplants, which required considerable maintenance, from the fleet. The main exceptions were carriers and large amphibious ships.

4. This is not easy to do. A ship well offshore must be able to hit a target designated by someone who is perhaps a hundred miles away. Key components include a satellite-based communications net, which extends far over the horizon; satellite navigation so the ship and the shell she fires know where the target is; and guns routinely firing at ranges of about a hundred miles, yet delivering the sort of payloads that ground howitzers currently deliver less than twenty miles away. One unresolved problem is the lengthy time of flight for shells fired over very long range; they may be unable to handle urgent targets.

5. Under existing Marine doctrine, helicopter-borne troops would isolate a beach area that is hopefully not yet occupied by large numbers of enemy troops. They could move seaward to help secure a nearby beach. It would take some time for an enemy to concentrate heavy units to attack the beachhead. The helicopter troops could not stand up to such units until their own heavy equipment, delivered over the beach, reached them. Thus the beachhead continues to be important.

6. In the Gulf War, the threat of a marine amphibious assault tied down several Iraqi divisions in defensive positions facing to seaward.

Chapter 12. Using Seapower

1. For example, as the United States withdrew forces from Vietnam, President Richard Nixon enunciated his doctrine: the United States would supply naval and air support to allies, but the allies would have to supply their own troops. That is, the U.S. commitment to places like Vietnam would not be open ended. Critics read Nixon's doctrine as a way of abandoning Vietnam, but in fact it was a statement of how the United States could keep engaged there and how U.S. seapower could make such a commitment affordable.

2. Soviet practice was to produce a stock of spares when a ship was completed. The spares would last the ship until planned half-life, then she would be refitted, with all systems rebuilt at the factory and a new stock of spares produced. Integral to this system was a guaranteed system lifetime, warranted by the producer. Soviet officers tried to keep from exceeding guaranteed lifetime in peacetime, for example, by running ships on one shaft instead of two in order to limit the number of hours on their gas turbines. The system encouraged the view that a military force was readiest before it had operated for many hours, that is, when it still had many hours remaining. By way of contrast, Western forces considered their elements unready *until* they had operated long enough. The system was adopted partly because it fit the planned economic system; producing new spares as needed would be difficult to plan. On the other hand, repair by replace-

ment required much less technical training. U.S. or British manuals generally explain how a device or system works, so that the person doing the repairs can diagnose problems and deduce the appropriate solution. Soviet manuals are cookbooks: plug in contacts A and B, turn the screwdriver until the display matches what is printed on the housing. If that is impossible, pull out the unit and find the spare, with its number, in the racks opposite the electronics. Such manuals do have the advantage of frustrating any intelligence officer who lays hands on them, because they reveal absolutely nothing of how the electronics in question function. Little or no specialized training is required for these types of repairs. In contrast, Western navies and other armed services operate large schools for technicians.

3. Stevenson, *Armaments and the Coming of War*, 85.

4. It took several decades for NATO navies to standardize on Link 11, and even now some NATO warships lack it. The coming tactical links are Link 16 (JTIDS) and the cooperative engagement capability (CEC) link. U.S. warships also use an internet-like system, called IT-21, for vital communication; it is the equivalent of e-mail. Without IT-21, it is difficult for a commander to discuss plans with a U.S. commander. IT-21 replaces numerous special encrypted radio links between ships as well as several important intelligence-sharing broadcasts. It is possible that interoperability will improve as more and more equipment is controlled by software that is much easier to modify. In an emergency the U.S. Navy can easily distribute the necessary software, so the key question for the future may be how flexible new communications and control hardware will be.

5. Because the new systems change the way the U.S. Army plans to fight, interoperability on land is likely to be more difficult to establish than interoperability at sea. Other armies may well choose not to follow the same path.

Appendix A: Naval Technology

1. This conclusion was apparently reached during the Seaplan 2000 study begun in 1977. By 1980, the U.S. Navy was calling for a six-hundred-ship fleet built around twelve carriers, which was the number the Carter administration appeared willing to accept. The successor Reagan administration adopted the six-hundred-ship goal, but with a different fleet composition; it called for fifteen *deployable* carriers, which actually meant sixteen or even seventeen in all.

2. For British attempts at reconstruction, see Norman Friedman, *The Postwar Naval Revolution* (Annapolis, Md.: Naval Institute Press, 1986). Friedman describes U.S. attempts throughout his series of Illustrated Design History titles, published by the Naval Institute Press, including *U.S. Destroyers* (1982), *U.S. Aircraft Carriers* (1983), *U.S. Cruisers* (1984), and *U.S. Submarines Since 1945* (1994).

3. See Michael C. Potter, *Electronic Greyhounds: The Spruance Class Destroyers* (Annapolis, Md.: Naval Institute Press, 1995).

4. The *Spruance* hull was large because it was conceived to include both antisubmarine and antiair variants. The idea was that building a common hull for both purposes would save money. The antiair version required far more weaponry, so the hull

was sized for that mission. The U.S. Navy did not order any antiair variants of the design, however; four, ordered by the shah of Iran, ended up as the U.S. *Kidd* class. In effect, then, the *Spruance* was an antiaircraft destroyer with the antiaircraft features removed. That removal automatically left the ship with considerable empty space, which was correctly evaluated as inexpensive. At the time, the ships seemed grossly underarmed for their size.

5. Moore's Law applies to signal processing. Stealth techniques reduce, but cannot altogether eliminate, signatures. The greater the signal processing power, the more effectively a given system can distinguish a weak signature from the surrounding noise. This reasoning suggests that the future of stealthy systems is quite limited, thus major operational sacrifices made in the interest of stealth, as in the current French *La Fayette*–class frigate, may be pointless.

6. For details of the standard NATO links, see Norman Friedman, *Naval Institute Guide to World Naval Weapons Systems,* 1997–98 edition (Annapolis, Md.: Naval Institute Press, 1997), 26–30.

7. There is also the cooperative engagement capability (CEC) data link, which transmits radar data on a more detailed level than Link 11 or Link 16. CEC will soon probably be a prerequisite for ships to work together in air defense, so the issue of which allied navies buy it is critical. As of late 2000 only the Royal Navy had decided to buy the new link, initially for seven Type 23 frigates, which thereby will gain an over-the-horizon radar picture, and later for the new Type 45 air defense ships. Likely candidates appear to be the new Norwegian and Spanish frigates, which have the Aegis system for which CEC was conceived, and the new Dutch and German air defense ships, whose active-array radars approximate Aegis performance.

8. For further information, see Friedman, *Seapower and Space.*

9. During the Cold War, the U.S. Navy relied heavily on convergence zone techniques; in the Atlantic this requires water depths considerably greater than four thousand feet. Effective bottom bounce requires even greater depths to achieve much range. It used to be said, then, that the U.S. Navy had designed itself as though the world was covered in cold water thirteen thousand feet deep.

10. Sonar frequency determines how quickly the water absorbs the signal, so low frequency offers range. Normally a sonar signal, however, will bounce off the bottom, then the surface, and so on; the sonar signal finds many paths between transmitter, target, and receiver. This multipath tends to smear out signals. One solution is to create very short pulses, so the small time differences inherent in multipath are detectable and cancelable. Another is to shape the beam so that it grazes surface and bottom at shallow enough angles, thereby minimizing reflection. The first requires a more sophisticated signal generator and processor; the second requires a new, generally dipped, array. Neither solution will necessarily deal with confused reflections off underwater terrain. Cooperative systems, involving a controllable sound source and multiple distributed receivers, may solve the problem. Both airborne and surface versions have been tried by the U.S. Navy.

11. A catamaran offers similar advantages of limited waterplane, but the bodies providing buoyancy pierce the water. In smooth water a catamaran can perform spectac-

ularly, achieving much higher speeds than conventional ships. For example, the 900-ton Australian HMAS *Jervis Bay* makes 43 knots on 9,656 BHP (brake horsepower). Because her deck is quite wide, thanks to the use of slender twin hulls instead of a single hull, she has enough deck area to transport five hundred troops or up to two hundred cars. As the catamaran rolls in rough seas, however, first one hull and then the other is much more deeply submerged, making the roll quite uncomfortable. The deck area near the sides of the ship becomes uninhabitable. The problem is equivalent to that of a simple surface-piercing hydrofoil; when it rolls, the area submerged varies. The solution in that case is to submerge the hydrofoils completely, and to add a complex electronic ride control system. No similar solution is possible for a catamaran, but a SWATH might be considered equivalent to a fully submerged hydrofoil. In a SWATH, the supporting bodies are completely submerged, so that buoyancy on each side does not vary much as a ship rolls. The bodies can be quite large, because they do not penetrate the surface and thus do not engender wave-making resistance. Thus the struts connecting them to the supported deck can be much smaller than catamaran hulls, and resistance is reduced. Hull forms like the catamaran and SWATH may be limited in maximum size by stresses felt by the deck structure connecting the hulls or struts.

12. As of early 2001, the British were building a *Trimaran* to test the concept. Much of the efficacy of the design depends on how wave trains created by the three hulls interact, not only with each other but with the sea through which the ship runs. No navy would build a full-scale warship using so radical a hull form without sea tests of this sort, precisely because unexpected problems may arise. For example, some analysis suggests that although the *Trimaran* will run very well through a bow sea, she rolls badly in a quartering sea; such rolling would be unacceptable. In addition, like a catamaran, a *Trimaran* might roll irregularly, because at large angles so much of one side hull and so little of the other would be submerged. That would make for a very uncomfortable ride.

13. A new generation of explosives may greatly increase the effectiveness of missile warheads. Missile size, however, is not proportional to warhead size. Even if, for instance, the Tomahawk warhead were reduced to a tenth of its current weight, the missile as a whole would not weigh only a tenth as much. An air-launched weapon devotes more of its weight to explosives, because the airplane acts as a booster. Similarly, a gun-launched projectile devotes more of its weight to payload, because the effect of the gun is to replace much of the missile powerplant and, often, its guidance.

14. The French strategic school pressing for a navy consisting entirely of torpedo craft and commerce raiders was called *La Jeune Ecole,* the "young school." Its most senior member, Adm. H.-L. T. Aube, lost much of his confidence in such craft after a series of winter exercises in 1886. See Ropp, *The Development of a Modern Navy,* 176.

15. This story is told in Rear Adm. Kemp Tolley's *The Cruise of the Lanikai: Incitement to War* (Annapolis, Md.: Naval Institute Press, 1973). Tolley was chosen to command the small schooner *Lanikai.*

16. The U.S. version is Outlaw Bandit. Reportedly, merely covering flat areas of the superstructure and dealing with major corner reflectors drastically reduces radar cross-section, probably below the cross-section offered by decoys.

17. HMS *Sheffield* was disabled, not sunk, by the Exocet that hit her. She sank later

in a storm, having lost too much stability due to a combination of accumulated fire-fighting water and the loss of oil fuel in her bottom; her gas turbine kept running after she was abandoned. USS *Stark* survived two Exocets but was nearly lost due to accumulated fire-fighting water that did not drain. Other ships lost to Exocets generally burnt out; they did not flood from the above-water hits. Overall, remarkably few ships have actually been sunk by antiship missiles.

18. Ironically, when the carriers were designed the U.S. Navy was unaware that the Soviets used proximity fuses for their torpedoes; it assumed that such fusing was impractical, because its own magnetic proximity fuses had failed so badly during World War II. The lesson is not that U.S. intelligence was poor, but that technical details of weapons are often very difficult to obtain in peacetime, when the weapons are not used.

19. Shkval was designed solely as an antisubmarine weapon, using a nuclear warhead set to go off at one of a very limited number of distance settings. Presumably it could be developed into a straight-running antiship weapon using a proximity fuse, but in that case it would still be too slow to be sure of hitting at any great distance. The noise generated when it fires would presumably ensure that the target was alerted, thus the target would have time to evade.

20. Not only were the motors and generators heavy, but about 10 percent of the power produced was lost before it reached the propeller. That was quite acceptable at the time, because alternatives such as single-reduction gearing were not much better. Modern gearing drastically reduces the loss, whereas electric transmission still entails a larger loss.

21. The big *Spruance*-class destroyers could not be fitted with vertical launchers aft because they would have interfered with the propeller shafts.

22. During the Gulf War, some ships were replenished without using a pier, by ammunition ships alongside, both ships having stopped altogether in very calm water.

23. The typical current support complement is a jammer squadron (four EA-6B), an airborne early warning squadron (four aircraft), an antisubmarine (now strike support) squadron (seven S-3B), an antisubmarine helicopter squadron (seven SH-60B/R), and one C-2 for carrier-on-board delivery (COD), so the total including combat aircraft is typically seventy-one.

24. When the Sea Harrier was modified for true multipurpose operation, it gained too much weight; the Royal Navy did not replace its engine to regain the necessary weight-lifting performance.

25. See Thomas Hone, Norman Friedman, and Mark D. Mandeles, *American and British Aircraft Carrier Development, 1919–1941* (Annapolis, Md.: Naval Institute Press, 1999), for further details.

26. Cell phone traffic, which is radio traffic, can be tapped, as was spectacularly demonstrated some years ago by Prince Charles, ironically an ex-naval officer, when his private conversations with Camilla Parker-Bowles were recorded and published.

27. Action can be subtle. During the Vietnam War, a U.S. submarine stationed off Haiphong repeatedly popped her sail out of the water alongside startled Warsaw Pact merchant ships going into the port. She was not permitted to torpedo any of the ships,

but it soon became clear that the North Vietnamese thought that ten or twelve U.S. submarines were offshore, ready to begin blockading the port.

28. In the computer-aided design of the U.S. *Seawolf* class, special attention was paid to keeping paths open for installing or removing computer consoles. In the past, some submarines, such as U.S. "fleet boats" converted to radar pickets, had neutral-buoyancy sections added amidships, to provide needed volume. There is current U.S. Navy interest in a modular submarine, which might have such sections added or removed without major reconstruction. There is also increased interest in towed pods and in external stowage.

29. The frigate, a modernized *Leander,* also had the vital Seawolf antimissile missile. That night the British made a carrier sweep toward the Argentine mainland, and the frigate was wanted as cover against a possible Exocet attack. One irony was that less sophisticated frigates, armed with a ballistic weapon (Limbo), could have destroyed a bottomed submarine, but probably could not have distinguished her from the clutter on the bottom.

30. Torpedoes such as Mk 44 were active pingers; when near the surface, they could home on pings reflected from the surface. Some versions of Mk 46 introduced an alternative passive mode (effective against surface targets), advertised in brochures showing a Mk 46 sinking a surfaced submarine.

31. The concept of prepositioning equipment and flying in troops was invented in the early 1960s; its first champion was Secretary of Defense Robert S. McNamara. Parallel to the European stockpile, a floating stockpile was built up at Subic Bay in the Philippines to support possible involvement in Southeast Asia. It was expended during the Vietnam buildup.

32. Some have argued that the Iraqis stopped at the Saudi border because their army could not have run much farther, due to lack of spares and maintenance. Perhaps it was more important, for subsequent events, that the Saudis saw the U.S. Marines as an invaluable line of defense. The other early U.S. troop presence, in the form of the U.S. Army airborne units, performed its intended role of securing key airfields so that further forces could be flown in. Such units were not, of course, positioned to stop an Iraqi attack across the border.

33. The first unsweepable mines used the pressure change (the suction) a ship produces as she moves along in shallow water. About sixty years after pressure mines were invented, there is still no effective sweep. Many current mines use microprocessors to store particular signatures, to distinguish the targets they are intended to destroy not only from sweeps but also from nontarget ships. For example, the standard German mine comes in two forms: the mine proper and a dud mine with the same sensing mechanism. The dud collects ship signatures, which can be inserted into the mine's microprocessor.

34. The exception is a group of Norwegian surface-effect hunters and sweepers, which needed high speed so that a small number could cover the entire Norwegian coast.

35. The Soviets developed several generations of rising mines during the Cold War.

The Chinese currently advertise a simple version, EM-52, for export and have reportedly sold it to Iran, to close the Straits of Hormuz. Other countries have their own versions. The U.S. Navy developed CAPTOR, an antisubmarine rising mine containing a Mk 46 torpedo, during the Cold War.

Appendix B: The Shape of the Fleet

1. Pakistan had long pledged an armored division and aircraft, all paid for by Gulf states, for Gulf defense. Full deployment was impossible because of Indian pressure. It can be argued that India saw likely Pakistani deployment as an opportunity. Similarly, North Korea applied pressure to South Korea, which precluded the deployment of substantial numbers of South Korean troops to Saudi Arabia.

2. The main components of the U.S. Navy budget are shipbuilding/conversion, navy (SCN); aircraft procurement, navy (APN); weapons procurement, navy (WPN); and operations and maintenance, navy (OMN). The Navy Department budget includes the Marine Corps budget. Thus Marine aircraft are included in APN, and Marine vehicles in WPN.

3. For example, before World War II the U.S. Navy in effect substituted a large force of seaplane patrol bombers for some carrier aircraft. The number of carriers was limited by treaty, whereas the number of sea-based aircraft was not. For example, seaplanes could scout for the fleet, thus reducing the load on the fleet's carriers. By way of contrast, the prewar Royal Navy had no seaplanes of its own, and those operated by the Royal Air Force were not intended to support the fleet; given the RAF's ideology, they were conceived as an alternative fleet. The Royal Navy therefore emphasized the long-range scouting role of carrier aircraft. This requirement helped shape the Fairey Swordfish, the biplane torpedo bomber with which the Royal Navy entered World War II. On a subtler level, the fact that the Swordfish enjoyed very limited performance, which was actually due in large part to the long-range scouting mission, convinced British naval policy makers that carrier-based aircraft necessarily had low performance—a disastrous and entirely misleading conclusion.

4. A few years ago a French account of maritime patrol aircraft was titled "Cruisers of the Air."

Index

189; base structure, 66; China in, 184–87, 189, 192, 195; coalition, 18–19, 44, 183; configuration of U.S. Navy fleet, 272–73; convoying, 86–87; Cuba and, 189–90; decentralized command and, 53; Europe and, 182–84; ideology, 10; Korea and, 192–93; main fleets, 90–91; mass forces in, 102; in the Mediterranean, 190–91, 199, 200; peripheral conflicts, 180; sea control and, 41; Soviet fleets, 59; strategies, 9, 108, 197–98, 201–6; surveillance in, 44, 79–81, 88; Taiwan in, 184–87; U.S. air defense and, 107; U.S. power projection during, 82–84; Vietnam and, 193–97

Cole (USS), 51–52, 218, 249, 255

Collins-class submarines, 238, 281

colonies, 144, 150

combat direction, 238–39

commanders in chief (CinCs), 278

command systems, 52–54, 232, 239–42

commerce raiding, 48, 84, 86, 87, 92, 93, 126

Communist Party, 182–86, 194

Constantinople, Turkey, 120, 150, 151

container ships, 68–69

continental system counterblockade, 117, 119

convoys, 57–58, 84–90, 112, 160

Copenhagen, Denmark, 122

Cornwallis, Charles, 74

Corsica, France, 63

corvettes, 160

Cox Bazar, 210

Crimean War, 6, 13, 39, 120–23

cruise missiles, 109, 237, 242, 246, 256–57, 259–60. *See also* missiles

Cuba, 205

Cuban Missile Crisis, 189–90

currents, water, 57–58

Danish Straits, 152, 198, 212

Danube river, 151

Dardanelles, 61, 120, 143, 150–51, 198

Davis, Jefferson, 129

deception operations, 160–61, 169

de Gaulle, Charles, 98

democracy as U.S. ideology, 11–12

Denmark, 18, 94, 116, 211–12

destroyers, 84, 225, 236, 245, 251, 252, 262, 279–80

deSuffren, Pierre André, 74

deterrence, 99, 181, 204, 228

Dewey, George, 69

Dien Bien Phu, 30–31, 74

drafting of mass armies, 104–5

Dreadnoughts, 65

Dulles, John Foster, 193

Dutch East Indies, 62, 70

East Pakistan, 208, 209, 210

East Prussia, 133

East Timor, 3

education of personnel, 229–30

Egypt, 117, 168, 190–91, 214, 216, 217

Eilat (destroyer), 216

Eisenhower, Dwight D., 107, 193, 194, 198

Eisenhower (USS), 273

electric ships, 254–55

e-mail, 241

embargoes, 3, 92–98; on Britain, 117; on Cuba, 189–90; on Iraq, 35, 95, 97, 190; on Japan, 97–98, 173; leading up to Gulf War, 80; as national strategy, 221, 222; on Serbia, 190

England. *See* Britain

English Channel, 41, 61

Enigma machine, 79

Enterprise (carrier), 210, 277

Ethiopia, 97

Europe, 134–35, 182–84, 217–18

expeditionary warfare, 41, 131

Falkland Islands, 50–51, 61

Fernandina, Fla., 126

Ferrol, Spain, 63, 115, 116

Fisher, Sir John, 6, 61, 65, 77, 123, 136, 141, 152

"fitting for but not with," 236

Flanders, Belgium, 146, 152

fleet command centers (FCCS), 54

fleet-in-being, 85, 88–92, 140

fleet trains, 175–76

flo-flo merchant ships, 268

"Forward . . . From the Sea" (1995), 219–25

forward deployment, 49–51

France: alliance with Spain, 70, 115, 119; Allied invasion of, 170–71; attack on India, 115, 117; avoidance of battle, 88–89; balance of power, 14–16, 20, 21; British blockade of, 61–62; British destruction of ships, 165;

France (continued)
    coalition with American colonists,
    71–73; coalition with Britain, 29–30,
    75, 137–47, 231; Communist Party in,
    182, 183; defeat by Prussia, 48;
    dependence on foreign shipping, 96;
    embargo against Britain, 117; gar-
    risons at Hansa ports, 118; ground
    force, 104–5, 114, 231; Louisiana Pur-
    chase and, 38; in Mexico, 127; multi-
    coast fleets, 59; relationship with
    Russia, 65, 116; in Vietnam, 30–31. See
    also Crimean War; Franco-Prussian
    War; Napoleonic wars; World War I
Franco, Francisco, 168
Franco-Prussian War, 15, 47–48, 211–13
French Revolution, War of the, 63. See also
    Napoleonic wars
frigates, 84, 236, 239, 245
". . . From the Sea" (1992), 219–22, 225
fused data, 80

Gallipoli, 104, 116–17, 151
garrisons, 26, 106–17
geography, 55–78; American Revolution
    and, 70–75; basing and, 62–70,
    277–78; Cold War, 198–201; modern
    warfare and, 45; of the Pacific, 75–77;
    position and dominance, 61–62;
    World War II and, 159–66
Germany: in Africa, 29, 32; air force,
    165–66; army-oriented general staffs
    in World Wars, 53; avoidance of bat-
    tle, 88–89; balance of power, 14–15, 21;
    blockade of, 94–95, 104, 139, 141, 153;
    colonies, 150; construction of fleet,
    131–32; destruction of British bases,
    66; economy, 132, 152–53; French gar-
    risons in, 118; invasion of Belgium,
    62; mutiny of High Seas Fleet, 155;
    surface fleet, 140; surveillance of,
    78–79. See also Franco-Prussian War;
    U-boats; World War I; World War II
Ghazi, 209, 210
Glennard P. Libscomb (turbo-electric sub-
    marine), 255
Global Positioning System (GPS)/guided
    bombs (JDAMS), 258
Gneisenau (battlecruiser), 86, 165
Goeben (battlecruiser), 147
Gorkiy on the Volga, 61

Gorbachev, Mikhail, 105
Gorshkov, Sergei, 87, 189
Graham, Sir James, 121, 122
Grand Mufti of Jerusalem, 32
Great Lakes, 38
Greece, 22, 147, 150, 169
Greenland/Iceland/United Kingdom
    (GIUK) gap, 66, 198, 199
ground forces, 113–29; British, 130–31,
    141–43; coalitions and, 44–45; com-
    mand of, 52–53; commitment of, 178,
    195; defense against, 111; detection by
    satellite, 80–81; in Gulf War, 101, 103;
    mass, 101–7, 114, 172; preferences for,
    230–31; support of, 41–42, 219–25. See
    also land wars
Guam, 277
Gulf of Aqaba, 214, 216
Gulf War, 2, 11–12, 17–20, 33–36, 101–2, 103,
    106, 108. See also Persian Gulf

Haiphong, port of, 194
Halsey, William, 89
Harriers, 258, 266
Hayward, Thomas, 202
heartland versus rimland, 138–39
Heligoland Bight, 132, 136, 212
Helsinki (Helsingfors), 122
high-frequency radio direction-finder sta-
    tions, 79
Hitler, Adolf, 97, 158, 159, 171–72
H. L. Hunley, 124
Ho Chi Minh Trail, 194
homeland defense, 99, 100
homeporting, 276–77
Hong Kong, 24, 77, 187
Hood (HMS), 79
Hornet (carrier), 176
hot wars, 181
Huascar (ironclad), 23
Hudson River, 73
hull design, 245–46, 285
hunting, 87. See also commerce raiding
Hussein, Saddam, 11, 12, 34–35, 97, 111

Iceland, 199–200
ideology, national, 10–14, 22–23
immigration by sea, 230
Inchon, S. Korea, 192
Independence (USS), 275
India: assistance to Iraq, 35; Crimean War

Maine, 38
main fleets, 84–85, 88–92, 216–17
major regional contingency (MRC), 31–32
Malacca Straits, 61, 97
Malaya, 27, 170, 173
Malta, 63, 118
Manchuria, 30–31, 178
Mao Tse-tung, 184, 185, 190
Marianas, 42, 89
"Maritime Strategy," 202–6
mass forces, 101–12, 114, 172
McClellan, George T., 128
McNamara, Robert S., 201
Mediterranean Sea: blockage of, 41; British
    in, 61–63, 161–66, 169; Cold War in,
    190–91, 199, 200; dominance of in
    World War I, 147, 151; Germany in
    during World War II, 168; Middle
    East War in, 214–18; as route to India,
    120; U.S. deployments in, 274–76
merchant ships, 56, 68–69
Mers-el-Kebir, 165
Mesopotamia, 151, 152
Mexico, 127, 145
Mid-Atlantic Ridge, 58
Middle East War, 214–19
Midway, battle of, 42, 176–77
Midway-class carriers, 59, 237
military operations other than war
    (MOOTW), 3, 22
Milosevich, Slobodan, 3, 20, 97
mines, 148–49, 223, 225, 267–70
Minnesota, 38
missiles, 18, 280; in Cold War, 82–83; in
    Gulf War, 19; in Middle East War,
    214, 216–17; replenishment, 255–56;
    ship design and, 246–54; U.S.
    defense system, 99, 100. *See also*
    cruise missiles
Mississippi river, 124, 127
Mobile, Ala., 126
mobility, 7, 43–44, 127–28, 175–76, 223–28.
    See also railroads
modernization as U.S. ideology, 11
Moltke, Marshal Helmut von, 133
Monitor (ironclad), 128
Monroe Doctrine, 23
Moore's Law, 238
Moslem countries, 27, 32
Mozambique, 205, 206
Mukhti Bahini, 209

Mussolini, Benito, 97

Napoleon, Louis, 121
Napoleon Bonaparte, 39, 113–20
Napoleonic wars, 14, 20, 36–37, 113–20, 159
Narvik port, 160
Nassau, Bahamas, 72
Nasser, Gamal Abdul, 180, 191
national strategy, 7, 9–39; Britain, 12–15,
    22–26, 33, 131; ideology and, 10–12;
    United States, 9, 11–12, 47–49
Nautilus, 264
naval expeditionary warfare. *See* littoral
    warfare
naval stores, 63, 71
Nelson, Lord Horatio, 63, 88, 115, 116, 117,
    118–19
Netherlands, 14, 94, 97–98
network-centric warfare, 8, 45, 52, 53, 241–42
New Army (British), 142–43
New Bern, N.C., 126
New Orleans, La., 37–39, 126
Newport, R.I., 73, 74
New York, 73, 74
New Zealand, 77, 144
Nicaragua, 205
Nikolaev, Ukraine, 59
Nimitz (carrier), 257, 274
Nixon, Richard, 184
no-fly zone, 35
Norfolk, Va., 126
Normandy, France, 161, 171
North America, 70–71
North Atlantic Treaty Organization
    (NATO), 3, 19, 20, 82, 91, 182–83, 189,
    200, 201
North Cape, 41
North Korea, 35. *See also* Korea
North Sea, 61, 85–86, 90, 93–95, 133, 136,
    139–41, 148–49, 212
North Vietnam, 102. *See also* Vietnam
Norway, 18, 94, 136, 160, 199–200
nuclear weapons, 5, 53, 107, 108, 182

occupation duty, 24, 46
oil, 69, 96–97, 126, 173–74, 216–18, 220
Okinawa, Japan, 26, 63
Omega radio aid, 68
Operational Intelligence Centre, 79
operational maneuver from the sea
    (OMFTS), 223–25

Scott, Winfield, 124
sea control, 40–43, 61–62, 82–91, 198, 201–3, 221. *See also* blockades; embargoes
sea denial, 40–41, 82, 83
Sea Knife, 245, 246
Seaplan 2000, 201–2, 203
seapower: advantages, 3–5, 17–18, 49–54, 227–28; ambiguity, 43–44; potential, 230–31
self-synchronization, 52, 53
sensors, 80, 81, 109, 241–42. *See also* surveillance
Serbia, 3, 20, 91, 97, 143, 190
Sevastopol, Crimea, 120, 121, 122
Seven Years' War, 70, 71
Sharm el-Sheikh, Egypt, 214, 217
Sherman, William Tecumseh, 128
shipping routes, 56–61, 64–66
ship to objective maneuver (STOM), 223, 225
Shkval (Squall) rocket torpedoes, 253
shore-based establishments, U.S., 282
shore based patrol aircraft (PBY Catalinas), 51
Sicilian Narrows, 61, 199
Sicily, Italy, 117
Sierra Leone, 9, 10
Sinai, 218
Singapore, 77, 157
"Sivuch"-class surface effect fast attack craft, 246
Skipjack-class ships, 264
smaller-scale contingency (SSC), 31–32
Solomons, battle in, 177
Somalia, 9–10, 24, 50
Somme, France, 42, 144
sonar, 243, 263. *See also* surveillance
SOUS system, 58, 79, 88, 283
South Africa, 144, 206
South America, 23, 62
South China Sea, 97
Southeast Asia, 172–73
Southern Army of Northern Virginia, 124
South Yemen, 205
Soviet Union: Baltic Fleet, 59; ban on land-based cruise missiles, 109; Black Sea Fleet, 61; defense of bastions, 91; economy, 105, 206–7; Fifth Eskadra fleet, 191, 218; geography of, 59; German invasion of, 159; mass army, 105; military build up, 155, 182–83, 206–7;

missile-equipped land-based bombers, 82–83; naval philosophy, 53–54; Northern Fleet, 59, 61, 199, 200; Pacific Fleet, 59; personnel, 229; surveillance operations, 79; in World War II, 167–68, 170–72. *See also* Cold War; Russia
Spain, 14, 23, 37–38, 70, 74–75, 88, 115, 119
Spratly Islands, 19, 97
Spruance, Raymond, 89
Spruance-class destroyers, 236, 245
S-3s, 282–83
Stalin, Joseph, 167, 170–71, 182–83, 184, 190, 206
stand-off weapons, 109
Stark (frigate), 96, 240, 249, 252
stealth, 108
steamships, 86
Stonewall (CSS), 127
St. Petersburg, Russia, 122, 123
straits, strategic, 58–61
Straits of Bab-el-Mandeb, 214, 216, 217
Straits of Gibraltar, 59, 61, 62, 168, 199
Straits of Jubal, 217
Straits of Magellan, 61
Straits of Malacca, 56
Straits of Otranto, 61
strategic air attacks, 110–11
Strategic Air Command (SAC), 44, 107
strategic defense, 98–100
strategic territories, 55, 58–61
strike cruisers (CSGNs), 260
Strike Fleet Atlantic, 200
submarines, 260–65; British concern about in World War I, 139–40; British fleet, 65–66; convoy escorts and, 84–88; design, 262; diesel-electric, 65, 66, 262–64, 281; nuclear, 51, 263–64, 280–81; Russian "Kilo"-class, 253, 265; strategic, 91–92, 99; surveillance and, 79–80, 87–88; U.S. requirements, 238, 280–81; use in Cold War, 91–92, 199. *See also* antisubmarine warfare (ASW); U-boats
Sudan, 28–29, 31, 32
Suez Canal, 13, 56, 61, 62, 77, 168, 214, 216–18
superports, 68
surface action groups (SAGs), 258–59, 279–80
surface fleets, 79, 140
surveillance, 43–44, 58, 78–81, 87–88,

282–83. *See also* radars; radios; satellites; sensors; sonar
SWATH, 245, 246
Sweden, 94, 116
Syria, 151, 152, 191, 216, 217

T-AGOS (surveillance ships), 58
Tagus river, 63
Taiwan, 184–87
Taranto, Italy, 165
targets. *See* centers of gravity
technology, 21, 22, 42–43, 229–30, 233–70; combat direction and, 238–39; command systems and, 232; in littoral conditions, 243–44; survivability of warships and, 249–59; in U.S.-Japanese war, 178
tenders, 281–82
Thailand, 194
Third World countries, 9–10, 90–91, 96, 102, 106, 180–81
Tirpitz, Alfred von, 131–32
Tirpitz (battleship), 84, 85
Tito, Josip Broz, 190
Tokyo, Japan, 176
Tomahawk cruise missiles, 237, 242, 246, 256–57, 259–60
Tonkin Gulf, 195
torpedoes, 247, 253–54
Toulon, France, 59, 63, 73, 115
Tracy, Benjamin, 48–49
trade routes. *See* shipping routes
trade warfare, 84, 94
Trafalgar, 88, 116, 118–19
Transvaal, 29
Treaty of Peace and Friendship, 208
Trimaran, 245, 246
Tripoli, Libya, 216, 217
Tripoli (helicopter carrier), 269
Truman, Harry S., administration, 192
Tsushima, 30, 69
Tu-16 "Badger" bomber, 200
Turkey, 32, 147, 150, 151. *See also* Crimean War
Turkish Straits, 120, 150, 199. *See also* Dardanelles
two-ocean navy act, 58
Type 23 ("Duke")-class frigates, 239

U-boats, 41, 56–57, 69, 84–90, 112, 139–40, 147–49, 159–60. *See also* submarines

Ukraine, 59
Ulithi base, 176
United Nations Law of the Sea, 220
United States: abandonment of draft, 105; air strategy, 108; balance of power, 16; ban on land-based cruise missiles, 109; bases in Pacific, 175–76; Civil War, 92, 123–29; concept of warfare, 41; dependence on foreign shipping, 94–96; economy, 11–12, 22, 24, 72, 155, 219–20; industrialization, 178; intervention in Russia, 24; intervention in Third World countries, 9–10, 24, 50; Iraq and, 96–97; Japan and, 45–47, 97–98, 156, 172–79; lack of goal in Vietnam, 33, 96, 102; national prestige, 26, 50, 195; national strategy, 9, 11–12, 47–49; post–Cold War strategy, 219–25; relationship with China, 16, 98, 99, 184; reliance on coalitions, 33; as rimland state, 138; support of Afghanistan, 187; support of Israel, 217–18; wars of choice, 26, 98; in World War I, 144, 145, 148–49, 154–56; in World War II, 166–67, 169, 170. *See also* American Revolution; Cold War; War of 1812
United States Air Force, 44, 107, 197–98
United States Army, 45–47, 102, 175, 197
United States Central Intelligence Agency (CIA), 192
United States Coast Guard, 230
United States Marine Corps, 175, 223–25, 265–66, 279–80
United States Navy: configuration, 271–85; development in 1889, 48–49; General Board on Philippines, 46; interoperability of, 232; main fleet, 89, 90; in Mediterranean Sea, 274–76; modernization, 235–37; Seventh Fleet, 49, 184–87; Sixth Fleet, 49, 191, 218; surveillance system, 80
unmanned air vehicles (UAVS), 67, 109, 283
Upholder-class diesel-electric submarines, 66
Ustinov, Dmitriy F., 206

Venezuela, 23
Verdun, France, 145, 150
vertical missile launchers, 237

About the Author

Norman Friedman is an internationally known strategist and specialist in the fields of weapons design and development. He has written design histories of U.S. Navy carriers, battleships, cruisers, destroyers, submarines, and small attack craft. Dr. Friedman also writes articles on a variety of defense subjects for journals worldwide and contributes a monthly column on world naval developments to the Naval Institute's *Proceedings* magazine.

Dr. Friedman, who holds a Ph.D. in physics from Columbia University, was a longtime consultant to U.S. government agencies and a former deputy director of national security studies at the Hudson Institute.